ORGANIZED LABOR

ORGANIZED LABOR

ITS PROBLEMS PURPOSES AND IDEALS

AND

THE PRESENT AND FUTURE OF AMERICAN WAGE EARNERS

BY

JOHN MITCHELL

[1903]

AUGUSTUS M. KELLEY • PUBLISHERS
CLIFTON 1973

First Edition 1903

(*Philadelphia*: American Book & Bible House, 1903)

Reprinted 1973 by
AUGUSTUS M. KELLEY PUBLISHERS
Reprints of Economic Classics
Clifton New Jersey 07012

Library of Congress Cataloging in Publication Data

Mitchell, John, 1870-1919.
   Organized labor.

   (Library of American labor history)

   Bibliography: p.
   1. Labor and laboring classes--United States.
2. Trade-unions--United States. I. Title.
HD6508.M6 1972   331.88'0973   68-56263
ISBN 0-678-00733-0

PRINTED IN THE UNITED STATES OF AMERICA
by SENTRY PRESS, NEW YORK, N. Y. 10013

JOHN MITCHELL
President of the United Mine Workers of America

Organized Labor

ITS PROBLEMS, PURPOSES AND IDEALS

AND

THE PRESENT AND FUTURE OF AMERICAN WAGE EARNERS

BY

JOHN MITCHELL

AMERICAN BOOK AND BIBLE HOUSE
PHILADELPHIA, PA.

CONTENTS

PREFACE ix

CHAPTER I
The Philosophy of Trade Unionism 1

CHAPTER II
Labor Unorganized 12

CHAPTER III
Trade Unionism—a Product of Modern Industry 17

CHAPTER IV
The Oppression of Labor under the Factory System 23

CHAPTER V
British Labor in Self-Defence 32

CHAPTER VI
Modern Trade Unionism in Great Britain 41

CHAPTER VII
Labor in the American Colonies 51

CHAPTER VIII
Labor from the Declaration of Independence to the Emancipation Proclamation 57

CHAPTER IX
Organized Labor before and since the Civil War 65

CONTENTS.

CHAPTER X
The Constitution of the American Trade Union 75

CHAPTER XI
American Trade Unions of To-day 83

CHAPTER XII
Organized Labor *versus* Unorganized Labor 93

CHAPTER XIII
The Benefit Features of Trade Unions 104

CHAPTER XIV
The American Standard of Wages 110

CHAPTER XV
The Day's Work 120

CHAPTER XVI
The Work of Women and Children 131

CHAPTER XVII
The Death Roll of Industry 142

CHAPTER XVIII
The Moral Uplifting of the Workman 153

CHAPTER XIX
How Trade Unions Benefit Employer and Public 160

CHAPTER XX
The Problem of the Unskilled 167

CONTENTS.

CHAPTER XXI
The Immigrant and the Living Wage 176

CHAPTER XXII
Organized Labor and Organized Capital 186

CHAPTER XXIII
The Union and the Trust 195

CHAPTER XXIV
Unions and Politics 205

CHAPTER XXV
Trade Unions, the State, and the Law 215

CHAPTER XXVI
The Incorporation of Labor Unions 222

CHAPTER XXVII
The Case against the Trade Union 233

CHAPTER XXVIII
The Right to the Machine 246

CHAPTER XXIX
The Restriction of the Output 254

CHAPTER XXX
The Passing of the Apprentice 260

CHAPTER XXXI
The Boundaries of Trades 264

CONTENTS.

CHAPTER XXXII
The Unionist and the Non-Unionist 272

CHAPTER XXXIII
The Label and the Boycott 286

CHAPTER XXXIV
Labor and Capital at War 299

CHAPTER XXXV
Strikes in their Moral and Economic Aspects 307

CHAPTER XXXVI
The Proper Conduct of a Strike 316

CHAPTER XXXVII
The Injunction in Labor Disputes 324

CHAPTER XXXVIII
The Strike *versus* Compulsory Arbitration 337

CHAPTER XXXIX
The Strike *versus* the Trade Agreement 347

THE COAL STRIKE OF 1902:

CHAPTER XL
The Advent of the Great Railroad Corporations 355

CHAPTER XLI
The Advent of the United Mineworkers of America 362

CONTENTS.

CHAPTER XLII
The Strike Declared 368

CHAPTER XLIII
The Indianapolis Convention 374

CHAPTER XLIV
The Intervention of the President 379

CHAPTER XLV
The Award of the Anthracite Coal Strike Commission 391

CHAPTER XLVI
Labor Federation in the United States 397

CHAPTER XLVII
The Work before the Unions 407

CHAPTER XLVIII
The Ideals of Organized Labor 412

CHAPTER XLIX
Organized Labor and Public Opinion 418

CHAPTER L
Trade Unionism and the American Democracy 424

CHAPTER LI
"The Universal Vital Problem of the World" 431

In the compilation of data and in the preparation of "Organized Labor, its Problems, Purposes and Ideals," I have been assisted by Walter E. Weyl, Ph. D., and we have consulted, among many others, the following authorities.

Webb (Sidney and Beatrice).
    Industrial Democracy. London, New York, and Bombay.

Webb (Sidney and Beatrice).
    The History of Trade Unionism. London, New York, and Bombay.

Stimson (F. J.).
    Handbook to the Labor Law of the United States. New York.

Ely (Richard T.).
    The Labor Movement in America. New York.

Engels (Frederick).
    The Condition of the Working-Class in England in 1844. Translated by Florence Kelley Wischnewetzky. London.

Wright (Carroll D.).
    The Industrial Evolution of the United States. New York.

Walker (Francis A.).
    The Wages Question. Boston.

Howell (George).
    The Conflicts of Capital and Labour. London and New York.

McMaster (James B.).
    History of the People of the United States.

Lloyd (Henry D.).
    A Country without Strikes.

Report of the National Conference on Industrial Conciliation. 1902 and 1903.

Report of the United States Industrial Commission. Vols. XVII and XIX.

PREFACE

THE average wage earner has made up his mind that he must remain a wage earner. He has given up the hope of a kingdom to come, where he himself will be a capitalist, and he asks that the reward for his work be given to him as a workingman. Singly, he has been too weak to enforce his just demands and he has sought strength in union and has associated himself into labor organizations.

Labor unions are *for* the workman, but *against* no one. They are not hostile to employers, not inimical to the interests of the general public. They are for a class, because that class exists and has class interests, but the unions did not create and do not perpetuate the class or its interests and do not seek to evoke a class conflict.

There is no necessary hostility between labor and capital. Neither can do without the other; each has evolved from the other. Capital is labor saved and materialized; the power to labor is in itself a form of capital. There is not even a necessary, fundamental antagonism between the laborer and the capitalist. Both are men, with the virtues and vices of men, and each wishes at times more than his fair share. Yet, broadly considered, the interest of the one is the interest of the other, and the prosperity of the one is the prosperity of the other. Where wages are high, capital and the conduct of business are not without their reward; where the industry of the country is carried on by broad-minded, far-seeing, adventurous leaders, the remuneration of labor increases, even to the common laborer on the streets.

The trade unions stand for the principle of united action and for the policy of a living wage earned under fair living conditions. In union there is strength, justice, and moderation; in disunion, nothing but an alternating humility and insolence, a state of industrial despotism tempered by futile and passing revolutions. Unions stand for the right of association, self-government, and free speech, for the dignity and self-respect of the workman, for the mutual esteem of capitalist and wage earner, and for a wide, far-seeing, open-minded, democratic conduct of industry. The living wage means the American standard of living. The world does not owe a man a living, but the man owes it to himself, and the industry that voluntarily employs and voluntarily retains him owes him the right to earn it under fair and living conditions.

In the pursuit of these ideals trade unionism has justified its existence by good works and high purposes. At one time viewed with suspicion by workman and employer alike, it has gained the affections of the one and the enlightened esteem of the other. Slowly and gradually it has progressed toward the fulfilment of its ideals. It has elevated the standard of living of the American workman and conferred upon him higher wages and more leisure. It has increased efficiency, diminished accidents, averted disease, kept the children at school, raised the moral tone of the factories, and improved the relations between employer and employed. In so doing, it has stood upon the broad ground of justice and humanity. It has defended the weak against the strong, the exploited against the exploiter. It has stood for efficiency rather than cheapness, for the producer rather than production, for the man rather than the dollar. It has voiced the claims of the unborn as of the living and has stayed the hand of that ruthless, near-sighted profit-seeking which would destroy future generations as men wantonly cut down forests. It has spoken for the negro slave on the plantation and the white slave in the factory. It has aided and educated the newly arrived immigrant, protected the toil of women and children, and fought the battle of the poor in attic and sweat shop. It has conferred benefits, made sacrifices, and, unfortunately, committed errors.

I do not conceal from myself that trade unionism has made its mistakes. No institution fully attains its ideals, and men stumble and fall in their upward striving. The labor union is a great, beneficent, democratic institution, not all-good, not all-wise, not all-powerful, but with the generous virtues and enthusiastic faults of youth. Labor leaders have erred, but the underlying impulse has been good, and the unions have sought the welfare of their class and of society.

I have mentioned these faults and errors of American trade unions, because I believe that they should not be glossed over by the men who love the unions in spite of their faults. I believe, however that many employers have been less than just and have closed their eyes to the virtues of unions while searching for flaws with a microscope. Capital should be as tolerant and fair to labor as labor is to capital, and the employer should cease to consider unions and their policy beneath his notice and should begin to study them in a frank, open-minded manner. What is required between these two factors in production are knowledge and mutual understanding. Ignorance is the mother of prejudice and strife, and peace may come only from an understanding of the attitude of an opponent. The labor problem cannot be solved by the benevolence of employers, but only by their justice and wisdom, not by gifts or donations, not by allotments or sales of stocks, not even by profit-sharing. However beneficent these may be, the problem can be solved only by a recognition of the rights of labor and a willingness on the part of employers to confer with their associated workmen and to formulate trade agreements covering the whole field of the labor contract.

The recognition of the rights of organized labor by the making of trade agreements will with the coming years become more and more general in the United States. The American employer is too broad-minded not to realize the advantage of such a method of securing stable conditions and of ensuring a spirit of friendly coöperation among his men. The manufacturer of the future will no more forego such an insurance of the good will of his workmen than he will permit his factory to remain uninsured against fire. The trade agreement makes for peace in the industrial world. Strikes will not entirely disappear, and the fear or possibility of strikes will still remain, but the frequent bickerings and constant irritation will vanish, and strikes themselves will be reduced to a minimum. To the present period of industrial war will succeed an era of peace, an era of peace with honor to both sides.

The recognition of the rights of organized labor should be to the employing class as much a principle as a policy. It is a recognition of the dignity of labor, of the equal rights of men engaged in manual toil. It is a second emancipation, freeing both master and slave. Former slave owners found it difficult to treat with freedmen, and it is no less difficult to men accustomed "to run their own business in their own way" to enter into contractual relations with representatives of employees associated into organizations of national scope and purpose. Such a broad recognition, however, binding, as it does, in indissoluble bonds of amity, employer and employee, would like mercy bless him who gives and him who takes, conferring a lasting benefit upon workingmen, employers, and the whole people of the United States.

I have written this book in the hope of contributing, though in the slightest degree, to the attainment of this result. I wish to see the interests and ideals of labor and capital fairly reconciled, not by surrender, but by mutual understanding, and to see the rights and responsibilities of all parties, the workman, the employer, and the public, clearly, completely, and unmistakably recognized. To the better comprehension of these rights and responsibilities, whether of labor or of capital, and to a better understanding between these two great factors in production, I dedicate this book.

John Mitchell

CHAPTER I

THE PHILOSOPHY OF TRADE UNIONISM

Apparent Complexity of Trade Unionism. Underlying Simplicity. The Fundamental Principle. The Right to Bargain Collectively. Its Importance. Its Necessity. A Minimum of Wages and Conditions of Labor for all Workers. Why Trade Unions are Opposed to Truck Stores. Arbitrary Fines, etc. Trade Unions Stand for Freedom of Contract. The Recognition of the Union. The Denial of Representation is Tyranny.

TO the ordinary man of affairs, immersed in his business and the daily routine of life, trade unionism may seem a bewildering maze of conflicting ideas and doctrines. Such a man, unless he has a special interest in the subject, is liable to have his opinions formed from disjointed, scattering, and often untrustworthy accounts. At one time he reads of trade unionists attempting to raise wages or reduce hours of labor in a particular factory, or demanding the recognition of the union, or urging a sympathetic strike, or resisting or denouncing a federal injunction. At other times the trade union seems to be taken up with such questions as whether the foreman shall or shall not belong to the union, whether the unionists shall or shall not work with non-union men, whether a particular factory is in a sanitary condition, whether a certain machine is speeded up too much or not enough, whether the temperature of a given factory is such as to endanger the health of the operatives, what differential should be paid for a new machine, and so on. At still other times, he reads of unionists leaving their uncompleted work at the stroke of the hour, demanding the abolition of truck stores, insisting upon the weighing or measurement of their product, refusing to work on goods made by non-unionists, or boycotting certain individuals or products. In some instances the unionists seem to be insisting upon pay by the piece, and in other cases, refusing absolutely to have anything to do with the piece system. At one time the unionists appear to be at war with one another or with employers, and at other times they are meeting amicably in gigantic federations, or legislating in conjunction with associations of employers for the conduct and management of great industries.

In the hundreds of trade unions that exist and the thousands of local groups into which these organizations are divided, various problems are encountered and various measures taken in each exigency. The result is a perfectly bewildering series of rules and regulations, in which the ordinary man sees neither rhyme nor reason, except, perhaps, that he observes in vague outline the ever-present desire on the part of the workingmen to improve their conditions and to raise their standard of life and labor. But even when the general public clearly understands this ideal, it fails to see why so simple an ideal requires so many and so elaborate regulations, and in many cases, though the good motives of trade unions are not impugned, their wisdom is questioned.

The complexity of trade unionism, however, is merely the complexity of human life itself. No matter how simple and fundamental the principles and constitution of an organization, its rules and regulations necessarily become complex as soon as they encounter the diverse conditions that characterize modern life. Law in its simplest form stands for a certain rough ideal of justice and for the maintenance under certain conditions of the life, liberty, and property of the individual. While, however, in primitive times the law is simple, direct, and easily recognizable, the cases being decided with the rough-handed justice of the monarch dividing the infant, the intricate complexity of modern life renders it necessary to decide even the simplest cases by reference to hundreds of precedents. The commandment, "Thou shalt not steal," contains a commentary running through hundreds of thousands or even millions of accounts of cases of men who have been tried and acquitted or convicted. Even a simple contract involves the most elaborate series of conditions, expressed or implied, in order to guard the interests of both parties.

In its fundamental principle trade unionism is plain and clear and simple. Trade unionism starts from the recognition of the fact that under normal conditions the individual, unorganized workman cannot bargain advantageously with the employer for the sale of his labor. Since the workingman has no money in reserve and must sell his labor immediately, since, moreover, he has no knowledge of the market and no skill in bargaining, since, finally, he has only his own labor to sell, while the employer engages hundreds or thousands of men and can easily do without the services of any particular individual, the workingman, if bargaining on his own account and for himself alone, is at an enormous disadvantage. Trade unionism recognizes the fact that under such conditions labor becomes more and more degenerate, because the labor which the workman sells is, unlike other commodities, a thing which is of his very life and soul and being. In the individual contract between a rich employer and a poor workman, the laborer will secure the worst of it; he is progressively debased, because of wages insufficient to buy nourishing food, because of hours of labor too long to permit sufficient rest, because of conditions of work destructive of moral, mental, and physical health, and degrading and annihilating to the laboring classes of the present and the future, and, finally, because of danger from accident and disease, which kill off the workingman or prematurely age him. The "individual bargain," or individual contract, between employers and men means that the condition of the worst and lowest man in the industry will be that which the best man must accept. From first to last, from beginning to end, always and everywhere, trade unionism stands unalterably opposed to the individual contract. There can be no concession or yielding upon this point. No momentary advantage, however great or however ardently desired, no advance in wages, no reduction in hours, no betterment in conditions, will permanently compensate workingmen for even a temporary surrender in any part of this fundamental principle. It is this principle, the absolute and complete prohibition of contracts between employers and individual men, upon which trade unionism is founded. There can be no permanent prosperity to the working classes, no real and lasting progress, no consecutive improvement in conditions, until the principle is firmly and fully established, that in industrial life, especially in enterprises on a large scale, the settlement of wages, hours of labor, and all conditions of work, must be made between employers and workingmen collectively and not between employers and workingmen individually.

To find a substitute for the individual bargain, which destroys the welfare and the happiness of the whole working class, trade unions were founded. A trade union, in its usual form, is an association of workmen who have agreed among themselves not to bargain individually with their employer or employers, but to agree to the terms of a collective or joint contract between the employer and the union. The fundamental reason for the existence of the trade union is that by it and through it, workmen are enabled to deal collectively with their employers. The difference between the individual and the collective or joint bargain is simply this, that in the individual contract or bargain one man of a hundred refuses to accept work, and the employer retains the services of ninety and nine; whereas in the collective bargain the hundred employees act in a body, and the employer retains or discharges all simultaneously and upon the same terms. The ideal of trade unionism is to combine in one organization all the men employed, or capable of being employed, at a given trade, and to demand and secure for each and all of them a definite minimum standard of wages, hours, and conditions of work.

Trade unionism thus recognizes that the destruction of the workingman is the individual bargain, and the salvation of the workingman is the joint, united, or collective bargain. To carry out a joint bargain, however, it is necessary to establish a minimum of wages and conditions which will apply to all. By this is not meant that the wages of all shall be the same, but merely that equal pay shall be given for equal work. There cannot be more than one minimum in a given trade, in a given place, at a given time. If the bricklayers of the city of New York were all organized and the union permitted half of its members to work for forty cents an hour, while the other half, in no wise better workmen, were compelled or led to ask for fifty cents, the result would be that the men receiving fifty cents would be obliged either to lower their wages or get out of the trade. To

SAMUEL GOMPERS,
President of the American Federation of Labor.

JAMES DUNCAN
Secretary of the Granite Cutters' National Union; First Vice-President of the American Federation of Labor

secure to any union man fifty cents an hour, all union men of equal skill must demand at least an equal sum. The man who wants fifty cents an hour is not injured by other unionists asking or getting ten or twenty cents in excess of this minimum, but he is injured by fellow-craftsmen accepting any wage less than the minimum. The same rule of collective bargaining applies to the hours of labor. If all union bricklayers in New York City were to receive four dollars a day and some were, for this pay, to work eight hours, others ten, and still others twelve and fifteen hours, the result would be that the employers would by preference employ the men who were willing to work fifteen hours. As a consequence, the men willing to work only eight or ten hours would lose their positions or be obliged either to reduce their wages or to work as long as their competitors, who were employed for twelve or fifteen hours. What is true of wages and of hours of labor is equally true of all the conditions of work. If some members of the union were allowed to work with machinery unguarded, whereas others insisted upon its protection; if some were to work in any sort of a factory, under any sort of conditions, with any sort of a foreman or master, while others insisted upon proper surroundings; if some were willing to be so over-rushed as to do more than a fair day's work for a fair day's wage, or would allow themselves to be forced into patronizing truck stores, to submit to arbitrary fines and unreasonable deductions, whereas others would rebel at these impositions, it would result that in the competition among the men to retain their positions, those who were most pliant and lowest spirited would secure the work, and the wages, hours of labor, and conditions of employment would be those set or accepted by the poorest, most cringing, and least independent of workers. If the trade union did not insist upon enforcing common rules providing for equal pay for equal work and definite conditions of safety and health for all workers in the trade, the result would be that all pretense of a joint bargain would disappear, and the employers would be free constantly to make individual contracts with the various members of the union. The trade union does not stand for equal earnings of all workmen. It does not object to one man's earning twice as much as the man working by his side, provided both men have equal rates of pay, equal hours of work, equal opportunities of securing work, and equal conditions of employment. The union does not object to an employer's rewarding especially efficient workers, or even favored workers, by paying them more than the union scale, or granting them shorter hours than provided for by the joint agreement. What the union does stand for is merely equal rates of pay—equal pay for equal work; and while it will allow a man to receive twice as much as his fellow-craftsmen, it will not permit him to do so by underbidding them in wages or by working under less favorable conditions or for longer hours. Neither does the union oppose competition among unionists for positions, although it demands that this competition be solely upon the basis of efficiency and not upon that of reduced wages, lengthened hours, or any abatement from the conditions fixed by the collective bargain.

This principle of trade unionism will explain many of the seeming peculiarities and many of the numerous rules of labor organizations. It will supply an answer to the question so naïvely put by many people, as to why the union will not allow a man to accept two dollars a day, while all other workers in that trade are receiving three dollars, or to accept forty cents for mining a ton of coal, when the minimum scale is fifty-six cents. "Why," it is inquired, "should not a man be allowed to accept a reduction of wages if he wish? Why should a man be compelled to take more wages than he wants?" The answer of the unions is that as a result of such individual bargains, the employer would give all the work to the men who were satisfied with two dollars a day, and, consequently, the men who demanded three dollars would be thrown out of employment, and therefore forced to accept a lower rate of remuneration. It is this necessity of equal pay for equal work that compels trade unions to say to the employer: "Either you shall pay three dollars to the man who only asks for two, or we will not work for you. We recognize your right to employ or not to employ whomsoever you wish, but either you must pay *at least* three dollars, or else all the members of our union will refuse to work for you."

This necessity of defending the collective bargain, or contract, explains many features of trade union policy. If the union is to maintain its standard of wages by collective bargaining, it must prevent the employer, by individual bargains with individual workmen, from making deductions from wages and thus breaking down the minimum wage agreed upon between the union and the employer. If trade unions are to tolerate truck stores, not only will unfair and extortionate prices be charged, but individual men desiring the favor of the employer will compete for their jobs by purchasing more and more goods in the company store. Instead of offering to work for two dollars a day when the standard rate is three, a man may simply take for his work an order on the store, which, though nominally worth three, will actually be worth two dollars. It is well known that companies operating truck stores for profit in connection with their factories, invariably give the preference in the matter of jobs to men who best patronize the stores, with the result that competition for jobs among workmen becomes as severe as ever, and the consequent undercutting or underbidding takes the vicious form of spending as much as possible at the company store. The toleration of the company store may thus come to mean a series of individual agreements, real but not expressed, by which individual workingmen permit themselves to suffer deductions from their real wages in the form of profits on the goods which they are obliged to buy.

The prohibition by unions of arbitrary fines and docking is due to this same desire to maintain a common minimum standard of wages and conditions. Apart from the direct evil and oppression that result from the unlimited powers of employers arbitrarily to levy fines or make deductions from wages, there is the added danger that, by this means, the employers will break down the collective bargain and substitute for it a series of individual bargains. If the trade unions secure from the employer a minimum daily three-dollar wage, the effect of this common action will be nullified and destroyed if some individual workmen submit in any form to an average deduction of ten cents a day, whether for fines or docking, others to a deduction of twenty cents, and others to one of fifty cents or a dollar a day. The union is not opposed to a deduction from wages in case of proved negligence or poor workmanship; but as these fines and this docking affect the union wage, they should be jointly determined upon by the employer and union, and not by the employer alone, nor between the employer and the individual workman. If the individual employee is permitted to make any rebate or allow any deduction whatsoever, under whatever guise, from the wages fixed as a minimum by the union, then the whole principle of a union scale of wages will fall to the ground.

The necessity of maintaining the collective, rather than the individual, bargain explains why the trade union is sometimes opposed to the piece system and sometimes not. When the piece price can be regulated collectively, as in bituminous coal mining, the unions are not antagonistic to, but actually in favor of, this system. Where, however, each separate job differs and a price must be put upon it separately, payment by the piece degenerates into a system of underbidding and undercutting and to the resurrection of individual bargaining in one of its worst forms. Where the price cannot be fixed collectively and where time wages cannot be paid, the union has solved the problem, at least partially, by having the shop foreman, a representative of all the men in the establishment, fix the price of the work in concert with the employer or foreman.

Like the wage scale, the length of the working day, as determined by the union and employers, must be protected from changes made by individual workmen. The individual workman cannot be allowed to work longer hours than the union prescribes as a maximum, or to work more overtime, or at different times, or for less compensation than is fixed by the collective bargain. If the individual workman is to decide for himself how much overtime he will work, and at what rate of compensation, he can just as surely underbid other workmen as by accepting a lower wage at the start.

There is hardly an action taken by the trade unions, hardly a demand made, which does not either immediately or ultimately, directly or indirectly, involve this principle. Whether the union demand a higher standard of healthfulness, comfort, or decency in the factories, or a greater degree of protection from machinery, or any other concession ministering to the health or safety of the employee, the demand is always in the form of a certain minimum for all workers. The union does not prohibit a man from being paid more wages for less hours than his fellows, but it does claim that no man shall work in union shops for less than a certain rate, for more than a certain number of hours, for more than so and so much overtime, or at a lower rate for overtime, or with less than a given amount of protection to his health, comfort, safety, and well-being. The employer may, if he wish, make special provision for the health of a favorite workman, just as he may pay above the union rate or allow an employee, in return for the minimum wage, to work less than the maximum number of working hours prescribed by the union. What the union insists upon, however, is that certain minimum requirements be fulfilled for the health, comfort, and safety of all, in order that the workingmen shall not be obliged to compete for jobs by surrendering their claims to a reasonable amount of protection for their health, and for their life and limb.

The trade union thus stands for the freedom of contract on the part of workingmen—the freedom or right to contract collectively. The trade union also stands for definiteness of the labor contract. The relation between employer and employee is complex in its nature, even though it appear simple. The workingman agrees to work at the wage offered to him by the employer, at, say, fifteen dollars a week, but frequently nothing is said as to hours of labor, pauses for meals and rest, intensity of work, conditions of the workshop, protection of the workman against filthy surroundings or unguarded machinery, character of his fellow-workmen, liability of the employer for accident, nor any of the thousand conditions which affect the welfare of the workman and the gain of both employer and employee. There has always been a general tacit understanding between employers and employees that these conditions shall roughly conform to the usual and ordinary custom of the trade, but in the absence of an agreement with the union, it is in the power of the employer to make such rules absolutely, or to change or amend them at such time as he thinks proper. Like the railroad timetables, the individual contract reads, "Subject to change without notice."

The recognition of the union is nothing more nor less than the recognition of the principle for which trade unionism stands, the right to bargain collectively and to insist upon a common standard as a minimum. Workingmen have a nominal, but not a real freedom of contract, if they are prevented from contracting collectively instead of individually. The welfare of the working classes, as of society, depends upon the recognition of this principle of the right of employees to contract collectively. An employer, be he ever so well-meaning, stands in the way of future progress if he insist upon dealing with his workmen "as individuals." While in his establishment wages may not by this means be reduced, owing to the fact that other establishments are organized, still the principle for which he stands, if universally adopted, would mean the degradation and impoverishment of the working classes. There are many employers who surrender the principle of the individual bargain without accepting the principle of the collective bargain. These employers state that they do not insist upon dealing with their employees as individuals, but that they must retain the right of dealing with "their own employees solely," and that they must not be forced to permit a man who is not their own employee to interfere in their business. The right to bargain collectively, however, or to take any other concerted action, necessarily involves the right to representation. Experience and reason both show that a man, even if otherwise qualified, who is dependent upon the good will of an employer, is in no position to negotiate with him, since an insistence upon what he considers to be the rights of the men represented by him may mean his dismissal or, at all events, the loss of the favor of his employer. Not only should workingmen have the right of contracting collectively, but they should also have the right of being represented by whomsoever they wish. The denial of the right of representation is tyranny. Without the right to choose their representative, the men cannot enjoy the full benefit of collective bargaining; and without the right of collective bargaining, the door is opened to the individual contract and to the progressive debasement of the working classes, and to the deterioration of conditions of work to the level of conditions in the sweated and unregulated trades. To avoid this calamity and to raise the working classes to a high state of efficiency and a high standard of citizenship, the organized workmen demand and insist upon "the recognition of the union."

CHAPTER II

LABOR UNORGANIZED

The History of Labor is the History of the Human Race. The Chronicles of Kings and the Annals of the Poor. Ancient Society. War and Slavery. The Military System. Character of Ancient Slavery. Serfdom. Free Labor and the Freedom of Contract. Free Labor, the Collective Contract, and Trade Unionism.

THE history of labor is the history of the human race. From the dimmest ages of antiquity, man has eaten his bread in the sweat of his brow and has toiled incessantly that he might live. There has never been a Golden Age when men lived without working or reaped fields that were not sown. All that the race has gained, the right to live and bear children, the improvement of existence, the securing of comfort, happiness, and civilization, has been the result of an unremittent, never-ending toil on the part of millions.

The reward of labor has not always been to the laborer. From the beginning some have worked and others played, some have tilled and others eaten of the fruits. The workers, however, have always been in a vast majority.

In reading the history of past ages, one might imagine that the world was comprised of kings and nobles and that the common people had no existence. History reads like the newspapers of fashion, which tell us each summer that "everyone is out of town," though hundreds of thousands of wage earners are sweltering at their daily tasks. The pages of history abound with narratives of the doings and sayings of kings and princes, while the life and labor of the vast, silent, unnumbered multitude of toilers are unrecorded and unmentioned.

The wage earners of to-day differ fundamentally from the men who in the early stages of society performed the rough work of civilization. The ancient workman had his position fixed by custom, law, or religion. There was no opportunity for free contract by free laborers, and society evolved along the lines of labor fixed by status. The very early history of man, moreover, is the story of an incessant struggle with poverty. Men did not sow crops nor breed animals, but subsisted on what roots or wild fruits they found in the woods, or such food as they managed to obtain by hunting or fishing. It was a hand to mouth existence. By such uncertain methods of obtaining the means of subsistence, large populations cannot be supported, but flourish only when man helps nature by domesticating animals and cultivating crops. The numbers of men, then, did not increase, and great wealth did not exist, until society reached the pastoral stage, when men drove tamed herds from one good pasture to another. But the possibilities of labor became still greater when the agricultural stage was reached, and clans or tribes settled on fertile plains. From this time on a high state of civilization became possible; yet the essence of early history is the poverty of society. Where the struggle with nature is hard, man prefers to take rather than to produce, and the dominant note of early history is war. Rival communities battled with each other for the means of subsistence. As in our days the distribution of wealth causes bloodless contests between various social classes, so in the greater poverty of those days the insufficiency of the food supply led to constant struggles between various tribes and nations and to a never-ending war. Unlike modern society, which is based on industry and the production of wealth, the nations of those days were organized on a military basis, and the levying of tribute which plays so great a part in ancient history, shows that conquering nations lay emphasis upon the forcible acquisition rather than upon the production of wealth. With war came slavery. The conquering tribes in their raids secured not only the goods produced by the vanquished, but equally their means of production, most of the captives becoming slaves.

At first this slavery, unlike that of modern times, was merely incidental, and for a long time the number of slaves remained small. It increased, however, with the development of society. Servitude was not only forced upon the victims of war, but was used as a punishment for crime or failure to pay debts or taxes. Slavery became a system, which had at least one merit, that it trained millions of men to work. It is probable that the slavery of ancient times was not so harsh as it became in modern days, although many individual instances of excessive cruelty are recorded. The hard work of the community was performed by enslaved labor, without which there seemed to be no possibility of carrying on industry. The comparative absence of money prevented the toiler from receiving any pay except his food, clothes, and lodging, and the system was justified by philosophers and philanthropists. The number of slaves grew by natural increase, and communities flourished and attained to power under a system based upon the enforced labor of men.

Under slavery, of course, there could be no democratic organization of labor, such as exists in modern times. Certain rights, it is true, were accorded slaves among some tribes and nations, but never were they free agents with the right of combination. Though often subject to be beaten or slain by their masters they, in some places, enjoyed the protection of the law and might even obtain money and save it. Still, as long as they remained slaves the direction of their labor was in the hands of their masters and they were necessarily obliged to perform such services as were demanded of them. Frequently, the growth of rights among slaves led to the emancipation of individual bondmen. The right to save money was followed by the right to purchase freedom. As a consequence, even in ancient times, there existed a certain number of free workmen consisting of emancipated slaves, their children, or unfortunate representatives of other classes, though, as long as slavery endured and as long as war remained the chief concern of the nation, work was regarded as degrading and dishonoring.

At a later stage in the history of labor came the system of serfage. The distinguishing characteristic of serfage is that the laborer, while not actually a slave, is attached to the soil, and though more or less free in his domestic and private relations, is compelled to remain upon the land upon which he was born or to which he was allotted, and to work under conditions prescribed *for* him and not *by* him.

It is not to be supposed that the serfs, or even the slaves before them, necessarily desired freedom. Among some races the slaves looked with contempt upon the man without a master, and even in Anglo-Saxon England, the law prescribed that a lordless man be allotted to a lord in the neighborhood. Present day ideals did not govern society at that time. The system of serfage involved a greater independence than did slavery, but the character and routine of work were prescribed, not decided upon by negotiation or contract, the workingman being born to his position and to his work. The distinguishing mark of ancient labor is a fixity of relations, a determination of conditions by law, custom, or religion, and no more than slavery was serfage conducive to democratic organization. Free workers, it is true, even in ancient times apparently associated themselves into bodies, yet nothing in the nature of modern organized labor, with its potentiality of regulating conditions and remuneration by concerted action, could possibly have existed.

The story of modern labor begins with the gradual emancipation or freedom from serfage. This development took place at various times in the various countries, being earlier in England than elsewhere, owing to the fact that the English were the least military of nations. The growth of England's industries and consequently of its towns permitted the formation of groups of city workmen who acknowledged no lord. The obligation to remain upon the land and to pay certain labor dues to the lord was commuted into money payments. Instead of giving a specified number of days of work, the laborer now made a certain money payment, which came to be regarded as rent, while the property right came to be invested in the man himself. The right of contract was greatly extended and the establishment of a fixed money or medium of exchange aided in the emancipation of the laboring masses.

The evolution from serfage, as the evolution from slavery, was due to the greater efficiency of free labor. Where a man is not free there can not be the same incentive to work as where he is free. The prospect of gain is a stronger incentive than the fear of a master. The freedom of the laborer and the right of free contract changed entirely the relation between the workman and his work. Under slavery there had been no necessity for a labor contract. The master owned the worker, as he owned the tools and the material to be worked upon; the slaves worked as many hours and under whatever conditions the master prescribed, and all questions of the interpretation of the relations between the two men were settled by the crack of the lash. With the emancipation of the slave, however, the freedom of the individual contract was assured, and the way was paved for ultimately securing the right of forming trade unions and making collective contracts.

The rise of free labor did not mean the immediate establishment of labor organizations. As long as the laborer worked for himself, or as long as he worked for a master approximately his equal, and as long as industry was conducted upon a small scale, trade unionism was not essential or even possible.

Trade unionism is based upon the idea of the association of free workingmen, united for the purpose of fixing the conditions of labor. Where workingmen are not free or where the conditions of labor are fixed by law, custom, or religion, or by the action of individual workmen or employers, there trade unionism cannot exist. Trade unionism is a late product of the development of free labor employed in industry upon a large scale. The organization of labor results only from the organization of industry. The conditions giving rise to trade unionism and the steps by which labor organizations grew to their present position in England and the United States will be the subject of succeeding chapters.

CHAPTER III

TRADE UNIONISM—A PRODUCT OF MODERN INDUSTRY

Trade Unionism Bound up with Modern Factory System. What is Modern Industry? What is the Factory System? The Steam Engine and Machinery Revolutionize Industry. Canals, Railroads, Telegraph, Telephone, Electricity. Growth of Cities. Education. Political Democracy. Increase of Poverty and of Wealth. This Development takes place first in England. Reasons for English Domination: Internal Peace, Rivers, Good Roads, Harbors; Political Development. The creation of a New World. Modern Trade Unions and the Mediæval Guilds.

NO one can understand the true nature of trade unionism without understanding the industrial revolution and what it accomplished. The history of mankind has been more vitally affected by changes in its machines and its methods of doing business than by any action or counsel of statesmen or philosophers. What we call the modern world, with its huge populations, its giant cities, its political democracy, its growing intensity of life, its contrasts of wealth and poverty—this great, whirling, restless civilization, with all its vexing problems, is the offspring merely of changed methods of producing wealth. All that is good and all that is bad in the new order of things is due to these changes. The rapid progress in arts and sciences, the advance in technical processes, the change from wood to iron, from iron to steel, the girding of the earth by the iron rail, the copper wire, the vivified air itself, the education of the people, the massing of millions in cities, the abject misery of legions of the poor, the whole change from a monotonously simple to a bewilderingly complex and intricate life—all this is a part and a consequence of the industrial revolution.

This revolution did not break upon society in the dawn of a morning. Like all revolutions, it was merely the last stage of a long evolution. During the protracted winter of the dark ages England, like the rest of Europe, was hibernating, to awake only in response to a series of shocks from the outside world. With the discovery of America in 1492 and its subsequent settlement by European nations, the death-knell of the feudal system in Europe was sounded, and from that time on modern political conditions began to exist in the Old World. The little principalities were swallowed up by great states and the modern nations of Europe took their rise, while similar changes took place in the world of industry and business.

During the middle ages industry had been circumscribed by the limits of a province, or even of a village. In most countries of Europe toll-gates were to be found on every road. Little commerce was carried on, and that was limited to things of small bulk and large value. At mediæval fairs there was some little trade, but this was small and consisted chiefly of articles of common consumption. The bad state and insecurity of the roads and the excessive cost of haulage, the burdens laid upon transportation and commerce, and the comparative lack of money or of any means of credit, conspired with the poverty of the nations to prevent the growth of trade. As a consequence, much of the production of a household was for the use of that household, and most of the production of a village for the use of that village. There was no opportunity for a division of labor, since division of labor is possible only where production is large and the market extended. Not until the beginning of modern times, with the discovery of America and the foundation of colonies did markets expand.

At the dawn of the eighteenth century a capitalist class began to exist in England. These capitalists consisted of men of some wealth who contracted for the purchase of raw materials and for the sale of articles and gave out the work to be done in cottages in the various villages. From this time on there developed a separate class of workingmen, who had no hope of eventually becoming masters of their craft. As time went on the independent contractors became employers in the modern sense of the word, assembling their employees in workshops or small manufacturing towns. Henceforth the workman grew more dependent upon the employer, becoming a subject of the tolling factory bell.

The industrial revolution was more rapid and complete in England than elsewhere, because at that time England was of all nations the most advanced. Prior to the invention of the railway and the improvement of the common roads, commerce was practically confined to traffic by sea and river, and much of England's progress was due to its being an island, an island, moreover, with a meshwork of navigable streams. Furthermore, the possession of one of the strongest fleets in the world guaranteed England against foreign invasion, and politically and industrially, the country led the nations of Europe. For centuries no foreign army had set foot upon English soil, and thus unmolested the Englishman could till his farm and pasture his flocks. The country grew in population and wealth, woolen and silk mills arose, and the nation was able during the course of many generations to work out its political and economic salvation.

The really important industrial changes, or what is called the industrial revolution, occurred during the middle of the eighteenth century, and especially during the period from 1760 to 1785. During this quarter of a century, there came a series of revolutionary inventions, the like of which had never before been witnessed in the history of the world. This generation saw the invention of the steam engine, which revolutionized the production of power, and the discovery of the process of puddling and rolling iron and smelting by coal. The invention of the spinning jenny, the power loom, and the carding machine gave an impetus to the cheap and wholesale production of textiles, while other inventions in the pottery trade, in printing from cylinders, in bleaching by chemical agents, furthered the rapid development of industry. The market was extended by improved methods of digging canals, and the stupendous development of commerce, which was later to follow through the introduction of railway and steamship locomotion, was already foreshadowed. These inventions placed England in a position to produce for the civilized world and to break down the barriers which had previously restricted commerce. The veins of old England were filled with new blood, and industry was stimulated as never before. Business became wholesale instead of retail, and labor was affected exactly as all other commodities of sale or purchase. In mediæval times wages had largely been determined by custom and tradition, when not actually legally fixed by justices of the peace. The inventions and discoveries of this period created an enormous demand for labor, especially the labor of women and children. The peaceful, sleepy villages of Southern England were emptied of their inhabitants; the English yeomen, displaced by the political and economic development of the preceding century, flocked to the factories and to the busy upgrowing towns of the North. The new industrial world with all its latent good and evil had been born.

It was thus in England that the revolution first took place; it was therefore, this country which first acquired great wealth and industrial preeminence, and was first visited by the modern labor problem. Just as the factory system in England produced trade unions and the labor problem, so the same cause was followed by the same result in other countries. France, Germany, Belgium, Holland, and Switzerland were from fifty to seventy-five years behind England in their industrial development, but, with the advent of the factory in these countries, there came also the labor problem and the trade union. What was true of England and of continental countries was also true of the United States; and in every country where the industrial revolution occurred, an entire readjustment of the conditions of labor and capital was found necessary. Thus modern industrial conditions gave rise to the need of modern trade unions. In Russia, Hungary, Servia and other backward countries, the industrial revolution is as yet only in its initial stages, and in these lands trade unionism can hardly be said to exist, since the organization of labor is necessarily founded upon a high state of industrial development.

It is vain to deplore, as many have done and still do, the evil effects of a movement of the stupendous magnitude of the industrial revolution. Whether for weal or woe, the change was inevitable, and reform could be found only in further development and not in a return to the past. For some time the people of England looked to the past for relief from the evils which the factory system had brought upon them. Workingmen destroyed machinery, committed violence, and applied for the reënactment or reenforcement of obsolete and impracticable laws, while the foremost men of the time wrote impassioned invectives against the new régime. Only gradually was the true method of reform for the evils of the factory system seen to lie in factory legislation and in the organization of labor. Gradually the evil conditions produced by the factory system brought, at least in part, their own corrective, and the creation, through production on a large scale, of a separate working class with separate working class ideals formed the origin and basis of trade unionism as it exists to-day.

Centuries before the advent of the modern trade union, there had existed certain trade organizations called guilds. These guilds, however, while in some respects similar to trade unions, differed from the modern labor organization as fundamentally as the ancient slave or mediæval serf differs from the modern workingman. The guilds were composed not only of workmen, but of masters, and these latter usually exercised control over the organization. In the days of the guilds, the division of society was not one of journeymen against masters within the trade—because the journeyman expected in course of time to become a master himself—but rather of one guild or trade against another. The guilds were semi-public bodies with the power of government within the trade and often partaking in the government of the city itself. The old guilds could be better likened to organizations composed of employers and workingmen, and even the public itself, than to an association of workmen alone. Guilds had benefit features, as have many of our modern trade unions, and, like them, fostered a fraternal spirit among the workmen. Furthermore, they regulated wages, the hours of labor, the character and excellence of the work, the number of apprentices, and other conditions of trade, thus resembling in at least some respects the trade union of to-day. The modern labor organization, however, differs from the guild, in that it is a union of workingmen banded together not primarily in the interests of the masters of the trade, but in their own interests, and in the further fact that the workingmen so united are likely to remain workingmen for the rest of their lives. It is not believed by men who have studied this question that the trade unions which sprang up in the eighteenth century and began to flourish extensively in the nineteenth had any direct historical connection with the old guilds, and the history of the guilds is chiefly interesting as showing that at all times some form of organization has been deemed necessary by workingmen. The character of the organization, however, has changed fundamentally with the change in the character of industry and in the position and prospects of the workingman. Modern trade unionism must therefore be considered as a product of modern industry and as the direct offspring of the factory system.

CHAPTER IV

THE OPPRESSION OF LABOR UNDER THE FACTORY SYSTEM

Merrie England before the Factory System. Growth of Cities. Wheat Famines. Dear Bread and Low Wages. The Disappearance of the Old Handworkers. Fifteen Hours a day for Women and Children. The Parishes Sell Pauper Children to Manufacturers. Degradation of Labor. Terrible Death Rate. The Birth of the City Slum. Sickness and Plagues. The Manufacture of Cripples. Uncertainty of Work. No Room for Old Men. Immoral Tone of the Factories. Opium for Babies. No time for Childbirth. Death-dealing Machines. Deterioration of the Workingman.

THE factory system gave birth in England to a rarely paralleled oppression of the working classes. It had been predicted that, were there no artificial checks upon human action, the welfare of the whole nation would be attained by allowing each individual to pursue his own interest. This policy of permitting one section of a population to seek its ends at the expense of another culminated in a state of affairs incredible but for the testimony of thousands of witnesses before the various Parliamentary investigating committees appointed during the first half of the nineteenth century. These investigations were as a blinding light suddenly cast into a deep Inferno, photographing a swarming mass of torturing fiends and tortured victims. Even after the lapse of over half a century the mind recoils with horror from the most superficial description of these conditions.

With the coming of the factory, England began to change from a country of farms and pastures to a land of manufacturing towns. During this time towns and cities, especially in the manufacturing districts of the North, grew at a rapid pace, while the farming population failed to increase in proportion. The growth of the towns meant the growth of a labor supply for the factories, and everything conspired to produce this result.

For half a century before 1760 crops had been unusually good and harvests plentiful, but the decades immediately following that date contained a series of years of unprecedentedly short crops. Times were bad in the country districts. The yeoman, or small farming class, was gradually driven from the farm to the town. The common land for the pasture of cattle was rapidly enclosed and appropriated, and with the advent of the factory, the women of the farm were deprived of their winter earnings from spinning and weaving. The old hand weavers, who worked in their own homes and cultivated a small plot of ground, were driven out by the competition of the power loom, and these as well as the yeomen moved in droves to the towns. The grinding poverty of these newcomers did not prevent but rather accelerated the increase in population. There was "a devastating harvest of babies," doomed to a premature end in the city slum or to a living death in the rapacious factories. Taxes increased, the cost of living rose, and the real wages of workers fell, during the early years of the nineteenth century, to a point below which they had probably never before sunk during the five centuries preceding.

So low did wages fall that men came to believe in the idea of an iron law of wages, a cruel, immutable law, by which the pay of workmen was fixed at the lowest point compatible with mere existence. The actual conditions of the period seemed to warrant and verify the most dismal and pessimistic theories. The attitude of manufacturers under the stress of competition was that of masters toward slaves gratuitously obtained. As long as a slave is a valuable commodity, costing, let us say, a thousand dollars or more, it pays his master to be as careful of him as of an ox or a horse. At the beginning of the last century, however, what were practically white slaves were delivered free of cost and in almost unlimited numbers. Frequently manufacturers, far from paying for the use of pauper children, were actually compensated for ridding the parish of them. In one case an employer contracted to take one idiot child for each twenty sane children. The ruthless waste of human life under such conditions scarce finds a parallel in the chronicles of peace.

The change from a rural to a city residence on the part of hundreds of thousands of men was attended by widespread and acute misery. The

JAMES O'CONNELL
President of the International Association of Machinists; Third Vice-President of the American Federation of Labor

MAX MORRIS
Secretary of the Retail Clerks' International Protective Association; Fourth Vice-President of the American Federation of Labor

crowded slums of contemporaneous New York and London find their prototype in the overcrowding of the manufacturing towns of the England of that day. No one was concerned for the wellbeing of the newcomers. They lived in the smallest of dingy, filthy, foul-smelling rooms, in ill-built houses on ill-kept streets, in cellars and over open drains. In these dens, reeking with accumulations of filth, destitute of the primary conveniences and fundamental necessaries of health, families of artisans crowded under conditions destructive of morality and fatal to life itself. All ages and sexes herded together; there were as many people in a room as there was impure air to breathe. Refuse and filth littered the streets of the workingmen's quarter, which became a breeding place for the most virulent diseases. Epidemics of typhus and scarlet fever periodically ravaged these precincts and at times invaded the aristocratic portions of the towns.

The misery of the workingmen was aggravated by their numbers. The birth rate both in England and Ireland was high, and population mounted by leaps and bounds. At the same time, the change from manufacturing by hand to manufacturing by machine released a large surplus labor force, which was suddenly thrust into the labor market. The failure of the crops, the devastating effects of the Napoleonic wars, the sinews of which England was providing for all Europe, the heavy taxes, and the cruelly oppressive poor law—all tended to depress the real wages of agricultural workers and to force them into the factories.

The condition of these workmen in the textile and other factories was incredibly bad. The day's work was constantly lengthened, in some cases to fourteen, sixteen, and more hours, and while not difficult, the labor was confining and nerve-wearing. There was little provision for the safety of the workman, and terrible accidents were a matter of daily occurrence in the crowded mills and factories. Periods of feverish activity, during which men were worked beyond the limit of human endurance, were succeeded by still more harassing periods of depression, when thousands of men were thrown into the street. The low wages and the long hours of toil left the workmen with desire for no healthful pleasures and unfitted them for moral and mental development. The drunkenness which prevailed at that time—when in some cities one out of every ten houses was a tavern—the growing sexual license of the population and the rapid increase of illegitimacy characterized the manufacturing towns throughout the length and breadth of England. The terrible handicap under which the adult population was laboring was reflected in a veritable floodtide of criminality, the number of criminals increasing almost sevenfold within a period of thirty-seven years.

To the male operative, however, the worst feature of his work was its insecurity. Not only was he liable in bad times to lose his position, but in addition, with each advance in technical processes thousands and tens of thousands lost their livelihood. True, with the increase in manufacturing, some of these men regained positions, yet there were always many permanently deprived of the means of subsistence. The number of men forced to leave the region, to become tramps, or to seek refuge in poorhouses, grew with each decade, and even in good times there was a tendency in the factories toward the displacement of the men by their wives and children. The light, confining work of the textile factory was one to which the physique of women and children was peculiarly adapted, and this labor had the additional advantage of being cheap and docile. In the textile factories men worked side by side with their wives and children, and in other cases were supported by their wives who had taken their places at the whirling machines. The mad rush for exorbitant profits, unchecked by Government or by the concerted action of workingmen, led to tragic situations. The unrestricted play of "the *natural* law of supply and demand" of labor reversed the law of Nature, unsexed men and women, and made the child the father of the man, and his breadwinner. In many cases, full-grown men stayed at home minding babies or mending stockings, while the women were engaged all day at the wearing work of the mills. There was no room in the factories for old men. Of sixteen hundred operatives employed in several factories in Harpur and Lanark but ten were over forty-five years of age, and of over twenty-two thousand operatives in Stockport and Manchester less than one hundred and fifty were of that age. The result was not only an increase in the number of paupers and criminals, but a humiliating dependence of men upon women, in many cases resulting in the breaking up of the home.

Much of the burden of these evil conditions, unrestrained by law or by trade unions, fell upon the shoulders of women. The factory knew no regard for sex or weakness. The hours of labor were frequently extended to fourteen and over, and the women were obliged to be at their work on the minute, irrespective of the distance from their homes or the domestic duties which they were thus obliged to neglect. The condition of the factory rooms was ill adapted to foster feelings of delicacy or the finer womanly instincts. No special provision was made for wants of the operatives—no attempt to secure privacy or decent accommodations. The dangers which beset women in industrial life were increased by the attitude of the employers, and the moral atmosphere of the factories became absolutely intolerable.

The physical conditions of work were equally bad. The air of the textile factories, warm, humid, fetid, unventilated, and, in the cotton and linen mills, laden with irritating fibrous dust, exerted an enervating effect upon the operatives and produced a series of chronic affections. The women of the factory, insufficiently clothed, were exposed, upon leaving, to the rain or cold, and diseases of the lungs became frequent. Over the heads of these women hung the constant fear of losing their positions, and with them their grip upon life, and the employer used this dread as a whip to goad them on to new exertions and to the suffering of new indignities. In the eyes of some manufacturers no illness and no condition excused the worker for non-attendance or lateness. Instances are even recorded of children born in the noise and the whirl and the filthiness of the factory itself. The testimony of many women separated from their offspring, and frequently working at exhausting labor during this critical period, presents the most fearful indictment against unrestrained and unregulated competition in female labor that can be well conceived.

The effect of such conditions upon the children of the factory operatives may be imagined. Even before birth the chances of these babes were lessened by the excessive work of their mothers. The mortality of the newborn was deplorably high. Unable to attend to their children, mothers would frequently give them in charge to others or leave them in the care of children scarcely older than the infants themselves. The death-rate among infants so given out reminds one of the terrible mortality in baby farms. Children were quieted with spirits and even opiates, and if left at home they were necessarily neglected in the absence of both parents. The number of children burnt or mangled rose to astounding proportions. In Manchester some 52 per cent. of all children of the working people died before the age of five years, while the death-rate for the well-to-do classes amounted to only 20 per cent. Even those who survived and lived out their childhood in the damp, dark, filthy, reeking dwellings of the poor held an insecure lease upon life. The poor children of Manchester and other factory towns presented an appearance woefully pallid. Insufficient in quantity and lacking in nutrition as was the food of the adults, that of infants was even worse. Furthermore, in the absence of all suitable medical attendance, owing to its dearness, the working people were obliged to resort to patent medicines containing deleterious substances.

At an early age children of the working classes were graduated from the dangers of the street to the dangers of the mill. In the cotton mills children began to be employed at nine years of age, while in the silk mills boys of six and even five were employed for interminably long hours. The necessity imposed upon all workers, even children, of standing through the whole course of their employment, often in constrained and confining postures, their attention riveted upon a monotous, infinitely self-repeating process, crippled both mind and body. The manufacturing towns of the North were full of deformed children suffering from rachitis and from affections of the spinal column. A peculiar dislocation of the legs, in which the knees were bent backward and inward, manifested itself frequently. The excessive hours also resulted in an arrested development of both sexes, amounting frequently to permanent immaturity, and in many other ways the sins against the adults were visited upon the children. The whole physique of the working population was debased and degraded. The ill health of the people became proverbial, and the streets of the factory towns were haunted by pale, sallow faces. The recruiting officers of His Majesty's army found few to choose from among the throngs of undersized, stoop-shouldered, narrow-chested workmen whose youth and strength had been spent in the factories of England.

The condition of the miners of that day was even worse than that of the factory hands. The factory population had the advantage of living together, in touch with or at least in sight of civilization; but the miners were collected in miserable, lonely, out-of-the-way villages and were beyond the reach of justice and of public opinion. Consequently, there was no limit to the oppresssion to which these underground workers could be subjected. The mines swallowed up children at an age when they could not even have been admitted to school and threw them back upon the pauper rates of the parish at an age when they should have been in the full vigor of manhood.

The work of the mines was appallingly difficult. The miner was obliged to descend deep shafts, often requiring an hour for descent and ascent, and to work eleven, twelve, even fourteen hours and more at the most arduous labor and under the most atrocious sanitary conditions. The mines of those days were inadequately ventilated. The miner worked in an atmosphere deficient in oxygen and full of dust, powder, smoke, sulphur and carbonic acid gas. No wonder that he aged rapidly and that at thirty-five or forty he was cast aside, dismissed from his employment. The excessive work in such environment by men alternately exposed to the torrid heat of the mines and the cold and damp of the outer air, induced consumption as well as other affections of the lungs, heart, and stomach. The living conditions of the men were as evil as their working conditions. The miners lived in squalid huts or huddled together in barracks, in one instance fifty-six men and boys sleeping in one large-sized room.

The men employed at hewing coal were practically serfs, attached to the mine, and, as serfs, were exploited to the uttermost limit. The men were obliged to engage themselves for a year and during that period were not allowed to work for any other mine owner. The mine owner, for his part, however, did not guarantee them any particular amount of work, or, indeed, any work at all. Any breach of this unequal contract was harshly punished by justices of the peace, who were either mine owners themselves or relatives or pliant tools of mine owners. The miner who sought employment from any one except the mine owner to whom he was hired was summarily sent to jail or to the treadmill. The abuses which have always characterized the employment of men in lonely places, the truck store, infrequent payment, withheld wages, company houses, and unfair docking were carried on openly and shamelessly. Accidents were shockingly frequent, and, despite the manifest and criminal negligence of the mine owners, the resulting deaths were invariably ascribed by complaisant juries to "the act of God" or the carelessness of the victim.

The system bore especially hard upon the children. Over one-quarter of the employees in the coal mines were children or boys under twenty, and some of these entered the mines at six, five, and even four years of age. Nothing could surpass in horror the life of these children of five or six, sitting in the dark, damp passages of the mines, for twelve hours at a stretch, with no one to speak to, nothing to do to break the maddening monotony, nothing to lighten the black, terrifying solitude save the occasional opening or shutting of a mine door.

The whole population of the mines was cruelly overworked, even women not being immune from harsh treatment. Several thousand women and girls were employed in the mines, many of them engaged at hauling tubs of coal over the narrow and uneven underground passages. Frequently the women were obliged to push these tubs with their heads or haul them by a chain placed around the neck like a halter and passing between the legs. In many cases, especially in the thin veins, this work of pushing and dragging heavy loads was done by women or boys working on their hands and knees.

The severe strain of this work was aggravated by the conditions under which it was carried on. No provision was made for regular meal times, and men ate their food cold whenever they could snatch a chance. The heat of the mines was so intense that in some places men, women, and children worked throughout the whole day divested of their clothing. The thirst produced by the character of the atmosphere and the nature of the work could be slaked only by the dirty, lukewarm water underground, and the overexertion of the employees provoked the worst excesses of drunkenness and sensuality. The population of the mining region became bestialized. Men and women worked like galley slaves, without thought of a future, and without hope of escape from the remorseless tyranny of the mine owners. It was not until the year 1844, when the miners organized and for five months maintained an heroic though unsuccessful strike, that a ray of hope penetrated into the gloom of their life. The strike, although lost, fastened the attention of the community upon the utterly horrible conditions prevailing underground, and for the first time in their history, the miners of the United Kingdom awoke to the fact that they were men and not beasts.

CHAPTER V

BRITISH LABOR IN SELF-DEFENSE

Trade Unionism before 1760 Unimportant. The Growth of a Common Sentiment. Policy of the Early Unions. Fruitless Appeals for new Legislation for Workingmen. Repeal of the Old Laws in 1813 and 1814. Persecution of the Trade Unions. Savagery of the Courts. Imprisonment and Deportation for Unionists. Result—Greater Secrecy and Intensified Bitterness. Repeal of Conspiracy Laws. The First Waves of Unionism. Recession. National Revolutionary Unionism in 1834. Farm Laborers Unionized. Unions of Women. Robert Owen. The Hope of a Universal Strike. Persecution of the Unions. Defeat and Apathy. The End of the First Struggle.

IT is indicative of the lack of effective organization of the workingmen of those days that the first impulse toward improvement of factory conditions came from members of the aristocracy and of the middle class, rather than from the workingmen themselves. This legislation consisted of laws limiting the age at which children could be employed, the hours of work and the times of work of women and children, and providing for the health and safety of the toilers. Although the unionists felt the evil of the new conditions, they had not as yet learned the remedy, nor were they in a position to apply it had they known. Until 1824 trade unionism was unlawful, hence weak, and the bill for legalizing the formation of trade organizations was in that year carried through Parliament without the support and almost without the knowledge of the unionists. Subsequently, however, the unionists aided, and eventually assumed the leadership in, the agitation for the improvement of factory and mining conditions.

Trade unions in the sense of "continuous associations of wage earners for the purpose of maintaining or improving the conditions of their employment"[1] existed in England since the beginning of the eighteenth century,

---

[1] This definition, as much of the historical matter in this and the succeeding chapters, has been taken from "The History of Trade Unionism," by Sidney and Beatrice Webb. This book, as well as "Industrial Democracy," by the same authors, is a veritable storehouse of information upon the subject of trade unionism, especially in Great Britain.

Thomas I. Kidd
General Secretary of the Amalgamated Woodworkers International Union of America;
Fifth Vice-President of the American Federation of Labor

DENIS A. HAYES
President of the Glass Bottle Blowers' Association of the United States and Canada;
Sixth Vice-President of the American Federation of Labor

although their vital importance in the economic world was not felt prior to the year 1760. Long before that time, unions of journeymen were to be found in the building trades and among such artisans as tailors, woolworkers, silk weavers, and gold-beaters, where the extensive organization of the industry or the cost of materials or other capital, created a class of men who permanently remained wage earners. With the separation of the man from the machine, however, and the creation of a special capitalist or machine-owning class, trade unionism rapidly increased; and this movement was greatly accelerated by the assemblage in factories and towns of large bodies of men engaged in similar trades and their consequent awakening to a sense of their common interests.

At the beginning of the industrial revolution and for a considerable time thereafter, British trade unions were in theory and practice reactionary. They constantly appealed to Parliament to enforce obsolete laws limiting apprenticeship and permitting justices of the peace to determine wages. The labor organizations felt that the new conditions were their destruction, and they pleaded with Parliament to put a stop to the changes of the time and to reëstablish by law the conditions of life and labor existing before the introduction of machinery. In this endeavor the workingmen were, prior to the year 1756, not entirely unsuccessful, and many laws were placed upon the statute books in the hope of remedying the evils created by the new methods of production. After 1756 or thereabouts the attitude of the government underwent a change. The old statutes proved unenforceable, and the logic of circumstances drove Parliament into a practical policy of "hands off." This theory, which was based upon the idea that industry would develop more harmoniously without interference from the national legislature, was reënforced in 1776 by the appearance of a book written by Adam Smith, entitled "The Wealth of Nations," in which the doctrine of "let-alone," or "no interference," was propounded as the correct relation of government to industry. From 1760 to 1814, however, the unions did not desist from attempts to prosecute employers under the old laws or to secure new laws of greater stringency. These efforts were vigorously and successfully resisted by the employers. The laws in question were suspended during a series of years, and, finally, in 1813, the statute empowering justices of the peace to fix wages was suddenly and completely repealed. In the following year, despite vigorous protests from the working classes, the law limiting the number of apprentices was also removed from the statute book.

But the principle of "let-alone" did not work both ways. From 1814 employers were granted entire immunity from burdensome laws, but the same privilege was not extended to the workmen. The employers were given complete freedom of contract and were empowered to buy labor in their own way, but the workmen were refused the similar right to sell their labor as they saw fit. The British courts declared all combinations of workingmen illegal, in restraint of trade, and in violation of the common as well as of the statute law. The courts resurrected an obsolete law against conspiracy passed some five centuries before, the statute entitled "Who be Conspirators and Who be Champertors," and another law passed in 1549, directed against the maintenance of "trust" prices and styled "Bill of Conspiracies of Victuallers and Craftsmen."

The use against trade unions of the common law, as well as of these old statutes, was an innovation in those days, just as the application of the injunction to labor conflicts has proved to be in these. During the eighteenth century it had not been believed, or at least not clearly understood, that the courts would hold trade unions illegal; and the hostile employers appealed to Parliament for new legislation instead of applying to the courts for the enforcement of the old. To these demands of employers, Parliament lent an attentive ear. From time to time, during the eighteenth century special laws were passed against various individual unions, and in 1799 and 1800 general combination laws were enacted which rendered illegal the formation of trade organizations or the performance of any act for which they were created.

Laws, however, be they ever so stringent, cannot suppress a popular movement and unionism survived all attacks upon it. The trial of trade unionists in those days was carried on with barbarous and almost inconceivable savagery. Both judge and jury were recruited from the same class in society as the employer, and no leniency was extended to the "troublesome fellows" who had the hardihood to join labor organizations. In the harsh administration of a cruel law, the judges failed to temper injustice with mercy. Even where the union had been recognized by the employer, a vindictive prosecution might ensue. In 1798, five journeymen printers, who had been invited by their employers to meet with them and discuss grievances, were upon their arrival arrested and were subsequently tried, convicted, and sentenced to penal servitude. The efforts of striking workingmen were crippled from the outset, and unions were obliged to enter each struggle with their hands bound. The combination laws as they worked out in the textile industries were described as a tremendous millstone round the neck of the local artisan. "which had depressed and debased him to the earth: every act which he has attempted, every measure that he has devised to keep up or raise his wages, he has been told was illegal: the whole force of the civil power and influence of his district has been exerted against him because he was acting illegally: the magistrates, acting, as they believed, in unison with the views of the legislature, to check and keep down wages and combination, regarded, in almost every instance, every attempt on the part of the artisan to ameliorate his situation or support his station in society as a species of sedition and resistance of the government: every committee or active man among them was regarded as a turbulent, dangerous instigator, whom it was necessary to watch and crush if possible."[1]

Notwithstanding persecution and endeavors to disrupt them, the unions, especially among the skilled workmen, remained intact. This was due to the inefficient administration of the laws in England and to the further fact that in times when there were no strikes, there was little incentive to employers to persecute unions. Attacks were made upon labor organizations whenever a strike was threatened, but associations of hatters, coopers, cur-

[1] This is quoted from an anonymous pamphlet printed in 1823, the citation being reproduced in "The History of Trade Unionism," by Sidney and Beatrice Webb.

riers, compositors, shipwrights, and other workmen survived all assaults and continued to maintain their organization. Persecution, however, resulted, as it invariably does, in making organization more secret, discipline more rigid, and treatment of outsiders more harsh and arbitrary. In many unions no one knew who were the leaders, and men were expected to strike and did strike as the result of a hint and without a word being spoken. In 1812 forty thousand weavers struck upon a signal because the employers would not abide by the decision of the courts upon the matter of wages; but the leaders of this movement were cast into prison for the crime of combination, and, as a consequence, the strike collapsed.

During the years which followed the Napoleonic Wars, especially from 1816 to 1819, the depression in trade and the consequent fall in wages provoked a large number of strikes, and repressive measures were again carried out with unheard of severity. The attack on workingmen led, as has frequently been the case, to an assault upon the liberties of the people at large. In 1819 the so-called "Six Acts" were passed, which effectually suppressed public meetings, permitted magistrates to search for arms, strengthened the law against seditious libels, and placed an excessive stamp tax upon all publications owned by or friendly to labor organizations. These repressive measures aroused an intense hostility among the working classes, and this bitterness was responsible for many ill-advised strikes and indiscreet acts committed by trade unionists after the repeal of the combination laws.

It was not until 1824 that the law against combinations was repealed. This victory for the working classes was due in large measure to the indefatigable labors and remarkable astuteness of Francis Place, a retired master tailor and one of the most successful political managers of the age. After ten years of work and agitation, he secured the appointment of a Parliamentary committee of inquiry and caused to be introduced a bill repealing the combination laws and legalizing trade unions. Through the astonishing address and skillful manœuvring of Place and his coadjutors, this bill was steered through Parliament without debate and without division. The result was instantaneous. Trade unions, suddenly legalized, sprang up in all parts of the country, and employers awoke to the fact that almost without their knowledge these organizations had been given the sanction of the law. In the following year, attempts were made to reënact the old combination laws, but by this time organized labor was aroused, and the efforts of the opponents of trade unionism were fruitless. The unions were freed for all time.

Unfortunately, many of the organizations which sprang up after the repeal of the combination laws, were without experience, and, as a result, unwise and occasionally arrogant. Their growth was greater than their success. Following the legalization of the trade unions there came a serious commercial depression lasting from 1825 to 1829, and, as a consequence, the new unions failed in their efforts to improve materially the conditions of labor. A feeling of discouragement took possession of the working classes, and the commercial depression was marked by apathy on the part of workmen toward the organizations. The factory system extended rapidly throughout the length and breadth of England; the oppression of workingmen continued practically unabated; the strikes of the ill-organized unions were largely unsuccessful, and the revolutionary spirit, then so prevalent in France, crossed the Channel and found its way into England. During the succeeding years the trade unions became imbued with political and revolutionary aspirations, while the trade policy was more and more shoved into the background.

The new spirit of semi-political organization of wage earners manifested itself in the demand for a union of all workmen, irrespective of trades and extending throughout the country. As a result, in 1830, the National Association for the Protection of Labour was organized, its members consisting largely of textile workers, molders, blacksmiths, mechanics, and miscellaneous laborers. Despite a number of defections, this organization spread rapidly among coal miners, potters, wool workers, and others; and within a short time it claimed a membership of one hundred thousand. But the union was inherently weak, incapable of solving the problems with which it was confronted, and within a few years it had declined and disappeared.

During this period, however, other large organizations were being formed upon more permanent lines. The cotton spinners and textile workers in general, the potters and the members of building trades were rapidly organizing in many parts of the country. The message of these new organizations, composed of men who, for many years, had been repressed, was not always the soft answer that turneth away wrath. "We consider," so runs a proclamation of the Builders' Union to the employers, "that as you have not treated our rules with the deference you ought to have done, we consider you highly culpable and deserving of being severely chastised." The employers were equally arrogant. To all union demands they replied by insisting that the men, before securing work or re-entering upon employment, should forswear all present and future allegiance to trade unions. The promise not to join a union was called the "document," and for a quarter of a century the presentation of a document accompanied a number of labor disputes.

Notwithstanding the failure of the National Association for the Protection of Labour, an attempt to form a similar organization was made in 1833; and in the following year the Grand National Consolidated Trades Union came into being. This organization grew as probably no union or federation ever grew before or since. Within a few weeks half a million workers, it was claimed, became enrolled, and a fever for organization spread through all the working class world. Common laborers and farm hands were swept into the union, and store clerks, chimney sweeps, and many grades of unskilled and irregular workers became members. Women, too, were rapidly organized. The central idea of the union was crudely socialistic, it being proposed to secure for the workingmen possession of the means of production, though by other methods than those contemplated by the socialistic parties of to-day. The working class was still disfranchised, and the government was so corrupt and non-representative that little was to be hoped by workingmen from an extension of its functions. The plan of the trade unionists, therefore, was not to work through the state, but to secure to the workers in each particular trade the capital and machinery of that trade. The plans of the organization, however, were not consummated, and its ideals remained ideals. The panacea of the laboring class was sought not in the use of the ballot or in free education, but in a universal strike of all the workers throughout the Kingdom. It is needless to say that this universal strike did not materialize. Its possibility was never seriously entertained by the skilled laborers, and its success was despaired of from the beginning. The Grand National Union accomplished but little. It lost its first strikes and before long became of no importance or moment in the trade union world.

Although the combination laws had been repealed in 1824 and 1825, the employers had by no means reached the end of their devices for invoking the law against workingmen, and employees could still be indicted for simply notifying their employers that a strike was imminent. Picketing in almost any form was a criminal offense, and men were punished under the common law for the heinous offense of leaving their work unfinished. Any charge was good enough against a striker and any distortion of the law valid against a unionist. Following an ancient custom the unions admitted members under oath; and consequently an old law against the administration of seditious oaths was pressed into service. In the Dorchester case, in which an attempt was made to organize the agricultural laborers, the leaders were arrested and tried, and although there had been no intention or intimation of outrage or even a presentation of grievances, the men were convicted according to "due process of law" for administering an oath and were deported. The persecution of the unionists was found to be efficacious in putting down strikes, and recourse was had in those days, as in these, to all the subtleties and perversions of the law in order to stamp out the "odious" doctrines of trade unionism.

While the unions in 1834 increased their membership to an unprecedented extent, they were still not sufficiently strong to win substantial victories in their conflicts with capital. Some victories, it is true, were won, but the newly organized trades were not in a condition to struggle advantageously, and most of their members had too little experience of trade unionism to undertake the arduous task of carrying a strike to a successful finish. If, during the good times following 1834, many strikes were lost, the failure of the unions in the lean years from 1837 to 1842 was even more apparent. Politically, the unionists were disappointed in not securing the franchise when in 1832 this privilege was extended to the middle classes; and the success of the Liberal party over the Conservative was of no advantage to workingmen. It was found that at this time the Liberals, representing the great manufacturers, were even more hostile toward labor unions than had been the Conservatives, representing the landed gentry. The ambitious plans of the unions and their hopes and aspirations for a reorganized society retarded their real internal development. The Grand National Union had striven toward productive coöperation, but nothing came of it. True, a few labor bazaars were opened, where goods were exchanged according to the labor cost, and attempts were made, and for thirty years sporadically repeated, to compete with employers by means of coöperative factories. A feeling of apathy toward the legitimate aims of trade unionism manifested itself, and while the skilled trades maintained their organization and other unions continued to exist in skeleton form, membership declined and for several years remained below the level of 1834. Many of the men threw themselves into the revolutionary Chartist movement in the hope of securing industrial reforms through political action, but for the most part the unions in their official capacity held aloof. Thus within twenty years of the emancipation of trade unionism from the burden of the combination laws, the friends of labor had begun to despair of a peaceable escape from the misery which everywhere prevailed; and to the leaders of that day, the political skies of England seemed to be tinged with the blood of a coming upheaval.

CHAPTER VI

MODERN TRADE UNIONISM IN GREAT BRITAIN

Modern Trade Union Growth begins in 1842. Greater Stability. Growth of National Unions. Greater Strength and Consciousness of Unions. Miners' Strike of 1844. Financial Policy. The Lockout of 1852. "Presenting the Document." Prosperity. Steady Development. Permanent Trade Councils. Legal Persecution. Parliament Inquires. Victory for the Unions. Legalization. Unionists and the Criminal Law. The Era of Good Feeling. The Crisis of 1875. Lockouts. The Old Unionism and the New. The Great Dock Strike. Present Position of Unionism in England. The Employers' Liability Act of 1897. The Taff Vale Decision of 1902.

WHAT is known as the typical modern trade union has developed largely since the year 1842. Prior to that time the British trade unions were more or less unstable bodies, oscillating between economic and political ideals and without fixed, conscious aims. To a large extent they were local in their scope and temporary in their nature, and the organization of such federations as existed was loose and fluctuating. From 1842, however, the unions developed internally, the local bodies growing into organizations of national scope and becoming more powerful and responsible.

It was about the year 1843 that the unions first recovered from the depression which followed the great advance of the preceding decade. In that year the Potters' Union was reëstablished, and immediately afterwards the Cotton Spinners' Organization began to embrace the greater part of the industry of the Lancashire towns. The Miners' Association of Great Britain and Ireland also dates from this period, and the strikes which followed resulted in an elevation of the miners out of the condition of practical serfage to which the truck system and the system of yearly hirings had reduced them.

The time was propitious for the advance of trade unions. The generations following the close of the Napoleonic Wars had been marked by a series of commercial depressions hitherto unknown in the history of British trade; but from 1846 on the enormous expansion of English commerce, the conquest of foreign markets, the rapid extension of railways, and the wonderful development of manufacturing created a general prosperity, which was reflected in the condition of the workingmen. During this period, from 1842 to 1900, a period practically coeval with the reign of Queen Victoria, British labor and British trade unionism made gigantic strides. The small, local unions of the early part of the century expanded into national organizations; the seat of authority passed from the local to the central body; the insurance and benefit features of the unions were developed and widely extended, and organization upon a solid, permanent basis spread from the skilled to the semi-skilled and unskilled trades. During this period labor organization as well as most of the purposes and policies of trade unionism, received the definite sanction of the law, and unionists came to be regarded not as outlaws, but as responsible and law-abiding subjects. The workingman was vested with the franchise, and the schools were gradually opened to his children. Under the guidance of the unions, the workingmen successfully strove for higher wages, shorter hours, protection to life and health, regulation of the labor of children and women, and, in general, for the improvement and betterment of the conditions of work and life. Despite recessions and retrogressions, the membership, prestige, and power of labor unions grew, and the close of the century found trade unionism in England an established, recognized, and beneficent institution.

This development of modern British trade unionism may be said to have begun about the year 1842. Prior to that date the unions were, on the whole, without fixed ideals, and the modern spirit of trade unionism, a combination of aggression and conciliation, appears to belong to the latter period. The growing consciousness of power and self-worth was evidenced by the heroic but unsuccessful strike organized in 1844 by the Miners' Association. This was one of the most remarkable contests in the history of labor and a notable instance of the power of miners when organized to resist oppression. At this time, also, renewed attempts were made to form federations, and in 1845 the National Association of United Trades for the Protection of Labour was created. This association, which remained intact for fifteen years, did not seek to supersede the old unions, but to bring them together for common action. A great change had come over the spirit of trade unionism since 1834, and the new federation unlike its predecessors, was extremely conservative. The National Association opposed recourse to indiscriminate strikes and was inclined to seek a good understanding with employers rather than to antagonize them at every point. The organization proclaimed a policy of avoiding politics, except where certain definite labor aims were involved.

During this period the unions were becoming broader in scope and more representative and responsible; but the hostility of employers did not abate. Indeed, the opponents of trade unions made the very improvement in union organization an excuse for their antagonism. Hostile employers now claimed that they did not object to local unions, but that they opposed all national organizations, since the latter exercised tyranny over labor and set limits to its freedom. During this period employers answered strikes by legal proceedings and by general lockouts and endeavored to force upon the unionists the universally odious "document." The employers in the London engineering trades met the formation of the Amalgamated Society of Engineers and its protests against piecework and systematic overtime by a flat refusal to arbitrate or even to consider the propositions. In 1852 they locked out the whole trade and persisted in the presentation of the "document," and in April, the men were obliged to submit and to return to work after a three months' struggle.

The Amalgamated Society of Engineers, which survived this lockout and prospered thereafter, was the prototype of a large number of organizations in England during this generation. It was created by the amalgamation of a number of rival unions in various branches of engineering work and was organized upon a national basis. The earlier trade unions had been based upon the idea of a number of completely separate or loosely combined local clubs, each exercising a large measure of individual freedom, controlling its own funds and acting on its own initiative and in its own behalf.

The Amalgamated Engineers represented an advance beyond this primitive form of organization. The new union was not only built upon national lines, but the central government was strengthened at the expense of the locals, and the power of these smaller groups to declare strikes and involve the whole body of engineers in national conflicts was effectively restricted. The union built up an admirable, though somewhat cumbersome, system of financial management, preserving the initiative of the locals, but giving the real control to the central executive. The dues were a shilling (25¢) a week; and with peace and the growth in membership, the funds of the organization steadily amounted to a hitherto unknown total. The wealth of the organization, however, and its resulting strength aroused bitter animosity on the part of many employers. Those who were hostile to the union inveighed against its benefit features, declaring them to be a fraudulent device for diverting the savings of workmen from their real purpose, the protection against old age, death, sickness, and accidents, and using them as a means of breeding discontent and subsidizing strikes and idleness.

These verbal attacks, however, availed no more than had the persecutions of former years. The union grew and prospered, its membership and wealth increased, and through its policy of courting publicity and even advertisement, it was enabled to assume a prominent position among the chief labor organizations of the time. The carpenters, tailors, compositors, and members of other trades organized upon similar principles, and in the years from 1852 to 1859, the development of these organizations was steady and continuous. In fact, this period of internal development of trade unions was also an era of good feeling between labor and capital, and it was confidently predicted in many quarters that conciliation and arbitration would take the place of industrial conflicts and that in the course of a short time strikes would practically cease to-exist.

These exuberant hopes, however, were doomed to be shattered. From 1859 there occurred a series of strikes and lockouts, in which the unions were for the most part worsted. The industrial depression of the years following the crisis of 1857 threw many men out of work, and lockouts became frequent and general. In the year 1859, twenty-four thousand men in the building trades of the metropolis were suddenly locked out because of a demand for shorter hours, the ensuing contest resulting in victory for neither side. Even where the unions were defeated, there was no permanent loss of strength. The process of gradually building up the internal structure of the organizations continued. At the same time, and more especially from 1867 to 1875, the unions became more generally victorious in the political field. It is during this period that the complete legalization of trade unions was secured. From 1858 to 1867 permanent trade councils had been established in the leading cities of England, and these councils, acting in coöperation with brilliant volunteers from other classes in society, threw themselves into a movement for the reform of the labor laws as well as for the betterment of the conditions of work. Largely through the efforts of these men the Reform Bill of 1866, which conferred the right of suffrage upon the hitherto disfranchised workmen of cities, was placed upon the statute books. Another victory almost equally important was the amendment of the old law of master and servant, under which the workman was liable to be imprisoned for breach of contract or for leaving his work unfinished. The political activity of the unionists was stimulated by the Parliamentary inquiry of 1867, which was directed against trade unionism, but resulted in its justification and vindication. The minority report of this committee recommended that trade unions be granted the right to register and to secure legal protection for their funds while retaining immunity from other litigation. This minority report further recommended that no act should be illegal when committed by workingmen if not illegal when committed by others, and that no act should be illegal when committed by a combination if not illegal when committed by a single person. In 1871 the recommendations of the minority were embodied in a statute, and the act of 1871 completely legalizing trade unions and securing them from being sued was believed to be the law of the land, until the House of Lords interpreted it out of existence in the Taff Vale decision of 1902. The success of the workmen at that time and later was due in no small measure to their enfranchisement in the year 1867 and to the effort of the Conservative party to secure their votes.

In 1871 Parliament passed the Criminal Law Amendment Act, directly aimed at picketing. By this time, however, the unions were thoroughly aroused, and after four years of agitation they secured in 1875 the repeal of the law. This repeal rendered picketing, if unaccompanied by violence or intimidation, entirely legal.

While Parliament was thus granting to labor organizations the full and equal protection of the law, other reforms and advances were being made through the efforts of trade unionists. The coal miners and cotton spinners, who were strongly organized and largely concentrated in well-defined districts, relied to a great extent upon legislation for the attainment of their ends. The miners secured laws against the truck system and against weighing and docking abuses, while the cotton operatives obtained in 1874 a fifty-six and a half hour week for female workers. Other unions, especially in the building trades and among the engineers, secured reductions in the hours of labor and a general improvement in the conditions of employment. The hours of labor in the building trades were reduced to nine, and a large section of engineers obtained the same working day through the efforts of a temporary organization called the Nine Hours' League.

During this period the membership of trade unions increased rapidly and continuously. The year 1874 was particularly noteworthy by reason of the great number of accessions to the ranks of organized labor. As in the movement of 1834, forty years before, a wave of trade union sentiment swept over the country, and wage earners of all classes formed themselves into labor organizations. It was even attempted at this time to unionize the agricultural laborers; but the isolation and poverty of these down-trodden rural workers prevented them from overcoming the bitter hostility of the farmers, aided by the clergy, the justices of the peace, and even the army itself. Toward the end of the decade, however, business everywhere suffered a serious depression, and in the strikes and lockouts which resulted, a number of the unions succumbed. The defeats of the unions were followed by reductions in the rate of wages, increases in the hours of labor, and recourse to systematic overtime; but, as in the past, trade unionism weathered the storm. The organizations which survived—and this was true of the majority—suffered in diminished membership, but the crisis passed without permanent injury, and at its close labor organizations rapidly regained their strength, and within a few years were as active, self-reliant, and formidable as ever.

The depression of 1878 and the succeeding years had at least one good result, an increased self-knowledge on the part of the unions. Prior to this time trade unionism had shown a certain tendency to over-emphasize its benefit features and to become unaggressive and torpid. Many of the unions were disposed to subordinate the proper aims of labor organizations to the ambition of accumulating a large reserve fund, and to a certain extent at least the ideals and philosophy of trade unionism had been abandoned. During the early eighties a spirit of discontent made itself felt, however, and large sections of the working classes protested against the exclusive and restrictive policy of many of the trade unions. The terrible, wide-spread poverty of London and of many of the provincial cities brought forth a demand for a fuller democratization of the trade union movement and for the unionizing of the great mass of unskilled workers. This movement, which was designated the "new unionism," held out as its ideal the organization of unskilled workmen and the subordination of the benefit features to a specific and well-defined trade policy.

The spirit of the new unionism became particularly marked in the early years of the eighties. From the beginning it was tinged with socialistic doctrines, and it grew with the discontent which especially after 1886 became prevalent in England. It was a time of depression and of general unemployment, and the drain of out-of-work benefits became more and more severe. Many unions sought to protect their funds by a policy of retrenchment and by dropping members who were in arrears; but the result of this action was merely to accentuate and increase the universal distress. The investigations of Charles Booth into the conditions of the working classes revealed an amount of poverty and degradation undreamed of. "Thirty-two per cent. of the whole population of London (in some large districts over sixty per cent.) were found to be living in a state of chronic poverty, which precluded not only the elementary conditions of civilization and citizenship, but was incompatible with physical health and industrial efficiency." The working people of the cities were in a ferment of excitement, and parades and gatherings of the unemployed startled the whole country. The radical element attempted to secure control of the trade unions, finally succeeding in this endeavor in the year 1890.

The greatest victory of the new unionism was achieved in the Dock Strike of 1889, one of the three or four most notable labor conflicts in history. The match girls and gas stokers of London had been successful in their strikes, owing to the sympathy of the public; and a strike was finally resorted to by the dockers in order to remedy the terrible conditions prevailing at the Port of London. The half-starved dock laborers demanded the abolition of the subcontract and piece system and a minimum wage of six pence (12¢) per hour, with the provision that they should be employed not less than four consecutive hours. Upon the refusal of the dock owners to grant these demands a strike was declared. There is probably no labor conflict in history, not even excepting the Anthracite Coal Strike of 1902, in which the sympathy of the general public was so aroused or became so potent. It seemed as though nothing short of a miracle could have won a victory for the oppressed and penniless men, who were but recently and incompletely organized. The leading men of England, men from all classes and ranks of life, subscribed large sums of money; the labor organizations throughout the country contributed generously, and thousands of pounds were telegraphed from Australia to the striking dock laborers. The pressure of public opinion proved too strong to be withstood; the dock owners found themselves facing a tempest of indignation and wrath, and the unexpected came to pass—the employers capitulated. Thus, the dock laborers achieved an unqualified victory.

The astonishing success of the London dock workers gave a great impetus to the trade union movement. The experience of this strike proved conclusively that the principles of trade unionism were becoming general and that even the unskilled workmen were better able to organize than they had been a generation or two before.

Since 1889 there has been a rapid growth among the organized laborers of the United Kingdom. The membership of British and Irish trade unions increased rapidly until 1892, when 1,503,000 persons were enrolled, then slowly declined until 1895, and since the latter year has again mounted steadily. In 1901 there were 1,923,000 members, and at the present time (August, 1903), the number of trade unionists in the United Kingdom is probably in excess of 2,000,000. The actual increase in the power of the unions, however, has probably been much greater than that indicated by the statistics. There is always a large number of workingmen in sympathy with the movement, although not a part of it, and these men vote and act with the unionists and follow their lead. The concentration of large groups of unionists in particular districts has also tended to increase their power and their political and industrial influence.

During the last decade the trade unions of the United Kingdom have increased not only in membership, but in stability, permanence, and power. In 1901 the principal unions, representing only three-fifths of the total membership of the organizations of the Kingdom, had accumulated funds amounting to over twenty millions of dollars and were enjoying an annual income amounting to ten millions of dollars. During the ten years from 1892 to 1901 inclusive, the principal unions, representing only a fraction of the membership of the Kingdom, expended upon dispute benefits, working and miscellaneous expenses, and unemployed, sick, accident, superannuation, funeral, and other benefits, the enormous sum of seventy-three and a half millions of dollars. This period has also been marked by the further development of labor federation, although this evolution has not progressed as far in England as in the United States. During the decade victories have been achieved in the field of politics, especially in the government of municipalities. The trade union has been successful in securing from the London

County Council and from a majority of municipal bodies important concessions in the matter of the maintenance of the union wage and the union working day. The chief victory in politics, however, has probably been the Compulsory Liability Law of 1897, by which workingmen in a large number of industries may receive compensation for accidents. The Taff Vale decision of 1902, which changes the legal status of unions, has temporarily thrown the movement out of joint. Although its full consequences cannot as yet be accurately foretold, this decision must be recognized as fraught with danger to the orderly and peaceful progress of trade unionism in England. Its first effect has been to cause the unions to participate more actively than formerly in the political movements of the time. Nevertheless, British trade unionism, which has outlasted so much persecution and so many attacks, will hardly fail to survive this final assault by the supreme judicial tribunal of the British Empire.

CHAPTER VII

LABOR IN THE AMERICAN COLONIES

Labour in 1700 and Labor in 1900 Simple Conditions in Colonial Times. Poverty. Slavery in the South. Labor in the North. Class Distinctions. Fixing Wages by Law. Two Shillings a Day. The Pay of Women and Indians. The Cost of Living. Poverty, Hard Work, Long Hours, but no Starvation. Indentured Servants. Apprenticed at Seven. No Labor Unions in the Colonies.

IN the American colonies land was plenty, but money scarce. There were many acres to till, but few men to till them. The needs of the people were simple, and were satisfied in a large, rough, substantial fashion. During the century and a half following the arrival of the Cavaliers in Virginia and the stern Puritans in New England, the history of American labor was the simple story of a conquest of nature by hardy pioneers. Scattered in settlements along the narrow fringe of coast line, venturing but a few miles up the navigable rivers, lived the English, French, Dutch, Swedes, Germans, and Spaniards, the inhabitants of the America of that day. These sturdy settlers spent their lives in subduing the wilderness, in trading with the Indians for furs, in raising tobacco, wheat, or Indian corn, in building ships, and in plying various rude handicrafts. In the Colonial days there was little wealth and less penury. The country was poor, but there was not the sharp contrast between fabulous wealth and abject misery, between the spacious mansions of the rich and the hiving tenements of the poor, which is a distinguishing characteristic of the present time.

Of course, differences and class distinctions existed, but the contrast was rather one of station in life than of the means of enjoyment. There were even then rich men and poor men. Favored gentlemen counted their laborers by the hundreds and their acres by the tens of thousands, while, on the other hand, the slaves, who in the South performed the hard work of colonization, owned neither lands nor tenements, neither the clothes on their backs nor their own bodies. But even the opulent could find no other outlet for their wealth than in the enjoyment of a rude plenty, for most of the luxuries of even the poor of to-day were unattainable to the wealthy of Colonial times.

During Colonial days and for four-score years under the Republic, the labor system of the South was based upon the institution of slavery. The relation of employer to workman was not that of one freely contracting person to another, but the relation of owners to property. On the vast tobacco plantations, stretching for miles from river to river, the owner was absolute lord and master over the hundreds of black slaves who worked for him in the field or served him in his household. There was no payment of wages to the slaves, and where a slave was loaned by one plantation owner to another it was not wages but a regular rent or hire which was paid, and not to the slave but to his master. In the South there was a sharp line of cleavage, not only between the master and his property, the slave, but equally between the slave owner and the slaveless man. The Virginian or Carolinian who owned no slaves was in the position of a landless man in Europe during the middle ages. He counted for nothing, had no political or social influence, and deteriorated into the so-called "white trash," which has shown its capabilities only since the Civil War.

In the Northern states the conditions were much better, but even here a line was drawn between those who worked with their hands and those who lived from the product of other men's labor. In the old Colonial days the toiler had no education and few political rights. His work was largely that of an unskilled man. He did not possess the means or the opportunity of educating himself or his children, and his wages, even when paid in money, were barely sufficient to feed and lodge him and to provide him with an annual suit of homespun clothing. The workingman at that time wore what was practically a distinctive dress, and there was no danger of confounding him with the "gentleman" who walked upon the other side of the way.

It is difficult to compare the wages of people living in one state of society or at one period of history with the wages of those living and working in another. Conditions change so as to render it almost impossible to say whether a class of men is better off at one time or at another. We know what wages were received by men in Colonial days, but the value of money has changed. The men themselves, their work, their methods of living, and their requirements of comfort and luxury have likewise changed. Roughly speaking, however, one may say that the workingmen of that day maintained an appreciably lower standard of living, that their wants and necessities were fewer, and that their wages, measured both in money and by what they could buy, were much less than at the present time.

In the colony of Virginia as in that of Massachusetts, the original idea was to form a society upon a crudely communistic basis. It was proposed to put all men to work at appointed tasks and to allow them to share in the products of labor, either equally or according to their needs. This attempt, however, was not successful, owing to the fact that many of the Cavaliers refused to perform their share, or indeed any part, of the work, and as a consequence the whole plan was abandoned. As Captain John Smith of Virginia declared, "He that will not work shall not eat." The colony shortly afterward imported slaves and no attempt was ever made to reëstablish communism in Virginia.

As early as 1633, or thirteen years after the arrival of the Mayflower, the policy of determining wages by law was put to the test of experience in Massachusetts. The General Court decreed that carpenters, sawyers, masons, brick-layers, tillers, joiners, wheelwrights, and certain other workmen should receive no more than 2s. (50¢)[1] per day, or, if furnished with living, not over 14d. (28¢) per day. Workmen of smaller capacity were to have their wages determined by the constables. The wages of skilled tailors were

---

[1] In giving the wages of Colonial workingmen, I have estimated the shilling at 25 cents, in order to enable an approximate comparison to be made between the wages of those days and of these. Any such comparison, however, cannot be exact, as different kinds of shillings were current at different times and places, and their values underwent change.

fixed at 12d. (24¢) per day and of unskilled tailors at 8d. (16¢). The better class of the common, unskilled laborers were to be paid 18d. (36¢) per day and the less skilled in proportion. At one time a penalty of 5s. ($1.25) was imposed upon employers paying higher wages, but this provision was subsequently repealed. The whole law, moreover, was commonly evaded and soon became obsolete.

Generally speaking, the average pay for mechanics' labor in the colony of Massachusetts at the beginning of the seventeenth century, was about 2s. (50¢) per day, and as late as 1672 the wages of common laborers did not exceed 2s. (50¢). Even at the beginning of the eighteenth century pay for common labor seems to have been at about the same level, although exceptionally skilled, all-round men occasionally averaged higher wages. The wages of women were, of course, much lower, amounting to four or five pounds ($20 to $25) per year, apparently with food, while Indians who worked in the fields received about a shilling and six-pence (36¢) per day. The wages seem to have remained almost stationary during the seventeenth century and not to have increased very rapidly until after the Revolutionary War.

The condition of a workman, however, depends not only upon the number of shillings or dollars which he receives for his labor, but upon the amount of things to eat and drink and wear that can be bought with these shillings or dollars. It is difficult to ascertain just what could be purchased in Colonial times with the 2s. which the workman earned each day. Prices fluctuated considerably. Nevertheless, it appears that many articles consumed by the working people were higher in price than at present. Thus, corn varied from 6s. ($1.50) per bushel in 1633 to 12s. ($3.00) per bushel in 1635. In other words, in these years it took from three to six days of work to buy a bushel of corn, whereas, at the present time, it would take only about one-third to one-half of the day's wages of an unskilled workman to buy the same quantity. Butter was cheaper, selling for 6d. (12¢) and cheese for 5d. (10¢) per pound; but on the whole the prices of the absolute necessities of life appear to have been at least as high, if not higher, than at the present time, while the number of things consumed by the average workman was less. There are, of course, many things of necessity to the workman at the present time, such as car fare, high ground-rents, etc., which were not elements of cost in those days, and it is probable that many of the workmen who, in Colonial times, daily received a couple of shillings, owned a little patch of ground and possibly a cow, a hog, or some chickens, which, in connection with their earnings, enabled them to provide for the wants of the family. Their clothing was usually made by their wives in their own households. While the living was rude and simple and many of the present day comforts and luxuries were not obtainable, and were not even desired, the general condition of the toilers was not an unhappy one. There was not much comfort and probably little refinement in the life of the workman of that day, but there was, apparently, also but little actual want and acute suffering, except, perhaps, when the corn crop failed or some other calamity afflicted the colony.

The hours of work for which the 2s. of the laborer stood were, in general, from sunrise to sunset. The illumination of houses was not such as to permit much work after sundown, but the men as well as the women and children worked as long as there was daylight. There was a plentiful demand for unskilled labor, but it was necessary to work long and arduously to get a sufficient living from the land. To a certain extent the work was done by indentured servants. There were many people in England, and in Europe generally, who, to benefit their condition or to escape oppression or persecution, were anxious and willing to leave their native country. These men and women usually received free passage on condition that upon their arrival in America they be indentured for a number of years, and so work out their passage money. During this time of indenture the redemptioners, as they were called, were obliged to work without wages at the dictation of their masters, their only compensation, as a rule, being a suit of clothes called the "freedom suit," given to them at the termination of their period of service. The position of the redemptioners was much better than that of slaves, as they possessed a number of rights well defined by law; but in many cases they were harshly treated and they were severely punished for running away. The system of indenturing workmen, moreover, led to a number of abuses owing to its being profitable to ship owners. Not only were men fleeing from justice, and outcast men and women generally, sold in this way, but youths were not infrequently kidnapped upon the streets of European cities and sold at a profit in Virginia or Massachusetts.

Another effect of the great demand for unskilled labor was the employment of very small children. In some cases boys were apprenticed at the age of seven and were obliged to labor, under rigid discipline and at difficult work, until the age of twenty-one, when they were supposed to receive full journeymen's wages.

The conditions of labor in the Colonies were by no means idyllic, but they were relieved by the fact that in the North, at least, a majority of the laborers were freemen. There was at that time no necessity of, or advantage in, forming trade unions and no considerable organizations of labor are known to have existed. The problem of the day was not how to distribute the wealth of the community but rather how to increase it. As long as the main brunt of the conflict of the workingman is to subdue nature and increase the productivity of labor in order to be able to live, there is small need for organization of the latter-day type. It is only where the laborer is deprived of his hire by the cupidity of employers or by the harshness of competition that organizations of workmen for their defense may be reasonably successful. It is thus that the general organization of American labor begins only after the Revolutionary War, and, in fact, only after the beginning of the nineteenth century.

The American workman has advanced with giant strides during the centuries which have elapsed since Colonial days. In the amount of his wages, in the length of his working day, in the things he can buy and the leisure he can enjoy, in his legal rights and political privileges, in his own skill, intelligence, enlightenment, and self-direction, and finally, in the esteem in which he is held and the humanity with which he is treated, the workingman of the America of to-day is infinitely better off than was his remote ancestor before the Revolution.

FRANK MORRISON
Secretary of the American Federation of Labor

JOHN B. LENNON
General Secretary of the Journeymen Tailors' International Union;
Treasurer of the American Federation of Labor

CHAPTER VIII

LABOR FROM THE DECLARATION OF INDEPENDENCE TO THE EMANCIPATION PROCLAMATION

Labor Conditions after the Revolution. Slavery in the South. The First Labor Problem—Slave versus Free Labor. Low Wages in the North. Depreciated Money. High Prices. Simple Food and Clothing. No Comforts or Luxuries. No Education and No Vote for the Workingman. No Mechanics' Lien. Imprisonment for Debt. The Right to Strike Denied. Gradual Improvement. Wages Rise. A Shorter Working Day. The Work of Women. The Beginnings of a Labor Movement.

THE Declaration of Independence did not make all men "free and equal," and the American Revolution did not throw off all the shackles of labor. Politically, America was free to enter upon her glorious career among the nations of the earth; economically, however, the Revolution did not effect a direct, immediate improvement in the condition of the workingmen. The new-born country awoke to the tidings of peace and independence, suffering, impoverished, and debt-ridden, and to the American workman the overthrow of British sovereignty did not, at least at the outset, bring higher wages, more regular wages, or wages in better money.

The history of the United States from the Declaration of Independence, in 1776, to the Emancipation Proclamation, in 1863, is the solution of a labor problem—the problem of slave *versus* free labor. From the founding of the Republic there had threatened an irrepressible conflict between the labor of freemen and of bondmen. Men saw that one of two things must come to pass: the freemen must break the shackles of the slaves or the slaves would forge fetters for the free. The Northern workingmen, and especially the trade unionists of that day, cried aloud for the abolition of chattel slavery, and it was in large part due to the patriotism of American workingmen that slavery disappeared from the North American continent.

At the time of the first census of the United States in 1790, seven years after the close of the Revolutionary War, there were in the country some 750,000 negroes, or almost one in five of the population. Of these negroes the great majority were slaves on the cotton and tobacco plantations of the South. The Constitution had not prohibited slavery and had even withheld from the Federal Government, before the year 1808, the right to prohibit the importation of slaves. At the time of the adoption of the Constitution it was generally believed that slavery would not continue much longer. So great was the expensiveness, ignorance, unreliability, and wastefulness of slave labor, that it seemed probable that the slaves would be largely liberated, or, at least, permitted to purchase their freedom. But the invention of the cotton-gin in 1793 changed this and made slavery exceedingly profitable. From this time on cotton growing paid well, and slaves were largely sought and became extremely valuable. The history of the United States from 1790 to 1860 is the story of a long industrial and political conflict between the states where slave labor prevailed and those in which labor was free. In other words, the principal question that demanded solution was a labor problem, the problem of slave *versus* free labor.

The evolution and solution of this first labor problem in the United States and the terrific struggle and awful sacrifice which accomplished it, are too well known to require repetition. For some time the slave states grew with great rapidity, owing to the phenomenal development of the cotton industry, and year by year slavery extended westward from the southern Atlantic coast to the Mississippi River. Thereafter the struggle took the form of a contest for the territory west of the Mississippi, and in this contest the states with free labor won. The European immigrants arriving in this country prior to the Civil War, settled in the states with free labor and held aloof from the states with slave labor. The population, intelligence and wealth of the free states increased more rapidly than those of the slave states and the opposition to chattel slavery grew so strong in the North that the South, despairing of the future, attempted to solve the problem by secession. With the close of the Civil War and the success of the North, the victory of free over slave labor was complete. It is a sign full of promise for the future that during the last two decades the South has made wonderful progress, and it cannot be doubted that the prosperity of the Southern States will be greater under free labor than was possible under a system of slavery.

While the chief labor problem of the United States during the period from 1790 to 1860 was the question of free *versus* slave labor, there was fought out during the same period in the North the problem of the proper status of free labor. The close of the Revolution found the workingmen of the North in a condition but little, if at all, superior to that in which he had been at the beginning of the contest. The ordinary unskilled workman still earned his two shillings (50¢) a day; he still worked from sun-up to sun-down; the commodities which he purchased were still expensive. According to Professor McMaster, the price of corn in 1784 was 3s. (75¢) per bushel and that of wheat 8s. 6d. ($2.12) a bushel, while the price of a pound of salt pork was 10d. (20¢), so that an ordinary unskilled laborer would have to work a day and a half for a bushel of corn, four days and a quarter for a bushel of wheat, and about two days for five pounds of salt pork.

The standard of living of the American workman at the close of the Revolution was extremely low. Staple articles of consumption seem to have been expensive and the variety of food, limited. Workingmen rarely tasted fresh meat more than once a week and even this was considered a luxury. The large number of fresh foods and vegetables which can now be obtained at reasonable cost were at that time either unknown or so expensive as to be beyond the reach of the poor, and such fruits and vegetables as the canteloupe, tomato, rhubarb, sweet corn, cauliflower, egg plant, and others were entirely unknown. The dress of the workman was simple and coarse. "A pair of yellow buckskin or leathern breeches, a checked shirt, a red flannel jacket, a rusty felt hat cocked up at the corners, shoes of neat's skin set off with huge buckles of brass, and a leathern apron comprised his scanty wardrobe." The wives and daughters of the workingmen were clothed and fed with equal economy, and with as little regard for taste or comfort. Their homes were extremely plain; the floors of the dingy rooms were sprinkled with sand, which took the place of a carpet, and the walls were bare of adornment. There were no pictures or prints of any sort and no glass or china, the dishes of the working classes being made entirely of pewter. There were no stoves, no coal, no matches, and fire for the modest cooking of the poor was lighted from the sparks of a flint.

In many other respects the workingmen of that day were at a great disadvantage as compared with their descendants of the present time. The facilities for securing an education were extremely meagre, and where schools existed the cost was usually prohibitive. There was no regularity in the payment of wages, and frequently a workman was obliged to wait many weeks or months for any pay at all. Even when he received his wages he was liable to be deceived into accepting depreciated currency or the notes of banks which had failed, money of all forms and kinds being in circulation. Further, he might be deprived of his earnings by the failure or dishonesty of his employer, and his situation was in every way precarious. In many parts of the country truck stores existed, and it was not infrequent for payment of wages to be made in commodities or in an order on a store instead of in legal tender. For such injustices as the workingman suffered there was small redress. In many states he did not possess the suffrage, and as a non-voter he had practically no influence in political and social life. There were no savings banks in which to deposit his savings, if he possessed any, and no beneficial societies or strong trade unions which could insure him against a rainy day.

Bad as was the condition of the average workingman in times of health and steady work, it was incalculably worse with the first buffet of misfortune. The law was extremely scrupulous about the rights of property and in those days even more than at present placed the dollar above the man. The wage earner whom misfortune overtook, whose wife fell ill, or who himself was crippled or disabled temporarily, was subjected to the severest penalties of the law for the crime of having no money. In the newly-freed

United States, as in England, a man could be thrust into prison because he was in debt. No matter how small the sum, there was no immunity from this punishment, if the creditor wished to take advantage of the law. The jails were filled with debtors, many of them workingmen. It was estimated that of the inmates of the prisons of Massachusetts, New York, and Pennsylvania in 1829, 20,000 were there for the non-payment of debts, most of these being small in amount. The average per capita indebtedness of 1,085 debtors in the Philadelphia prison in 1828 was less than $24.00, and one case is on record in which a man was confined in jail thirty-two days for a debt of two cents. The character of these debtors' prisons beggars description. The workingman who, through illness or lack of work, fell into arrears of rent, might be thrown into an indescribably filthy and unsanitary jail, amid a swarm of murderers, thieves, and hardened criminals. The miseries of some of the debtors' prisons can be compared only with the horrors of the slave ships.

While the American Revolution did not result in an immediate improvement of labor conditions, it rendered this improvement ultimately possible. As long as the Colonies remained under the dominion and tutelage of Great Britain, they were debarred from developing to the full their natural resources. The impetus to industry given by freedom and by the establishment of a stable home government was not immediately effective in materially bettering labor conditions. The administrations of Washington and Adams passed without marked improvement in the condition of the workingman. Even in the days of Jefferson the state of the American wage-earner was still far from satisfactory. The great mass of unskilled laborers in the cities were hired by the day, while on the farms and upon public works men were employed by the month and were given free board. The wages of such men did not average much over five or six dollars a month. The diggers on the Pennsylvania canals were wretchedly housed, were fed upon coarse, cheap food, and received six dollars a month in summer and a dollar less per month in winter. About the same wages were paid to the unskilled workers, hod carriers, mortar mixers, diggers and choppers, who, from 1793 to 1800 worked on the public buildings and streets of Washington. At Albany and New York wages were forty cents a day, at Lancaster, Pa., from eight to ten dollars a month, and at Baltimore, about six dollars or less. In Virginia the ordinary white laborer received, besides board and keep, about $5.33 a month, one-fourth less being paid for the hire of slaves. The work was arduous and lasted as long as daylight. The condition of skilled artisans was, of course, better, yet their wages were low in comparison with those of to-day. Typesetters were paid at a piece rate of 25¢ per thousand ems, and were thus enabled to earn as much as eight dollars a week. These wages were considered so excessively high that the newspaper companies felt justified in putting up the prices of their journals.

The first quarter of the nineteenth century brought an increase in wages to the laboring men of the country, but did not effectually settle the grievances of the workingmen. This period witnessed the beginning of manufacturing in the United States and the rise and gradual extension of the factory system. Many opportunities of labor formerly non-existent were created. The construction of canals and of public roads as well as the opening of the great West brought about a strong demand for unskilled labor. The policy of non-intercourse with Europe and the succeeding war with England had given an impetus to manufacturing, and industrial establishments sprang up in Massachusetts, New York, Pennsylvania, and elsewhere. At the same time there began, about 1820, that vast wave of immigration which has continued to flow unceasingly and has peopled the new world with the children of the old.

From 1825 to 1829, or in other words, during the administration of John Quincy Adams, the earnings of the American workingman were higher than ever before in American history. The unskilled workmen, such as sawyers and hod carriers, received about 75¢ a day for twelve hours of work, while on the canals and turnpikes, men who, a quarter of a century before, had earned six dollars, now received fifteen dollars a month and board. During the winter, however, wages were lower. Men who could earn in summer from 62½¢ to 80¢ per day were glad to receive a much smaller sum in winter. With each approach of cold weather the whole community seemed to shrink within itself; wages were reduced, and the expenditures of the workingmen curtailed. The remuneration of women was, as to-day, lower than that of men, and their opportunities for employment incomparably less. According to Professor McMaster,[1] these women "might bind shoes, sew rags, fold and stitch books, become spoolers, or make coarse shirts and duck pantaloons at eight or ten cents a piece. Shirt-making was eagerly sought after, because the garments could be made in the lodgings of the seamstress, who was commonly the mother of a little family, and often a widow. Yet the most expert could not finish more than nine shirts a week, for which she would receive seventy-two or ninety cents. Fifty cents seems to have been the average."

While wages had thus risen in the quarter of a century since the inauguration of Jefferson, and many of the abuses which had plagued colonial workers had disappeared, yet prices also had risen and not a few of the old grievances were unrelieved. Still, on the whole, work was better remunerated and the workmen better off. The condition of the entire nation was improved, life was easier, and many of the hardships incident to the earlier days of the settlement of the country, had disappeared. Canals and turnpikes threaded the land and abridged distances between the main cities, which were growing rapidly in wealth and population. The Erie Canal had been built, transportation cheapened, the West and East linked together. Everywhere the country was full with the new life of a coming era. In all parts of the East banking, insurance, steamboat, turnpike, and canal companies were being formed, and factories and mills established. There was a demand for mill hands, mechanics, machinists, engineers, clerks and bookkeepers, and for workmen in occupations which, a quarter of a century before, could hardly be said to exist. The wages of labor had risen, hours had shown a slight tendency to decrease, and a somewhat greater willingness was manifested to treat the workingman as a human being and not as a slave or a serf. In many states the law consigning men to jail

---

[1] History of the People of the United States, by John B. McMaster.

for small debts had been repealed or amended, and no man could now be imprisoned for a debt of less than $15, $20, or $25, according to the state in which he lived. In the larger cities savings banks had come into existence, and the workingman could secure not only a reasonably safe place of deposit, but also might receive interest upon his money. The old evils, however, had been lessened rather than removed. The workingman was still liable, in the absence of lien laws, to see his wages lost through the failure or fraud of a contractor, was still liable, under the old common law, to arrest for striking or for other acts of conspiracy or combination, and as he was still without a vote in many states, he could not secure the enactment of better laws or even the repeal of the old ones. The conditions in some of the factories which were now springing up in New England and elsewhere, were extremely bad, and women and children were harshly treated and cruelly exploited. The time was marked also by a vast amount of intemperance and much want, suffering, and degradation in the rapidly growing cities.

It was at this time, about the year 1825, when the conditions of the American workman had already begun to improve, that the first considerable unrest appeared among the laboring classes. Friends of the workingmen called upon the legislatures to "prevent the rich from swallowing up the inheritance of the poor," asked for protection for factory operatives, who were exposed to sickness, death, and mutilating accidents, and demanded better, cleaner, and healthier workshops for these people. "Such pleas," says the historian, Professor John B. McMaster, "had small effect on the public but more on the workingmen and women who, after 1825, began to organize in earnest." It was at this time that the American workmen embarked upon socialistic and communistic schemes, formed societies in various parts of the country, and endeavored to live according to the dictates of their conscience and their ideas of social justice. Societies were formed at New Harmony and elsewhere, the workingmen were stirred to higher ideals by the visit to America of Robert Owen, and a number of workmen in the large cities became interested in movements for reform, which, however, lacked elements of permanence and stability.

THE LATE P. M. ARTHUR
Grand Chief Brotherhood Locomotive Engineers

EXECUTIVE COMMITTEE OF THE ILLINOIS COAL OPERATORS' ASSOCIATION

This Association enters into yearly contracts with the Union, and since its formation there has been no strike

The improvement in the status and condition of American workmen becomes more apparent after 1825, when a number of local trade unions sprang up in the chief cities of the country. During this period and until the outbreak of the Civil War, there was a gradual evolution of the American workman toward a higher standard of life and labor. Money wages rose, as did also real wages, though to a smaller extent, since prices rose at the same time. The increase in wages during the period ending 1860 may be shown by a large number of instances. Thus, carpenters, who were paid less than 60¢ in 1790, received, according to Mr. Carroll D. Wright, United States Commissioner of Labor, from $1.13 to $1.40 per day during the period from 1830 to 1840, after which these wages remained fairly stationary. A similar rise took place in the wages of common laborers, who averaged about 43¢ a day in 1790, 62½¢ in 1800, 82¢ from 1800 to 1810, 90¢ from 1810 to 1820 and 87½¢ to $1.00 a day from 1840 to 1860. The wages of printers rose from an average of about $1.00 a day in 1800, to $1.75 in 1860, while the daily remuneration of shoemakers increased from 73½¢ to $1.00. The wages of the hands in the textile mills also advanced, in the cotton mills the average rising from about 44¢ in 1820 to $1.03 in 1860.

It must, of course, be understood that these statistics are not absolutely exact, owing to the fact that the records during this period are incomplete and, to a certain extent, untrustworthy. But there can be no doubt that a gradual increase took place in the rate of wages paid to most classes of workmen. While for certain commodities prices rose, other prices fell, and it seems to be unquestioned that the American workman could and did purchase more with his earnings in 1860 than was possible in 1800. In addition to increased wages, the working classes secured an extension of their political rights, better opportunities for education, and the amelioration of many onerous conditions which had formerly borne heavily upon them.

CHAPTER IX

ORGANIZED LABOR BEFORE AND SINCE THE CIVIL WAR

American Labor Unions Date from the Nineteenth Century. Reasons for Late Development. Agricultural Population. Smallness of Cities. New York and Haverhill. Early Unions Local. Slow Growth. Central Labor Unions. Political Progress of Unions. Persecution and Conspiracy. Union Successes. National Unions after 1850. The Civil War and the Unions. Growth of Unionism from 1866 to 1873. The Progress of American Unions.

PRIOR to the nineteenth century trade unionism could hardly be said to exist in the United States. There were in Boston and New York some small organizations of calkers and other artisans, and it was largely the turbulence and aggressive patriotism of these men that led, in 1770, to the Boston Massacre. Not until the beginning of the nineteenth century, however, did the unions become of sufficient importance to warrant much notice, and even during the period from 1800 to 1865 they at no time became an element of real power in the community.

This late growth of labor organizations in the United States was due to the primitive character of early American industry. Trade unionism, as we now know it, is the result of a highly developed industrial system. Only where industry is conducted on a large scale and is diversified, only where great cities exist and commerce between them flourishes, only, then, in highly organized industrial communities can trade unions prosper. The movement took rise in England earlier than in the United States, because in England industrial development was earlier, and for the same reason English trade unions are older and stronger than those of Continental nations.

At the time of the adoption of the Constitution of 1787 the United States was a thinly populated country stretching from Canada to Florida and from the Atlantic to the Mississippi, although the pioneers had, as yet, hardly crossed the Alleghenies. The total population in this area was but slightly larger than that of the City of New York to-day. The people were almost entirely engaged in agricultural pursuits, and at this time and for several decades thereafter, such industries as existed were small and were carried on for the local trade only. In 1790 there were but five cities in the country that could boast a population of 10,000 inhabitants, and the metropolis of that time, New York City, had a population of only 33,000, or less than the present population of Chelsea, Chester, Davenport or Haverhill. The total population of all the cities of the United States with 8,000 inhabitants or over, would not have amounted, in 1790, to the present population of Worcester, and even as late as 1820 the combined population of all the cities of the country was not as large as the present population of Baltimore.

The occupation and status of large sections of the population also tended to retard the growth of a labor movement. By far the greater portion of the population was engaged in agricultural pursuits, and the farm hands, whose relations to their employers were largely personal, were too widely scattered and too isolated to permit of any combined action. Agricultural laborers do not lend themselves as readily to organization as mining and manufacturing communities. Even at the present time farming in the United States is conducted on a small scale, the average farm being smaller than a homestead, and there being less than four wage earners or hired employees, to each five farms. The overwhelming agricultural population of the North did not, in the early days of the century, promote the spirit of labor organization, and the slave labor of the South proved an even more insuperable barrier to the progress of union ideas. With slave conditions and slave traditions the trade union movement was completely and utterly incompatible.

There were still other reasons for the absence of an effective trade union movement in the United States during the early part of the century. Not only was the population sparse and largely engaged in agricultural labor, but such industry as existed was on a small scale, and the workingmen were not sharply separated in feeling or in interest from their employers. The workingman of those days had a fair chance of becoming a small employer himself, and at the worst he could secure at little expense a small farm in the West. To a large extent the wage earners of the early days were without education, and in many cases they did not possess sufficient intelligence to understand their own interests or to act together in a spirit of common fellowship. What the great Scotch political economist, Adam Smith, said, in 1776, of British workmen, was equally true of the American workman at this time: "In the public deliberations, therefore, his (the laborer's) voice is little heard and less regarded, except upon some particular occasions, when his clamor is set on and supported by his employers, not for his own but their own particular purposes." At this period the American workman could be stampeded, paraded, or if necessary voted on a wholesale scale by his employers, and it was not until much later that workingmen, largely through the influence of trade unionism, developed a sense of the rights and dignity of their class.

What organizations existed at the beginning of the century were small and of merely local importance, being confined to the few coast cities. There was at that time no need for, and no possibility of, national organizations. The carpenter or shoemaker in Boston did not compete with his fellow-craftsman in Philadelphia, these two cities being further separated in the eyes of the workingmen of those days than are at present New York and San Francisco. There was little communication between the several cities, consequently but little competition for positions. Until about 1850, therefore, no need was experienced for any but local organizations.

The first authenticated instance of a trade union in the United States is that of the New York Society of Journeymen Shipwrights, which was incorporated on April 3, 1803. During the eighteenth century there had existed a number of clubs of local artisans, such as the Caulkers' Club of Boston, but it is believed that these organizations were for social and political purposes only and did not possess any trade policy. In the year 1802 a strike had occurred among the sailors of New York, but a union among them is not known to have existed.

A union of house carpenters of the City of New York was incorporated in 1806, and a printers' union, called the New York Typographical Society, appears to have existed from almost the beginning of the nineteenth century, although not incorporated until 1818. A similar society appears to have existed in Albany, where a strike was declared in 1821. The shipwrights and caulkers of Boston formed themselves into a labor organization in 1822, and in 1823 were incorporated under a charter granted by the legislature of Massachusetts. This charter was similar to those of the old friendly societies, giving the union the right to have a common seal, to protect its funds, and to assist unfortunate mechanics or their families by benefits of various kinds. There is, of course, no mention of the right to take aggressive action, the theory being that such organizations were solely for benefit purposes.

The growth of local trade unions during the first quarter of the nineteenth century was extremely slow, although doubtless there existed a number of local organizations of which we have no record. After 1825, however, the local unions became stronger and many small organizations in the various trades were formed in the principal cities, the chief centers of trade unionism being Boston and New York. About this time, also, the first labor journals appear, the *Workingman's Advocate* being published in New York City from 1825 to 1830, and being succeeded by the *Daily Sentinel* and by *Young America*. These papers seem to have adopted an aggressive, radical policy and to have exerted some influence, although their circulation was probably small.

The first traces of American central labor unions are not found until the thirties. In 1833 the various unions of the metropolis combined to form the Central Trades Union of the City of New York. It is not known that this federation exerted any power, or that it was more than a mere temporary gathering of representatives of the various trades, but it doubtless aided the movement of the workingmen towards a participation in politics. Even in those days the political platform of the unions was, on the whole, progressive and in advance of the time. The policy of the unions favored the freedom of the public domain, a homestead law, the grant to settlers of a right to the land, the making of homesteads inalienable, a national bankrupt law, a mechanics' lien law, the abolition of imprisonment for debt, the equality of women with men, the abolition of chattel slavery, the limitation of the ownership of land to 160 acres per man, the abolition of monopoly, especially the United States Bank, and the right of the government to carry the mails on Sunday. The workingmen also demanded free and universal education as a step toward the emancipation and elevation of their class. Many of these demands have since been granted, and the wisdom and political foresight of the unionists has been, at least in part, justified. Under Presidents Jackson and Van Buren the Democratic party was supposed to represent, to a certain extent, the interests of the workingman, and it was believed by many that the election of Jackson was in part due to the aid given to him by the organized workmen.

The trade unions of this time, however, were still weak and were obliged to overcome a considerable amount of opposition. In the United States, as in England, the old conspiracy and combination laws were invoked against them, and men were thrown into prison, for the crime of jointly refusing to work. The newspapers of the country were almost unanimously hostile to unionism, and there were but few workingmen's papers or journals which would represent fairly the attitude of the unions. Attempts were made to discredit the various organizations by misrepresenting them and claiming that they were opposed to religion and good morals, and efforts were made to suppress the unions altogether. Thus, a combination of merchants was formed in Boston for the purpose of crushing the local unions of shipwrights, calkers and engravers, $20,000 being subscribed for this purpose.

Late in the thirties a shortening of the general working day was won by large classes of toilers in Baltimore; but the first considerable success of the organized workmen was obtained on the 10th of April, 1840, when President Van Buren issued a general order limiting to ten per day the hours of work in the Navy Yards at Washington, D. C., and in all government establishments. This was followed shortly afterwards by the adoption of a ten hour day in many private ship-yards. Here and there the unions scored successes, raised wages, reduced hours, and improved conditions of employment, but the greater victories of American unionism were not achieved until after the formation of the national organizations.

It was in the year 1850 that the Journeymen Printers formed the first national trade union in the United States. This association, which subsequently became the International Typographical Union, rapidly extended its membership throughout New York, New Jersey, Pennsylvania, Maryland, and Kentucky, and eventually secured a foothold in all the states and territories of the United States and in Canada. The growth of this organization and its increasing strength led, in various parts of the country, to the formation of other national unions. In 1854 a national union was established by the hatters, in 1858 the iron and steel workers, under the name of the Sons of Vulcan, organized upon a national basis, and in 1859 a national union of iron molders was formed under the name of the Iron Moulders of North America.

The growth of labor organizations was interrupted for a few years by the outbreak of the Civil War. With the beginning of hostilities men's minds were diverted from everything but the preservation of the Union, and all projects for the betterment of the laboring and other classes in society were temporarily abandoned. Toward the close of the War, however, and especially during the latter part of the sixties, trade unionism received an impetus which carried it much further than it had ever gone before. The question of slavery, then being solved, naturally drew the attention of men to the position and problems of free labor, and with the opening up of the whole territory of the United States to the work of freemen, the question of the correct status of wage earners forced itself to the front. The expenses of the War had necessitated the issue of paper money, which had become depreciated, and this called for a readjustment of wages in order to enable the workingman to live. A surplus of labor was produced by the return of the soldiers from the War, and acute suffering was felt in many parts of the country. Moreover, cities were growing rapidly, division of labor had been widely extended, and the people of the United States were ready to launch into manufacturing on a large scale. This transition had gone on so gradually as to be almost unmarked, but from the close of the War until the crisis of 1873 the evolution began to be realized and trade unionism grew as never before.

The reason for this rapid development of trade unionism since the Civil War will be apparent from a comparison of the statistics of the present time with those of the beginning of the American government. In 1900 there were 76,000,000 people in the United States, or more than nineteen times the population of 1790. While, however, during this period the rural population increased thirteen fold, the urban population increased two hundred and twenty fold, the inhabitants of cities and towns increasing from 131,000 to over 25,000,000. In the United States at the present time one out of each three persons lives in a city or town, and in the North Atlantic States two out of three persons are urban dwellers. During this period, moreover, and especially since 1850, manufacturing and mining communities have grown apace and have furnished recruiting grounds for trade unions. During the half century elapsing between 1850 and 1900 the capital invested in American manufacturing has increased from half a billion to almost ten billions of dollars, the value of products from one billion to thirteen billions, and the wages of workers from two hundred and thirty-seven millions to twenty-three hundred and twenty-seven millions of dollars; the capital invested increasing eighteen, the value of products, thirteen, and the wages of workers, tenfold during the fifty years. The number of wage earners employed in manufacturing increased from less than one million to over five and one-quarter millions during the same period. The extension of mining has also been rapid. From 1880 to 1901 the yearly output of coal increased from 78,000,000 to 293,000,000 short tons, and the value of the output of minerals in the United States now amounts to considerably more than a billion of dollars a year. Railroads and street railways have also expanded to a remarkable degree. In 1830 there were but 23 miles of railroad in the

United States, and in 1850, only 9,021, while at the present time the mileage of American railroads is over 200,000, or greater than the combined mileage of all the railroads of Europe. The capital of American railroads is in excess of twelve billions of dollars, and over one million men are employed by them. The development of street railways has been equally rapid, and the capital invested therein and the number of men employed by them are steadily increasing. Hundreds of thousands of men are annually attracted to the expanding manufacturing, mining, and transportation industries, and it is from these wage earners that trade unionism is securing the majority of its adherents.

It was during the later years of the Civil War, when the progress above described was well under way, that many of the strongest national unions now existing were formed. The locomotive engineers organized in Detroit in 1863, under the name of the Brotherhood of the Footboard, which title was subsequently changed to the Brotherhood of Locomotive Engineers. In the following year the cigar makers organized upon a national basis, and in 1865 an international union of bricklayers and masons was formed. The Conductors' Brotherhood, which subsequently became the Order of Railway Conductors, was organized in Mendota, Illinois, in 1868, and in the next decade many of the national organizations now existing in the United States were instituted. During this period the unions became considerably stronger, and their purposes better known and more highly regarded. The last generation has witnessed a gradual improvement in the calibre of the men in the trade unions and a growth of intelligence in the management of the organizations. Despite occasional defeats and defections, the trade union movement has steadily grown in membership and has redressed many of the grievances under which workingmen formerly suffered. Much of the effort of the unions has been devoted to internal development, but wages have been increased, hours reduced, conditions reformed, and legislative concessions obtained from the national, state, and municipal governments. Since the early seventies many well-conducted trade union journals have been established, some of them being printed in German, French, Italian, and the various Slavic languages.

The growth of trade unions in the United States, as in England, has been gradual and permanent. There have been periods in both countries when the unions increased their membership at an extremely rapid rate, and other periods during which there was stagnation or actual decline. Each succeeding flow of the tide, however, carried the movement further and each ebb was less marked than its predecessor. The prophets who, with each advance movement, declared that trade unionism was temporary and would not live, have been confounded; each decade has strengthened the movement and rooted its principles deeper and deeper in the hearts of the workingmen.

The steady growth of trade unionism in the United States may be summed up in the language of Mr. Carroll D. Wright, Commissioner of Labor, who says: "No matter what the opposition of any particular period was or the character it assumed, no matter what antagonisms within disturbed their order, no matter how defections reduced their ranks at times, and jealousies prevented their immediate success, labor organizations from 1825 continued through success and failure, their propaganda extending first to all great cities and ultimately to all parts of the land."

CHAPTER X

THE CONSTITUTION OF THE AMERICAN TRADE UNION

Gradual Evolution of the Union. Government of Workingmen, by Workingmen, for Workingmen. The Elasticity of the Trade Union Constitution. Local, National, and International Unions. Nature of the Local Union. Its Democracy. Local Officials. Relations between Local and National Unions. Basis of Representation. ure of Office. Salaries. Who May be Members of Trade Unions. Initiation Fees Conventions. Delegates. Referendum and Initiative. Trade Union Officials. Ten- and Dues. Union Cards. Internal Government of Unions. A Typical Trade Union Constitution. Trade Union By-Laws. The Constitution Follows the Trade Agreement.

THE labor organization as it exists to-day is the product of a long evolution. Unions did not spring full-grown from the brain of man; they were not invented, not contrived. The constitution of the trade union, its by-laws, its customs and traditions, its practices and policies have all been the result of a gradual working out of particular remedies for particular problems.

The constitution of the trade union, moreover, has been evolved by and through the efforts of workingmen. The trade union is a government of workingmen, by workingmen, for workingmen, and the framers of its constitution have been workingmen. Although the supreme law of the union was not formulated by highly paid constitutional lawyers, nevertheless, it represents in a clear and definite manner the ideals, purposes, and aims of the great majority of the members of the organization.

The faithfulness with which trade union constitutions represent trade union sentiment is due to the elasticity of these constitutions. The government of trade unions is loose and flexible, and neither constitution nor by-laws are rigidly fixed and immutable. The object of the leaders, as of the rank and file of trade unionists, has been to preserve the largest possible elasticity and freedom of movement to the ruling majority of the organization. In trade union management, there is no tyranny of the "dead hand." Even the most conservative unions are not bound by a blind, unthinking worship of an outgrown instrument, but adjust their form of government to the changing needs and exigencies of the times.

To a certain extent, therefore, the formal written constitution of a trade union is rather a statement of principles and a formulation of the present policy of the union than a hard and fast determination of its future laws. Trade union constitutions are easily changed. The Constitution of the United Mine Workers may be altered by a majority vote in convention, and in a large number of other unions the fundamental law of the organization may be changed by a majority vote either of the delegates in convention or of the members voting by referendum, although in some unions a two-thirds vote is necessary.

American unions are either local, district, national, or international. The local unions ordinarily represent members of a single trade who live and work in a single city or small community. A district organization is a division of a national union usually exercising supervision over the locals in a particular state. It is chartered by, and subordinate to, the national. National organizations, as a rule, extend to the various states where members ply the particular trade, or are engaged in the particular industry over which such organizations exercise jurisdiction, although in a few cases, these national unions are concentrated in certain localities and do not seek to extend their sphere of influence. For instance, the organizations in the cotton spinning trade are practically confined to New England, and the membership of the Northern Mineral Mine Workers, although a national organization, is confined to the states of Michigan, Wisconsin and Minnesota. Many of these unions are styled international because they include Canadian, and, as among several of the railroad brotherhoods, Mexican members. There is no affiliation, however, of American international unions with organizations in Europe or in other parts of the world, with the exception of Canada and Mexico.

Historically considered, the local union is father to the national. Small local organizations existed half a century before national organizations were established, and these latter were usually formed by the amalgamation of existing locals combined for the purposes of common defense and general welfare; but the overwhelming majority of local unions in all trades have been formed by the national organizations.

The local union may thus be considered as the basis or foundation stone of the national organization. As might be supposed, these local bodies are extremely democratic and popular in their form of government. They are composed usually of men working at the same trade, men with approximately equal wealth, wages, and position in the community and connected, moreover, by ties of personal friendship or mutual acquaintance. It is perfectly easy in a town of one hundred thousand or less to convene meetings of local unions at short and regular intervals, and it is therefore possible for the local body to act directly upon all matters of interest to it. Every attempt is made by these local bodies to maintain their free and democratic nature. Most of the decisions and actions are taken by popular vote, and in many cases even the appointment of committees devolves upon the members instead of upon the chairman. The presiding officer, usually called the president, is elected, as a rule, for but six months or a year and is rarely paid a salary for his services. The secretaries and treasurers of local unions are required to give bond and are subject to the close supervision of the members. The walking delegate or business agent is usually a salaried employee elected for a term of six months or one year, but subject to removal at any time by a majority vote of the members of his union. Nearly all of the national organizations employ paid organizers, who are constantly engaged in forming local unions. The United Mine Workers of America has at present eighty paid, and about two hundred unpaid, organizers devoting their time to this work. The Union expended in 1902 the sum of $110,000 in the creation and maintenance of new unions. The American Federation of Labor, which is a federated body composed of the principal unions of the country, also pays a large force of organizers and secures the gratuitous services of a great number of volunteer organizers.

Upon the relation existing between the local and national organizations depend the character, power and prestige of the union. In some instances, the national organization has limited power and exercises but slight control over the actions of the local unions; whereas, in other cases, this control and supervision is effective. Where, as in coal mining, the industry is of such a nature that the employers in the various parts of the country compete with each other for the sale of their product, it is highly essential that power be concentrated in the national organization. In other industries, where there is less competition and less need of uniformity, the demand for the centralization of power in the national union is less keenly felt. Generally speaking, the relation of the local unions to the national is somewhat similar to the relation between the state and national governments. The local unions have somewhat less power than the state, but considerably greater power than municipalities. Broadly considered, they have the right to do anything not in conflict with the national constitution or with by-laws passed in accordance therewith. In many instances, the locals are supreme in determining the rates of wages, the shop or factory rules, the fining or disciplining of members, and the amount of dues and initiation fees. Even where the hours of labor are fixed at a certain maximum by the national union, the locals are frequently permitted to secure a still further reduction, and where the national union prescribes a maximum and minimum for fines and assessments, the local is generally allowed discretion in fixing these fines between the maximum and the minimum. The administration of the funds of the local, except such portion as is paid for taxes or assessments to the district or national organizations, is in the hands of the local. The punishment of members for offense against the union, for underbidding members, for working below the union scale, for working during strikes, for revealing the proceedings of the organization, for abusive language, for misappropriation of funds, for unexcused absence, or for other neglect of duty, is under the control of the local, although appeals may be made from these decisions to the national officers, or even to the conventions of the national organization. The punishment inflicted for failure to comply with the rules of the union may consist of reprimand, fine, suspension, or expulsion according to the gravity of the offense and the past record of the offender. Although this punishment is, to a large extent, a local matter, the national organization sometimes regulates the maximum amount of fines or makes other provisions to obviate occasional injustice.

Local unions are rarely vested with power to inaugurate a strike without the advice and consent of the national organization. As a general rule, the national officers do not have the right to call a local strike, but merely have the privilege of vetoing the application of a local union that contemplates engaging in a strike, thus acting as a brake upon, and not as a stimulus to, hasty action. In practically all unions, the national officers are more conservative and more desirous of maintaining peace than the local officials or members who, not feeling the same degree of responsibility, frequently overestimate the importance of a petty quarrel and thoughtlessly rush into strikes which may involve the whole organization.

The government of a national labor organization, like the government of the United States is composed of executive, legislative, and judicial departments. The power to direct and administer its affairs is entrusted to representatives selected by the local unions. These executive powers are vested in a president and a board of directors; the legislative, in a delegate convention, while the judicial function devolves upon the president or secretary of the organization, with the right of appeal to the executive board. The legislation of the national union is carried on by means of conventions composed of delegates from the various locals, or by the actual votes of the members of the union themselves. The representation of the locals is in some organizations based entirely upon the number of their members, resembling in this respect the representation of the various states in the United States House of Representatives. The majority of unions, however, give the larger locals a less than proportionate representation in the national conventions; for illustration, the Brotherhood of Carpenters gives one vote to a local having 100 members or less, two votes to locals having from 100 to 500 members, three votes to locals having from 500 to 1,000 members, and four votes to locals having over one thousand members. This system of giving the various locals a number of representatives increasing with their membership, but not increasing in proportion, is somewhat like the representation of the various states of the country in the electoral college, or in the nominating conventions of the Republican and Democratic parties. The conventions, like the meetings of the locals, are conducted in a broad and democratic spirit. The ordinary laws of parliamentary procedure are adhered to, but no attempt is made at "gag" rule, and every opportunity is afforded to all delegates to present fully the wishes and claims of their respective locals. Generally speaking, especially in the older and more firmly established organizations, the expenses of the conventions, including the railroad fares to and from the place of meeting, are defrayed by the national union.

In some organizations, the system of government is even more democratic. In many unions, there is a growing tendency to legislate by means of the referendum and to limit as much as possible the frequency of conventions. Ordinarily, conventions are called annually, but in several unions they are called but once in two, three, four, or five years, and in the case of the Granite Cutters there has been no convention since the year 1880. Legislation in some unions may be proposed by a given number of members or by the executive and may then be acted upon by the vote of the entire membership. Much of the legislation of a number of the unions is carried on in this way, and in a large percentage of organizations, amendments to the constitution are adopted either by a referendum vote alone, or by the action of the convention supplemented by a referendum vote. In other unions, including the Boot and Shoe Workers, the Cigar Makers, the Tailors, the Bakers, and the Mine Workers, officers are elected by referendum vote, with the result that lobbying and electioneering at the convention are done away with and the delegates are permitted to devote themselves exclusively to the more important business of the organization.

The officials of the national trade unions, whether elected in convention or by referendum, consist usually of a president, one or more vice-presidents, a secretary or a secretary-treasurer, and an executive board, who are ordinarily elected for a term of one or two years, but may be, and in many instances are, reëlected. The President of the Carpenters held office for twenty years, and the late Mr. Arthur remained Chief of the Locomotive Engineers for twenty-nine years. In the United Mine Workers this tendency of constantly reëlecting the same president has been less manifest—prior to my incumbency the term of office with one exception never exceeded two years.

The chief officials of the national trade unions are almost invariably on salary and devote their entire time to the work of the organization. In the case of the railroad brotherhoods, the rates of remuneration are high, amounting in some cases to $6,000 per year, but with this exception, I believe, no national officer receives a higher salary than $3,000. The probable range of salaries for trade union presidents lies, at the present time, between $1,000 and $1,800, although in a number of organizations the pay of officials is still less. Officers' salaries are regulated to a considerable extent by the numerical strength of the unions or by the wages of its members. In a few national unions having a limited membership the executive officers work at their trades, and in these cases their remuneration is purely nominal.

It is impossible in a brief chapter to give a complete account of any one of the one hundred constitutions of national trade unions in the United States. The constitution usually prescribes rules for such matters as eligibility to membership, times for holding meetings, initiation fees, dues and assessments of members, general finances, discipline, laws for expulsion and reinstatement of members, rules for the election of officers, duties of presidents, vice-presidents, secretaries, and treasurers conduct of strikes, lockouts, and boycotts, work of organizers, character and nature of supplies, use of the label, management of the official journal, times and causes for holding general or special conventions, administration of insurance, order of business, and a large number of other matters. The member of a trade union is ordinarily provided with a card to signify his membership and with a button or badge, which in many cases he is expected to wear about his person. Most constitutions prescribe methods for securing and controlling the collection of dues, the usual system being that of stamps affixed to a book.

Although the constitution of the United Mine Workers is supposed to represent the fundamental and organic law of the union, this constitution does not take precedence over the trade agreement. It is specifically stipulated in many contracts with operators that nothing in the national, state, or local constitutions will be allowed to conflict with any provision of the trade agreement.

CHAPTER XI

AMERICAN TRADE UNIONS OF TO-DAY

Various Kinds of Trade Unions. Trade Unions and Respectability. Trade Unions Affiliated with the American Federation of Labor. Centralized Unions. The Growing Necessity of Centralization. The United Mine Workers of America. Interstate Agreements. A Million Dollar Defense Fund. The Garment Workers, and the Sweated Trades. The Cigar Makers, the Label, and Trade Benefits. The Carpenters and Joiners. Various Other Unions.

MANY people speak of trade unionism as though all organizations of wage workers were identical in government, purpose, and action. A commendation of one union is interpreted as a commendation of all, and an attack upon one as an attack upon all.

There are almost as many kinds and varieties of unions as there are kinds and varieties of industries. Trade unions differ from one another with differences in the trades or industries which they represent. There is no more similarity between a union of glassblowers and one of waiters, or a union of typesetters and one of street laborers, than there is between the occupations engaged in by these men. Some organizations are formed merely on local, some, on national or international lines; some organizations have but a weak federal government, others are strongly centralized; some organizations are composed of men of the highest skill and training, others, of workmen whose training has been acquired in a few days. Even this does not exhaust the differences. There are unions composed chiefly of native workmen, others, almost entirely of newly landed immigrants; many unions consist chiefly or exclusively of men, others, overwhelmingly of women. Some unions—but these are few—do not admit negroes and make other discriminations, while the great bulk of organizations throw open their doors to men of every race, creed, or nationality; some unions are exclusive and aristocratic, other organizations—and these are the majority—are all-inclusive and extremely democratic.

Unions, moreover, are divided according to the status of their members and to the nature of their industry. There are unions of government employees, such as the letter carriers or, to a less extent, typesetters and pressmen in the government printing office. There are organizations of municipal employees, such as school teachers. There are many organizations which cannot resort to strikes and many which must depend entirely for their success upon the label. There are organizations in trades protected by the monopoly of the employers, and organizations in the superlatively competitive sweated trades. There are organizations with highly developed benefit features, paying their members or their families in case of death, sickness, accident, or loss of employment, and there are others which have no benefit features whatever. There are unions which insist upon strict apprentice rules and others which admit any man capable of earning the standard wage. There are a few unions which adopt the policy of limiting the number of their members or the amount of work which they may do, and there are others, the overwhelming majority, which place no such restriction. There are unions which embrace only persons who perform a particular function or who work at a particular trade or operation, and others which embrace all persons employed in a great and diversified industry. Finally, there are unions, the so-called "federal" unions, which unite into local groups men of diverse and entirely dissimilar occupation and skill, and which serve as a recruiting ground for other and more specialized unions.

Many persons, apathetic or hostile to trade unionism, seem either consciously or unconsciously to divide labor organizations into three classes, respectable, semi-respectable, and disreputable. These people speak of organizations like the Typographical Union or the Brotherhood of Locomotive Engineers, as being model institutions and regret that other trade unions are not of the same type and character. This classification is like dividing men into adults, youths, and children. The child becomes a youth, and the youth a man, and in the same manner the unions now denounced as radical and unreliable will in due time attain to complete and full fledged respectability. There was a time when the locomotive engineers and the typographical unions were assailed for their alleged violent methods, for their lack of respectability, for their failure to comply with the highest requirements of trade unionism, just as many organizations of more recent origin have since been attacked. The truth is that each organization of wage earners must gradually fight its way against the opposition of men who criticise instead of aid it to a position where its word is as good as its bond, and where its actions meet with the approval of well-intentioned men in all parts of the community. There necessarily is a gradual evolution, a gradual sifting out of the worst elements in the organization, and the acquisition of a sound and conservative policy. At the beginning, when the efforts of the new union are derided and decried, when the attempts to better the conditions of the workers are met with the scorn, hatred, and constant opposition of employers, it is small wonder that the organized men, new to the methods and the ideals of trade unionism and smarting under the sense of their weakness and inexperience, resort to measures unwise and injurious to themselves. A union becomes stronger with wisdom and wiser with strength. A union that succeeds in winning its strikes gains not only better conditions of life, but also the respect of its former antagonist and the wisdom and conservatism which comes from an assured position.

I desire in this chapter to give a brief account of a few of the various classes of unions. It would not, of course be possible to describe all the unions in the United States,[1] or even to give an adequate description of a small number of them.

---

[1] The following is a list of trade unions affiliated with the American Federation of Labor, together with the vote to which they were entitled during the last five years. To estimate the legally recognized membership of these unions, it is only necessary to multiply the number of votes to which they are entitled by 100. For reasons given in the chapter on the Federation of American Labor, these figures are probably 50 per cent. or more below the real membership. The actual membership of the unions affiliated with the American Federation of Labor at the present time (August, 1903) is probably two million.

Organization.	1898.	1899.	1900.	1901.	1902.
Amalgamated Association of Marine Water Tenders, etc.					*
Actors' National Protective Union				3	5
Allied Metal Mech. Bicycle Workers, International	7	9	22	5	6
American Agents' Association	7	9	*		*
Bakers and Confectioners' International	21	31	45	64	102
Barbers' National Union	30	40	69	116	160
Brass and Composition Metal Workers					*
Brewery Workmen, National Union	100	107	183	235	291
Broommakers' Union, International	1	3	4	8	
Boot and Shoe Workers' Union	94	43	47	88	146
Brickmakers' Alliance, National	5	10	14	17	41
Boilermakers and Iron Shipbuilders	22	27	51	73	95
Blacksmiths, International Brotherhood of	3	5	15	35	43
Bookbinders, International Brotherhood of	26	28	36	53	70
Bottle Blowers' Association of United States and Canada		42	42	47	59
Carpenters and Joiners, Amalgamated	16	18	20	26	32
Carpenters and Joiners, United Brotherhood of	200	200	200	400	800
Carriage and Wagon Workers	5	7	13	25	31
Cigarmakers' International Union	266	270	321	339	317
Clerks, International Protective Association, Retail	50	75	200	200	300
Coopers' International Union	15	27	38	49	57
Cloth Hat and Capmakers, United					20
Curtain Operators, Amalgamated, Lace	3	3	4	4	5
Coremakers' International Union	7	10	12	12	12
Carvers' Union, International Wood	9	12	18	20	23
Chainmakers' National Union			2	4	6
Clerks, Order of Railway			5	6	†
Car Workers, International Association of				10	24
Clothingmakers, Special Order of					60
Electrical Workers', International Brotherhood	20	20	48	73	115
Engineers, National Union of Steam	12	18	27	48	65
Engineers, Amalgamated Society of	19	18	18	18	19
Engineers, National Brotherhood of Coal Hoisting		5	7	10	8
Furniture Workers of America, International					*
Furriers' Union of United States and Canada					††
Firemen, International Brotherhood of Stationary		11	24	41	62
Furnace Workers and Smelters of America				14	9
Garment Workers of America, United	43	42	74	154	43
Glass Workers' Union, Flint	70	75	80	72	71
Grinders' National Union, Table Knife	2	3	2	2	2
Granite Cutters' National Union	46	48	59	70	82
Gold Beaters' Protective Union, National	5	5			3
Glass Flatteners' Association of North America, Window	5	6	6		†
Glass Cutters' League of America, Window	8	8			7
Glass Workers' International Association, Amalgamated			2	3	7
Horseshoers of United States and Canada	20	20	21	23	28
Hotel and Restaurant Employes	25	20	48	103	191
Hatters of North America, United	60	60	60	73	80
Hat and Capmakers, Cloth					20
Iron and Steel Workers, Amalgamated	80	80	80	80	150
Iron Workers, Bridge and Structural, International Association				60	
Jewelry Workers' International			9	9	10
Longshoremen's Association of United States	80	130	200	250	347
Leather Workers on Horse Goods	4	10	21	32	42
Lathers, International Union of, Wood Work and Metal			6	14	23
Ladies' Garment Workers, International				20	21
Leather Workers of America, Amalgamated				3	22
Metal Workers' International Union, United			10	21	43
Moulders' Union of North America, Iron	120	150	150	150	259
Machinists' Union of America, International	100	136	225	225	355
Mine Workers of America, United	160	400	1,010	1,891	1,854
Marble Workers, International Association of					5
Mine Managers and Assistants' Mutual Aid Association, National					4
Mineral Mine Workers, Progressive					3
Miners, Western Federation of	7	6	5	4	†
Metal Polishers, Buffers and Platers, etc.	42	48	50	56	84
Musicians, American Federation of	60	60	62	81	97
Meat Cutters and Butcher Workmen	10	17	32	55	84
Metal Workers' International Association, Amalgamated Sheet		15	29	45	66

Organization.	1898.	1899.	1900.	1901.	1902.
Painters of America, Brotherhood of	43	45	280	280	348
Papermakers, United Brotherhood of	1	1	4	18	41
Patternmakers' National League	13	15	22	23	23
Piano and Organ Workers' Union					57
Potter's National Union of America	2				
Printing Pressmen, International	53	72	91	100	119
Plumbers, Gas Fitters, Steam Fitters, etc.	40	40	45	87	128
Potters, Stoneware	1	1	1		†
Powder and High Explosive Workers					4
Printers, Plate, of United States of America, National	4	4	6	7	7
Potters, National Brotherhood of Operative		13	22	29	49
Paving Cutters' Union of United States of America				1	2
Oil and Gas Well Workers' Union, International			4	5	3
Quarrymen's National Union	4				††
Quarrymen's National Union, Slate	1				††
Railway Employes' Amalgamated Association, Street	30	30	35	43	98
Saw Smiths' Union of America					3
Seamen's Union of America, National	40	40	41	82	99
Spinners' Association, Cotton Mule	21	21	24	27	26
Stove Mounters' International Union	6	6	9	13	16
Stoneware Potters					††
Steam and Hot Water Fitters and Helpers		20	18	15	15
Shirt, Waist and Laundry Workers				21	42
Stereotypers and Electrotypers' Union of North America, Internat'l					18
Trackmen of America, Brotherhood of Railway					46
Tailors' Union of America, Journeymen	50	50	73	93	109
Theatrical Stage Employes, National	23	30	30	38	44
Typographical Union, International	289	310	329	365	393
Tobacco Workers' Union of America	46	41	60	43	41
Textile Workers of America, National Union o	25	22	31	27	106
Tile Layers and Helpers', International Union	2	3	4	7	11
Trunk and Bag Workers			3	3	5
Tin Plate Workers, International Protective		17	21	20	21
Team Drivers, International		17	47	94	138
Telegraphers, Order of Railroad		80	80	80	80
Tube Workers of United States and Canada					5
Weavers, Amalgamated Association of Web	3	3	3	2	2
Wood Workers', International Machine Union	51	68	121	151	184
Wire Drawers of America, Federated Association o	3	5			††
Watch Case Engravers, International			5	5	4
Wire Weavers' Protective, American			2	2	2
Watch Casemakers, International				3	††
Upholsterers, International Union of			13	13	13
American Federation of Labor:					
Locals	146	163	349	469	678
Centrals	81	117	218	324	425
State Branches	10	11	16	21	27
Total votes of affiliated unions	2,881	3,632	5,737	8,240	10,705

* Charter revoked.   † Suspended for non-payment of per capita tax.   †† Disbanded
** Merged with Amalgamated Wood Workers.

The strongest unions of the present day are those which are highly centralized. As in political government, so in the government of trade unions, there is always a contest between the advocates of a strong centralized government, in which the national union exercises effective control over its locals, and a decentralized government, in which the locals reserve a large amount of power. The fact that some unions are centralized and others decentralized is not accidental or arbitrary but is due to the character and nature of the industry. Where, in such industries as coal mining or steel manufacturing, competition between employers is keen and is felt in all parts of the field, it is essential that the government of the trade union be centralized, so that competitive conditions can exist in the labor market throughout the whole country. The rate of pay of Illinois coal miners is fixed in such a way as to enable the Illinois operators to compete on fair terms with those of Indiana, Ohio, Pennsylvania, and other portions of the country. Such a system of securing to all employers fair, competitive conditions in the labor market could be adopted only by a strongly centralized union, regulating the rates of pay, the hours of labor, the conditions of work, and the policy of war or peace in the various parts of the country. Even where employers do not compete, as in the building trades, unions have tended to become centralized by reason of the competition of the workmen themselves. The wages of New York carpenters cannot remain high so long as those of other cities are low, since a Philadelphia carpenter can go to New York or Baltimore at a cost less than a day's wage. The mobility of labor in the United States is such that unions are necessarily becoming more and more centralized, in order to regulate the competition between the men in a given trade, wherever their place of residence.

One of the most centralized labor unions is that of the United Mine Workers of America. This organization, the largest labor union in the world, now has 260,000 members upon its rolls, not including some 60,000 or 70,000 men who are in arrears for dues or assessments. It is organized upon industrial, rather than upon trade, lines. Every man or boy working in or about the mines, whether as engineer, fireman, ash-man, barn-man, teamster, blacksmith, carpenter, gate-man, oiler, inspector, loader, culm-driver, washery-man, laborer, slate picker, miner or any other of the scores of different occupations, is eligible to membership. The union is composed of men of many nationalities and races. Colored persons are freely admitted to membership and enjoy all the rights granted to other members, and representatives of twenty nations, speaking twenty different languages, are found upon its rolls. The union is highly centralized, the national organization exercising a veto power over the calling of strikes. The union has entered into inter-state agreements covering the competitive territory of Illinois, Indiana, Ohio, and Western Pennsylvania, in the one case, and the competitive territory of Missouri, Kansas, Arkansas, and Indian Territory upon the other; it also has trade agreements with the operators of Iowa Michigan, Alabama, Kentucky, Tennessee, Montana, Central Pennsylvania and portions of West Virginia. The dues are low, averaging about forty cents a month. The national union is supported chiefly by a monthly tax of ten cents per member, but additional assessments may be levied. Membership is open to boys, but under sixteen years of age, they pay only one-half dues and assessments and have only one-half a vote.

This organization has grown more rapidly than any trade union in the history of the world. It has locals in every coal producing state in the country and carries on its rolls over two-thirds of the 500,000 coal mine workers in the United States. It has been one of the most successful national unions in the country in its strikes, which have usually extended over a large territory. The organization has at this time a special defense fund of $1,000,000 but has no insurance or benefit features.

One of the typical unions in the sweated trades is the United Garment Workers of America, an organization composed of tailors, cutters, trimmers, lining cutters, and other men engaged in the clothing trade. There is no industry in the United States that has so lent itself to sweating as the manufacture of ready made clothing. The conditions which have prevailed in this trade, especially in New York, Chicago, Philadelphia, and other large cities, have been terrible, and have been the subject of a number of legislative investigations. By the organization of the Garment Workers, however, and of several other trade unions, these abuses have, to a certain extent been mitigated. The union is composed largely of immigrants, especially of Russian and Polish Jews, Scandinavians, Italians, and Poles. It is an organization chiefly centered in a few large cities.

The greatest difficulties which the Garment Workers have experienced have arisen from the fact that a steady flow of immigration is continually pouring in upon them, and from the further fact that the industry is broken up into a number of small establishments. On the other hand, the union has derived support from the factory laws in the various states, and more especially from the successful and extensive use of the union label, without which it is doubtful whether the organization could have attained its present strength. The Garment Workers' label, in existence since 1891, has been largely advertised, and there is a strong demand on the part of workingmen and other members of society for label-made goods. The organization has a well-edited monthly journal. The local dues are fixed at a minimum of 25¢ a month, or 50¢ a month for cutters. Special facilities are extended to women workers, and lower initiation fees are charged to unions with a majority of female members.

The Cigarmakers' International Union of America is the classic instance of an American organization depending largely on its insurance features. This union has for more than a generation attempted to strengthen the economic condition of its workers by developing an extended system of benefits. The initiation fee is $3.00, the dues 30¢ a week, or over $15.00 a year, which are exceptionally high payments, especially in view of the fact that the cigar makers are not particularly high-paid workers. During the last twenty years the union expended over eight millions of dollars. The Cigar Makers' Union has gradually and steadily increased in membership, and through its out-of-work benefits, the organization maintained its strength even in the bad years following the crisis of 1893. It has fought a number of strikes, winning a large percentage of them, and it has secured for its members an eight-hour day. By means of the label, of which over three hundred million have been issued, the union, despite the great influx of immigrants, has maintained relatively high wages.

The United Brotherhood of Carpenters and Joiners of America is a typical organization of the building trades. After unsuccessful efforts in

1854 and 1867, a national union was finally established in 1881 with a membership of two thousand. This number has increased to over sixty-eight thousand in 1900, and in July 1 of that year, there were 679 local unions, with an approximate membership of 150,000. Of these locals, 40 were conducting business in the German language, 6 in French, 2 in Bohemian, 2 in Jewish, and 1 in Scandinavian. The union has benefit features, having expended over $53,000 in 1900 for funeral and disability benefits. It has been in numerous conflicts and has had a series of jurisdictional disputes, the last of which was with the Amalgamated Wood Workers. This dispute has attracted wide-spread attention in labor circles, owing to the refusal of the Brotherhood of Carpenters to accept the award of a board of arbitration, which rendered a decision adverse to its claims.

There are many other unions deserving of discussion and meriting extended study. Among these are the International Typographical Union of North America, which has had over fifty years of interesting history; the International Longshoremen's Association, which comprises all the dock laborers on the Great Lakes and forms trade agreements with the shippers; the Amalgamated Association of Street Railway Employees of America, which is a comparatively recent organization, but one whose growth has been very rapid; the National Amalgamated Association of Iron, Steel, and Tin Workers, which in 1901 conducted a struggle against the United States Steel Corporation. There are numerous other organizations in the building, printing, textile, glass and pottery, wood working, metal and machine, and transportation industries. The various railroad brotherhoods have had a long and interesting history and have grown yearly in power and prestige. There are also organizations of retail clerks, team drivers, horse shoers, jewelry workers, letter carriers, theatrical stage employees, and scores of other classes of employees. One of the most interesting forms of trade unions is the federal union, which consists of men of various trades and serves as a temporary union from which permanent organizations are formed as soon as there are sufficient members in a given trade to warrant the creation of a new union. The members of all these various unions, international, national and local, represent the rank and file of organized labor. At the present time there are probably more than two and a half million trade unionists in the United States. As has been shown, these organizations differ in many respects, but, underlying all, there is a certain spirit in common, a desire for concerted action, and a more or less clear conception of solidarity and brotherhood.

CHAPTER XII

ORGANIZED LABOR VERSUS UNORGANIZED LABOR

An Age of Organization. Organization Especially Necessary to Workingmen. The Separation of Wage Earner from Wage Payer. Defenselessness of the Individual Workingman. The Track Layer and the Pennsylvania Railroad. Free Competition for Jobs at its Worst. The Influence of the Employer upon the Life, Health, Safety, Manners, Morals, and Character of the Workingman. What Freedom of Contract Means to Unorganized Workingmen. It Takes Two to Make a Contract. Advantages of Trade Unionism. Its Absolute Necessity.

THE age is an age of organization. Not only in industry, but in every field and phase of human life, have men combined into groups and worked as a unit. Thus, we have political organizations; organizations of men engaged in various trades or industries; organizations of lawyers, doctors, ministers; organizations of men into clubs, into friendly or benefit societies; organizations for the pursuit of arts, of science, of education; organizations of men into universities, organizations of men into cities, states, and nations, and, finally, organizations extending over national boundaries and reaching all sorts and conditions of men, the organizations called churches. Everywhere, look where we may, we see men of all classes and all characters organizing for all purposes, and effecting by concerted action what cannot be accomplished by individual action. The age is an age of organization, moreover, of the representation of the many by the few, of conventions, of the interchange of thought among men united in purpose, of unity of action and concert of management. What is true of all other classes is true to no greater and no less extent of workingmen. What these organizations are to various classes of men in society, trade unions are to the workingmen in the pursuit of their industrial happiness.

Were the workingmen of the United States not a separate class, with **separate class interests**, there would be less necessity for their separate organization. If the modern wage earner evolved into the capitalist, as the boy into the man, or the caterpillar into the butterfly, he might not be obliged to associate with his fellow-craftsmen in order to improve his conditions. There is, however, a growing separation in interest and feeling between employers and workingmen. "The business men in the present generation," says Professor Arthur Twining Hadley, President of Yale University, "have in large part risen from the ranks of labor to their existing position of leadership; but whether the same thing can be predicted for the next generation is very doubtful. Certain it is that the prospect of becoming capitalists does not act as so powerful a motive on the laborers of to-day as it did on those of a generation ago. The opportunities to save are as great or greater; but the amount which has to be saved before a man can hope to become his own employer, has increased enormously. When a man who had accumulated a thousand dollars could set up in business for himself, the prospect of independence appealed to him most powerfully; when he can do nothing but lend it to some richer man, the incentives and ambitions connected with saving are far weaker—too weak, in many cases, to lead the man to save at all, except through the medium of a friendly society or trades-union." We thus have a separation of the community into more and more rigidly defined groups, different in industrial condition, distinct in ideals, and oftentimes antagonistic in ambitions and sympathies.

Not only is the individual workingman's chance of becoming an employer rapidly disappearing, but with every advance in industry, with each new development of enterprise upon a large scale, his importance is diminishing and his power to bargain individually, growing less. The industrial development of the past century and a half has made the employer grow and the workman shrink. When the man who received wages and the man who paid wages worked side by side on the same wooden bench, the present inequality between the individual workman and the employer did not exist. The employer who formerly owned thousands of dollars, however, is now the possessor of hundreds of thousands or millions, and the employer of the future will no longer be a man, but a vast corporation with a capital of hundreds of millions, if not, as in the case of an existing corporation, with a capital of over a billion of dollars.

Owing to the present growing inequality between capitalists and individual workingmen, the advantage, the necessity even, of trade unionism becomes apparent. The United States Steel Corporation can better do without the services of an individual puddler or roller than the puddler or roller can do without the wages of the United States Steel Corporation. A tracklayer or brakeman upon the Pennsylvania Railroad is more anxious to keep his job than the Pennsylvania Railroad is desirous of retaining his services. The very freedom of contract which the workingman now possesses is, if he is unorganized, at least to a certain extent, a disadvantage. It was formerly supposed that as soon as all restrictions upon the inalienable right of a man to work were removed, the workman would become prosperous, since free competition and the play of supply and demand would work out to his advantage. What has actually occurred, however, is that the individual workman, unprotected by a union, is more and more at the mercy of the large employer and more and more defenseless with every advance made by modern society.

There is no doubt that upon the whole the American workingman receives better wages, both in money and in what money will buy, than the workingman of any of the nations of Europe. But, like all men who are dependent upon their earnings, the American wage earner standing alone is in a precarious condition. There are at work hundreds of thousands, if not millions, of Americans, whose entire belongings do not amount in value to more than two or three weeks' wages, and there are many who draw their present week's pay with the intention of liquidating their last week's debt. In all employments, and especially in large cities, work is precarious and uncertain; and in hard times particularly, the fear of enforced idleness acts as a terrible weight upon the mind of the workingman. The majority of workingmen do not hold their own and do not have a fixed income sufficient to support them in case of loss of work. There is no prospect of aid from the government or from charitable societies, in case they become ill or prematurely aged.

Under such conditions the unorganized workman in the United States, as elsewhere, is frequently obliged to accept extremely low wages, to work for excessively long hours, and to labor under unsanitary and dangerous conditions. Of course, the unorganized workman may, in periods of exceptional prosperity, draw advantage from an abnormal demand for labor; but in ordinary times, and especially in periods of depression, he must accept the wages that are offered. The free competition for labor frequently works great hardship. A man with a family at home and without a dollar in his pocket will be willing to work for almost any wage, and the men in the same trade who have greater resources will be obliged to accept the same rate of remuneration. The strength of the chain is the strength of its weakest link, and the power of resistance of unorganized workmen is the power of the poorest and least resourceful of them. The competition of women and children, willing to work for spending money, drives down still further the wages which unorganized men and women, solely dependent upon their own work, will be forced to accept. The pin money of the farmer's wife fixes the amount of the needle money of the city seamstress. The unrestricted competition for the opportunity to work in the ready-made clothing and other sweated trades before the existence of the union was such as to reduce whole masses of the population to a level of wages, and force them to an intensity and duration of work, inconsistent with health, morality, or the propagation of the species. The competition for jobs in unorganized and unregulated trades brings forth a struggle which is pathetic and from a moral point of view, unutterably brutal and anarchic. An eye witness, writing prior to the famous dock strike of 1889, says: "There is a place at the London Docks called the cage, a sort of pen fenced off by iron railings. I have seen three hundred half-starved dockers crowded round this cage, when perhaps a ganger would appear wanting

EMIGRANT'S LANDING
857,000 emigrants arrived last year

A Group of Miners Through Work for the Day

three hands, and the awful struggle of these three hundred famished wretches fighting for that opportunity to get two or three hours' work has left an impression upon me that can never be effaced. Why, I have actually seen them clambering over each other's backs to reach the coveted ticket. I have frequently seen men emerge bleeding and breathless, with their clothes pretty well torn off their backs."

The scene above described is true not of London alone, nor of dock hands alone. During the bad times of 1893 and 1894, groups of half-starved workingmen were seen in the large cities surrounding newspaper offices at daybreak, waiting for the first edition of the paper, with its want "ads.," and then racing to the place where the job was offered to be the first to take the position at any price. Wherever unorganized, unskilled workmen strive for jobs, they do so under the burden of this blind, merciless, remorseless competition from men who are unemployed or men who are but partially employed. This competition is no less terrible because unseen. When in bad times an employer advertises for a clerk and receives, as is often the case, a hundred or more applications, the misery that produces so unregulated and excessive a demand for the position offered is no less fearful because its effects are not immediately visible.

To a very great extent trade unionism regulates this unrestricted competition and directs it into socially advantageous channels. In union there is strength. Through trade unionism the wages of workmen cease to be regulated by the wages of the man with the least resources and the greatest needs, and become the remuneration that the average man in the trade might demand. Trade unionism takes labor from the list of perishable articles that must be sold on the spot and immediately, or not at all, and gives to the workingman a reserve power and to his labor, a reserve price. Through the trade union, the workingman bargaining for a position gets his second wind. By emphasizing the solidarity of labor the union renders the competition of workmen with each other less keen. The instinctive feeling among workingmen against underbidding one another is crystallized by trade unionism into the commandment, "Thou shalt not unfairly take thy neighbor's job." The union changes the individual bargain between the man who needs a job immediately and the employer who may hire him to-day, or a month from now, or not at all, into a collective bargain between all the workingmen and all the employers in the trade. The union, further, gives to the workingman the services of men especially trained to the work of making bargains with employers, men who, as officers of the union, devote their lives to the sole task of getting the best possible conditions. The union in so doing acts upon the principle that the advantage of the workingman will not come to him of itself, as the rain comes to the parched fields, but will flow only from the persistent and combined efforts of workingmen. As General Francis A. Walker said, "If the wage laborer does not pursue his interest, he loses his interest."

It is only when we comprehend the influence which labor conditions exercise upon the physical, mental, and moral life of the workman and his family that we realize the vital necessity of trade unionism. The wage contract is not merely a contract to deliver certain labor for a certain sum of money, but is an arrangement regulating a thousand and one details of life and vitally affecting every phase of the existence of the workman. The question of organized labor *versus* unorganized labor is the question of the right of workmen to determine some of the conditions under which they shall work and live, instead of leaving the whole matter to the greed or necessities of an employer or to the whim, cruelty, or sordidness of a tyrannical foreman.

Labor, it is said, is a commodity to be bought and sold, and it is as idle to attempt to regulate the price of this, or of any other commodity, as to seek to stop the flow of the tides. Labor, however, is a commodity of a peculiar sort. It is a part of the very being of the man who sells it. The commodity sold is a human creature, whose welfare in the eyes of the law should be of more importance than any mere accumulation of wealth on the part of the community. It is a commodity, further, which it is difficult to sell to advantage. The workingman cannot know the best market for this ware, his labor, nor can he sell it at any place, except where he himself is. He cannot send a sample of it, nor can he, without organized effort, regulate the supply. As long as he lives and is without resources, he must work, and for many years in succession he may be forced to sell his product at a price considerably less than the cost to society of reproducing it. When the demand for cotton or wheat decreases, this very fact lessens the supply, since it becomes less profitable to raise it; but when the demand for labor declines, this very fact creates an added supply, since women and children and other persons ordinarily unemployed are now forced on the market, and men will be willing to work longer hours, because there is less work to do. The commodity labor is one which can be supplied by women and children, and if there is no limit set either by organization or by the force of law to its use or exploitation, it can very well result in the wholesale destruction of the commodity itself, and in the permanent deterioration of the workmen of the community.

Without organization and without the interference of the law, therefore, the individual workman is practically at the mercy of the employer. It does not follow that the employer will always abuse this privilege, or that he will seek to secure labor at less than a reasonable and humane remuneration. At the same time the force of competition will in many cases compel the unprotected and unorganized workman, rather than starve, to accept a wage insufficient to maintain a decent standard of living or to keep him in a state of industrial efficiency. The experience of the sweated trades illustrates this tendency. In the manufacture of ready-made clothing in New York City, Philadelphia, Boston, and Chicago, one class of workmen has been displaced by another willing to take lower wages, and this latter by another, and so on, until the most meagre wages compatible with mere existence have been paid. The employment of women and children in the manufacture of paper boxes, of matches, confectionery, artificial flowers, brushes, and numberless small articles also illustrates this tendency. Where labor is unorganized and competition exists, the effect is not only felt in decreased wages, but also in longer hours, in unsanitary conditions, in the excessive employment of women and little children, and in every possible abuse of the workingman.

In many ways other than the amount of wages and the hours of labor, does the employer exert a strong influence upon the welfare of the workingman. Wherever there has been unorganized or disorganized labor, there have been cases of unfair advantage taken of employees by means of delayed payments, compulsory credit, and truck stores. If the employer refuses to pay frequently, but pays his workmen at long and irregular intervals, it is practically certain that a large number of them will be obliged to receive goods on credit, and, as a consequence, will fall prey to the extravagance which the presence of credit and the absence of cash invariably breed. Indebtedness to the employer means dependence upon him. It also means opportunity to reduce real wages by increasing prices at the company store. The unwarranted and unjust profit obtained from the truck stores has firmly imbedded the system in the arrangements of many employers. These stores have also enabled the employers to charge exorbitant prices and to cheat the workingmen in the matter of both quality and quantity of the goods offered. In many cases the truck store arose, in the first instance, from the actual needs and necessities of the workingman; but where a benefit becomes a curse, it should be abolished, whatever its original advantage. It is one of the principal achievements of trade unionism that it has, to so large an extent, inaugurated the system of weekly or semi-monthly payments in cash, and that in large measure it has done away with the system of paying in scrip or in commodities and has in many cases abolished the truck store.

The vital importance of trade unionism cannot be evident unless the full and true meaning of the labor contract is understood. The labor contract with the individual, unorganized workman is a loose verbal arrangement, stating nothing definitely with regard to the protection of the workman against disease, death, or accident. The employer practically dictates to the unorganized workman where he shall live, where he is to work, the condition under which the work shall be done, the amount of heat or dampness or ventilation, and whether or not there shall be guards upon the machinery to protect his life. It is not specifically stipulated in the contract with a brakeman or other trainman that each year one out of every one hundred and thirty-seven shall be killed, and one out of every eleven shall be maimed or injured; but the railroad company assumes the right to set the conditions which shall make this proportion of deaths and injuries inevitable. The employer also retains the right to choose unreservedly the companions and fellow-servants of the unorganized workman; and thus, the man who may put the new employee's life into jeopardy is entirely of the employer's choosing. The employer also influences by his regulations the hours of labor, the right of the employee to absent himself in case of sickness, the age and the task at which children shall be employed, and thus the health, not only of the present, but of future generations. In the same way, if unrestrained by organized labor or by the authority of the state, the employer can seriously impair the moral health of his workpeople, and that without violating the labor contract. The ordinary contract with the individual, unorganized workman states nothing with regard to the manner in which men and women shall work together in the factories, during the day or at night, the sanitary conditions, the presence or absence of separate toilet rooms, or any other provisions for the maintenance of the moral conditions of the workwoman. One of the advantages of trade unionism has been that it has aided conscientious employers and compelled negligent employers to maintain in their establishments a certain minimum of decency in these matters.

The labor contract, as it exists to-day, for the great majority of unorganized workingmen is merely a verbal agreement between the individual employee and the foreman, and each side reserves the right to quit at practically a moment's notice. There may be some advantages in this system, but one of the many disadvantages is the insecurity which it brings into the life of the person so employed. The unorganized workman is subject to the private spite and malice of his employer or foreman, although this is probably less true than was formerly the case. The position and wages of the unorganized workingman are entirely subject to fluctuations in the industry, and he is liable to be thrown out of employment with the first appearance of a shrinkage. The whole tendency of employment under the capitalistic régime has been, at least until recently, to make the position of the workingman more and more insecure. The crises and commercial depressions which have swept over this country during almost every decade, have resulted in intense suffering on the part of workingmen, a suffering accentuated by the competition of great masses of immigrants who come here during more prosperous times. Even apart from such crises, the workingman is subject to the loss of his job through sickness, accident, or other contingencies beyond his control; and in the vast majority of cases he can secure no compensation from the employer for injury inflicted by an accident, no matter how free the workman himself is from carelessness or contributory negligence. The employee is also subject to the loss of his position through advancing age, and in the case of the majority of unorganized workmen, no provision is made for him in this event.

To a considerable extent the unions steady and modify these influences and thus ameliorate the condition of the workmen at such times. By the payment of out-of-work benefits, which is common in England and becoming more prevalent in the United States, they lessen the hardship of a temporary unemployment, and by death and funeral benefits, they protect the widow and the orphans upon the demise of the wage earner from absolute destitution. The payment of old-age benefits, which is also more common among English than American trade unions, relieves the workingman of a portion of the anxiety with which he looks forward to approaching disability through age.

Trade unionism thus gives to workingmen increased power to modify to their advantage the terms of the labor contract. This is frequently styled by unreasonable employers as "interfering with my business," but the workman might with justice retort, "the employer is interfering with my life and happiness." The employer is now willing to concede, though he was not always willing to do so, that the workman has the right to determine what wages he will accept and how many hours he will work. What it has taken the employer much longer to learn, and what he has not even yet mastered, is the fact that the organized workman has just as much right to make suggestions and stipulations with regard to other conditions of employment. It takes two to make a contract, as it takes two to make a quarrel, and both parties to an agreement should have equal rights in determining how, when, with whom, at what time, and under what conditions work shall be carried on. Through the instrumentality of the trade union this right has been gradually, though as yet imperfectly, secured for the wage earner.

CHAPTER XIII

THE BENEFIT FEATURES OF TRADE UNIONS

Direct Benefit of Insurance. The Benefit Features of American Trade Unions. British vs. American Trade Benefits. Death and Funeral Benefits. Unions and Insurance Companies. The Unions and the Actuaries. Insurance and Union Discipline. Trade Unions and Assessment Insurance Companies. Death Benefits and Permanent Membership. Insurance and Union Control. Local Sick Benefits. Other Benefits. The Finances of British and American Trade Unions.

THE most direct, although not the greatest, benefit derived by workmen from their unions is insurance against death, accident, sickness, and in some cases loss of tools or failure to secure work. From their inception trade unions to a greater or less extent have adopted the policy of insuring their members, and, in fact, many of the earlier unions were formed and conducted under the guise of purely friendly societies. This system of trade union insurance has reached a high state of development in England. American unions, owing to their comparative youth, have not yet evolved as complete a system, although they are making steady progress in that direction.

An entirely false conception of the whole subject of trade union insurance is inevitable, unless one bears in mind that insurance is always subordinate to the trade policy of the unions. Trade unions are interested in protecting their members and paying them benefits in case of death, sickness, or disability, but they are even more vitally interested in raising wages and improving conditions of employment. Out-of-work benefits, for instance, are conceived entirely in this sense. The workman may derive an advantage from the support of his family when he is out of work; yet the primary object of the union is not to bestow charity or assistance upon the unemployed man, but to protect the wage of the men actually at work. Thus, if wages in an occupation are twelve dollars a week, the union prefers that an unemployed man receive from union funds an out-of-work benefit of four or five dollars a week rather than accept employment at ten dollars a week, or at any other rate below the union scale.

Even where benefits are not directly connected with loss of work, the insurance feature is subordinated to the trade policy of the organization. This constitutes one of the drawbacks and also one of the advantages of the system. From the point of view of the workingman there appears at first sight a certain disadvantage in being insured by the union, since he has no absolute guarantee of receiving the insurance for which he has paid. The funds devoted to life insurance and the money which may have been contributed for the purpose of insuring against sickness or old age, while as a rule kept separate and distinct from the general funds of the organization, may be used in a great strike or expended in out-of-work benefits during a prolonged commercial depression. Moreover, a member of the union, after paying his dues for a number of years, may have his assessment increased, or, by reason of a flagrant violation of the laws of the organization or for other misconduct, may be expelled from the union, and his rights to insurance benefits may thus be forfeited.

In point of actual practice these theoretical disadvantages have not materialized, and trade unions have been able to meet the obligations which they have incurred toward their members. From the point of view of the trade union, however, this system of insurance is of great benefit. By means of it a large number of the best workmen are attracted to the organization, and the enthusiasm of the members is maintained by the hope of securing relief in times of sickness or accident or provision for their families in case of death. The accumulation of a large reserve fund derived from insurance also strengthens the union in the event of a strike or of negotiations which may lead to a strike, while the hope of securing insurance benefits tends to render the members of the union more conservative and less willing to jeopardize its funds in useless or unwarranted labor conflicts. The possession of large funds for the payment of benefits further aids the union in establishing and maintaining discipline. Expulsion from a trade union is a much more serious punishment if it involves the loss of future insurance benefits than if no such losses are entailed. The trade union also possesses an advantage over the ordinary assessment insurance company in being able, by means of assessments levied upon members or otherwise, to adjust the income of the union to the demands put upon it by its insurance policy. In the case of an ordinary assessment insurance company, in which membership is voluntary, the increasing demand made upon the organization as men grow older and as the death rate increases, causes the assessments to become so high that the younger members gradually drop out, while other young men refuse to join, with the result that the average age of the members becomes constantly higher. On the other hand, in the case of the trade union, where participation in insurance is obligatory upon all members, there is no possibility for the young men to remain out, and the steady influx of new blood causes the average age of the members to remain constant. The actuaries and leading insurance experts of England predicted in 1867 that the trade union insurance companies would all become bankrupt, but this prediction, like many others regarding trade unionism, has been proved untrue by the subsequent experience of the organizations.

The development of trade union insurance by British organizations has beeen gradual but constant. During the ten years preceding 1901 the one hundred principal trade unions of Great Britain spent almost $45,000,000[1] in unemployed, sick, superannuated, funeral, and other benefits. Of this sum $15,900,000 were spent in payments to unemployed; $13,100,000 for cases of sickness and accident; $7,300,000 for superannuation, and $8,300,000 upon funeral and other benefits. The unemployed benefit is paid by a great majority of the unions and amounted, in the year 1902 to $2,230,000. Expenditures for this purpose fluctuate with the state of the trade, increasing in seasons of depression and decreasing in periods of industrial activity. In England they reached the highest point in 1893 and fell to the lowest

---

[1] In making this computation the pound sterling is held to be worth $4.85.

point in 1899, since which time they have beeen steadily rising. The expenditure for sick and accident insurance, paid usually as a weekly benefit in cases of sickness or allowed in lump sums in cases of disabling accident, or in other instances made as grants to hospitals, have steadily increased from $1,020,000 in 1892 to $1,670,000 in 1901, 69 out of 100 unions paying these benefits in 1892 and 77 unions out of 100 in 1901. The superannuation benefit consists of payments ranging from 50 cents to $3.00 per week, but usually averaging from $1.25 to $2.50 per week. It is given to men no longer able to work at their trades, or, at all events, to earn full wages, but is paid by only 38 of the 100 principal unions. The sum so expended, however, is largely increasing. In 1892, less than $500,000 was spent in this way, whereas in the year 1901 the sum so expended had increased to almost $1,000,000. Funeral benefits are the most widely diffused of all forms of trade union insurance in Great Britain, 89 out of the 100 principal unions, comprising 89 per cent. of the membership, paying benefits of this character. This benefit is also gradually increasing, amounting to $330,000 in 1892 and to $480,000 in 1901.

The policy of paying extensive benefits and of charging high dues has resulted in a rapid increase in the wealth and the membership of British trade unions. During the nine years from 1892 to 1901 the funds in the hands of the one hundred principal British unions increased from $7,785,000 to $20,185,000. Each year, therefore, enables the labor organizations of England to extend the scope and amount of their insurance and to guarantee the workingman greater immunity from life's vicissitudes.

The system of insurance, as already indicated, is not as fully or as perfectly developed in the United States as in England. This is accounted for not only by the fact that unions in the United States are younger but also by the fact that the dues in this country are much lower in proportion to the wages received. The average member of a British trade union pays about $8.50 per year, or about seventy cents per month, which is considerably in excess of the average dues of trade unionists in the United States. The American trade unions have adopted, however, at least in principle, the insurance features of British trade unions. The Cigar Makers and the German-American Typographia are perhaps the only American unions paying out-of-work benefits from the funds in their national treasuries, although in the case of victimized members a number of trade unions provide relief. The usual form of insurance on the part of American trade unions is the death or funeral benefit. This benefit is common because death itself is inevitable and brings a burden to the family of the deceased, and because a death or funeral fund can be administered much more easily and with less risk of fraud than a sick or accident fund. Some of the railroad brotherhoods pay large insurance in case of death and charge accordingly; the death benefit of the Locomotive Engineers ranging from $750 to $4,500; of the Conductors from $1,000 to $5,000; of the Firemen from $500 to $1,500; of the Trainmen from $400 to $500, and of the Telegraphers from $300 to $1,000. These organizations charge a uniform rate of assessment, irrespective of the age of the members, although they permit the younger men to insure more heavily than the older. The only trade union which establishes different rates of assessment for men of different ages is the National Association of Letter Carriers.

The majority of American trade unions pay but a small death or funeral benefit. The Glass Bottle Blowers and the Cigar Makers pay $500 as a maximum, the Lithographers from $50 to $500, while a number of unions pay $200 or less, and some pay only from $50 to $100. A number of unions also pay small amounts on the death of a member's wife.

About a dozen national organizations pay sick insurance and these benefits are also given by a considerable number of local unions whose national organizations have no insurance features. The sick benefit usually amounts to $4.00 or $5.00 per week, and the length of time during which a member may receive it is limited. Great care is also taken that the demand upon the union may not be fraudulent, a physician's certificate being required before an applicant can secure his benefit, and local committees being appointed to visit the sick in order to prevent deception.

The American trade union which has developed the most extended insurance features is the Cigar Makers' International Union. From 1879 to 1900 it expended $838,000 for strike benefits; $1,453,000 for sick benefits; $794,000 for death benefits; $917,000 for out-of-work benefits, and $735,000 for loans to members while traveling (90 per cent. of these loans having been repaid); the total benefits given and loaned amounting to $4,737,000.

Trade unions in the United States are largely extending the scope of their insurance and will, in the course of time, become much stronger by this means. Several of the unions have already adopted the superannuation benefit for men incapacitated by old age and long service, although the system has not yet had time to develop. However, in the future trade unions will continue to widen the scope of their activity in this direction, protecting the workingmen from the effects of sickness, accident, loss of activity, incapacitation, and old age, and will also provide in case of death, for the payment of funeral benefits. This policy will lead to an increased popularity of trade unions and will result in a growth in membership, although, as is absolutely necessary, the dues of the organizations will be raised in consequence. Founders of such insurance, if wise, will avoid the error of promising inordinately large benefits in return for small assessments. With the avoidance of this error and with the increase and extension of the insurance features, the strength of the union, its conservatism and its capacity for maintaining fair conditions of work will immeasurably increase. But trade unions which now have benefit features and those which may, in the future, adopt them, should exercise great care in keeping the insurance features incidental to the trade policy and to the primary objects of the unions, which are and must always be to raise wages, lessen hours, and improve the general conditions of employment.

CHAPTER XIV

THE AMERICAN STANDARD OF WAGES

Trade Unions have Maintained and Elevated the American Standard of Living. Increased Wages, especially in Organized Trades. Unionism Necessary for Higher Wages. The American Standard of Living. 1803 and 1903. Food, Clothing, Shelter, Instruction, and Amusements of the American Workingman. $600 a year for the Unskilled. Will it Pay? The Economy of High Wages. Increases not Taken from Capital. High Wages, National Prosperity, and the Welfare of the Middle Class. The Upward Tendency of Wages.

ONE of the greatest benefits conferred upon wage earners by trade unionism has been the elevation and maintenance of the standard of living. In the United States, as in England, organizations of labor have constantly rallied about this standard and numberless strikes have occurred in its defense. The history of American trade unions in the nineteenth century has been the story of a gradual increase in the wages of American workingmen.

Trade unions have swelled the pay envelope of the workman, both by enforcing increases and by preventing reductions in his remuneration. During the last twenty years, thousands of strikes have resulted in the granting of higher wages, and these victories have been supplemented by the concession of semi-monthly and weekly payments in cash and by the abolition of truck stores and credit payment. Scores of other strikes, or threatened strikes, have prevented reductions in wages, and many advantages have been gained through conference and negotiation. These advances, it must be admitted, have not been due wholly to trade unionism. The greater skill and effectiveness of workmen, the invention of machinery, the improvement and increased productiveness of manufacturing have all contributed to this result. But without the active intervention of trade unions, the increase in wages which has marked the progress of American industry in the nineteenth century, would not have taken place.

It is not possible in the course of this chapter to give even the barest outline of the manner in which, and the extent to which, trade unions have increased wages. This tendency is so apparent that it hardly requires extended proof. No one can pick up a newspaper without reading accounts of increases of wages obtained in the organized trades. In many cases workingmen, who had hitherto been unorganized and had no opportunity to compel increases, found their wages suddenly raised as soon as they had perfected an organization in their defense. In the various building trades, in transportation, in mining, in the several sections of our highly developed manufacturing industries, wages have been largely raised through the activity of trade unions. Many of these increases have come without strikes, and some have been granted even in advance of a specific demand upon the part of the trade unions. The increases in wages obtained in one industry, through the efforts of trade unions, have rendered it less difficult for other organizations to obtain like concessions.

"An overwhelming preponderance of testimony before the Industrial Commission," says that body in its report dated 1902, "indicates that the organization of labor has resulted in a marked improvement of the economic condition of the workers." Many specific instances were cited by witnesses before the Commission. These advances in wages obtained by trade unions are, of course, acknowledged by employers as by all well-informed and reasonable people in the United States. There are, however, some theorists who claim that this increase in wages is merely apparent and of no real benefit to the workman, since if all wages rise, all prices must rise in proportion, and the workingman who receives an advance in his wages must pay it all out because of the consequent increased cost of the necessities of life. It is thus urged that a general increase in wages is nothing but a wearisome march around a circle, ceaseless and leading to nowhere. There are several reasons, however, why this objection is not valid. In the first place, wages do not always increase the cost of production, since the workingman becomes more efficient when he is better paid, better fed, better clothed, and better housed. In many industries prices have nothing at all to do with wages, but are arbitrarily fixed at a monopoly figure and remain the same whether wages are high or low. Moreover, when wages actually raise prices, the resulting increase is never in proportion to the rise in wages, since the cost of many of the materials, the ground rent, the interest on capital, taxes, the cost of supervision, and the profits of employers are not necessarily affected by an increase in wages. Finally, workingmen do not consume all, or even nearly all, of the articles which they produce; and an increase in the wages of diamond cutters, of makers of grand pianos, of weavers of fine carpets, as well as of men engaged in performing personal services for the rich, does not in any way affect the purchasing power of the money in the ordinary workingman's envelope. If this argument were true, and an increase in wages all around did not benefit the workman, then a decrease would not injure him, and the workingman would be as well off if he did not receive wages or remuneration at all.

It is claimed by some that labor organizations do not raise or even maintain wages, but that the rate of remuneration is fixed entirely by the law of supply and demand. This law, however, does not work automatically. Without trade unionism, the workingman does not derive full advantage from an increased demand for labor, and he suffers a disproportionate injury with each lessening in the demand for, or each increase in the supply of, labor. Those who assert that trade unions have no influence upon wages, appear to assume that in point of intelligence, knowledge of the market, and power of resistance, the workingman and the employer are upon an equality. But this is not the case. The employer knows the state of the market both for his goods and for the labor which he wishes to purchase, and he, or at least his foreman, has probably made a practical study of the art of bargaining for labor, whereas the unorganized workman, unaccustomed to haggling or bargaining, is consequently at a disadvantage. The result is that the competition of unorganized workmen for a job tends to reduce wages to the lowest point. Even if the employer is not disposed to take advantage of his workman, he is frequently impelled to do so by the force of competition. Back of him stand the jobber, the wholesaler, the retailer, and, finally, the great, careless, bargain-hunting, indiscriminate body of consumers, who are constantly pressing upon him and forcing him to cut his cost price, and, consequently, the wages of his labor. There is competition and cutting of profits all along the line, until the point is reached where the burden finally settles its crushing weight upon the shoulders of the individual workman or workwoman.

Formerly it was believed that the tendency to lower wages would work its own remedy automatically, since if wages fell below a certain point, the workmen would stop marrying and the birth rate would decrease, with the result that eventually the number of workmen would diminish and wages would again rise. We now know this theory to be false, as conditions in the low paid industries have demonstrated that, up to a certain point, the number of children actually increases with growing poverty. The doctrine that wages will be maintained in one generation by the fact of a smaller number of workers in the next, is about as convincing as the theory that it does not pain a lobster to be boiled alive, since he has become used to this process in the course of many generations.

As before stated, the history of the past century has been the story of a gradual increase in the wages of the working classes. When, in 1800, Thomas Jefferson was elected president, the workingmen of the North were in a condition but little superior to that of colonial days, a condition in which they worked long hours, at hard toil, for small pay. From this state of affairs the invention of machinery and the improvement of production on a large scale, as regulated by law and trade union action, have gradually emancipated the workingman, and wages have risen, while the prices of many articles of consumption have declined.

This progress, however, to which the trade unions have largely and nobly contributed, is not yet complete. Until within the last generation, the problem confronting the United States as an industrial nation, was how to increase the public wealth; now, the question is how to distribute the vast riches which have accumulated, very largely as a result of the efforts put forth by workingmen. In this evolution, society has reached a stage where, in return for his day's toil, it is possible to give the workingman a wage upon which he may live with reasonable comfort and decency, and with which he may obtain the necessaries and some of the pleasures of life, which, in the past, society was too poor to provide for him. The enormous increase in the productivity of labor, due to the invention of machines and to the increased intelligence of the workers, has now made possible a condition which will permit the wage earner to enjoy a small, but fairly comfortable home, and to secure a reasonable amount of nourishing food. The realization of this possibility is contingent only upon the formation of strong, compact trade unions and upon the demonstration to the American people of the fact that the necessary wages can be paid without threatening the industrial supremacy of the nation.

Much that has been said about the American standard of living has been vague, but to a large extent this vagueness is inevitable. It is easy to state what sum of money a given man should earn, but it is hard to define just exactly what necessaries, comforts, and small luxuries a whole working population should receive. And yet, notwithstanding all the vagueness, there remain in the mind of the workingman certain more or less definite things which make up to him what he calls the American standard of living, and a certain sum which, he feels or believes is a living wage. It is not reasonable to compare the American standard of living with the British, the German, the Russian, or the Chinese standards. The American demands and receives better wages and better conditions of life than either the Englishman or the German, and there is no comparison possible between his standard and that of the Russian or of the Chinaman. The American public has always sympathized, and will continue to sympathize, with the demand of the American workman that he maintain his superiority over the conditions of life which prevail in other countries. The American people, with that far-sighted, practical idealism characteristic of them, have come to realize that it pays to maintain workmen at a high standard of excellence, just as they realize that universal free education pays; but even apart from this, and whether or not it pays, the American people are committed to the policy of the American standard of living and will vigorously defend it, if the workingmen, through their trade unions, will but insist upon its maintenance.

The American standard of living of the year 1903 is a different, a better, and a higher standard than the American standard of living of the year 1803. The American workman of the present day is a better workman, more intelligent, more industrious, and more efficient than his forefather of a hundred years ago. Moreover, the productivity of the American workman of the present day is, by reason of better organization and the use of machinery, enormously in excess of the productivity of the workman of a century ago. The man who formerly turned out twenty articles a day now turns out a hundred or five hundred; and in every department of activity men have become increasingly able to perform more work and to obtain greater output.

While the standard of living has risen, it has not, by any means, kept pace with the increased productivity of labor. The larger product which society now obtains from industry is more than sufficient to enable the workingman of the present time to maintain a higher standard of living. To attain this standard, he must become organized and must maintain his organization through good and bad seasons. Of course, for different classes of workingmen, trade unionism recognizes different standards. For the skilled workman it stands for wages commensurate with his skill and knowledge, whether these wages be three, four, five, or ten dollars a day. There are even now men who are receiving five or six dollars a day, who are not obtaining nearly all to which they are fairly entitled. No union seeks to regulate wages for any but its own trade; and because a definite minimum is set for unskilled labor, it does not follow that much higher wages should not be paid to men engaged at more difficult work, or work requiring a higher degree of skill and intelligence.

In the following pages I shall attempt to define what I consider the American standard of living for unskilled workingmen and the minimum wage upon which this standard can be maintained. I do not mean that some unskilled workingmen, employed in extra hazardous occupations, should not receive much more than the ordinary unskilled worker; and the sum suggested would be totally inadequate for workmen in trades requiring years of training or a high degree of skill. It would also be inadequate for workmen living in very large cities. Further, I believe that what should now be considered as the American standard and as a minimum wage, will, in the course of ten or twenty years, cease to be so considered, since it is reasonable to anticipate that the earnings of workingmen and their requirements for comfort, will, with the progress of the age, increase in the future as they have in the past.

In cities of from five thousand to one hundred thousand inhabitants, the American standard of living should mean, to the ordinary unskilled workman with an average family, a comfortable house of at least six rooms. It should mean a bathroom, good sanitary plumbing, a parlor, dining-room, kitchen, and sufficient sleeping room that decency may be preserved and a reasonable degree of comfort maintained. The American standard of living should mean, to the unskilled workman, carpets, pictures, books, and furniture with which to make home bright, comfortable, and attractive for himself and his family, an ample supply of clothing suitable for winter and summer, and above all a sufficient quantity of good, wholesome, nourishing food at all times of the year. The American standard of living, moreover, should mean to the unskilled workman, that his children be kept in school until they have attained the age of sixteen at least, and that he be enabled to lay by sufficient to maintain himself and his family in times of illness, or at the close of his industrial life, when age and weakness render further work impossible, and to make provision for his family against his premature death from accident or otherwise.

This, or something like this, is the American standard of living, as it exists in the ideals of the unskilled workingmen. There are, of course, differences in the way in which men regard their wants, and no matter how closely the majority attain to this standard, there will always be a small minority, who will waste their money through intemperance or other indulgences, or whose children are so many that a reasonable standard cannot be maintained upon any attainable wage. For the great majority of men, however, who are willing to work and are not incapacitated by physical, mental, or moral defects, the manner of living above described is an approximate statement of what their standard should be; and with the great productivity of American labor, I believe it not unreasonable to say that these things should now be possessed by every workingman, however unskilled.

Life under these conditions would mean the removal of much of the temptation to drunkenness which arises from the absence of a comfortable dwelling place. It would mean the decency and morality which come from the proper separation of the sexes in the homes of the poor, and the cleanliness and health which arise from having proper bathrooms, proper drains, and suitable conditions in and about the house. These comforts and conveniences, which are already possessed by many artisans in the skilled trades, should be within the reach of any workingman in the country who is willing and able to perform some useful service to society. In this way the American standard should mean for the great mass of unskilled workmen life under conditions which would permit them to enjoy some of the comforts and pleasures of life and to avail themselves of some of the opportunities for intellectual development.

The American, as a practical business man, always asks what a desired innovation will cost, and until he hears the price, reserves his opinion as to whether a thing is Utopian or a practicable idea. What wages, therefore, are necessary to maintain this American standard? This question was put to me by the attorneys for the coal companies during the sessions of the Anthracite Coal Strike Commission, and at that time I stated that the very least upon which an unskilled workman could maintain a desirable standard of living, was $600 a year. Since that time I have had no occasion to change this estimate. It is, of course, true that this estimate applies more exactly to workmen in towns of from five thousand to one hundred thousand inhabitants, than it does to other places. In speaking of $600 for unskilled workmen, I do not mean to include farm hands or men in rural communities, where the cost of living is less and the standard of living not so high. On the other hand, in cities of over one hundred thousand, and especially in cities of over half a million, $600 would, in my opinion, be insufficient to maintain this standard for unskilled workingmen. This is more particularly true of the city of New York, where the cost of maintaining a fair standard of living would be much greater, owing to excessive rents, and where the ideal of a separate small house for the workman must itself be given up. For the great mass of unskilled workingmen, however, residing in towns and cities with a population of from five thousand to one hundred thousand, the fair wage, a wage consistent with American standards of living, should not be less than $600 a year. Less than this would, in my judgment, be insufficient to give to the workingman those necessaries and comforts and those small luxuries which are now considered essential.

At the present time the organized skilled workman is securing a larger, although by no means a sufficient, share of the reasonable satisfactions of life. Through the cheaper building of houses and through the extension of electric railways, which permits a lowering of ground rents, the workingman is now able to secure a comfortable house built according to modern requirements and with modern appliances, more cheaply than was possible a dozen years ago. The department stores, with their free delivery system, have tended to bring down the prices of many articles of furniture and household service; and the transportation facilities of the country, the railroads, wharves, docks, and markets, have brought within reach of the workman many things formerly withheld from him. However, the man with an income of less than $600 a year can profit but little from these improvements; and owing to his meagre pay, the unskilled workman has been deprived of the ability to take advantage of them. When he receives a wage of $600 a year—and at this time the unskilled workman should receive this wage—opportunity for better living will come within his reach. The effect of this will be of great benefit to society at large, as well as to the unskilled workman himself. Not only is the workingman who has a comfortable home with proper sanitary appliances a better and more efficient workman than he who sleeps in a dirty lodging house or is crowded into a tenement, but society gains in other ways. Once the workingman obtains this income and learns how to use it, the drink bill of the community will be diminished, the expenditure for apprehending, trying, and imprisoning criminals will be reduced, and many other evils of society will be lessened. The most important result, however, of such an increase in wages upon the part of the unskilled workman would be an enormous incentive to industry, a vast increase in the demand for goods, and a more rapid march of the United States towards industrial supremacy.

The American trade unionists, therefore, should keep constantly in mind, and should, within the coming years, attempt to realize the ideal of a $600 minimum wage for unskilled workmen, whether of native or of foreign birth. The increase will pay for itself. A $600 man, working even as a common laborer, will be a better workman and a better citizen than the $450 man now doing this class of work, just as the latter is better than the Mexican peon working at twenty-five cents a day, or the Chinese coolie toiling for five or ten cents a day. The employer and the community in general will be better off when the conditions of labor are improved and the wages of the workingmen are increased.

High wages mean more than industrial efficiency, more than the gratification of the reasonable desires of the working population. They contribute to the wealth and future of the nation, which are not to be measured by its palaces and millionaires, but rather by the enlightened contentment and prosperity of its millions of workers, who constitute the bone and sinew of the land.

CHAPTER XV

THE DAY'S WORK

Trade Unions Lessen the Hours of Labor. Work from Sun to Sun. Work of Government Employees. The Building Trades. The Working Day in Factories. The Struggle for the Eight-hour Day. Victories of the Cigar Makers and the Bituminous miners. Short Hours in Australia, the United States, England, and the European Continent. The Day's Work in the Sweated Trades. Advantage to the Capitalists and the Public. The Economy of Short Hours. The Experience of the Soft Coal Fields. Better Work and Better Men. Are Short-hour Laws Constitutional? "Decreasing the Hours Increases the Pay." Difference between Manual and Mental Workers.

THE success of organized labor in increasing the wages of workmen has been brilliant and signal, but has not been more important than its success in reducing the hours of labor. An increase in the rate of wages means more of the comforts and luxuries of life; a decrease in hours, the opportunity to enjoy these comforts and luxuries. The shortening of the working day, further, stands for freedom from toil at the time when it becomes most exacting, nerve wearing, and dangerous; still further, it stands for leisure, recreation, education, and family life.

Reductions in the hours of work have been the more significant because such decreases, once gained, have been well defended and rarely surrendered. An increase in wages may perhaps be nullified in part by increased prices, a thing which cannot well occur in the case of a decrease in hours. Again, there is always a strong temptation for employers to seek to reduce wages as soon as bad times come, whereas at such times there is not so strong as the same incentive to increase hours, because there is less demand for labor.

During the nineteenth century American trade unions diminished the length of the working day from twelve, and in some cases fourteen, to ten, nine, and eight hours. At the beginning of the century man worked from sun

MINER DESCENDING SHAFT BY ELEVATOR OR "CAGE"
To work hundreds of feet below ground. Notice lamp and drills

Miners Going to Work in an Empty Mine Car

to sun, but in one industry after another the trade unions secured a radical reduction in the hours of labor. In this movement the Federal and State Governments aided. In 1840 President Van Buren instituted in the government navy yards a maximum ten-hour day, which was also accepted by other ship builders, and in 1867 the hours of labor were further reduced from ten to eight.

In the reduction of hours by means of trade unions the building trades have led all other organizations, owing to the fact that the unions in these trades were among the first to organize and to grow strong, and to the further fact that they were federated and acted in concert. Moreover, there was little competition between men employed in the building trades of one city as against those employed in the building trades of another city; that is to say, the building trade employees of New York or Philadelphia did not compete with those of Baltimore or Charleston, and, therefore, no tendency could exist for the worst paid workmen in the country to set a standard for the best paid. At the beginning of the century the men in the building trades worked as long as daylight lasted, but shortly after the second war with Great Britain, the ship carpenters attempted to secure a reduction of work to ten hours, and by means of strikes, succeeded in the year 1825. During the next quarter of a century one victory after another was achieved by the various building trade organizations, so that at the close of the Mexican War, the general working time in the industry was ten hours a day. From that time on, especially after the close of the Civil War, a demand arose for a still further reduction of the working day from ten to eight hours. The cities had grown apace, and the distance from a man's home to his work had become so great that the trip amounted to a considerable deduction from his real leisure. The struggle for a maximum eight-hour day was accordingly taken up by the men in the building trades. Spurred on by the successes already achieved and encouraged by the gradual reduction of the hours of labor in England and Australia, the American building operatives, by means of a series of strikes, by negotiation, conciliation, and in other ways, reduced the hours of labor to eight per day and in a number of trades to forty-four per week.

The same development has taken place, although to a somewhat less extent, in the factories. At the beginning of the century the factories frequently worked their hands twelve and fourteen hours, and for a long time they maintained an average of about eleven hours per day. The trade unions had attempted to secure a reduction of these hours by means of legislation and otherwise, but it was not until 1874 that the first law, by which the hours of labor were reduced to ten, was enacted. This law, passed in Massachusetts, was directed against the excessive labor of women and children, but in actual practice applied to workers of all ages and both sexes. During the next fifteen years one state after another, following the example of Massachusetts, adopted a working day of ten hours or less. In New Jersey the legal working time for women in factories is fifty-five hours per week, and in Massachusetts a reduction has now been made from sixty to fifty-eight hours. The Southern States, however, which have made rapid progress, especially in cotton manufacturing, have, as a general rule, not responded to the demand for a shorter working day—the South lacking effective labor organizations to compel such legislation.

Since the Civil War the task of securing shorter hours has devolved to an increasing extent upon trade unionists. After the close of the War, eight-hour leagues were established in various parts of the country, and hours were reduced in many places, but the activities of these leagues were interrupted by the crisis of 1873 and the bad times following, and it was not until the early years of the eighties that the work was again undertaken, in this instance by the Knights of Labor, and it is now being vigorously prosecuted by the unions affiliated with the American Federation of Labor. The benefits of the eight-hour day are being extended to many classes of workmen hitherto deprived of them. The Cigar Makers succeeded in obtaining the eight-hour day in 1885, the great majority of the bituminous miners in 1898 and 1899, and in 1903 the Anthracite miners obtained a nine-hour day. The New York State Department of Labor found that of 647,000 persons employed in factories inspected by it in 1901, 38%, and in New York City 54%, were working 9½ hours a day or less. Among the organized laborers, the working hours were considerably less than this, almost one-half of the organized workmen and workwomen of the State of New York enjoying a maximum eight-hour day.[1]

The same struggle for a shortening of the working day is going on in England and Australia, in France, Germany, Belgium, and even in such backward countries as Italy, Spain, and Hungary. Generally speaking, the Englishman has secured shorter hours than the American, and the Australian shorter hours than the Englishman. The average length of the American working day may be fixed at about ten hours. In deciding upon this number it must be taken into consideration that, while the vast body of organized laborers work a shorter time and while hundreds of thousands in the building trades work only eight hours or less, there are, again hundreds of thousands employed on steam railroads, on the docks, on street railways, and elsewhere, whose working day is in excess of ten hours.

Owing to the fact that the work of the modern world is becoming more and more a matter of nervous energy, of skill, and intelligence, and less a matter of mere brute force, the reduction of hours is not only of advantage, but of absolute necessity. Even when work is simply and purely physical, it is not economical to work long hours, but a shorter day of labor is imperative when work is intense or when intelligence, ingenuity, and inventiveness are required. You cannot get more out of a man than is in him, and if you take too much one day, there will be so much less to obtain on succeeding days. As stated by Professor Clark of Columbia University: "If you want a man to work for you one day and one day only, and secure the greatest possible amount of work he is capable of performing you must make him work for twenty-four hours. If you would have him work a week

---

[1] The efforts of trade unions have also been directed towards maintaining Sundays and the usual holidays as days of rest.

it will be necessary to reduce the time to twenty hours a day; if you want him to work for a month a still further reduction to eighteen hours a day. For the year, fifteen hours a day will do; for several years, ten hours; but if you wish to get the most out of a man for a working lifetime, you will have to reduce his hours of labor to eight each day."

The most curious feature about the history of the reduction of hours is that in almost all cases the trade unions have been obliged to force employers, strongly against their will, to grant reductions which have ultimately proved to their advantage. The English mill owners in the beginning and middle of the nineteenth century claimed that they would be ruined if hours were reduced; and the same complaint was made by the New England manufacturers in the seventies and is being now repeated by the Southern mill owners. Wherever the reduction has been made, however, the result has been a decided benefit not only to the workman but to his employer. In a succeeding chapter I shall endeavor to show how short hours, like other demands of trade unions, have benefited employers, and how an absolute increase in the amount of work performed during a day has frequently resulted from a shortening of the working day.

In so far as lessened hours mean increased production and cheapened cost, there can be no question as to the advisability of shortening the working day, and in such cases employers should be compelled to seek their own permanent interest by adjusting themselves to reasonable conditions. Even where the advantage to the employer is not so apparent, an excessive number of working hours should not be tolerated. A reduction in hours means a strengthening of the workman, the growth of a keener intelligence, and an improvement in his home life. The workingman's self-appointed protectors among the employing classes have from the beginning alleged that a reduction in hours means more time spent in drinking and dissipation, since the employee will not know what to do with his newly acquired leisure. This assertion, reiterated incessantly, has been completely contradicted by everyday experience and by the history of the working classes. When the workingman comes from mill or mine, having taxed to the utmost his muscular and nervous energy, depressed by an excessive expenditure of vital force, it is small wonder if he seek a stimulus in alcohol or in other crude pleasures. A man who has labored for ten or twelve hours at exhausting toil is in no fit condition to enjoy books, pictures, music, or the sane pleasures of a well-regulated family life. The unanimous testimony of all competent observers, teachers, ministers, and sociologists, has been to the effect that a reduction in the hours of labor almost invariably means an improvement in the whole moral tone of the community, a raising of the standard of living, a growth of the self-respect of the workingman, and a diminution, not an increase, in drunkenness, violence, and crime. If the American workman can be entrusted with the suffrage, it is certainly safe to entrust him with a few hours of leisure. The laborer is worthy not only of his hire, but also of the right to live.

An attempt is frequently made to ridicule the demands of trade unionists for a reduction of hours by exaggerating these demands. When an employer is asked to reduce the hours of his workmen to eight, he frequently asks, "Why not to six, or four, or two, or one?" The workingman might with equal justice retort, "If you demand that we work ten hours a day, then why not fifteen, or twenty, or twenty-four?" Trade unionists do not demand or desire an unreasonable reduction of the hours of labor, and they are willing that each demand for such reduction be considered on its own merits and be granted or withheld accordingly.

The attorneys who cross-examined me before the Anthracite Coal Strike Commission asserted that they themselves worked fourteen to fifteen hours a day, and they believed that I also was in the habit of working for an equal number of hours. They said they did not believe that the trade union has any moral right to decree that a free American citizen, whether he be carpenter, miner, or conductor, should not work more than a given number of hours. It is true that the lawyer, doctor, or minister does frequently work excessive hours and that he has no desire for their limitation by law or by concerted action. There is a difference, however, in the conditions under which the work of professional men and that of the manual wage earners is performed. As a rule, the lawyer receives increased remuneration for increased hours of work, and this is true also of the independent farmer. The manual wage earner, on the other hand, receives, in the long run, not more but actually less pay for more work. The rhyme of trade unionists, "Whether you work by the piece or work by the day, decreasing the hours increases the pay," while seemingly paradoxical, is, in the majority of cases, absolutely and literally true. An individual wage earner may gain a temporary advantage over his fellow-craftsmen by making an exception and working a few hours extra, but as soon as all men have increased their hours to the same limit, it will usually be found that wages for the day are not higher and wages for the hour are, of course, actually lower. Statistics show that the occupations where short hours prevail are, upon the whole, those in which wages are highest and localities in which hours are longest are those in which wages are lowest.

Still another difference exists between the labor of the employer who claims that "I work more hours in a day than any man in my employ," and the labor of his employees. The employer, as frequently the professional man, works when he will, how he will, where he will, and usually at what he will, while, as a general rule, and with exceptions, the manual workman labors, when, where, how, and at what he *must*. The difference between working at what interests you and brings you profit and at tasks given to you by others is as great as the difference between recreation and toil.

The successful attempts of trade unions to reduce hours of labor have encountered violent opposition. It is held by many otherwise well-informed men that it is immoral and un-American to restrict the number of hours of workingmen. The ordinary critic says, "It is all right for the unionist to refuse to work over eight hours, but he should not refuse to permit an unusually industrious man to work ten or twelve hours." Unless the union establishes a maximum, however, the employer will establish a minimum. If some men are willing to work for eight and some for twelve hours a day, it will soon be found that the men who refuse to work for more than eight hours will find it difficult or impossible to secure work, and the final result will be that all men will work as long hours as the most subservient and cringing of them, and will not receive more wages for the long than for the short working day. There is no alternative in this matter between the establishment, either by the union alone or by the union and employer combined, of a maximum number of hours and the establishment by the employer alone of a minimum number of hours. Unless all workingmen are to be chained to their work as long as it pays or seems to pay the employer to keep them there, then they must fix among themselves or with the employer the maximum number of hours that any man will be allowed to work.

To maintain the limit fixed by wage earners to the number of hours which they will work, it is absolutely essential to regulate the question of overtime. The ideal of an agreement upon the working day should be to limit its length to a reasonable number of hours, while at the same time permitting the employer in cases of emergency to keep his men at work for a longer period. It has been shown in practice, however, that where overtime is paid for at the same rate as ordinary time, so-called emergencies multiply, overtime is resorted to systematically, and the normal working day is broken down. The men who have thus secured an eight-hour day find that they are regularly working eight hours per day plus, say, two hours overtime, and after a few years, they may receive for their ten hours no more, if not actually less, than formerly for their eight hours of work. To remedy this evil and to avert this peril, trade unionists have in many cases been obliged to charge for overtime at a considerably higher rate, such as time and a quarter, time and a half, or double time. This is fair to the wage earner, since the last hour of work is harder for him than any other, whereas to the employer, who pays most for this last hour, it is the least valuable, since the workman is tired. Theoretically therefore, the employer will work overtime only in especially good seasons or in emergencies. In actual practice, however, overtime, even when paid for at a higher rate, tends often to become systematic and to lengthen the working day without permanently increasing wages. Consequently, unions have frequently been compelled to prohibit overtime entirely, to limit the maximum amount of overtime per week or month, or to make other provision that overtime, while serving the employer's purpose, may not be used to break down the standard working day.

Occasionally, the arbitrary fixing of the length of the working day causes inconvenience to the public. A man who wants to get shaved at eight o'clock in the evening or on Sunday finds that the union rules forbid it, and a householder who wants repairs made in his home and would like the workmen to stay "just fifteen or thirty minutes longer" and "be paid for it," finds it extremely annoying that they refuse to do so. In these matters, however, the public is frequently unreasonable, or, at all, events, unknowing. The breaking down of a working day is always gradual and insidious. The men begin by conceding ten minutes here and ten minutes there, until the eight-hour day becomes nine and eventually ten hours in length. But while the workingman should struggle always to maintain his standard working day, there is a point beyond which it is not fair, wise, or reasonable to go. The workman should try to finish the job and have the place cleaned up by the close of the hour, and the ending of the working day should not be made the excuse for being discourteous, disobliging, or arbitrary. A lady told me that once she was obliged to walk down from the top floor of a high building, because the elevator man refused to extend his working day by a few minutes. Acts like these, though fortunately rare, result in the exasperation of the public and in the weakening of its sympathy for the reduction of the working time.

Upon the whole, unions have been more successful in reducing the hours of labor by means of strikes or trade agreements than by means of the law. Where these reductions have been made by agreement, it has re-

STRIP BANK WORKING

Preparing a blast which will be fired by electric battery

MINE CAVE-IN

Fire boss testing, with safety lamp, the amount of gas accumulated

quired months, or even years, of patient and protracted effort. In a number of cases the organized workmen have agreed to accept a gradual reduction in the hours of labor, the working day being lessened by fifteen minutes or one-half hour each year, thus enabling the employer to adjust his business to the new conditions. Reduction of hours by means of legislation has advantages, since, if the law is enforced, it applies equally to all the employers in the state, although competition between the various states renders this advantage less, on the whole, since the industry usually extends over state lines and the laws of the various states differ.

The great disadvantage of legislation limiting hours, however, apart from the difficulty of obtaining it, has been the danger of its being declared unconstitutional. Laws limiting the hours of labor of children have usually been held valid, owing to the fact that minors are not in possession of full legal rights, and, according to the law, are not capable of making binding contracts. Until recently there was no question raised as to the complete constitutionality of laws limiting the hours of labor of women, and where a reduction in hours was obtained for the female workers, it became practically operative to the advantage of the men working with the women in the same factories. The Supreme Court of the State of Illinois has held that, as a woman is a citizen and a person, she comes under the constitutional provision that "no person shall be deprived of life, liberty, or property without due process of law," and a limitation of her hours of labor is held to be a deprivation of her liberty, discrimination against her as compared with men, and, therefore, unconstitutional. This is the only instance on record in which a court has rendered a decision of this character.

By reason, however, of the decision of the United States Supreme Court in the case of Holden vs. Hardy, the question of the right of the state under its police power to limit the hours of labor of all the workers, men, women, and children, in a special industry, is definitely settled to the advantage of the workman. Laws have been passed in various states regulating the hours of labor of railroad and street railway employees, of bakers, barbers, and other persons, and these laws have been upheld on the ground of the police power of the state. The Supreme Court, in its decision, takes the high position that the state is interested in the individual health, safety, and welfare of the workmen and can protect them by means of the police power, even in apparent violation of the freedom of contract. The decision of the Court is a strong endorsement of the position maintained for many years by trade unionists, and I have therefore quoted a portion of it, italicizing certain words: "The legislature has also recognized the fact, which the experience of legislatures in many States has corroborated, that the proprietors of these establishments and their operatives *do not stand upon an equality,* and that their interests are, to a certain extent, conflicting. The former naturally desire to obtain as much labor as possible from their employees, while the latter are often induced, by the fear of discharge, to conform to regulations which their judgment, fairly exercised, would pronounce to be detrimental to their health or strength. In other words the proprietors lay down the rules and the laborers are practically constrained to obey them. In such cases *self-interest is often an unsafe guide,* and the legislature may properly impose its authority. It may not be improper to suggest in this connection that although the prosecution in this case was against the employer of labor, who apparently, under the statute, is the only one liable, his defense is not that his right to contract has been infringed upon, but that the act works a peculiar hardship to his employees, whose right to labor as long as they please is alleged to be thereby violated. The argument would certainly come with better grace and cogency from the latter class. But the fact that both parties are of full age and competent to contract does not necessarily deprive the state of the power to interfere where the parties do not stand upon an equality, or where the public health demands that one party to the contract shall be protected against himself. The state still retains an interest in his welfare, however reckless he may be. The whole is no greater than the sum of all the parts, and *when the individual health, safety, and welfare are sacrificed or neglected the State must suffer.*"

CHAPTER XVI

THE WORK OF WOMEN AND CHILDREN

Women in Industry. From Home to Factory. The Protection of Women by Trade Unions. The Wages of Women. Life on Five Dollars a Week. Number of Women Unionists Small, but Increasing. The Teachers and the Trade Union Movement. Equal Pay for Equal Work. The Exploitation of Children. Its Wastefulness. Its Immorality. Child Labor and Vagrancy. The Unions Struggle against Unrestricted Child Labor. Wages of Children Deducted from the Wages of their Parents. In School until Sixteen.

IF trade unionism had rendered no other service to humanity, it would have justified its existence by its efforts in behalf of working women and children. Unfortunately, society does not seem to feel itself capable of conducting its industries without the aid of its weaker members. With each advance in production, with each increase in wealth and the capacity of producing wealth, women and children, in ever larger numbers, are drafted into service. In this development, the woman, like the child, has been torn from her home and has been put into factories, subject to the dictation of an employer or task-master. The integrity of the home, in which the woman formerly played her part and performed her quota of work, has been shattered by the invasion of the machine and the factory system. Through the cheapened production which has resulted from the organization of industry on a large scale, woman has become incapable of performing at home the work to which she was once accustomed, and has been compelled to seek her means of subsistence in competition with men. To a certain extent woman is now simply doing by machine in the factory what she formerly did by hand at home, but the conditions of her work and life are different. Carding, spinning, and weaving have long since ceased to be profitable as home occupations, and laundry work, dairy work, the canning of fruit, and the like, are rapidly passing from the household and being elevated into special industries.

While it is probable that in the household of former days the circumstances under which the work of women and children was carried on were by no means idyllic, the movement from home to factory was accompanied by an aggravation and intensifying of these evils. This development has been caused not by the greed or ill-will of men, but by conditions which could not have been avoided and by a force which was irresistible. It is, however, useless to deplore the past, or seek to reconstruct conditions of a by-gone age.

It is to the credit of trade unionism that it has to some extent alleviated the conditions of women in factories. Not only in England, but in the United States, not only in the past, but in the present, have women been doomed to suffer, and by reason of their very weakness have been forced to engage in arduous toil for excessively long hours. The rate of remuneration for women has always been low. In almost all countries they have received from one-third to one-half less than men, by reason, it is said, of their lesser strength, their greater liability to sickness, the reduced scope of their employment, and the fact that to a certain extent, husbands, fathers, or brothers contribute to their support. As a result of these disabilities, women have suffered in more ways than in submitting to lowered wages. Their weakness has been an excuse, not for reduced but for extended hours of work, and the wages of women solely dependent upon themselves are no better or higher than those of women receiving support from relatives.

The chief effort of trade unions in ameliorating the hardship of women's work has been in the direction of excluding them from certain kinds of employment, in improving the sanitary conditions of their work, and in reducing the length of their working day. At one time, women were employed in mines, but through the efforts of trade unions this inhumanity was done away with. Women workers have also been excluded from some trades which impair their health or injuriously affect their morals.

Even at the present time, the wages of women are woefully deficient, although they have been increased to some extent through the efforts of trade unions. As the result of an investigation to ascertain the wages of skilled and unskilled women workers, made in 1888 by the United States Department of Labor, it was found that in twenty-two cities of the United States, wages of women varied from a minimum of $4.05 a week in Atlanta to a maximum of $6.91 in San Francisco, the average wages appearing to be less than $5.50 a week. Of course, in some instances these were supplemental wages, that is, wages in addition to those earned by relatives, but, in most cases, they were the sole support of the women, often even of women with dependent children. Anyone acquainted with the cost of living in large cities will be aware that these wages were entirely insufficient to meet the cost of the barest necessaries of life. That hundreds of thousands of girls and women should work in factories for ten hours a day, possibly in a vitiated atmosphere and at depressing labor, and earn but five or six dollars a week, seems hardly credible in a prosperous and civilized community. With her five dollars such a girl could not live even a plain, monotonous life under conditions that would maintain her efficiency as a worker and as a citizen. Five dollars a week means less than a proper amount of nourishing food, less than a room to herself, less than sufficient clothing to protect her from the wet and cold, or a proper change of clothing when it is warm. Five dollars a week means that she must perhaps share with other girls a small, bare, ill-lighted room in some tenement in a squalid and unclean quarter of an overcrowded city. It means food oftentimes adulterated and at best ill-cooked and ill-served. It means the sacrifice of most of the comforts and many of the decencies of life. And when this sum is meted out, not to the girl dependent upon herself, but to the widow with children, the effect is utterly crushing and annihilating.

The burden of our civilization bears with heaviest weight upon the shoulders of women. Through constant association with it, we have become hardened to the degrading and humiliating truth that in our society, as at present constituted, hundreds of thousands, if not millions, of girls, depending exclusively upon their own resources, are compelled to work unduly long hours for a beggarly pittance. The temptations besetting a woman, particularly in our modern industrial life, are multiplied a hundredfold in the case of these shamefully underpaid workers. There is no cessation of toil, no surcease from the wearisome round of exhausting labor, no pleasure or diversion in the few hours of leisure. The salient fact of present-day existence, not only in our large cities, but in small towns as well, is the incentive offered to all, especially to young people, to entertain themselves and to secure a modicum of the attractions everywhere set before their eyes. But a girl earning in a factory or store the sum of four or five dollars a week must resolutely avert her gaze from all that is pleasant or attractive in life, and toil on without the prospect or hope of a better and fuller existence.

From the low wages which are now paid to women there is no hope of escape through the benevolence of the individual employer. To a certain extent the employer with a soul can improve conditions of work within his establishment and even increase pay, so that his workwomen may enjoy a little more comfort. There can be no doubt, however, that the employer who pays larger wages than his competitor for the same character of work is at a certain disadvantage, and the wages of women are, as a consequence, regulated by those which the most grasping competitor gives to his employees. The only hope of a permanent increase is from the organization of women workers into trade unions and the attainment and maintenance through their efforts of a higher standard of life.

Up to the present time, women, while materially benefiting from trade unions, have not joined in as large numbers as they might. In England, of a total of 2,000,000 trade unionists there are only 120,000 female members. In Germany the percentage is still less. It is probable that a slightly larger percentage of women are enrolled as members of trade unions in this country, but the proportion is not as yet what it should be. The men in the various industries should to their utmost endeavor to secure the enrollment of women workers, and the women themselves should take the initiative in this movement.

In the future there will probably be an increase in the number of women trade unionists. At the present time women are largely engaged in trades which are difficult to organize, but they are rapidly joining unions of which men are already members, and are also organizing into separate bodies. It has been shown in the few organizations of women which exist that they are even more willing to make sacrifices for a cause than are men, and they frequently make the best unionists.

An interesting phase of the changing attitude of women toward unions is revealed by the action of the Chicago Federation of Teachers. The teachers of Chicago, recognizing that they were wage earners and realizing the similarity of their aims and ideals with those of the great body of trade unionists, threw their fortunes in with their fellow-workers and became affiliated with the Chicago Federation of Labor. This action was repeated in three other towns and is doubtless only the forerunner of a general movement of school teachers to the ranks of organized labor. The influence for good which may result from this bond between the working people and the teachers of their children can now be only faintly forecasted.

The women who toil in this country are beginning to recognize clearly that their improved conditions are due in large part to the action of trade unions. The trade unions have always stood for the principle of equal pay for equal work irrespective of sex, and the various national and local unions, coöperating with the American Federation of Labor, have done all in their power to aid the cause of woman. The success of the labor organizations in reducing the hours of labor of women has been shown in another chapter, but these attempts represent only a portion of the work which has been accomplished, and the future will undoubtedly show a vast strengthening of the labor movement through the compact organization of the women employed in American industries.

Even more important than the benefits conferred by trade unionism upon women workers have been its efforts in behalf of the toiling children. The employers of labor have drafted into their service not only masses of newly arrived immigrants, not only married and unmarried women, but also children of a tender age. Since the birth of the factory system, children have been mustered by thousands into factories, and on account of their nimbleness, their docility, their powerlessness to resist oppression, and the low wages which they were forced to accept, have been permitted to displace men and to ruin themselves by work unsuited to their age and strength. This has also occurred in the anthracite coal regions, where thousands of boys are employed in the breakers.

It is hard to reconcile the humanity and vaunted intelligence of this era with the wholesale employment of children in industry. Childhood should be a period of growth and education. It should be the stage in which the man is trained for future efforts and future work. With each advance in civilization, with each improvement of mankind, the period of childhood should be extended in order that the men and women of the next generation shall be mature and developed.

It is difficult to conceive of anything more fatuous, anything more utterly absurd and immoral, than the wholesale employment of children in industry. Apart from the particular and special evils of the system as it exists to-day, the policy of extracting work from children and exploiting their slow-growing strength is utterly vicious and entirely self-destructive. A state of society might be conceived in which poverty was so intense that even the little children would needs be drafted into the industrial army, in order to produce enough to enable society to eke out its existence. But in a nation which has its millionaires, almost its billionaires, the utter inhumanity of any system which permits the exploitation and degradation of children is horrible.

Largely through the influence of trade unionism and through the gradual awakening of an enlightened sentiment on the part of the public, the evils of child labor both in England and the United States have been somewhat ameliorated. The conditions which formerly prevailed in England and in the New England and Middle Atlantic States of this country are now no longer possible in any civilized community, with the exception of the Southern States. Through the efforts of the trade unionists and other disinterested and public-spirited men and women, laws have been passed in the various states restricting the evil of child labor and ameliorating the conditions of the little ones in the mills, mines, and factories. This legislation has usually taken the form of laws compelling school attendance, prohibiting children's work before a certain age, limiting hours of labor above that age, obtaining proper conditions for children during the hours of their employment, and, finally, excluding children from certain dangerous and unhealthy occupations. In the majority of the American states, laws have been passed compelling children to attend school until their tenth, twelfth, or fourteenth year, but, unfortunately, these laws are not always rigidly enforced, and the school term is not invariably as long as it should be. The laws regulating employment usually prescribe that a child shall not be employed in a mine, a factory, a work-shop, or any establishment in which the manufacture of goods is carried on, below a minimum age, ordinarily fixed at ten, twelve, thirteen, fourteen, or sixteen years, the average being probably about twelve or thirteen years. Even above this age it is usually provided that a child shall not work for more than eight, nine, or ten hours, and provision is made for the posting of notices definitely stating the hours of beginning and ending work, and the times for meals. In various states the employment of children has been entirely prohibited in some occupations, and in certain states it is legally forbidden to inflict corporal punishment upon the child.

Important, however, as has been the work of trade unions in this direction, there still remains much to be done. Even at the present time, there are over 168,000 children employed in the manufacturing industries of the country, and there are many thousands more engaged in mines, shops, and mercantile establishments, and at work in the streets of the cities. A third of the children engage at manufacturing are employed in the cotton industry, but many more are employed in tobacco factories, in the manufacture of cigars, paper boxes, picture frames, furniture, feathers, neck-ties, artificial flowers, and boots and shoes. Although the age at which children may begin to work is gradually being raised, the factories in the Southern States still employ children of ten and even of eight and seven years. By means of trade union activity, the number of children engaged in manufacturing in the Northern States of the Union has gradually been reduced, and the total so engaged throughout the country appears to have been less in 1900 than in 1880. But the labor force of the cotton and tobacco factories of the South is being constantly recruited from the small children of those regions, and exploitation there is practically unrestricted. The character of some of these mills, operating at enormous profits and building upon the unmerciful exploitation of children, beggars description. The children are subjected to the harshest and most brutal tyranny, are compelled to overstrain and overexert themselves, and to wear out their young lives in the eternal struggle to keep up with the machine.

The effect of this employment of child labor is not only to reduce wages of adult workers, but absolutely to preclude the possibility of the children themselves growing into sane and healthy adults. Miss Jane Addams, of Hull House in Chicago, has pointed out the intimate connection between exploited child labor and vagrancy. Thousands of men who tramp about the country and live off society, instead of for it, are the product of a system of unregulated child labor. In the factory the spring of the child's life snaps and his spirit is completely broken. The outlook upon life of a child of twelve or fourteen, emerging illiterate and listless from five or six years of work at deadening, monotonous labor is hopelessly blank, and it is not to be wondered at that many children with such a past develop into tramps and criminals. The constant throwing off of these worn out, prematurely aged children is a terrible indictment against a society claiming to be civilized.

There is no hope for the poor children of the South, except the possibility of succor from trade unions. While the sentiment of the entire country is one of righteous indignation against the cold-blooded, money-seeking owners of Southern cotton and tobacco mills, it needs the constant stimulus of a strong union movement to crystallize this sentiment and render it effective. Many of the owners of these mills, drawing their dividends from an anonymous company, are growing rich upon the flesh and blood of thousands of emaciated wretches, whom they have never seen. The sentiment of the community should be directed against these persons as individuals as well as against the industries they represent, and a concentrated effort should be made so to educate the legislators of the states that they will assume a virtue if they have it not, and in spite of their own selfish ends and aims legislate for the protection of these children.

I wish, even at the risk of tiresome repetition, to insist upon the absolute wastefulness and the utter depravity of this system of child labor. There is no need to search for extreme and exceptional instances of hardship. The ordinary life of the ordinary child in the factory run under ordinary and usual conditions is such as no society should permit. It is a well-known fact that children in mines and factories are much more exposed to accidents than are adults, capable of avoiding recognized dangers. They are also more liable to disease, more liable to the poisoning and infection of their young bodies, more liable to premature death or complete disability. The utter ruinousness of this parasitic exploitation of children before they can arrive at strength or maturity should animate statesmen to legislate against this abomination and destroy it root and branch. We are daily seeing the spectacle of children taken out of school and thrust into factories, with the result that a few years of ineffectual work are added and a great many years of productive and effective labor are lost. If the whole community were enslaved to a single lord who cared not for the happiness of his subjects, but wished merely to increase his own wealth, he would not do as we do now—exploit the labor of little children; he would prohibit their employment until such time as they were enabled to perform the greatest amount of work throughout their lives. The policy of rendering men unfit for work by squeezing out of them the last iota of strength when they are children, is an extreme case of slaying the goose that lays the golden eggs.

In its attempts to ameliorate the conditions brought about by this cruel exploitation of child labor, trade unionism has met with opposition not only from the more unscrupulous manufacturers, but also from the less intelligent workmen. It is unfortunately a fact that many workmen and even a few trade unionists are still so ignorant that they do not perceive that a prohibition of child labor will improve their own condition, as well as save their children from a useless, if not a vicious, life. The father of a family sees only the two, three, or four dollars which his little boy or girl brings home, and fails to see that these same dollars are taken from his own wages by the employment of his children. It is a fact proved over and over again that the wages of men whose children are not employed are greater than the total wages of the families of men who permit their children to work. The investigation of various bureaus of labor throughout the United States have clearly demonstrated that the entire wages of workingmen's children, and even more than this amount, are deducted from the wages of the workingmen themselves. This is indisputable, but even if it were not, the workingmen of the country should be—and in the majority of cases are—above the temptation to obtain a temporary increase in the income of their families by means of the sacrifice of their own flesh and blood.

The trade unions of this country should stand for education laws in the various states, compelling all children below the age of sixteen to attend school for the full term. They should also insist upon the enactment of laws establishing a minimum age of sixteen years below which children might not work in mills, mines, factories, or mercantile establishments. These laws should be rigidly, strictly, and equably enforced, and the various evasions due to the deliberate perjury of parents and employers should be guarded against. Provision, I believe, should be made for cases in which such a prohibition of child labor would work undue and exceptional hardship, but these regulations should be of such a nature that no favoritism could result and that no large body of children could be employed. There are a few cases, amounting, perhaps, to two or three per cent. of the children drafted into factories and mines, in which the establishment of a minimum age of sixteen might work needless hardship, but, as has been shown by the laws of several states, these cases may be provided for without opening the door to numerous evasions and to the practical nullification of the law.

Whatever the specific measure taken by trade unions, their policy must always be based upon the fixed determination to keep children out of the factory and the mine. The prosperity, the very existence, of our civilization depends upon the safeguarding and protection of the child, depends upon the immunity of the weak from the oppression and aggression of the strong and unscrupulous. No trade unionist is loyal to his cause, who is not solicitous for the welfare of the least of the little children in industry, and no permanent progress can be attained until all workmen and all well-intentioned members of society are united in a determined effort to protect children and to guarantee to them a happy, healthy, and useful existence.

CHAPTER XVII

THE DEATH ROLL OF INDUSTRY

The Perils of Peace. Accidents Increase with Industry. The Killing, Maiming, and Poisoning of Workingmen. Accidents Inevitable and Preventable. Trade Unions and the Health and Safety of the Workingman. Public Opinion Favors Factory Legislation. Factory Legislation in England and the United States. The Ounce of Prevention and the Pound of Cure. Liability of Employers for Accidents. The Doctrine of Common Employment. Its Injustice. Employers' Liability Laws. Cheaper to Kill than to Save. The Killing of Workingmen not a Matter of Private Agreement. An Argument for Trade Unionism.

THE bread of the laborer is eaten in the peril of his life. Whether he work on the sea, on the earth, or in the mines underneath the earth, the laborer constantly faces imminent death. His peril increases with the progress of the age. With each new invention the number of killed and injured rises; each increase in the number and size of our great engines, each new speeding up of the great mechanisms of industrial life brings with it fresh human sacrifices.

The victories of peace have their price in dead and maimed as well as the victories of war. As the intensity of life increases, as the hold of the weaker becomes feebler, as the struggle for existence grows ever sharper, so the peril to the life and limb of the worker is enhanced with every mechanical advance. The stage coach was more dangerous to the individual passenger than is the railroad; but where the stage coach slew its thousands, the railroad has slain its tens of thousands. Each year the locomotive increases the number of its victims, each year the factories maim more and kill more, each year lengthens the tale of miners who go down into the mines and do not come up again.

The death roll of industry is longer than is evident from official figures. Many are killed without violence. Thousands of men, women and children lose their lives in factories and mills without the inquest of a coroner. The slow death which comes from working in a vitiated atmosphere, from inhaling constantly the fine, sharp dust of metals, from laboring unceasingly in constrained and unnatural postures, from constant contact of the hands or lips with poisonous substances, lastly, the death that comes from prolonged exposure to inclement weather, from overexertion and undernutrition, from lack of sleep, from lack of recuperation, swells beyond computation the unnumbered victims of a restless progress.

However sure the precautions, however perfect the arrangements, it is inconceivable that the gigantic industrial movements of the American people could be conducted without some fatalities. No movement of an army, no great parade, no celebration, hardly a picnic, without attendant danger of life lost or mangled limb. The industrial structure is a huge machine, hard-running, and with many unguarded parts. It would not be possible to conduct our railroads without a single accident, and many of the fatalities in industry, as many deaths in general, are simply and solely the result of "an act of God," inseparable from the ordinary course of existence.

While, thus, some fatalities of our industrial life are inevitable, while many are maimed, many sickened, many poisoned because of conditions beyond the reasonable power or control of employers or of the state, yet there is no doubt that a vast amount of entirely unnecessary and easily avoidable injury is inflicted upon workingmen. The evil is at present greater in volume and extent, although less in intensity, than in the early days of the factory system. When steam began its triumphant march through the industries of the world and production on a large scale drove the small workshops into backward villages, the fate of the wage earner was put in the hands of men concerned singly with the ideal of money getting. The struggle of competition drove each employer to speed up his machines, to drive his workmen, to do all in his power to increase output and reduce expenses. Machinery left unfenced was frequently tended by small children, whom it seized and mangled like some huge, malicious monster. The sanitary conditions of the factories and workshops of the day were indescribably bad, and women and children as well as men were exposed to all the maladies which excessive work with noxious materials under unspeakably unsanitary conditions would produce.

The task of converting the factories of civilized nations from noisy, whirling dungeons into the better, cleaner, and more sanitary workshops of to-day fell to the lot of organized labor. For a time, it is true, the impetus to reform came largely from other classes in society, but as soon as trade unions became strong enough to take up the task, they prosecuted it with vigor and in many industries carried it to a successful issue. Both in England and in the various states of this country, the unions have had more success in obtaining from the government legislation regulating sanitary conditions than in any attempt to reduce by law the hours of work. The law has not permitted the fixing of a standard of wages either in the United States or in England, and with the exception of a few trades and barring one or two recent decisions, no legislation regulating the hours of labor of adult male workers has been held constitutional. From the first, however, public sympathy has been with the workingmen in their attempt to make their working places less dangerous to life, limb, and health. It was clearly seen that the individual, unorganized workingman could not in his wage contract or otherwise, regulate the condition in which the factory of his employer was to be kept, and that in order to secure reforms of this sort, recourse must necessarily be had to legislation or to the direct negotiation of a trade union. The public also perceived that for the preservation of its own health and strength, improvement in the sanitary conditions of work was indispensable. It was feared that by permitting the working places of the people to become pests, the door would be open to infectious diseases of all kinds, resulting in ultimate injury to all classes of society.

Even in England no general attempt was made on the part of trade unions much before 1840 to better the sanitary conditions of workshops, and it was not until about thirty years ago that this became universally a part of the settled policy of trade unions. The argument occasionally raised against insurance, that it is impious, seemed also to apply to attempts to regulate the conditions of work, since the sickness of workmen or their death from accident was attributed to the "act of God," rather than to unsanitary or dangerous conditions. The political economists, who at this time were all arrayed upon the side of the capitalists, stated that the more dangerous and unsanitary the conditions of work, the higher the remuneration, and, therefore, any attempt to improve the sanitary conditions of work would attract new workmen and would consequently lower wages.

Notwithstanding all arguments to the contrary, the desire for reform grew rapidly, as the effect of unsanitary work became more clear. It was soon seen that many of the accidents and much of the disease incidental to various occupations were avoidable, and it also became recognized by the workingmen that the effect of dangerous and unsanitary labor was not to increase wages, but merely to degrade the workers compelled to perform tasks of that nature. The effect of improving the sanitary conditions of work has not been, as was anticipated, a decrease in the wages of the men performing the safer work, but has been, rather, an increase in the efficiency of the workers and an improvement in their general character and calibre.

Gradually, in England and in this country, the legislatures passed laws providing for a number of reforms tending to make the conditions of work more healthful, safe, and comfortable. These acts varied with the nature of each industry and have been more or less sweeping and more or less rigidly enforced in various industries and in various states. The factory laws passed by the legislatures of American states have generally been justified and declared constitutional as coming under the police power of the state.

Factory legislation has been so wide in extent and manifold in character that it would be impossible in a book of this size to consider it in detail. In his Handbook to the Labor Law of the United States, Mr. F. J. Stimson has thus summarized the principal classes of laws of this sort passed by the American states: "Statutes providing for the preservation of the health of employees in factories by the removal of excessive dust, or for securing pure air, or requiring fans or other special devices to remove noxious dust or vapors peculiar to the trade; statutes requiring guards to be placed about dangerous machinery, belting, elevators, wells, air-shafts, etc.; statutes providing for fire-escapes, adequate staircases with rails, rubber treads, etc.; door opening outward, etc.; statutes providing against injury to the operatives by the machinery used, such as laws prohibiting the machinery to be cleaned while in motion, or from being cleaned by any woman or minor; laws requiring mechanical belt shifters, etc., or connection by bells, tubes, etc., between any room where machinery is used and the engine room; laws aimed at overcrowding in factories, and at the general comfort of the operatives; and many special laws in railways, mines, and other special occupations, such as the laws requiring warning guards to be placed before bridges upon railroads, requiring the frogs and switches or other appliances of the track to be in good condition and properly protected by timber or otherwise, providing automatic couplings to both freight and passenger trains, and, in building trades, providing for railings upon scaffolds and for suitable scaffolds generally.

"There are most elaborate statutes and several constitutional provisions regulating the conduct of mining industries, the condition of mines, the use of safety cages, etc., in the states where the mining industry predominates.

"Both manufactories and mines are, in nearly all these states, submitted to some kind of public inspection to see that these regulations are in force, and in many states there are special inspectors appointed for the purpose; in others the matter is left to the state labor bureaus, the board of health, the local authorities, or the chief of police. An appeal from their decisions or orders may be taken to the courts."

The most usual, direct, and efficacious manner of protecting the life, limb, and health of the worker is by legally compelling the employer to do or refrain from doing certain things and to appoint inspectors to see that these things are done or omitted. Thus, to prevent men from being needlessly killed in coupling cars, the easiest and best method is to compel the railroads to provide automatic couplers and to punish by fine, imprisonment, or otherwise any refusal to comply with this regulation. To prevent men from being needlessly mangled by machinery, it is only necessary to compel by law the fencing of such machines and to appoint inspectors to see that the fencing is properly done. This has been the method usually adopted in the factory and mining laws of many nations and of the various states of this country. New York and Massachusetts have been especially energetic in passing good laws and securing their enforcement. Where it has been found difficult, however, to obtain the enactment or effective enforcement of factory laws, attempts have been made to protect the lives of the workmen indirectly, by making the killing of employees too expensive a pastime. This has been accomplished in England by the passage of a compulsory insurance law, and in France, Germany, Austria, Italy, and a number of other Continental countries, provision is made for compulsory compensation of injured employees. A necessity for some form of compensation undoubtedly exists in the United States, owing to the inadequacy of the law in this regard.

Under the common law of England and of the United States, an employer is responsible for the action of his workmen in the course of their employment, very much as a principal is responsible for the actions of his agents. However, in the celebrated case of Priestley *vs.* Fowler, decided in 1837, the law was laid down by a certain learned judge that a servant could not recover from his master when the injury was due to the negligence of a fellow servant; and this decision has become imbedded in English law through a succession of judgments adverse to injured workingmen. Even at that time the decision was unjust, but with every advance in industrial development, it has become more grievous. When two journeymen carpenters were working on the same job with their employer, it might or might not be just to relieve the employer of responsibility for injury inflicted in the course of employment by one workingman upon the other;

but at the present time the distinction is utterly vicious. Under the law as it exists to-day, where not modified by statute, all the passengers in a train may recover for an accident due to the carelessness of a switchman or the negligence of a telegraph operator, except only the engineer, fireman, brakeman, and conductor, though killed in the performance of their duty and without any contributory negligence. No matter though the person guilty of negligence has never been seen or heard of by the injured workman, no matter though he serves in a different department or in a different country, no matter though he is the workman's superior and capable of giving him orders, there is still no possibility of recovering, because all are covered by the blanket of common service. In the large industrial establishments of to-day, employing thousands of workingmen, one hand cannot know what the other hand doeth; yet, as the law stands in most American states and as it stood in England until recently, no workingman can recover damages for injury inflicted upon him by any one of five, ten, twenty, or fifty thousand fellow-servants. The employer is, of course, responsible for his own individual carelessness or malice, but in the huge, anonymous corporations of to-day, such as the Pennsylvania Railroad and the Standard Oil Company, who *is* the employer?

About thirty years ago, the trade unionists of Great Britain, especially the coal miners and railway employees, despairing of the enactment and rigid enforcement of laws safeguarding the workingman, determined to remedy the employers' liability law and to mulct the companies in damages for injuries to their workmen. After much agitation, they secured, in 1880, the passage of an employers' liability law, making the employer in certain industries responsible for injuries to workmen when the accident was due to the negligence of superintendents, managers, foremen, or through obedience to improper rules or orders. Within two years, however, the decisions of the court rendered the law nugatory by allowing the employers to "contract out." By these decisions, it was held that if a workman received notice that he must forego his rights under the act and accept instead a claim to a benefit club established by the employer (to which the workman himself was obliged to contribute largely), he was held to have entered into a valid contract to surrender his rights. In 1897, however, the act was widely extended and compelled employers in the trades affected, including about one-third of all British workmen, to compensate their workmen for all injuries suffered in the course of their employment, whether caused by negligence or not.

This legislation, however, while extremely beneficial to the employee, has not been successful in compassing its original object. It is unfortunately true of modern industrial life that in the majority of cases it is cheaper to kill men and pay for them than to go to the expense of making suitable provision for preventing accidents. It is useless for trade unionists to shut their eyes to the fact that an employer, if unscrupulous, will pay occasional damages for employees who are killed and injured, if compelled to do so by law, rather than take the expensive precautions necessary for preventing the accident. The employer can and does insure himself against accidents to his workingmen and thus finds it cheaper, if less humane, to kill than to save. In the matter of accidents, it not infrequently happens that an ounce of prevention costs more than a pound of cure.

But what the workingmen desire and demand is not so much compensation for injury as prevention of injury. The workingman who, through no fault of his own, is killed or maimed or permanently disabled in an industry should receive from that industry or from the state, either directly or through his heirs, a suitable compensation, whether the injury is due to the negligence of the employer or not. It is inhuman to permit disabled workingmen to starve, it is inhuman to permit widows and orphans of men who have died in the performance of their duty to be left without suitable provision for their future maintenance. The workman however, demands even more strenuously and justly that all possible measures be taken to prevent accidents. It is well to receive a thousand dollars for the loss of an eye or a leg, but it is better by far for the man, as for society, that the eye and the leg be not lost. As Frank P. Sargent, U. S. Commissioner of Immigration, says, "We would prefer to prevent the injuries rather than to secure indemnity therefor." The trade unions must continue by agitation and education, by appeals to legislatures, and, if necessary, by strikes, to enable good and compel bad employers to do everything within their power to lengthen the life and maintain the health of their workers.

In the matter of the health and safety of the workingman, society has not yet learned its full lesson. There was a time when the criminal law was a matter of private settlement, and a man could relieve himself of responsibility for the murder of his neighbor by making a blood payment of so much money to the kinsmen of the murdered man. Our attitude toward preventable accidents is still much the same. If the employer pays a ludicrously inadequate sum to his injured employees or to the widow of a workman who has been killed, society assumes that he has performed his full duty and that his concern in the matter has ceased. The commission or permission of preventable accidents should be considered a public crime, an injury not only to the workingman but to society at large. The factory laws of all states, which at the present time are frequently inadequate and sometimes remain a dead letter upon the statute book, should be greatly extended and should be enforced with the utmost rigor; and when men are killed or maimed or injured on railroads, in factories, or in mines through a violation of the plain letter of the law, as frequently happens at the present day, the employer should not only suffer in pecuniary damages, but should be liable to prosecution for a penal offense. No country, however powerful or formidable, can be considered truly great which does not hold important the life and happiness of its citizens, even if they be the humblest of untrained workingmen or the least of the little children in the factories.

There is nothing which so justifies the existence of trade unions as the work which they have done and are still doing in improving the sanitary conditions of the workingmen and saving them from premature or violent death. The solution of these problems in so far as the state does not take the direct initiative can be left to no one but the organizations of labor. The individual workingman cannot regulate the conditions of his work. The textile workers of the United States, if organized into one vast, all-comprising union, could enforce proper sanitary conditions in all the textile mills; but a single weaver or spinner would be utterly unable to make any impression whatsoever. A weaver who offered to work only on condition that all the machinery of the mill be fenced, that the temperature of the rooms be not above a certain maximum, that such and such sanitary conditions be maintained, would find that his prospective employer would be able and willing to do without his services. No single workingman could determine upon, even if he could enforce, the hundreds of reasonable conditions which enter into our factory or mining laws or into the shop rules incorporated in trade agreements.. The shop and mining rules agreed upon in conference between employers and unions are, in many instances, absolutely essential to the health and even to the life of the workingman, and these rules require united action on the part of all workingmen. It would be impossible for the employer to treat with each workingman as to what shop or mine rules he would be willing to accept, however possible such an individual agreement might be in the case of wages. The rules relating to sanitation and safety are common, general rules, and serve to demonstrate clearly that the workingmen in a factory or in an industry are not to be considered as individual men contracting separately, but as members of one united group.

Even if it were possible for the individual workingman to contract upon the matter of safety and health, it would be contrary to public policy and public welfare to permit him to do so. The state refuses to allow a man to sell himself into slavery, even though he is an adult, in full possession of his faculties and not acting under duress. The law also refuses to permit a man to make any contract by which he will maim himself or allow himself to be maimed. If, however, the law is to permit a man to accept any risks of employment which his employer is willing to force upon him, the position of the workingman so contracting is practically identical with that of a man selling himself into slavery or offering for a consideration to kill or maim himself. If it is against public policy to permit a brakeman by private agreement to relieve a railroad company of the obligation to use automatic couplers, then it should also be against public policy to allow an individual workingman to relieve the employer of the obligation to take such precautions for the health and safety of the workingmen as have been agreed upon jointly by the employers and the employees of the trade. The action of trade unionism in these matters should become increasingly universal, and to a greater and greater extent must secure a sanction like that given to the law itself.

LOADED CARS READY FOR HAULING TO THE MOUTH OF THE MINE

The coal must be nine or ten inches above the water edge of the car

Loading Coal in Strip Bank in Anthracite Region

CHAPTER XVIII

THE MORAL UPLIFTING OF THE WORKMAN

Trade Unions Raise the Moral Tone of the Workingmen. Effect upon Character and Habits of—Higher Wages—Shorter Hours—Decreased Peril—Better Sanitary Conditions. Can the Workingman be Trusted with Leisure. Labor as a Commodity. The Laborer as a Man. "Hands" and Men. Morals and Insurance. Morals and the Standard of Living. The Dignity of Labor. Self-respect, Democracy, and Morals in Industry. The Educating Influence of Trade Unions. Self-sacrifice and Unionism. The Erasure of Lines of Race, Creed, and Nationality. The Lesson of Universal Brotherhood.

THOSE who look only at the surface of things and judge trade unionism by an occasional glimpse are likely to fail signally to appreciate the uplifting influence of this institution upon the character of the wage earners. Many who admit that trade unions have been successful in raising wages, shortening hours, and improving the material conditions of the worker's life still believe that their effect upon his intellectual and moral tone has been either bad or entirely nil. Many deplore what they are pleased to call the "tyrannizing" of trade unions, their alleged reduction of all men to the same level, their supposed tendency to "breed" discontent; and it is asserted that the strike and the boycott, which are laid at the door of the trade union, also affect injuriously the *morale* of the wage earner.

To all, however, who do not view these matters superficially, it must be evident that trade unionism has had exactly the opposite effect. The increased wages and shortened hours of labor have in themselves brought about a vast improvement in the mental and moral status of the workers. Workmen who formerly went from their twelve hours of work to the nearest saloon now spend their time with their families, improving their minds, or enjoying a sensible and sane recreation. In most instances increased wages have meant the gratification of the intellectual and artistic sense of the workers; have meant books and pictures; have meant a few extra rooms in the house and more decent surroundings generally; have meant a few years' extra schooling for the children, have meant, finally, a general uplifting of the whole working class. The same is true of the measures taken by trade unions to prevent disease and accidents in factories. There is nothing so demoralizing as the recklessness which comes with the constant peril of one's life. A man who may be cut down at any moment by the sinking of his ship, by a bullet from the enemy, by a mine explosion, by the crash of cars without automatic couplers, or by the deadly clutch of an unfenced factory machine is apt to take little heed of the morrow and is not unlikely to spend the present day in a reckless debauch, which will injure him physically and degrade him morally. The measures taken by the trade unions to prevent the killing, maiming, and poisoning of the toilers, to prevent the men, women, and children of a factory from being huddled together indiscriminately with insufficient air, in an overheated or overmoist atmosphere, and with insufficient sanitary arrangements, have had a distinctly beneficial effect upon the morals of the persons affected.

Trade unionism has benefited the worker and raised his whole intellectual and moral tone by the emphasis which it has laid upon the welfare of the workingman. The employer, like the political economist of former days, was interested solely in the amount of production. He forgot the producer in the goods produced. Trade unionists and other reformers have thrown the emphasis not on the goods, but on the men by whom, and ultimately for whom, they are produced. It is no longer the machine, but the man at the machine, that is now taking the center of the stage in economical thought.

Formerly and, in fact, until quite recently, all discussions upon the subject of labor, its rights, and duties assumed the workingman to be a mere animate machine. The comparison was frequently made between the sale of labor and that of any other commodity, without reflection that the seller of a bushel of wheat cares not how, when, where, or by whom it is consumed, whereas the seller of a day's labor may be affected throughout his life time by the manner, place, and circumstances of the use of that day's labor. The workingman was considered a machine which cost so many dollars per day, which was to be used so many hours, which was to be given the smallest amount of care, attention, and fuel necessary to keep it in fair working order. He was an organism without a soul, composed, in fact, wholly of hands and stomach. Even now an employer speaks of so many hundred "hands," meaning thereby that number of individual workmen.

As long as the ideal of society was to produce as much as possible above the cost of living of workingmen, it became an object to keep wages as low as possible. The whole emphasis of the statesmen of three generations ago was laid upon saving, and the workingman was even urged to save from his scanty earnings in order that the amount to be devoted to production should be as great as possible and the amount devoted to consumption, as small as possible. The crises which has swept over the civilized world during the last fifty years have shown the falsity of this policy and how dangerous and useless it is to stimulate production and discourage consumption; thus, trade unions have been justified in their successful attempts to raise the wages of the workingmen and to increase consumption.

The trade union is to the wage earner what the school is to the child, or the army to the raw recruit. It is a means of discipline and of education. In the trade union the workingman learns to subordinate his own wishes to the will of the majority and to aid intelligently in the formation of this will. No institution is perfect, and no group of men, however educated or however cultivated, can work with complete smoothness and absolute perfection. In actual practice the trade union may be a less perfect school than in theory, but on the whole it does bring out the qualities of mind and heart that tend to produce good men and good citizens. The individual unionist soon realizes that he cannot force his fellow-craftsmen in the local meetings to do his will. To carry them with him he must convince them, and to convince them he must know the facts and know how to present them. A system of Parliamentary law is in use in even the rudest and simplest of these meetings, and all men receive a respectful hearing, no matter how opposed their views to the general sense and will of the meeting.

The workingman in the meetings of the trade union also learns the lesson of subordination. The man who will strike rather than submit to injustice on the part of employers will cheerfully bow to the will of the union in which he himself has cast his vote. Gradually there grows up in the local meetings, and especially in national affairs, a feeling of tolerance and a just appreciation of the other man's side. In their agreements with employers unionists are on the whole more conservative and reasonable than are unorganized workmen. It is an argument for the educating influence of trade unions that it is always the newer organizations which are most turbulent and most intractable, and even employers hostile to the spirit of trade unionism laud the older and better established organizations and acknowledge the superiority of their methods and practices.

The trade union, like the Church, teaches the lesson of brotherhood. Before the union came, the mining regions and other fields of industry were rife with the mutterings of discontent and full of internal jealousies among the various nationalities. The Irish, English, and Scotch hated the Italians, Poles, and Hungarians, and the Catholics and Protestants were equally at war. The non-English-speaking laborer was indiscriminately dubbed "John," and cases were not rare in which the more defenseless foreign workmen were made to bear the brunt of the displeasure of their fellow-craftsmen. The union, however, soon changed this. In the meetings of the labor organizations men of all nations, languages, and religions sit or stand side by side. Italians or Poles will remain for hours listening to English speeches, which they cannot understand, and will patiently wait for the Italian or Polish speeches which may close the meetings. It is in something of a religious spirit that many of the men join the unions and it is in this spirit that they make sacrifices for it. The recognition of the union has a sentimental as well as a practical meaning to these men, and, as in the case of all sentiments, the men are willing to sacrifice for it tangible and immediate benefits.

If the morals of a man may be gauged by his willingness to make sacrifices, then the uplifting influence of trade unionism must be acknowledged. Men who year by year devote their scanty leisure to increasing the strength and power of the union, who without remuneration toil into the night after the enervating work of the day, who risk the blacklist and even imprisonment for the sake of a principle, show the extent to which this influence is felt. A cause that can inspire so much self-sacrifice cannot be wholly bad. There are many men to-day who are blacklisted and utterly unable to secure work because of their loyalty to their labor organization. No one who is not a workman can realize how terrible this punishment is. It is like a fearful, silent machine which strikes at all times and in all places, or like an invisible, deadly coil thrown about the man and ever tightening. This dreadful punishment, which in the case of a man with a family may mean condemnation to death by starvation, has been meted out over and over again to unionists; yet, notwithstanding this fact, men are willing to risk all for the sake of the cause. Union officials have gone about the country talking during the day and trudging during the night, living off the scantiest of food for the sake of propagating unionism. At one time the secretary of the Illinois District of the United Mine Workers of America, which is now one of the richest branch organizations in the United States, went about the country at his own expense and, without hope of repayment, lent to the cause his last hundred dollars. At that time the headquarters of this district were in the pockets of Mr. Ryan's coat, the righthand pocket being used for letters received and the left, for letters answered. This is but one of thousands of similar cases which might be cited. The mutual help of unionists, the donations made by prosperous unions to organizations in trouble, the willingness with which the members of a trade union will take up the scrip of their organization, and many other facts show this readiness to make sacrifices. The supreme test, however, of the willingness of men to forget their own interest in their love of a cause is seen in the case of strikes. More especially is this true in sympathetic strikes, where men frequently risk the savings of years for the sake of workers whom they have never seen and from whom they expect no benefits in return.

The trade union distinctly raises the moral tone of the wage earners by infusing into them a sense of the dignity of labor. There is much lip service paid to the ennobling effect of labor and to the dignity which it confers upon the worker, but it is the trade union, and the trade union alone, which translates these mere professions into actual deeds. The same man who prates about the worth of labor and the dignity of work often refuses to raise wages, lest the money so earned will be spent in drunkenness and dissipation; or to reduce hours, lest the workman, dignified by his labor, will resort immediately to some unworthy place and waste his new-gained leisure in a foolish or vicious manner. The same man who discourses eloquently upon the dignity of labor is unwilling that his employees shall have anything to say with regard to the conditions of their work or the manner in which the greater portion of their waking hours shall be spent. The working man, like the voter, is treated with occasional deference in after-dinner speeches, but not infrequently with contempt in ordinary times. Although a sovereign crowned with the dignity of labor, the ultimate repository of power and the real producer of the wealth of the nation, he is not considered worthy of a voice in the disposal of his own time.

In one sense the labor unions believe earnestly in the dignity of labor, and in another sense they do not. They believe that no matter how menial the work, no matter how deadening, how monotonous, how onerous, or even how filthy, the man who performs it faithfully is deserving of the praise and the thanks of the community, and is not paid in full when he receives his wages. The unionists feel that it is not the work itself, but the spirit in which the work is accepted and performed, that ennobles the worker. The unionist does not believe that man was put upon this earth for no better purpose than ceaselessly to push a piece of wire through a little hole, or end-lessly repeat the same simple, uniform operation. He believes, on the contrary, that man should be, as far as possible, relieved from work partaking of the character of drudgery, but that such work as is necessary should be performed unhesitatingly, uncomplainingly, and conscientiously.

The principal element which gives to labor its dignity and ennobling quality is its voluntary character. There is nothing ennobling about the toil of the slave crouching beneath the lash. There is nothing ennobling in the work of the serf bowed down by the weight of centuries. There is little of the dignity of labor in the forced work of the convict, or of the man toiling under the *padrone* system. The greater the initiative and the more complete the independence of the worker, the greater the pleasure in his work and the more educating and ennobling it becomes. We cannot do without subordination; we cannot carry on our great industries without the subjection of the individual workman to the will which directs the whole machinery. When, however, the wage earners have themselves fixed upon fair and reasonable working rules, voted upon by them in joint convention and obtained as a right from the employer, when the workingman is responsible to his fellow-craftsmen for the excellence of his work and is enabled to perform it under conditions which permit efficiency and self-satisfaction, work becomes a pleasure, and what was formerly a stern duty becomes, as in the case of artistic or intellectual work, the joy of achievement.

CHAPTER XIX

HOW TRADE UNIONS BENEFIT EMPLOYER AND PUBLIC

Workman's Gain is not Employer's Loss. Interests largely Identical. How the Trade Union Benefits the Employer. Cotton Spinners in India and Massachusetts. Cheerfulness and Profits. Why Slavery does not Pay. High Wages, Short Hours, and Great Efficiency. Waste and Wages. Trade Unionism Increases Demand for Products of Industry. Works for Good Times and against Crises. The "Most Favored" Employer. A Premium on Scruples. The Improvement of the Employing Class.

IT is a mistake to assume, as is often done, that a gain to the workman is a loss to the employer. In a large and very real sense, the interests of employers and workmen are reciprocal, and in benefiting the wage earner the trade union may secure quite as important and permanent an advantage to the employer. The workman labors shorter hours, and the output of the factory is enlarged; the workman gets higher wages, and the manufacturer produces more cheaply; the workman secures protection to life and limb, to health and morals, and profits increase. The trade union protects not only the workingman but the better class of employers, as well, from the unfair competition of the avaricious; it has thus tended to weed out the most unscrupulous employers and to raise the moral tone of the employing as well as of the laboring classes. It places business upon the firm basis of a fixed, definite labor cost, it indirectly increases the demand for the product of the manufacturer and steadies industry in general.

It has been repeatedly shown that the advance in wages and the shortening of hours have resulted not in an increased, but actually in a reduced cost. In most industries it has been clearly demonstrated that a workman really accomplishes more in ten hours of regular work than he formerly accomplished in twelve; and in many industries the reduction of hours from

TYPICAL GROUP OF BREAKER BOYS IN A PENNSYLVANIA MINING TOWN

These boys pick the slate and other impurities from the coal as it passes through the chutes and screens. They begin at an early age and reach manhood with but little schooling

MALTBY BREAKER

This is a building through which the coal passes on its way from the mines to the railway car. The slate is picked out by breaker boys, and by screens and chutes it is cleaned, and sorted into various sizes for market

ten to eight has meant increased production as well as greater profits to the employer. Witnesses before the Industrial Commission testified to the fact that in their establishments output increased with the shortening of the working day. Weavers in silk mills produced more in nine hours than in ten, workmen in a large drop forge establishment also increased their output upon a reduction in the hours of labor, and other cases were cited which prove the same point. As a result of reducing the hours of labor from ten to eight the output of bituminous coal per miner has largely increased. The same truth, the economy of a short working day, has been manifested in England, where the reduction of the hours of labor has been coincident with a cheapening of production and a rapid extension of foreign markets.

There are several reasons for this increased output on the part of men working shorter hours. The body and mind of the workman are in better condition when he is not overstrained and overtaxed during an excessively long working day, and the increased intensity and intelligence of the work is accompanied by an increased cheerfulness, which makes difficult tasks easy. If in a comparatively small number of hours the workman can earn enough to educate himself and children, his ability and efficiency during these few hours will be greater than when he worked a longer time; consequently the cost of his production is lessened, and his children will in turn stand a better chance of becoming good workmen. In a short working day, also, there is less waste as regards materials, time, and supervision, the men commencing on the minute instead of "soldiering" or dawdling for a portion of the day. The necessity of economizing labor, moreover, is felt much more keenly when the working day is short. As a result, machinery is introduced wherever possible, and work is better organized, better conducted, and better supervised.

What applies to the hours of labor is equally true of advances in wages. The organization of labor has had the effect of largely increasing wages. This increase has represented an advance not only in nominal but in real wages, not only in the actual amount of money paid to the workman, but in the quantity and quality of the goods which the workman can secure for such money. There is a difference, however, between the wages of labor and the cost of labor. The employee is interested only in the amount of his earnings; the employer, on the other hand, not in how much he pays any particular workman or even the whole body of workmen, but how much he obtains in return for that payment. It is far better for an employer to pay two dollars a day to a man who can make ten articles of a given kind than to pay one dollar to a man who can make four. No labor is so cheap as that of the well-paid workman, no labor so dear as that of the under-paid workman. A starving employee is dear at any price.

Many critics of trade unionism argue as though all workmen were endowed with the same capabilities, as though the Massachusetts or Lancashire cotton spinner were no more efficient than the East Indian, or the work of the farm laborer of Nebraska, no more productive than that of the Russian or Hungarian peasant. It is not true that all men are equally capable. The productivity of labor varies in different countries and depends upon a number of conditions—the liberality of the workman's diet, his general education, his technical training, his hopeful or despondent outlook upon life, and his attitude toward work. To pay such wages as make it impossible for a workman to procure sufficient food is as poor economy as to underfeed a horse or to understoke an engine; and to increase the laborer's intelligence and his chances for securing a technical education is to increase by so much his working capacity and to lower the actual cost of his labor. An even more important factor is that when labor is well paid and hours short, the man is apt to be infused with intelligent hopefulness and contentment. I do not mean the blind, stupid contentment of the man without ambition, who takes what is offered and gives in the form of labor what he must. I mean the contentment and hopefulness of the man who looks forward to increasing his wage by augmenting his efficiency and his power of work. It is a well-known fact that slave labor is usually unable to compete with free labor, though the master pays the slave only what will keep him alive and exacts from him as many hours of labor as he, the master, chooses. The ignorance, unreliability, and lack of hopefulness of the slave make him dear at any price. The same is true of serfs or of persons in a semi-slavish condition. The history of modern Europe shows that a serf is always worth more to himself than to his master, and where the law allows, the serf can actually purchase his freedom by the difference between what he can create as a free man and what he would produce when not free.

In the present state of society, only those are stimulated to the extent of their powers who receive the full benefit of all that they produce. The peasant proprietor or the small American farmer will work long hours, under severe strain, because he realizes that the full advantage of his labor accrues to himself. For the same reason, the lawyer, the doctor, and other professional workers are also willing to apply themselves for excessively long hours. Of course, it is not possible to give the great majority of wage earners that exclusive interest in the result of their labor which will incite them to work inordinately long hours. It is doubtful whether under present conditions such an unusual stimulus would be advantageous even if possible. However, a healthy incentive is given to labor by trade unionism, which increases the wages of the workingmen and encourages their reasonable anticipations of a still further betterment in their conditions, and consequently results in an enhanced cheerfulness and an increased product. The ideal of the trade unions should always be high wages, short hours, and great efficiency, and the realization of these ideals means higher real wages for the men and cheaper production for the employer.

Trade unionism tends to improve workmen not only directly, through an increase in wages and a reduction in hours, but it attains the same end in an indirect manner. The general policy of trade unionism, as has been explained before, is the establishment of a minimum wage, safeguarding, as a rule, the right of the employer to discharge for proved inefficiency. The result of this is the gradual creation of a dead line or a standard of efficiency, to which all who work must attain. When there is a minimum wage of four dollars a day, the workman can no longer choose to do only three·dollars' worth of work and be paid accordingly, but he *must* earn four dollars, or else cease from work, at least in that particular trade, locality, or establishment, the consciousness that he may be employed for a varying wage permits many a man to give way to his natural idleness and carelessness, whereas the maintenance of a rigid standard causes a rapid and steady improvement. The minimum wage acts upon the workman as the school examination upon the child. If a child falls, by however small a margin, below the standard set by the school, he fails of promotion, and the stimulus which is strong in the case of a school child is infinitely more intense in that of a worker with a family dependent upon him. The principle of the survival of the fittest through union regulations, works out slowly and unevenly; nevertheless its general effect is toward a steady and continuous progress of workingmen to a permanently higher standard of efficiency.

The trade union confers still another benefit upon the employer in definitely setting a price upon the cost of his labor. The union practically says to the employer, "You shall pay at least so much for each man you employ, and we guarantee to you that no one competing with you will receive his labor at a lower rate." Each employer is guaranteed a wage cost as low as the most favored employer in the trade and district. In former times, and even to-day where trade is not organized, the employer is sometimes driven by a power which he cannot resist, to force down wages, to defraud employees, and to resort to all manner of tricks, cheating, and evasions, which he finds distasteful but necessary. In unorganized trades, the honorable employer is at a disadvantage in competition with an unscrupulous employer, and the man who will not grind the face of his workpeople, may find himself undersold by men of lower moral calibre. The establishment by trade unions of a definite and irreducible minimum of pay and an equally definite maximum of time, places competition where it should be—upon a plane of legitimate business activity and upon a basis of business acumen and foresight. The minimum wage and other union regulations, place a premium on scruples. The employer who cannot gain an advantage by robbing his workmen is obliged, in order to secure profits, to obtain the latest machinery, to effect economies in production, to seek a wider or a better market, to improve the quality of his goods, or to branch out into new industries. Thus, the necessity imposed by the trade unions becomes the mother of invention in all legitimate fields of business activity. The establishment of a fixed minimum price for labor acts upon the employer like the establishment of a fixed charge for transportation. It prevents men from securing unfair rebates from workmen, just as the law prevents or seeks to prevent, shippers from securing rebates from the railroads, and it thus puts all employers upon an equal footing, where the fittest may survive. There is nothing so certain, nothing so advantageous and promising as the gradual improvement in the mental and moral calibre as well as in the business methods of the employing class, and in this improvement trade unionism has played a not unimportant part.

Trade unionism not only increases the ability of manufacturers to produce, but equally their ability to sell. To an ever increasing extent, the working classes are becoming consumers of the nation's products, and with every increase in their wages, there comes an increase in their ability and willingness to purchase the products of labor. The industries of the country flourish best when there is a large and constant demand for the products of labor, and this demand can best be stimulated by increased wages and shorter hours. The consumption of wealth by the very rich is more inconstant and less beneficial to the community than is that of the great wage earning class. Most of the articles made by machinery are purchased by the working classes, and periods of great prosperity are those in which the producers of wealth themselves furnish the demand for the articles of consumption.

If we look about us at the present time, we will notice an ever increasing demand of the working classes for the products of labor. Even a millionaire cannot wear many more shoes, hats, coats, or shirts than a poor man, and his consumption of food is also not much greater. The majority of the articles offered for sale in a store are purchased by men of small or moderate income, and most of the public services, such as street-car transportation, are for the benefit of men of limited means. The crises which periodically visit modern communities result from an unequal distribution of the wealth of the community—too large a share being in the control of employing and investing classes, and too small a portion in the hands of the consumers, especially of the working classes. Society can escape from such a crisis only by one of two ways—by destroying or decreasing the amount of capital invested in production, or by increasing the ability of the consumers to pay more for necessaries and comforts. Unfortunately, when such periods of depression come, they are rendered more grievous by a lowering of wages, which decreases the purchasing power of the workingman. These ever recurring crises may be moderated to a certain extent by the action of trade unions in raising wages, increasing consumption, and creating and maintaining a permanent stimulus to production by increasing the popular demand for the articles produced.

CHAPTER XX

THE PROBLEM OF THE UNSKILLED

The Problem of Poverty. The Dilemma of the Unskilled. What Trade Unionism has Already Accomplished. The Unemployed and the Partially Employed. Raising Sections of the Unorganized. Progress by Selection. The Limited Possibilities of the Untrained Workmen. The Incapables. The Duty of Society. Will the Unions of the Unskilled Live? Mutual Aid.

"THE great problem of poverty . . . . . resides in the conditions of the low-skilled workman. To live industrially under the new order he must organize. He cannot organize because he is so poor, so ignorant, so weak. Because he is not organized he continues to be poor, ignorant, weak. Here is a great dilemma, of which whoever shall have found the key will have done much to solve the problem of poverty."[1]

In the above paragraph a noted political economist sums up the problems of poverty as they exist to-day in the more advanced nations of the world. The author of this book believes that the destruction of the unskilled workingman is his lack of organization, and that owing to his absence of skill and his lack of intelligence, it is impossible to bring him into labor organizations. Trade unions have always recognized that in this question of the unskilled lies the very essence of the trade union problem. The great mass of unskilled, untrained men residing in a community, living by odd jobs, and willing to take any work at any price at any time, is a serious drawback to the trade union movement and a menace to the society in which they live. In the slums of our great cities reside hundreds of thousands of men, brutalized by poverty and forced by their needs to lead an anti-social life. There is in every city an army of men who, by reason of their lack of means, are forced to perform work unsteadily and fitfully,

---

[1] Hobson, John A. Problems of Poverty (London, 1891), page 227.

who are subject to unemployment, and to all the ills of modern industrial life.

It is urged against trade unionism that it does nothing, and can do nothing, for the great mass of the unskilled. It is claimed that the unions exist only for a small minority of workingmen, namely, those who are skilled, and have a particular trade, and that for the great mass of men there is no hope and no salvation in labor organization. It is stated that trade unionism merely raises a small section of workers, creates a new class of skilled workmen out of a fragment of the entire laboring population, and thus fulfills only the aims of a new and moderately small class, instead of working for the welfare of humanity.

Those who argue in this way—and they may be said to be the majority—fail to see what trade unionism has already done for these masses and the possibility of further action in the future. It must be admitted that this problem of the unskilled and untrained is intensely difficult, and that it is only partially solvable by direct trade union effort. There can be no doubt that it constitutes a menace to the trade union world and that it raises difficulties compared to which all other problems of trade unionism sink into insignificance. However, trade unionism has essayed the solution of the problem and has already accomplished at least something toward minimizing it and improving the conditions of large groups within this class.

The activity of trade unionism in this matter may best be observed by a study of conditions as they actually exist in England and in the United States. It has been shown that one-third of the whole population of London earn only about five dollars per week per family. Investigations in other English cities also prove conclusively that vast sections of the population live below what is called the poverty line, in other words, receive a wage less than that which will purchase ordinary necessaries of life and will maintain health and vigor. While the conditions in American cities have not been investigated so carefully, they also show an enormous amount of poverty. The slums of our large cities contain vast armies of men living below what is necessary for health. The number of men who can do unskilled work but can not secure it permanently is enormous and the number of men unable to do even this kind of work is equally great. The conditions of life of many of these unfortunates are such as to destroy utterly hundreds of thousands. Many of these people live crowded together in unspeakable dwellings and obtain a quantity of food insufficient to maintain vigor or sometimes even mere existence. The cost of necessary articles of consumption is exorbitantly high to these classes owing to the fact that they must make their purchases in small quantities, and as a result of their frequent unemployment they are not able to maintain life decently at any time. Our vast army of criminals and tramps, recruited from the temporarily unemployed and the entirely unskilled, bears witness also to the existence of these multitudes of penniless men. The Jacks-of-all trades, men who can secure no permanent position, but shift from place to place, as though tossed by the waves of the sea, form a regiment in this vast army. All classes, kinds, and sorts of men are merged in this great group, men unskilled and untrained, men, used by industry when necessary and thrown aside when the necessity ceases. Broken down men from other ranks of life, men of small physical or mental strength, men afflicted by disease or with deformity, professional idlers, men bankrupt in health and spirits, men broken by the wheel of industrial life, worn-out factory children grown up—all these enter into this enormous group. These men, if they work at all, work at some form of unskilled labor, labor which can be learned in two or three days or, it may be, in two or three hours, and form an army reënforced enormously by the annual advent of hundreds of thousands of immigrants, willing at the start to work at any price, and to perform any labor, however menial and however ill-paid.

The problem confronting trade unionism is how to raise these men to a position where they can demand and maintain a minimum standard of wages and conditions; how to elevate them so that they will do efficient work for sufficient remuneration and become regularly enrolled as members of a permanent industrial army. The very existence of a minimum wage presupposes the ability of the workman to earn it, and trade unionism itself, therefore, apparently renders the hold on life of many of these wretches more precarious by depriving them of the opportunity to earn a small portion of a minimum wage in the hours or days which they are willing or able to devote to the work. At first sight it would appear that trade unionism, far from benefiting, has the effect of actually injuring these poor wretches. By fixing a minimum wage of two dollars a day, the union practically shuts the gate upon men who could earn a dollar a day for a dollar's worth of work, but who cannot earn two dollars a day, because their work is not worth two dollars. These unskilled workmen are thus precluded from earning a fraction of the minimum wage by doing a fraction of the work expected of them. The attitude of the unions in this matter is like their attitude towards the question of immigration, when they propose the exclusion of all immigrants who do not attain a certain standard of proficiency and efficiency, and seek to shut out from the country men incapable of earning fair wages.

In the long run, however, trade unionism actually benefits these workmen, and by this very policy. Trade unionism has been successful in raising one trade after another out of the profound slough of unskilled, untrained, and unregulated labor. Much work which was formerly absolutely unskilled and at which men were employed a few hours at a time to be taken on or discharged, fined or suspended at will, has now become organized so that the men secure fair wages and by reason of that very fact earn and deserve them. As soon as an unskilled trade of this sort becomes organized, wages are raised, the calibre of the men is improved, and their ability to *earn* as well as to *secure* good wages, is greatly increased. The organization of a hitherto unskilled trade restricts the opportunities of incapable men by debarring them from it, but it takes from the mass of unorganized workmen a large section and improves their condition.

This gradual elevation of one industry after another has widened the field of union activity and progressively reduced the scope, and sets limits to the extent, of the influence of the great body of unorganized and unskilled workmen. With every decade the trades which can be organized are increased in number and membership, and the opportunities of employment for the absolutely incapable are decreased, their absolute destitution becoming more obvious. The only progress which trade unionism can make in this direction is successively to take out one section after another from the mass of the unskilled and unorganized, and thus to show society more and more clearly its duty towards the incapables who can not enter any trade.

This elevation and improvement by selection takes place sooner where large groups of unskilled men are aggregated, or where by reason of a good strategic position they can secure more favorable terms. For example, unskilled workmen engaged in transportation have a certain advantage owing to the fact of their function and activity being so essential to the prosperity of the country. Other bodies of unorganized workmen rise out of their depressed position owing to help given to them by members of more skilled trades. Where a body of men have work which is contributory to the work of employees more skilled, it frequently occurs that the skilled workmen make an alliance with them and aid them in securing higher wages. What is called the industrial union or the union composed of all men in an industry, as distinguished from a "trade" union, which comprises only the men at a given special occupation, is especially favorable to the protection of the unskilled men. An industrial union composed of fifty thousand skilled and one hundred thousand unskilled men could by a strike or through negotiation secure better conditions not only for the skilled, but for the unskilled men. This has been one of the great advantages of the industrial unions, that they have the possibility, and frequently exercise the power, of raising the standard of the unskilled while improving the conditions of the skilled men.

The result of this activity of the trade union is to decrease the number of men who are suffering from want of the protection of labor organizations, but not actually to improve the conditions of those that remain. The men who are utterly incapable, whether through misfortune or otherwise, of holding a permanent position, cannot perhaps be greatly benefited by any direct action of trade unionism. Trade unionism improves the conditions of the unorganized, unskilled workers by lessening their numbers, rather than by bettering the condition of those who are below the line of organization.

To a certain extent, however, trade unions appear to benefit even the unorganized workmen who are not yet ready to be unionized. While the unions actually restrict the number of positions to which these men are eligible, they at the same time definitely diminish the competition for the positions of these unorganized men by making their unsteady jobs undesirable to men who have been organized and whose work has been elevated into a trade. In another and more subtle way the trade unions effect an increase in wages, and an improvement in the condition, of unorganized workmen. The standard of living and the demands of even unorganized and exploited workmen increase by reason of the improvement in the organized industries. By and through trade unionism, not only unorganized workmen, but employers and the general public as well, have been educated to a point where conditions which would once have been acceptable now are deemed intolerable. The wages of unskilled men are increased not only by actual membership in a trade union, but by the *possibility or potentiality* of becoming members. Just as the wages of unorganized domestic servants have been increased with each increase in the opportunities offered to women to secure more remunerative occupations elsewhere, so the wages of unskilled men outside the unions are increased by the *possibility* of their entering the organized trades, composed of men of about equal capacity. The good which unions do is never limited to their own members but is extended to those who are sufficiently capable workmen to *become* members.

The men, however, who permanently remain below the level of trade unionism by reason of incapacity are destined to be exploited by profit-seeking employers. Trade unionism attempts to prevent this evil also by factory legislation and by forbidding men to work under certain unhealthy and evil conditions. The result of this is still further to increase the number of men obtaining reasonably fair conditions of work, but still further to deprive a certain small section of workmen from securing any employment whatsoever. Trade unionism progressively separates the capables from the incapables, extending the work of capable men, preventing the incapacitation of tens of thousands of workers, and limiting with the formation of each union the opportunities for work of the men who remain below. The effect of this is to reduce the number of men who are incapable and to render the condition of each of these less desirable, his hold upon life more precarious.

In this tendency trade unionism acts as does the physician who separates the healthy from the diseased. It may be of comfort to the man suffering with a contagious disease to have healthy and cheerful men about him, but if the healthy man catch the disease, both are worse off in the long run. At the present time the thoroughly unskilled Jacks-of-all trades, the men who are chronically unemployed, act as a terrible deadweight upon the working population of the United States. These men driven by the pangs of hunger accept work at any price and thus break down the scale painfully built up by workmen, so that their poverty, distress and chronic unemployment become contagious and others are reduced to their level. This vast army of men, many of them half supported by charity, many of them living below the standard of any reasonable human being are employed, at least partially, during the good times, and at all times are used to break down the wage scale and lower the standard of living of the more efficient workmen. In this respect they may be likened to the state-supported convict, the product of whose work in the prison shop lowers the wages of free men regularly employed. It is largely from the ranks of the entirely unorganized and partially subsidized workers that the professional strike-breaker is drawn.

Trade unionism will, it is to be hoped, eventually teach society its full lesson in this matter. The progress of trade unionism means the comparative lessening of the group below the unions and the more obvious recognition of the fact that it consists of incapables. Trade unionism must continue to lift up this great submerged mass slowly and by degrees, and the remainder must be cared for by the State. There must be some method of relieving industry from this vast incubus. It would pay society to support every person who was found to be incapable of supporting himself, rather than to permit these men to secure a partial and incomplete living as at the present time. In its treatment of the very poor, society acts like the ostrich which buries its head in the sand; it attempts to remedy the evil by refusing to recognize it. Everybody in society must be supported in some way or other, and it would be far more economical to adopt a definite policy of isolating the incapables and supporting them in some manner or other than to allow them to be a drag on industry, to fill our sweat shops, to throng our streets needlessly selling needless articles, to beg, steal, or help build up the vicious, hoodlum element in our great cities. The problem can only be solved by an extension of trade unionism which raises one class after another from this mass by the insistence, through trade union action, upon a minimum wage and steady work, by a restriction of immigration to men, or to the families of men, capable of holding a steady job, and by a definite determined and courageous policy on the part of the State, looking towards its direct assumption of the burden of supporting these men, which burden must in all events fall upon the State in some form or other.

The elevation of these groups from the great mass of the unskilled and unorganized is shown in the development of federal unions organized by the American Federation of Labor. The federal union is the kindergarten of trade unionism. It is the ungraded school in which miscellaneous workmen of all sorts combine and from which group after group is raised and organized into separate and independent unions. Just as the separate unions grow out of federal unions, so do groups of organized workmen grow out of the great mass of the unorganized and unskilled.

It is frequently predicted that the success of trade unions in organizing unskilled workmen is only temporary and that the result of bad times will be to destroy the new unions. There is some truth in this statement, although it is greatly exaggerated and magnified. With every advent of bad times, a number of the unions which have grown up during the preceding periods of prosperity, fall to the ground, yet, nevertheless, the progress made is not entirely lost. It is of benefit to a man to *have* belonged to a union, even though that union subsequently die. The ideals once implanted in the breast of a man by his trade union live longer than the union itself. Moreover, while unions of unorganized workmen are frequently weak internally and are subject to dissolution in times of prolonged depression, these organizations grow stronger with each decade. As it advances, so does the wave recede, but at each recession the low water mark is at a higher level. The unions which might have been destroyed by a commercial depression twenty years ago would have survived one ten years ago, and many which would have died ten years ago would survive a commercial depression to-day. There are unions which will go to pieces with the next commercial depression which, formed again, will in the not remote future become sufficiently strong and stable to withstand any possible crisis or depression.

Trade unionism advances by an advance of all its parts. The men who once stood on the lowest rung of the trade union ladder have mounted higher, and, in turn, have made room for men from lower ranks of life. With each succeding decade, other sections of workingmen from lower and lower ranks of industrial life will advance toward trade unionism and will form unions, which with the progress of years, will gradually grow in strength and increase in stability.

In this advance the members of the trade union world should act as a unit. By means of the label and the boycott, by moral and financial support during strikes, by sympathy and encouragement at all times, the more skilled workmen can aid the less skilled and can indirectly promote their own welfare by promoting the welfare of their less fortunate brethren.

CHAPTER XXI

THE IMMIGRANT AND THE LIVING WAGE

Enormous Influx of Immigrants. 857,000 in One Year. The Promised Land and the Millions of Europe. Ebb and Flow of the Tide. Change in the Source of Immigration. The Nationality of Immigrants. Where the Immigrants Go and What they Do. The Congestion of Cities. Opportunities for Immigrants. The Good Side of Immigration. The Evil Side. Regulation Not Prohibition. The Immigration of Contract Laborers. Chinese Immigration and Chinese Exclusion. Illiteracy. Assisted Immigration. The Foreign Born Citizens of the United States. Immigration and the Living Wage. Immigration and Trade Unionism. The Lowering of Wages. Immigration and Bad Times. The Broadening Waves of Influence. Restriction without Prejudice and without Hatred. The Welfare of America and the Good of All Nations.

THE present year has witnessed an immigration to this country greater than any that has ever occurred in the history of any nation. During the year ending June 30, 1903, eight hundred and fifty-seven thousand people from various parts of the world landed at the ports of the United States and either settled in the sea-board cities or made their way into the interior. At no time in the history of the world has a movement of such stupendous proportions taken place. The immigrants to this country in the single year 1903 were probably much in excess of the total number of arrivals in the present territory of the United States during the two centuries from 1607 to 1820.

The movement of immigrants from Europe to the United States during the last three generations has dwarfed by comparison all former movements of populations. During this period over twenty million immigrants have landed on these shores. These men, hailing from all the countries of Europe and of the world, have peopled the vast territory of the United States, have intermarried with one another and with the native stock, and have formed the American nation as it exists to-day. In the cities of our sea-board, in the Middle West, on the trans-Mississippi prairies, and through-

LABELS OF THE DIFFERENT TRADES UNIONS

CHILD WORKERS IN THE SOUTHERN COTTON MILLS

out the broad expanse of our North-west, in almost every state north of Mason and Dixon's line, and extending from the Atlantic to the Pacific, large sections of the population are either foreign born or the children of immigrants. In the year 1900 there were over ten million persons in the United States of foreign birth and over twenty-six million of foreign birth or foreign parentage. About two-fifths of all the white inhabitants of the United States are the sons or daughters of parents one or both of whom are foreign born. These immigrants and children of immigrants represent some of the best elements in the American population, and the American citizens of foreign birth and parentage are, on an average, as patriotic, as loyal, and as valuable citizens as those of native ancestry.

The tide of immigration to the United States has had many ebbs and flows. Immigration has steadily increased, reaching a maximum point in periods of prosperity and falling off greatly in periods of depression In the year 1854, immigration reached a high water mark with the arrival of four hundred and twenty-eight thousand immigrants, and in 1882 seven hundred and eighty-nine thousand landed. This point was not again reached until the present year, 1903, when eight hundred and fifty-seven thousand immigrants arrived.

Within the last two decades a change has taken place in the character of immigration, which in the eyes of many people portends evil for American workmen. In the early years of immigration, when it was difficult, if not actually dangerous, to come to the United States, there was a natural selection of the best and hardest inhabitants of the old world, men willing to risk their all in going to a new country. The greater ease and cheapness of transportation have now given a stimulus to large classes of persons who in former years could not have come. The cost of transportation and the time required have, upon the whole, been reduced, and the sources of immigration have also shifted. Formerly, the great majority of immigrants came from England, Ireland, Germany, and the Scandinavian countries, from countries, in other words, where conditions of life and labor were, to some extent, comparable to those of the United States. At the present time, the source of immigration has shifted from northern and western to eastern and southern Europe, and from men with a higher to men with a lower standard of living. I do not desire to state that the moral character and mental capacity of the new immigrants are lower than those of the immigrants of former days; but it is quite clear that the standard of living has been reduced in consequence of the change in the source of immigration from countries in which wages are high to countries in which wages are low. The amount of money which the average immigrant brings with him has steadily decreased, and the immigrant from southern and eastern countries has, at the start, a smaller sum to protect him from starvation or the sweatshop than has the immigrant from northern or western Europe. The illiteracy of the immigrant has also become more pronounced. This illiteracy, amounting in some cases from sixty-five to seventy-five per cent., debars the newly arrived immigrant from many trades, makes it more difficult for him to adapt himself to American conditions and American manners of thought, and renders it almost inevitable that he fall into the hands of the sweater and exploiter. The efforts made by steamship companies to incite and over-stimulate the immigration of thousands of illiterate peasants tend to inject unnaturally into the American labor market a body of men unskilled, untrained, and unable to resist oppression and reduced wages.

The practically unrestricted immigration of the present day is an injustice both to the American workingman, whether native or foreign-born, and to the newly landed immigrant himself. As a result of this practically unrestricted and unregulated immigration, the congestion of our large cities is so intense as to create abnormally unhealthy conditions. In New York, which has at present a foreign-born population of over one and one-quarter millions, the congestion has resulted in the erection of enormous tenement buildings, in the fearful overcrowding of the slums, and in the normal presence of an over-supply of unskilled labor. The arrival in great numbers of immigrants without knowledge of English, without the ability to read or write the language of their own country, without money, and sometimes without friends, renders it inevitable that they accept the first work offered them. The average immigrant from eastern and southern Europe brings with him from eight to ten dollars, which is about the railroad fare from New York to Pittsburg and is hardly sufficient to support him for two weeks. It is inevitable, also, that he remain where he lands and take the work offered him on the spot. The result is a supply of labor in the large cities in excess of a healthy demand, and a consequent lowering of wages, not only in the cities in which the immigrants remain, but in those in which the articles are produced that compete with the sweat-shop products.

From the point of view of the great employers of labor there is an apparent advantage in keeping the doors wide open. The great manufacturers of the country, while anxious to shut out the products of the pauper labor of Europe, desire to have as much cheap labor within their own factories as possible. The great mine owners have eagerly taken advantage of the ever-flowing current of low-priced labor, not only to reduce wages, but to hold this reserve army of unskilled workers as a club over the head of the great mass of employees. The immigrant, who comes here in the hope of bettering his condition, is subjected to the exhausting work of the sweat shop, is forced to toil excessively long hours under unsanitary conditions, or is compelled to perform work under the *padrone* system, and is liable to be exploited and defrauded in many ways. The apprenticeship of the newly arrived immigrant is hard indeed, but it could very well be remedied if the state should so regulate immigration as to enable the newcomer to protect himself from extortion and exploitation.

The extent to which immigration, if unrestricted, might go was foreshadowed by the influx of Chinese which began about a generation ago. For a number of years the doors of the United States were thrown wide open to the importation of immigrants, practically, if not legally, under contract, from a country with a population of four hundred millions. The result of this immigration was seen in a reduction of the wages of labor upon the Pacific coast; and there can be no doubt that the admission of Chinese, if unchecked, would have resulted in the creation of an enormous Mongolian population in our West and the practical industrial subjugation of that portion of the country by the Chinese. It is a well-known fact that the cheaper worker, when he is able to compete tends to drive out the better, just as in the currency of a nation, bad money will drive out good money. Through the activity of the trade unions, however, the Chinese, were in 1882, excluded and in 1902 this law was reënacted.

The trade unions also secured in the year 1885 the enactment of a law rendering illegal the importation of workmen under contract. Formerly, in the case of a strike, the employer was able to contract for the importation of large numbers of foreigners, who, with lower ideals and without any knowledge of American trade unionism, took the places of the strikers and effectually aided the employer. The trade unions have also been energetic in their attempts to secure a further regulation of the conditions of immigration in such a manner that both the present inhabitants of the United States and the immigrants who come, will be in a better position to resist exploitation by employers in the sweated or unskilled trades.

The attitude of trade unionists upon this question favors not prohibition, but regulation. The trade unions do not desire to keep out immigrants but to raise the character and the power of resistance of those who do come. There is no racial or religious animosity in this attitude of unionists. The American trade unionist does not object to the immigration of men of a high standard of living, whether they be Turks, Russians, or Chinese, Catholics, Protestants or Jews, Mohammedans, Buddhists, or Confucians, whether they be yellow, white, red, brown, or black. In certain cases, as in that of the Chinese, it was absolutely essential to the success of the law that it discriminate against the whole nation, but the attitude of the unionist was not hostility to the Chinaman, but a determination to resist the immigration of men with a low standard of living.

The trade unionist believes that the policy of regulating immigration is justifiable on both ethical and economic grounds. It is admitted that the immigration of the past has to a large extent and for a long period benefited the American workingman. Especially was this true during the period before the public domain was exhausted, when men could secure a homestead for the asking. The trade unionist also realizes that a large percentage of the most worthy citizens, and probably a majority of the white manual laborers of the United States, are either foreigners or sons of foreigners. The American unionist sympathizes with the oppressed workingmen of foreign countries and feels that everything should be done to ameliorate their condition, provided it does not hinder the progress of the nation and the welfare of the human race. Cosmopolitanism, like charity, begins at home. The American people should not sacrifice the future of the working classes in order to improve the conditions of the inhabitants of Europe, and it is even questionable whether an unregulated immigration would improve the conditions of Europe and Asia, although it is certain that it would injure and degrade the conditions of labor in this country.

This point might be illustrated by the supposition of an unrestricted immigration from China. That country has a population of about four hundred millions and a probable birth rate of about twelve millions a year. It is quite conceivable with unrestricted immigration and with the cheapening of fares from Hong Kong to San Francisco that within fifty or a hundred years a third of the people of the United States could be Chinese, without in any way reducing the population of China. The creation of an outlet for a million or two millions of Chinese immigrants each year would merely have the effect of increasing the birth rate in that country, with the result that within a century a majority of the working people of this country would be Chinese, while the congestion of population in the Celestial empire would be as great and as unrelieved as ever. To a large extent the progress of nations can best be secured by the policy of seclusion and isolation. By means of barriers which regulate, but do not prohibit, immigration, the various countries of Europe and America can individually work out their salvation, and a permanent increase in the efficiency and remuneration of the workers of the world can thus be obtained. By the maintenance of these barriers the best workingmen in each country can rise to the top, and the great mass of the workingmen can secure a larger share of the wealth produced. If, however, it is within the power of employers to draw freely upon the labor of the world, while protecting their products from the competition of foreign manufacturers, the result will be that the workingmen of the world will have their wages reduced, or, at all events, will not have their remuneration increased, as would be possible under a policy regulating the importation of immigrants.

The trade union desires to regulate immigration partly in order to prevent the temporary glutting of the market, but to a much greater extent in order to raise the character of the men who enter. The glutting of the labor market through immigration is, I believe, temporary, and not permanent. It causes a temporary over-supply of labor in the large cities, a breaking down of favorable working conditions, a disintegration of trade unions, and a wide-spread deterioration and degradation in large circles of the community. Gradually, however, the market absorbs the fresh supply of labor, and the newly arrived immigrants create a demand for the products of their own work. While this temporary glutting of the market is disadvantageous and may result in a deterioration of the calibre of the workingman, the injury that comes from permitting the inflow of vast bodies of men with lower standards of living is infinitely worse. The policy of trade unions in this matter of immigration is in perfect harmony with other features of trade union government. Trade unionism seeks not to restrict the numbers, but to raise the quality, of workingmen. Any one may become a bricklayer in New York city, whether there be a hundred, a thousand, or five thousand, but whosoever enters the trade as a unionist must agree not to accept less than a certain rate and must, therefore, be an efficient worker with a high standard of life. The American workingman believes that there is ample room in this country for all men who are able and willing to demand wages commensurate with the American standard of living.

By a wise policy of restriction of immigration and by a careful sifting of immigrants according to their ability to earn and demand high wages, the country would secure annually, let us say, two or three or four hundred thousand good immigrants, instead of being forced to absorb, as at present, six or eight or ten hundred thousand immigrants, many of them undesirable. The result of this policy might lead eventually even to an actual increase in the number of immigrants, owing to the fact that if there were a wise selection of immigrants with a high standard of living, wages in the United States would rise to a point which would attract the most capable workmen of all Europe. A contingency of this sort would be looked forward to with hope rather than with apprehension, since the American nation need never fear the immigration of Europeans so long as that immigration does not involve or threaten a reduction in the standard of living.

The competition of the immigrant with a low standard of living, is felt not only in the trade, wherein the immigrant is employed, but in all the trades of the country. The immigrant, with his low rate of wages, drives out of his trade men formerly employed therein, who are either forced down in the scale of wages or else obliged to compete for work in higher occupation, where they again reduce wages. Thus the effect of the competition of immigrants is felt not only in the unskilled, but also in the semi-skilled and skilled trades, and even in the professions. The immigration of great bodies of unskilled workmen, moreover, of various races tends to promote and perpetuate racial antagonisms, and these racial jealousies are played upon by employers in the attempt to reduce wages, to prevent the formation of trade unions, and to keep the workmen apart.

I do not desire in this book to outline what I consider reasonable measures of regulation for the ever-rising tide of immigration. The American Federation of Labor has done excellent work in advocating wise measures, and the work should be continued along these lines. Restriction, however, should be without prejudice and without hatred. It should be as much in the interest of the immigrants as in the interest of the American citizens of to-day, whether of native or of foreign birth. Restriction should be democratic in its character, and should not exclude any man capable of earning his livelihood in America at the standard union rate of wages. It should not be directed by racial animosity or religious prejudice, and the laws that are passed should protect the immigrant from deception by steamship or employment agents, as well as protect the home population from undesirable immigrants. The law should be so arranged as not needlessly to separate members of the same family. Finally, trade unionists in their advocacy of immigration should not be actuated by a short-sighted policy, but by a consideration of the probable effect that such restriction will have upon the future prosperity of the working classes or of Americans in general.

The task which trade unions have accomplished in securing and enforcing laws regulating immigration has been hardly more important than their excellent work in raising the tone and increasing the efficiency of the immigrant upon his arrival. More than any other single factor, except the common school, the trade union has succeeded in wiping out racial animosities, in uniting men of different nationalities, languages, and religions, and in infusing into the newly landed immigrant American ideals and American aspirations. The United Mine Workers of America, for instance, has had marvellous success in creating harmony and good feeling among its members, irrespective of race, religion, or nationality. The meetings of the locals are attended by members of different races and are addressed in two, three, or even more languages. The constitution and by-laws of the organization are printed in nine different languages, and by means of interpreters all parts of the body are kept in touch with one another, with the result that a feeling of mutual respect and confidence is promoted.

Breaker Boys at Work

Typical Row of Company Houses in an Anthracite Village

The fences are usually made by the miners themselves, to protect their gardens

In no other country have trade unions had to face a problem of such enormous difficulty as the fusion of the members of these various nationalities, crude, unformed, and filled with old-world prejudices and antipathies. No higher tribute can be paid to American trade unions than an acknowledgment of the magnificent work which they have accomplished in this direction in obliterating the antagonisms bred in past centuries and in creating out of a heterogeneous population, brought together by the everlasting search for cheap labor, a unified people with American ideals and American aspirations.

CHAPTER XXII

ORGANIZED LABOR AND ORGANIZED CAPITAL

Organization of Capital a Justification of Trade Unionism. Capital Follows the Lead of Labor. Principles, Purposes, and Tactics those of Labor Unions. The General Strike and the General Lockout. The Sympathetic Strike and the Sympathetic Lockout. Disciplining the "Non-Union Employer." Internal Dissension in Organizations of Employers. Less Loyal than Workingmen. Labor Unions not Opposed to Unions of Employers. "The Recognition of the Union" of Employers. Advantage of Concerted Action on both Sides. Employers' Associations Unincorporated. Hostile Employers' Associations and the "Un-American Institution of Trade Unionism." Insurance against Strikes. Peace between Organized Labor and Organized Capital.

PERHAPS the fullest recognition of the power and necessity of trade unions is furnished by the organization of employers. Just as labor was obliged to organize in order to secure fair terms from capital, so employers have found it advantageous to form themselves into associations in order to adjust their relations with their workmen.

In the matter of organization workingmen took the initiative and trade unions originated before associations of employers. In fact, the trade unions were largely instrumental in calling employers' associations into being. This earlier formation of trade unions was due to the greater feeling of solidarity and brotherhood among wage earners, and the unorganized employers found themselves at a disadvantage in their dealings with their organized workmen. The first associations of employers, like the first associations of workingmen, were temporary in character and intended to meet special emergencies. Gradually, however, employers learned a lesson from their workmen, and groups or associations of manufacturers and other employers became a fixed institution. Many of these associations enforced discipline by securing from each member a deposit of funds and by fining some for disobedience to their rules and indemnifying others for losses incurred in strikes declared against them. In many other ways the associations of employers pursued tactics which had been a feature of trade union policy. In the case of a threatened dispute between one of their members and his workmen, the associations of employers investigated it and decided upon the justice and wisdom of his position and whether or not they would support him in his contest. In other cases, where an attack was made upon a single firm, all other members of the association were ordered to lock out their employees, whether or not there were grievances against these employees. Instead of the system of picketing and boycotting adopted by workingmen, the associations of employers occasionally resorted to the blacklist, sending notices broadcast for the purpose of preventing the employment of striking or locked-out workmen; and while employers now frequently criticise union men for applying opprobrious epithets to non-unionists who, during a strike, have entered the field and taken away their means of livelihood, the jealousy and hatred aroused among employers when a concern turns traitor resolves itself into curses as loud and as deep.

In one respect associations of employers are stronger than trade unions. The former have the advantage of greater wealth and therefore greater power of resistance, and by reason of their restricted numbers, can act with more secrecy than organizations of workingmen. Notwithstanding these advantages, however, the associations of employers, when they are not a trust or a monopoly, have invariably proved to be weaker than associations of workingmen. They have had the same or even greater power of disciplining the non-union or "scab" employer by expulsion or otherwise, and they have been able to use the power of ostracism to reenforce pecuniary penalties, but in spite of this, these associations have frequently broken down or been entirely debilitated by internal dissensions and trade jealousies. Whatever employers may say about the irresponsibility and unreliability of workmen and trade unions, it cannot be denied that the superior strength of trade unions, even without funds, over associations of employers with all manner of financial backing, is due to the fact that the workingmen show better faith and more honor in their dealings with one another than do employers in their associations.

Unions should not adopt an antagonistic policy towards organizations of employers, unless such organizations show themselves distinctly and unmistakably hostile to labor. It is, of course, natural that where trade unionists are assailed they should endeavor, as far as possible, to limit the power and avert the blows of their assailants; but in a general way the trade union, in the matter of friendliness to employers' associations, sets an example to the employers which the latter could advantageously follow. There are many employers who refuse to deal with trade unions because they render labor more formidable and, possibly, more exacting, even though they realize that the effect of trade unionism is also to make the men more reasonable and more conservative. Trade unions recognize that an association of employers is better able to combat them than a number of individual competing employers; but they also recognize that the association is, as a rule, more responsible, more conservative and better disposed than the individual employers of whom it is composed. The incentive to oppress labor is less strong and less direct. It is an undoubted fact that many an employer would be willing to do things in his own shop or mine which he would hesitate to submit as a proposed plan of action to the members of his association. In many cases, organizations of employers can, by the very fact of their association, make concessions to their workmen which none of the individual employers could separately have made. It frequently occurs that no one employer will raise wages because of the competition of other employers, whereas if all are united into a single organization, it is possible for them to make this concession simultaneously.

In stating that trade unionists should not adopt an antagonistic attitude toward organizations of employers, it is not meant that they should not take such means of defense against aggressive organizations as they may deem fit and proper. Where an association of employers is formed which has for its object the rooting out or crushing of trade unionism, the unions would be perfectly justified in meeting attack with attack. If an organization specifically urges that "employers' associations set about the task of pulling up root and branch the un-American institution of trade unionism as at present conducted,"[1] it may fairly be said that it does not invite and will not receive the hearty cooperation of trade unionists. I do not believe that any such association, even if formed with an avowedly hostile policy toward unions, will, in the long run, do any thing but good for the trade union movement. An association of employers that does not recognize the essential merits and advantages of trade unions, but seeks to destroy or injure them, will sooner or later be confronted with the absolute undesirability and impossibility of the attainment of its aims and will either change its attitude or cease to exist. Some of these organizations, instituted originally for the purpose of "fighting labor," have been persuaded by the logic of circumstances into adopting at first a tolerant and, finally, a distinctly friendly attitude.

In many cases the hostility of associations, as of individual employers, is concealed under the guise of a plan or program apparently for their own protection, but really directed against labor organizations. For some time past, there has been considerable talk in capitalistic circles of a system of strike insurance by which employers could be insured against, and compensated for, the losses occasioned by strikes. This is, of course, merely an extension of the general idea of insurance. The plan has been recommended by a number of newspapers, including several insurance journals, and according to the public press it appears that a company has already been organized for the purpose of insuring employers against strikes.

Three arguments may be urged in opposition to such a plan: first, that it is impracticable; second, that it would fail to fulfill its purpose; and finally,

---

[1] Quoted from the Annual Report of the President of the National Association of Manufacturers of the United States of America, April, 1903. Its President, Mr. D. M. Parry, goes on to say that the attack should be made not against "unions in themselves" but against modern trade unionism.

that it would probably lead to unfairness and to evils worse than those which it sought to remedy. A company of this nature would have to be mutual, since if it were a company for profit, it would be perfectly possible for adverse unions to destroy it if they so desired. Whether it were mutual or not, however, there would always be dissension, as between employers in various trades. A hardware store does not desire to assume the same risk against fire as a manufacturer of chemicals or the owner of a powder mill; and the stove manufacturers, who have had hardly a strike for twenty years, would not be willing to insure against strikes on the same basis as the building contractors. There would be constant internal trouble with regard to the fixing of assessments and premiums and the determination of both the physical and moral risks. As in fire insurance, many risks are refused, because the proprietor is believed to be willing to burn down his own place, so it would always be necessary to exclude from strike insurance men who would wish to have strikes and be compensated for them. Many men who would not commit arson would willingly incite strikes at their own works, and it would be precisely those industries and precisely those employers who were most fractious and strike loving who would most desire insurance. When one imagines the effect of such a strike as the anthracite suspension of 1902 upon an insurance company of this character, however large its capital, the utter impracticability of the plan will be realized. At the first call for assessments the membership of the company would rapidly disappear. Moreover, such an organization, if hostile to labor, would necessarily be secret, since otherwise its members could be punished by strikes or possibly ruined by boycotts. Even if such an insurance company were practicable, it would not work for social equity, because it would tend to support strong rather than just employers.

Trade unions are not averse to an insurance of employers of one trade by employers in the same trade, since in this development they see nothing but an association of employers banded together for mutual defense and acting on the same principle as the trade unions. It is true that trade unions may be antagonistic to certain individual associations of employers on account of their expressed or covert hostility, but it is merely because of this hostility and not because of the organization or mutual insurance itself, that the unions feel resentment. Anything which aims to make employers act harmoniously in labor matters and to assume moral or even financial responsibility for each other's action, is a step in the direction of a final settlement of the labor problem. I do not believe, however, that a general association of all employers is any more practicable than a general association of all workingmen. On the contrary, I believe that the most effective organizations of either employers or employees are those which limit their membership to a given trade or industry; and I do not regard general insurance of employers against strikes as any more practicable than general insurance of workmen against lockouts or reductions in wages.

In the case of employers, organization will have the same tendency to widen and strengthen moral responsibility as it has had among workmen. It frequently happens in a strike that some of the employers struck against are men who have always treated their employees fairly and for whom their work people entertain the highest feelings of regard and affection. This is unfortunate, but in many cases inevitable. The position of the employer who thus suffers for the transgressions or omissions of his fellow-employers, is identical with that of the workman who may be locked out on account of the actions of other workmen over whom he has no direct control. In many cases a strike or a lockout to be effective must involve the whole industry. The good employer who suffers thereby cannot secure relief because of his having treated his workmen fairly, but is held responsible by the course of events for the actions of other employers. In industry, as in life generally, it does not suffice that a man keep his own skirts clean. The tendency of such strikes, however, is to create among employers a recognition of the necessity of united action and a feeling on their part of solidarity and of responsibility for one another, as well as a determination upon the part of good employers that their fellow-employers shall maintain the same fair conditions that they themselves maintain. In the agreements between the bituminous coal miners and operators, every effort is made by employers to raise the standard of fellow-employers and by employees to raise the standard of fellow-employees. The trade union and the association of employers, the representatives of organized labor and organized capital, acting together in a trade agreement, thus work for a higher and broader justice than could be attained by a series of independent and separate contracts between individual employers and individual workmen.

The attitude of organized workingmen should not be, and as a rule is not, hostile to the organization of employers. True, rare instances occur of trade unions, generally in the hey-day of their youth and inexperience, assuming a superior attitude, refusing to have anything to do with associations of employers, and insisting upon treating with their employers "as individuals." Nothing could be more subversive of union ideals, nothing more contrary to union traditions. Workingmen in asserting their right to combine are obliged, by the logic of their own demands, to concede an equal right to employers. The associations of employers have resulted from the formation of unions of workmen, and each organization should be of benefit to the other. Harmony in the industrial world will be best obtained by the creation and strengthening of labor unions and employers' associations, and by the inculcation of a permanently friendly feeling between organized labor and organized capital.

One of the most potent influences in establishing amicable relations between organized labor and organized capital has been the National Civic Federation. This Federation, composed of the leading public-spirited citizens of the country, has, through its industrial branch, attempted with much success to create friendly relations between employer and employee. The Federation has upon its various committees members representing the employers, the workmen, and the general public, so that the interests of all are conserved and the interests of none, sacrificed. The Federation has

Worst Class of Miners' Houses in Anthracite Region

The newly arrived immigrants usually occupy these dwellings. The kitchen is on the left

This miner's home, propped up to keep it from falling, is valued at about $10, but the tenant pays $2.25 per month rent

been eminently successful in a number of attempts to create better feeling and to avert strikes, and as long as it pursues its present policy, it will undoubtedly continue to deserve and receive the hearty support of the community.

Of late certain sections of the public have scented danger in the possibility of this friendly feeling leading up to an offensive coalition of organized labor and organized capital against the general public. If, it is claimed, the unions agree to work for no other than employers organized into associations, and if these employers agree to hire none but union men, the inevitable result will be that non-union men and independent employers will be crushed out. As a consequence, competition, which is the life of trade, will cease to exist, and a reign of extortionate prices and unreasonable charges will be inaugurated. It is claimed that such coalitions already exist and that by means of combinations between furnishers of raw material, manufacturers of the finished product, and organizations of workmen, the public is forced to pay higher prices than are reasonable or just.

Notwithstanding these fears, combinations of labor and of capital are not fraught with danger to the public. There may occasionally arise coalitions which temporarily extort undue and unusual profits, but such a policy cannot be permanently successful. The mutual recognition of the employers' and employees' associations and the agreement by these associations not to employ or be employed by any except members, are not dangerous, but are actually beneficial as long as both the union and the employers' association keep their doors open to the admission of new members. In the coal industry any man who has a mine may open it and may join the coal operators' association, and any man who wishes to become a miner may join the organization and obtain employment. Where a different policy is pursued it will sooner or later be broken down. If employers cannot enter the associations on fair and equal terms, and if workmen cannot get into the unions under reasonable conditions, the result will be a building up of new associations of non-association employers, operating with non-union men, who will be able to compete upon equal terms with the closed corporations employing union labor.

I do not believe, however, that this policy of extortion will be tried upon any large scale. While, to further their own ends, officials of the union may consent to a plan of this sort, the great body of union members will not willingly lend themselves to a clique of employers, and any attempt to create and perpetuate a monopoly of this sort will be quickly frustrated.

It is my firm conviction and, what is more important, it is the conviction of a great majority of the workmen of this country, that no such coalition of organized labor and organized capital can or will permanently exploit the public. The ideal of trade unionism, however, will be attained when a strong organization, supplied with an ample reserve fund and embracing every workman in the trade, will find itself face to face with an equally strong association of employers embracing every employer in the trade. The two will then meet upon the basis of absolute equality. The result of such a state of affairs, which we are now rapidly approaching, will be that without incorporation, whether of the trade union or the association of employers, the agreements arrived at will be kept inviolate; and thus strikes and lockouts, with their attendant sufferings and losses, will be reduced to a minimum, and peace and prosperity firmly established in American industry.

CHAPTER XXIII

THE UNION AND THE TRUST

The Growth of Trusts. Their Origin and Nature. Industrial Combinations. Trusts and Public Opinion. Trusts from the Standpoint of the Consumer, the Investor, and the Workingman. The Trust and the Cost of Production. Trusts and Workmen. Trust Prices and the Cost of Living to the Poor. Trusts and Wages. Trusts and the Organization of Labor. The Phantom of a "Labor Trust." Are Trade Unions Monopolies? The Anti-Trust Law. Trusts and Publicity.

THE most striking feature of present day industry is the trust. During recent years there has been a sudden, rapid growth of industrial combinations upon a scale wholly unprecedented and hitherto unimagined. These gigantic corporations, with capital stock aggregating, in some cases, hundreds of millions or even a billion of dollars, have completely transformed and revolutionized industrial conditions. The competition of former times has given way to combination, consolidation, and "community of interest," and for good or for evil, the old order has changed, giving place to the new.

This rapid development of gigantic corporations, controlling a large proportion of the output of industry, has given rise to the wildest fears and the most sanguine hopes. Upon the one hand, there are regrets for the passing of a former period of competition and fears of what the new era may bring forth. The trusts are assailed because of their largeness and their power. It is alleged against them that they adopt secret and unscrupulous methods, that they secure rebates, mercilessly crush out rivals, deprive thousands of their livelihood, indulge in wild-cat financiering, charge extortionate prices, defraud and mulct investors, corrupt legislatures, and in every way imperil the rights and liberties of the American people. On the other hand, there is unbounded hope and unlimited confidence in the new combinations, and the trusts are lauded for producing needful articles in a more economical manner than heretofore, for doing away with ruinous competition, for substituting a responsible concern for a number of less trustworthy separate or independent companies, and for introducing modern methods into the conduct and management of business.

Whatever the advantages or disadvantages, the merits or faults of trusts as they exist to-day, it is inevitable that industrial combinations continue to exist. The industrial organizations of the future may not be run in the same way, or with the same freedom, or for the same purposes as at the present time, and it is probable that eventually they will be under a more effective control by the government. Some form of industrial combination, however, is inevitable. The system of competition, which for many decades reigned supreme, has now to a certain extent destroyed itself, or rather has changed its scope and its direction. Free and uncontrolled competition has in many phases of industrial life been weighed in the balance and found wanting. It is now seen that in the case of railroads, street railways, telegraph, telephone, gas works, and many other industries, men will not compete where they can combine. Competition in many industries has proved itself wasteful. It has led to the wildest excesses of production, has created alternating periods of exaggerated prosperity and extreme depression, and has forced men to produce in the dark, to furnish the supply without being able to calculate the demand.

The great industrial combinations, if properly organized, would have a number of advantages. They could purchase their raw material in much larger quantities, or could themselves produce it. They could also sell their articles in the same wholesale manner and, therefore, more cheaply and more intelligently. The production of the country, both as to quantity and quality, could be regulated according to the demand, and the factories or mills might be situated in the locality most advantageous for supplying the market. Operating expenses could be reduced in consequence of the volume of business, and the entire industry, if controlled by one organization, could wisely regulate conditions of production so as to decrease the effect of any depression. Further, a corporation controlling a given industry could carry on experiments, install expensive machinery, and equip its factories in a manner impossible to a single competing firm. It could specialize its products, initiate new methods of production, and, by reason of its very largeness, could protect and insure itself against fire, or against any other wide-spread calamity. The absence of competition would save the corporation from the necessity of making unprofitable sales or accepting bad credits, and would allow a better adjustment and adaptation of the products to the needs of the community. The advantage which a large concern now has over a small one would accrue in still greater measure to a well-managed industrial combination controlling the whole industry. The larger the plant and the greater the number of plants, the greater is the opportunity for comparative tests of methods, for a wisely regulated *competition within the combination*, and, in general, for a more efficient management of the whole plant. An intelligently directed industrial combination could reduce prices, insure a safe investment for the savings of the people, pay high wages, and grant favorable conditions of labor, while, at the same time, paying to the men in charge munificent salaries for their services in creating and conducting the combination.

I have above described trusts as they might be, not as they are. The actual industrial combinations have not always effected every possible economy. They have been managed sometimes inefficiently, sometimes dishonestly; the individual manufacturer has in many cases been supplanted by an official with no interest in the establishment; and the profits derived from large combinations have frequently been diverted from the stockholders to the pockets of an inside ring. Many of these combinations have been enormously over-capitalized, and the profits of future years have been monopolized in advance by the promoters of the trust. In many cases, the trusts have shirked the publicity which they owed to the public, and in a number of instances they have shown a hostility to the workingmen and to labor organizations as short-sighted as their other methods of obtaining temporary gain at the expense of permanent advantage.

The trust question is not whether we shall have industrial combinations but how, in what manner, and to what extent, trusts shall be regulated by the government. The anti-trust laws and other measures directed against combinations in restraint of trade or of competition are reactionary and utterly futile. We can no more stop the tendency toward industrial combination than we can sweep back the waves of the sea. The continued existence of industrial combinations in some form or other is absolutely assured, but the question agitating the people is the amount of control which the public shall maintain over these organizations and the proper manner of directing their gigantic activities into profitable and beneficent channels.

There are three points of view from which the trust question may be approached—those of the investor, the consumer, and the wage earner. The investor realizes that in some form or other, whether he invests in the stocks of industrial combinations, in the savings bank, or in life insurance, his capital must eventually be invested in the industries of the country. The proper management of industrial combinations affects the rate of interest upon, and the security of, all investments, in whatever form they are made, since the great bulk of the capital of the country must sooner or later be invested in industry, and the capital invested in other forms, such as houses, real estate, etc., will be affected by the rate of interest and the security of investments made in the great industries. Unfortunately it is a fact that even while the country is enjoying a period of unexampled prosperity, the ordinary man with small capital cannot, on account of the ignorance in which he is kept, obtain an opportunity for investment at once safe and remunerative. The man with small income is invited to invest his funds in large combinations many times over capitalized, only to find after a few years that dividends cease and the value of his dearly bought stock declines. The trust problem may also be approached from the point of view of the consumer. If the trust is enabled to secure economies in production, the result should be manifested in reduced prices. But it is felt that in the past this has not taken place to the extent which might have been expected. From the point of view of the wage earner, the trust problem is of interest, since the amalgamation of competing employers may have the effect of raising or lowering wages, of increasing or decreasing the field of employment, and of granting or withholding from the workingman a larger or smaller share in the determination of the conditions of his work.

The wage earners of the country are interested in the trust problem from all three points of view. They are interested to a slight extent as investors, to a greater extent as consumers, and to a still greater extent as wage earners. About one year ago, the United States Steel Corporation, doubtless with the best of motives, granted to its employees the right to purchase a certain amount of its preferred stock at $82.50 per share. Many workmen took advantage of this opportunity, under the belief that the stock they purchased would maintain, if not increase, its value. At the present time (September 28, 1903) this stock is selling for $59.25 per share, and, as a consequence, if one of these workmen were to sell his stock at market value he would receive $23.25 less per share than he paid for it.[1]

The workingmen of the country are interested in securing for themselves and other small investors an opportunity to place their savings in a reasonably secure and profitable manner, and any policy which looks toward rendering the attitude of trusts to their investors more responsible would receive the favor of the trade unions.

To a greater extent than ever before workingmen have become consumers upon a large scale, and as purchasers of trust goods, therefore, they are greatly interested in the trust problem. The wages of the workingman are measured in the final instance, not by the mere amount of money con-

---

[1] I do not mean to belittle the offer of the United States Steel Corporation. The proposition was doubtless generous and intended to benefit the men, but the fluctuations in the value of the stock, as a result of conditions over which the workmen had no control, indicate one of the worst features of coöperation.

tained in his envelope, but by what that money will buy. If the interests of the country are to be monopolized and to be beyond the control of the law, it is possible that, despite economy of production, prices will rise and the cost of living to workingmen be increased. Fear of potential competition may, perhaps, keep industrial combinations from unduly raising prices, and prices may be maintained at a low level in order to prevent other capital from entering the field. It is not wise or safe, however, to trust to the generosity or enlightened self-interest of the men in control of these industries, and the fullest publicity should be afforded, so that workingmen, as well as other citizens, may know what prices are being charged and what prices are reasonable.

The most vital interest of workingmen, particularly of organized workingmen, in the new industrial combinations, is the attitude which the trusts will adopt toward the men in their employ. Wages, it was once feared, would fall when the number of employers in a given industry was reduced by the formation of these industrial combinations, but this result is not inevitable, or even probable. The wages of workingmen are influenced, not by the number of employers, but by the amount of employment, and it is not probable that the amount of profitable employment will be decreased by the creation of combinations. Moreover, it has been feared that great bodies of men might be permanently displaced, but this dread also is not well founded. The creation of industrial combinations has the same effect upon the demand for labor as has the invention of machinery. It causes temporary displacements of labor, forces many men to lose their positions for the time being, but in the end does not apparently reduce the scope of, or opportunity for, employment.

A more reasonable fear entertained by the wage earners is that trusts, by reason of their enormous strength, may be able and willing to oppress the workingmen in their employ. There can be no doubt that the trusts are immensely stronger than the individual members entering the combination, since they have the advantage of unified management and are not deterred in a struggle with labor by fear of competitors. Moreover, where the trust has a number of plants, of which some are unionized and others not, it may play off the non-union shops against the union establishment, or pit one section against another. When in 1899 the men employed in the Colorado smelters struck for better conditions, the American Smelting and Refining Company temporarily transferred its production from its union to its non-union establishments, and the strike collapsed. During the course of the steel strike of 1901, the United States Steel Corporation simply concentrated its production in shops where the union was weak or non-existent, and even threatened to dismantle certain plants where the unionists were in control. The possibility of injuring or black-listing an individual employee, or group of employees, is also increased when the various establishments are under one management. In law, a blacklist does not exist unless there is a conspiracy of separate persons with the object of preventing a man from obtaining employment; but where all the opportunities of work are under the control of a single concern, the same result may be obtained without technical violation of the law.

The lesson which the labor union should learn from the trust is the absolute necessity of complete organization upon a national scale. No union has the slightest hope or chance of success in its struggle with a trust, unless it is completely organized and covers the whole field. Competition between the non-union and union establishments of a trust may be as severe and destructive to the wage scale and to union conditions of labor as competition of unionists and non-unionists within the same shop. A strike by a union against a trust which has non-union shops merely transfers the profits of the trust from one pocket to another and the wages of the men from the unionists on strike to the non-unionists not on strike. No union can effectively enforce proper conditions of work in an industry controlled by a trust, unless it is at least co-extensive with the trust itself.

The attitude of the great industrial combinations of the country is not yet sufficiently clear to enable one to prophesy with confidence as to the manner in which they will conduct themselves toward trade unionism. It is evident, however, that at least a large number of the men in control of industrial combinations are opposed to dealing or treating with labor organizations. This is unfortunate, not only for the labor union, but even more so for the trust. The trust, by reason of its comprising the great majority of the plants in the industry, is enabled to treat on more favorable terms with labor than could a separately competing manufacturer. The trust cannot refuse to raise wages or improve conditions by reason of the fear of competition, and it has the power of rendering any agreement that it makes with workingmen general and universal throughout the trade. On the other hand, by opposition to trade unionism, industrial combinations will endanger their own future. The public is beginning to realize that trade unions represent one of the chief bulwarks of democracy, and in a conflict between a trust, apparently autocratic, and a union of employees, struggling for democratic institutions, the sympathies of the public will be with the latter.

If it comes to a conflict between the trust in its present form and the labor union, the trust will not be the victor. It is possible, though, I think, not probable, that the trust might be able in a number of industries to root out the unions at least temporarily; but the victory would be a boomerang, which would rebound with destructive force against the conqueror. So long as workingmen in their trade unions can find a solution of the problems which beset them, just so long will they adopt the conservative and unaggressive policy toward industrial combinations which they have hitherto maintained. If, however, it were to be demonstrated that trusts were bent upon the destruction of the legitimate aspirations of workingmen, if it were once to be felt by the community that the trusts were tending to become autocratic and despotic rings of large capitalists, tyrannizing over and fleecing the men who provided the capital, the men who provided the labor, and the men who purchased the products, the reign of this class of leaders would be short-lived. I believe that in the long run nothing which obstructs the general will of the people of the United States can be maintained. The trusts must respect the interests of the workingmen, of the stockholders, and of the consumers, and if they fail to do so, if they antagonize all or any of these classes, their doom is absolutely and irrevocably sealed.

As before stated, I do not believe that the trusts should be proceeded against as trusts, or because they are trusts, but simply and solely in such a manner as to prevent abuses. Trusts are not bad because they prevent or change competition. As a matter of fact, they merely transform the field of competition from without to within the trust, and their potency for good, if well-managed, is almost immeasurable. The Anti-Trust Law of 1890 and other laws like it are blind, unthinking attempts to reconstruct conditions irredeemably gone. The fact that several of the anti-trust laws have been used against legitimate combinations of workingmen in no wise monopolistic, shows clearly that the very essence of this legislation is wrong.

The essential feature of trust legislation must be compulsory publicity. The old idea that a man's business is nobody else's business has been entirely exploded by the creation of trusts, the business of which vitally affects the welfare of every man in the community. The fullest light should be thrown upon these combinations, and the people of the United States should become thoroughly acquainted with their anatomy and physiology. Not only the amount and method of capitalization, the disposition of funds, the prices of raw materials, the cost of production, the amount of railroad charges, the rates of wages, but every other fact connected with the management of the business in any one of its details should be perfectly clear and manifest. The right of the government at any time to inspect any and all of the books of the trust, or those of any of its constituent companies, should be established and maintained. So long as we know what is happening within these huge combinations, to which we contribute our savings, devote our labor, and pay for our purchases, so long as we may inform ourselves upon each and every action taken by them, we need not fear the existence of great evils, or at least we may be assured of knowing how to correct them when they become apparent. The people of the United States, irrespective of party, should insist upon the fullest publicity being given to each and every act of each and every industrial combination, to the end that the interests of the investors, the interests of the consumers, and the interest of the wage earners be safeguarded.

It is claimed by many that the trade union is in itself a trust, and the phantom of a vast trust monopolizing the labor of the country has terrified a number of newspaper editors. If by this is meant that labor is organizing in such a manner as to deal collectively, it may freely be acknowledged. If, however, it is meant that trade unions are building up a monopoly, then it is entirely false.

Monopoly is the policy of the closed door with the monopolist and the key inside. The policy of trade unionism is the open door without a key. Trade unionism stands for unity and solidarity, but not for monopoly. A trade union is no more a monopoly than are the public schools, which any child may enter. Any wage earner who wishes to join a labor organization can do so upon practically the same terms as those upon which men already in were admitted; and the members who are now in will have no advantage over those who enter at any future time. The men who capitalized the Standard Oil Company are not willing that any other individual should buy their stock at the price which the originators of the company paid for it. No one may enter the company on the terms on which Mr. Rockefeller entered it. The great monopolies have capitalized their franchises and immersed them in water. The trade unions, on the contrary, have nothing which is not free to all, which may not be shared by any and every capable workman. The American unionists have invested in their organizations a large capital composed of gratuitous efforts and unrecorded sacrifices, but those who have been faithful from the beginning are willing to throw open the door to those who wish to enter at the eleventh hour. If this is monopoly, the enemies of unionism may make the most of it.

CHAPTER XXIV

UNIONS AND POLITICS

Political Methods and Industrial Methods. A Separate Labor Party Inadvisable. Concessions from the Dominant Parties. Labor Leaders in the Legislatures. Political Duties, not Political Preferment. The Advantage of Political Isolation. The Policy of Position grabbing. Its Dangers. The Necessity of a better Political Organization for Workingmen. Political Needs of Labor. Industrial Organization by Industries—Political Organization by Territorial Districts. The Strengthening of the American Federation. The State Federation and the City Central Bodies. Program and Propaganda. The Unionist at the Polls and in the Primaries. Summary.

TRADE unionism can secure its legitimate aims in two ways, by industrial methods, that is, by strikes, boycotts, or peaceable negotiation with employers, or by political methods, that is, by action on the part of the state.

Much controversy has arisen concerning the wisdom of the participation of trade unions in politics. The diversity of opinion concerning this matter is due to the vagueness of thought upon the whole subject. The very men who claim that unions should not engage in politics advocate, and actually secure, reforms through political action. The reason of this apparent discrepancy is that they do not distinguish between various kinds of political action. There are certain steps in politics which it would be wise for unions to take and other activities which all unions should avoid.

There can be no question of the advisability of unionists being represented in the councils of the nation. The only possible question is the method and manner of that representation. A certain section of the working class population believe that workingmen have interests that cannot be harmonized with those of other classes of society and that, as a consequence, a labor party should be created, which would devote itself entirely to the purpose of securing labor reforms. This plan of action might be advisable, if political conditions in America were like those in France or Germany, where the votes of the country are divided among a dozen or more different parties, each representing the interests of more or less distinct classes. In France, as in Germany, the welfare of the workingmen might perhaps be best conserved by the creation of a separate political party devoted exclusively to labor interests. Even though this party were not sufficiently strong to commit the government to a strictly labor policy, it might be powerful enough to secure, in conjunction with other parties, some measure of legislative protection for workingmen.

Conditions, however, in the United States, as apparently in England, are entirely different from those existing in France or Germany. In the United States, there are, practically speaking, but two parties, the Republican and the Democratic, and the entire electoral vote for the president is usually divided between these two. There are, of course, a number of other parties, such as the Socialist and the Prohibitionist, which poll each year a few thousands or scores of thousands of votes, but these parties are not sufficiently strong to obtain even a single electoral vote. The third parties which have arisen from time to time have either disappeared or been merged into other parties already existing, so that with but few exceptions, elections in the United States have been decided by the comparative strength of two contesting political parties. I do not wish to pass judgment upon this system, or to say whether or not the two-party system is advantageous. It appears, however, to be a permanent part of our political institutions. The effect of this two-party plan is to compel groups of men with special interests to seek concessions, not by direct action, but from one or the other of the two dominant parties. A strong, well-organized group of men determined upon a given line of policy can usually obtain either all or a portion of their demands from one or the other of the parties by maintaining neutrality between them. Each party is necessarily thrown upon the adherence of any large, compact, well-organized group of voters, and, as a rule, the group, if well-directed, can secure pledges and obtain their fulfillment. I therefore do not believe that for the present at least a third or labor party would be of benefit to the workingmen. Such a party, even if it secured the adherence of every organized worker in the United States, would not obtain a majority and could not, therefore, enforce its will upon the community at large. It is true that the presence in Congress of even a few men absolutely and completely committed to a distinct labor policy would be advantageous, since they would leaven the mass of legislators and would compel a vote and a show of hands upon any question involving the welfare of the laboring people. In my judgment, therefore, the wage earners should, in proportion to their strength, secure the nomination and election of a number of representatives to the governing bodies of city, state, and nation. And workingmen who are members of trade unions—whether they be laymen or officers—should be appointed to fill such positions as Commissioner of Labor, Commissioner General of Immigration, Chiefs of Bureaus of Labor Statistics, Factory and Mine Inspectors, and many other positions in which, by the enforcement of laws enacted especially for the protection of wage earners, the interests and the welfare of the working classes could be safe-guarded.

At the present time, trade unions can in all probability secure greater advantages and more important concessions from the existing political parties than by forming a third party. To a certain extent, both parties are desirous of securing the labor vote, and much legislation is proposed and carried out along these lines. There does not appear to be any clear division as between two dominant parties in this country, the Republican party being more favorable in some states and the Democratic party more favorable in others. Trade unionists should adopt a policy of building up a strong outside sentiment, and in this way influence the nominations of the two parties. The Anti-Saloon League and several other organizations adopt these methods, and their success justifies them in so doing. In declaring against a third labor party, however, I wish it to be understood that this refers only to the immediate policy of the unions. One cannot foresee what the future of the dominant parties in the United States will be, and if it should come to pass that the two great American political parties opposed labor legislation, as they now favor it, it would be the imperative duty of unionists to form a third party in order to secure some measure of reform. I regard the formation of a third party at the present time as inadvisable, owing to the clearly marked disposition on the part of the two dominant parties to grant a large number of the requests of the workingmen; but if these conditions should cease to exist, then it would be advisable for the unions to organize a third party.

One of the great disadvantages of the organization of a third party is that it means, at the same time, the organization of all men opposed to or apathetic to labor unions. The creation of a party means the establishment of a shining mark for the attacks of all persons antagonistic to unionism and the alienation of the sympathies and the loss of the support of the present parties. A third party should, therefore, be formed only in case of absolute necessity.

While, however, the workingmen could not as a separate party secure a majority or even a respectable minority of the legislators, they could do far more efficient work and could influence legislation far more effectively, by organizing with the purpose of influencing one or the other or both of the dominant parties. If the workingmen of the country were properly organized at the present time and were imbued with the absolute necessity of insisting upon wise labor legislation, neither of the dominant political parties could resist them, and wise legislation benefiting the toilers would undoubtedly be enacted. There is no doubt in my mind that the purposes of the workingman can better be attained by the formation of a solid group of men united in their political aspirations and their political demands, but not committed to the policy of forming a third party, than in any other way. It takes a majority of workingmen in any district to elect their own representative, but it takes only a small minority to insist upon the election of a proper man by one or the other of the parties already constituted.

Another form of political activity which the trade unions should avoid is that of committing the movement to any one political party. No union or federation, whether local or national, should commit itself to the Republican or Democratic party, because the majority of its members are Republicans or Democrats, or to the Socialist or Prohibition party, because the majority of its members are Socialists or Prohibitionists. You cannot thrust political convictions down a man's throat by a resolution, however unanimous, or by a vote, however binding. The attempts to commit the American Federation of Labor to the Socialist platform should be vigorously repelled, even by Socialist unionists themselves. Such a resolution has usually failed by a decisive vote, but even if it were passed, it would not mean that the majority of unionists would vote for socialism, and it certainly would not mean that the minority opposed to it would so vote. The proper method of creating and solidifying a political sentiment is not to commit a man to a single political party, but rather to create in them of their own conviction a sense of the necessity of working to carry out a particular and definite program.

As time goes on, it is not improbable that labor organizations will have increased influence upon the government of our states and especially of our cities. The day is past when government in the United States is considered the prerogative of a specially favored class. The history of all nations shows that one class after another has been admitted to the suffrage and has been invested with a larger and larger share of the responsibility of government. Up to the present time, the workingmen of this country, through lack of organization and, therefore, of a central, intelligent direction, have been unable to secure as much real control over, or advantage from, the government of our cities as they should. Workingmen have voted for one party or another according to habit, tradition, or personal friendship, or for some other reason not connected with the welfare of their class. In the past it was always possible to play off one body of workmen against another, just as in a strike the non-unionists are pitted against the unionists. With the growth of organized labor, however, it should be possible for strong trade unions and central federated labor organizations to secure from the legislators of our cities the enactment of fair and reasonable laws beneficial to workingmen. Such a participation of trade unions should be strictly and rigidly limited to obtaining measures for the advantage of their class and of the community in general, and should not degenerate into a scramble for office on the part of individual leaders. The path of politics is strewn with the ruins of high enterprises and the dry bones of noble characters, and a union once launched upon the perilous seas of office-grabbing is sooner or later bound to lose its hold upon the esteem and allegiance of its members and to be finally shattered by the force of internal dissension.

There is nothing wrong if a labor leader for the good of the cause accepts a political position for which he is fitted, and in which he can benefit his fellow-workmen. There should, however, be no contest for the placing of workingmen or men of any other class in "fat jobs." When a labor organization has grown strong, especially in a city, there comes even to the conscientious leader a feeling of power and a recognition of his ability to secure a position or political favors in return for his influence. It occasionally happens that political activity, begun with the highest ideals, degenerates into a policy of mere position-grabbing. The inevitable result of such action is demoralization and disintegration. The men who have not secured positions are jealous of the men who have, and the adherents of the political party not favored begin to feel that their union has been used as a tool for evil purposes and has been diverted from its original aims. When a union is launched upon this course, the result in too many cases is that the important and even vital demands of the workingmen are surrendered to the political ambitions of the labor leader himself.

By this I do not mean to say that a union official may not enter the service of the national, state, or municipal government, but the contest for such a position, especially where it involves the use of the prestige and power of the organization, is utterly demoralizing. Once embarked upon such a course a union can find no stopping place, no means of resistance to the temptations and dangers which beset it. At first it seems to be plain sailing, and no conflict appears between the interests of the candidate and those of his union; but little by little concession must be made, until in the end the contest is seen to be fought purely in the self-interest of the man and not to any extent for the welfare of those whose interests are entrusted to his care.

By holding aloof from the struggle for spoil, by maintaining a dignified neutrality upon matters of no import to trade unionism, by evading the wars of personalities, and keeping above the grime and mire of local politics, unions through their city federations may place themselves in a position to exact from the municipal government measures for the advancement of the working classes. The election of councilmen from workingmen's wards should be conditioned upon actual past services to the cause of labor. A constant effort should be made to commit the municipalities to the doctrine of a living wage, and no city work should be done and no city contracts awarded without provision that union wages and union conditions prevail. The cities, like the state and national governments, should take their place among the fair employers of labor.

In many other departments of city life the union could exert a beneficent and far-reaching influence. In the great field of education, for instance, this influence should make itself felt; for the schools of the city should not in any case be antagonistic to the principles of organized labor. By this I do not mean that organized labor should swagger into city government and attempt to do what is not within its fair province. But in this field, as in business, the rights of labor should be crystallized and formulated, to the end that the true interests of all members and all classes of society may be harmonized.

The political influence of organized workmen can be increased only by more wide-spread interest in political matters and more efficient organization. The machinery for influencing legislation already exists, but it needs to be perfected and to be used by men who are united in their efforts to secure political action. The workingmen of the country should be constantly appealed to, should be instructed upon questions of import to them, and should be kept continually informed of the records of the men for whom they vote.

The political influence of trade unions should be exerted, primarily, not through the several national organizations, but through the American Federation of Labor, the state federations, and the city central bodies. Trade unions are organized on the lines of trades or industries, but political action is carried out on territorial lines. The carpenters or Locomotive Engineers might each have enough votes to secure the election of representatives, if these votes could be concentrated in a few districts. As a matter of fact, however, the members of these unions—and this is true of the majority—are scattered all over the country and in no one place are sufficiently strong to carry an election. The world of organized labor must therefore exert its political influence through federations, which group the votes by districts, rather than through unions, which group the votes by industries.

To accomplish political reforms, the American Federation of Labor must be greatly strengthened and must receive the unqualified support of the national unions. The various unions should submit proposed legislation to the Federation in order to secure the support of all unionists upon any wise and just proposal of any single group; and no legislation should be advanced or fought for by national unions unless it secure the endorsement of the Federation.

The political activity of the union should always be carried on by the American Federation of Labor where it involves national legislation; by the state federations, where it involves state legislation; and by the city central bodies, where it involves municipal laws or ordinances. The program which has been carefully and thoughtfully prepared by the national unions, or their delegates, in the conventions of the Federation, after being drawn up by the best constitutional attorneys and subjected to the criticism of experts, should be sent to the various state federations and local bodies. The Federation should report to the national unions the progress of legislation and of the votes of various representatives upon the measure proposed, and the state federations and city central bodies should be kept constantly informed of the vote of the members from their districts upon each individual question. Before election every representative in the United States Congress should be presented with a list of questions concerning his attitude toward the specific demands formulated by the American Federation of Labor, and through the city central bodies and the constituent locals, this statement should be submitted to the workingmen of his particular district. Thus, in a Congressional election in any district, the replies of all candidates for the office should be placed in the hands of every workingman in the particular district, so that he could judge of the attitude of both candidates towards each of the demands formulated by the organized workmen. Pamphlets should be issued upon the various demands of the American Federation, and these pamphlets should be circulated by the state federations and the city central bodies, so that each of the two million trade unionists of the country would have in his possession a statement of the demands of the Federation, the reasons therefor, the progress already made toward their attainment, and the votes of various congressmen, senators, or members of legislatures upon the questions brought up. The Federation should devote a considerable sum of money to the sole purpose of political propaganda, and the national unions should strengthen it and hold up its hands in this work.

To accomplish political reforms, however, more is necessary than mere machinery. The trade unionists of the country must realize that little can be accomplished by political activities unless every man takes an interest. The men must go to the polls and vote. I would not desire to see and would strongly deprecate the slightest compulsion or the least exercise of undue influence upon the individual voter. Every unionist must retain the right to vote absolutely according to the dictates of his conscience and intelligence, even though his vote be directly in opposition to the political inclinations and political aspirations of the trade union world. While, however, every unionist should be at perfect liberty to vote as he will, the trade union ideas and the trade union program, simple precise, and unified, should be perfectly known to every unionist. The men should not only go to the polls, but should also go to the primaries. Politics can only be reformed by real interest on the part of all well-intentioned members of the community. A man who is now willing to go on a six months' strike and make heroic sacrifices for the good of his class will frequently not take the trouble to attend the primaries of the political party, to which he belongs, in order to help shape the policy of that party in a manner calculated to advance the best interests of his class and of society.

At the present time trade unions, and the labor movement in general, are stronger and have a greater influence in the legislative than in the judicial sphere of governmental activity. The present tendency of the political parties seems to a certain extent to be to allow the corporate interests to nominate the elective judges. Trade unions should attempt, as far as possible, to exert such influence and control upon political parties as will preclude the nomination for the judgeship of men who are notoriously opposed to the interests of organized labor.

In conclusion, trade unionists can effect much by political action. Such political power, however, cannot at the present time be best secured by the formation of a separate labor party, and no good, but much harm may result from committing the labor movement to any particular political party. The unions must avoid the danger of allowing their political activity to degenerate into mere position-grabbing, although the policy of choosing qualified men for elective or appointive positions in which they can be of real and obvious assistance to the movement should be encouraged. To accomplish political reforms the workingmen must be organized in an efficient and thorough manner, in a system which will concentrate the entire voting power of all unionists; and the individual men, while retaining fully their own initiative, must be encouraged to vote at all elections and to attend the primaries of their respective parties.

CHAPTER XXV

TRADE UNIONS, THE STATE AND THE LAW

Protection Under the Law and Protection From the Law. Prosecution and Persecution. The Right to Form Unions. The Right Not to Work. Trade Unionists and the Courts. The Question of the Militia. Attitude of Unionists toward Militarism. Labor Reform through Legislation. The Difficulties of American Legislation.

THE efforts of workingmen to assert their rights and better their conditions have been met from the beginning by the invocation of the law and the adoption of repressive measures. In England, as on the continent of Europe, the slightest indications of unrest called forth harsh laws, cruelly enforced; and only gradually, as the result of continued strife and effort, were the workingmen enabled to secure even a portion of their just dues. In this repression of labor, the law was not infrequently diverted from its original intent, so that often the need of labor became less protection under the law than protection from the law.

Long before the rise of trade unions, the law was used to depress the conditions of workingmen. When, in the fourteenth century, the Black Plague cut off hundreds of thousands of toilers and the survivors demanded higher wages, the English government answered the demand with the so-called Statutes of Laborers. These laws fixed the maximum rate of wages and made it a penal offense to offer or accept more.

During several centuries there appeared to be a conspiracy on the part of the governing classes in England to reduce wages and to retard the advancement of the workingmen. During the eighteenth century, especially at its close, oppressive measures were enacted against trade unionists, and even after the unions were legalized, their members were prosecuted for conspiracy, for picketing, for administering oaths, for not finishing work, and on many other pretexts.

Since the Revolution, there has never been in the United States a law fixing wages, but the inferior courts have held that combinations of workingmen were illegal, have punished laborers for striking, and for other justifiable actions. At a later period, however, certain legal decisions affirmed the right of workingmen to combine into unions and to strike for higher wages or better conditions, but it was not until after the Civil War that this right was finally and definitely guaranteed.

At the present time the right of workingmen to strike is perfectly clear. The common law, as it now exists, is summarized as follows by the Department of Labor in its Bulletin dated November, 1895.

"Every one has the right to work or to refuse to work for whom and on what terms he pleases, or to refuse to deal with whom he pleases: and a number of persons, if they have no unlawful object in view, have the right to agree that they will not work under a fixed price or without certain conditions. The right of employees to refuse to work either singly or in combination is balanced by the right of employers to refuse to engage the services of any one for any reason they may deem proper."

Even the most uncompromising opponents of unionism now recognize the legal right to strike. In its issue of May 14th, 1903, the *New York Sun,* in reply to this question from a well-known multi-millionaire, "Shall employers be permitted to conduct a lawful business in a lawful way without the dictation of walking delegates from irresponsible and lawless unions?" replied in an unqualified negative: "If unions prefer to conduct their business through walking delegates and become strong enough to dictate the conditions on which they will trade their labor for the employers' cash, their legal right so to dictate is no more questionable than is the right of each individual member to decide how much he is willing to pay for his hat. If they will work but an hour a day, at $10 an hour, prescribing at the same time that their employers shall wear green caps and drink no beer, no one can say them nay."

While the right to strike has now been conceded, the courts have, in many cases, declared illegal various actions necessary to the successful con-

Better Class of Company Houses in the Anthracite Region

These are double houses, renting for six dollars a side

MINERS' WIVES AND CHILDREN PICKING COAL FROM CULM BANKS
Many anthracite miners provide their household fuel in this manner

duct of a strike. It is perfectly just that all forms of violence be visited with condign and summary punishment, but it is unjust that, as frequently happens, peaceful picketing should be castigated. By picketing is meant nothing more nor less than the stationing of a few men before, or in the vicinity of, the establishment struck against, in order to inform prospective employees or patrons that a strike is in progress, and to convince or persuade them not to accept employment, or not to purchase articles, in the particular establishment. The right of picketing, which is merely the right of free speech, has been wilfully confounded with the use of violence, and has been over and over again interpreted as a malicious attempt to injure the employer struck against. Both by injunction and otherwise, trade unionists have been punished simply for doing what they had a perfect right to do, namely to picket, and many strikes have been lost and many lockouts won through the attitude of the courts on this matter.

In many other ways, the trade unionists and the working classes in general have been injuriously affected by the interpretation of the laws. Many legal measures for the protection of the workingman and the betterment of his condition have been declared unconstitutional, and in their decisions higher tribunals have appeared to interpret every attempt to improve the conditions of workmen as a violation of the right of contract or as special or class legislation. By the invention of the doctrine of common employment the courts have in the vast majority of cases taken away from workingmen all legal redress for accidents, no matter how serious the injury, or how innocent the victim of contributory negligence. The majority of the decisions of the courts, especially of the superior tribunals, have been clearly against workingmen, and especially against trade unionists.

The attitude of trade unionists toward the state and the nation should be and is that of all good citizens. The workmen should, and I believe do, realize that they form an integral part of the state and nation, and they should cast their votes and should agitate constantly for the attainment of the aims and ideals of their class.

The general attitude of the trade unions towards the state has been misunderstood in consequence of the attitude of a few unions towards the militia. A considerable amount of criticism has been aroused within recent years by the action of the Schenectady Trades' Council in expelling a member for joining the state militia, and it has been popularly claimed that the trade unionists as such are opposed to the military system of the various states.

This, however, is a very grave exaggeration. A few labor organizations have rules refusing membership to persons who join the state militia, but the vast majority of trade unions take no action whatsoever in regard to this matter. The feelings of those unionists who are opposed to the militia are summarized in a provision of the constitution of the Journeymen Stone Cutters of North America. "This association does not approve of, or sanction, any of its members belonging to any volunteer military organization, except on a call from the Government for the defense of their country." The cause usually assigned for this antagonism is that the volunteer military organizations have in the past been called out not only to suppress disorder but actually to put down strikes. There are instances in which certain officers have proceeded to the scene of a labor dispute and have congratulated themselves and their loyal and admiring fellow-countrymen upon "breaking the back-bone of the strike." The Stone Cutters, one of the few organizations refusing to admit militiamen, are proud of the fact that upon the outbreak of the Civil War their union at Washington enlisted in a body and fought throughout the conflict.

Whatever may be the sins of the militia against strikers, the attitude of unions towards them should be, and almost invariably is, one of tolerance if not of friendliness. There is, it is true, throughout the whole trade union world, a certain opposition to militarism, an opposition founded upon patriotism and good judgment. Labor organizations, however, should not oppose the establishment or creation of state militia, but should leave their members free to exercise their own judgment in the matter of enlisting. Unions could not, if they would, destroy the military organizations of the **several states,** and they should not if they could. A large number of the militiamen ordered to the anthracite region during the late strike, were members of the miners' organization, or in sympathy with its aims and purposes, and while they maintained peace (in which they were given the assistance of the United Mine Workers' organization), they did not try to break "the backbone of the strike." The strength of the labor unions will be largely increased by a friendly spirit between them and the militia. Fortunately, the number of unions discriminating against militiamen is extremely small, but it would be far better if there were none at all. The unions who do oppose the militia fail to recognize that they, as unionists, are a part of the State, interested in the maintenance of the institutions of the State, and vested with the right of determining in part the policy of the State. The trade union movement in this country can make progress only by identifying itself with the State—by obeying its just laws and by upholding the military as well as the civil arm of the government.

From the beginning trade unions have been law-abiding institutions and have endeavored by political action to secure the reforms which they desired. In the United States some of the progress already made by trade unions in bettering the condition of workingmen has been due to direct political action by trade unionists, but this is true to a far greater extent in England. The greater success of British unions in this regard is owing partly to the comparative youth of American organizations and to the fact that conditions in the United States for securing effective and far-reaching laws beneficial to workingmen are far less favorable than in England. There are many difficulties in this country in the way of securing and enforcing such laws. Unlike England, France, Belgium, and other countries, the United States is not a single, unified nation, but its powers of government are divided between the nation and the several states. For certain reforms it is necessary to go to the national government, for others, to the state governments, and for still others, to both. A victory gained in one state may sometimes be nullified by the failure to gain a like victory in neighboring states. A British law regulating hours of labor in the cotton factories applies to all the cotton factories in the United Kingdom; but a Massachusetts law has no validity in Pennsylvania or in Illinois. Whenever legislation for benefiting the workman is sought in one state, it is contested on the ground that its passage and enforcement will drive the industry in question from that state. If similar legislation could be obtained simultaneously in all states this objection would be groundless, but this has never been possible and legislation in one state has been hampered by the failure to secure similar legislation in another.

The powers of government in the United States, moreover, are not only divided but limited. In England a law passed by Parliament is by that very fact constitutional; but in the United States the courts can overthrow any law which in their opinion is not constitutional. In this country legislation secured by the unions has been repeatedly declared in violation of the constitution of a state or of the United States and, therefore, void. Legislation protecting the workingmen has been enacted in England, while similar legislation has been declared unconstitutional in the United States, because it was held to abridge the freedom of contract. The decisions of the courts has been so divergent that the workingmen have never been sure that they have secured an enforceable law until it has been tested in the courts.

The ordinary advantage of labor laws as compared with reforms obtained by strikes or negotiation is their more general application and validity. This, however, is very much less the case in the United States than in other countries, owing to the subdivision of the powers of government and, sometimes, to inefficient and even dishonest administration. Many laws tending to improve the conditions of workingmen remain a dead letter, or are enforced so unequally and unfairly that benefits which might otherwise arise from them are lost.

There can be no doubt, however, of the advisability of securing wise and reasonable legislation for the protection of wage earners, especially of working women and children. The laws should be so amended as to prevent excessive work by either adults or minors, and in all cases the health, safety, and reasonable comfort of the workman should be sought and obtained. The state should exercise supervision over the character and condition of the mills, mines, workshops, and factories, in which a large portion of the population spend the greater part of their waking days. The state should prevent overcrowding of factories, useless sacrifice of life, working with noxious and harmful materials, and the maintenance of evil conditions of work which undermine the health and destroy the happiness of the working classes. There are also many laws not directly connected with factory legislation which would be of great benefit to the wage earners. The provision of proper education for the children of the working classes, the adherence of national, state, and local governments to the principle of the living wage, the collection of useful data and information concerning wages and conditions of work, the efficient administration of laws regulating immigration, and many other matters of common interest should be directly influenced by the wishes and votes of the workingmen of this country.

CHAPTER XXVI

THE INCORPORATION OF TRADE UNIONS

Associations of Employers Unincorporated. The Claim of Employers. Incorporation Voluntary or not at All. Trade Unions Maintain Agreements. Moral Responsibility. Senator Hanna on the Indianapolis Convention. Responsibility Increased by Trade Agreements. Incorporation does not Create Responsibility. A Man's Word and his Bond. The Limits of Union Responsibility. Contradictions. The Taff Vale Case. Vagueness of the Law. Hostility of Judges. Fears of Workingmen. How Incorporation Laws should be Framed. Hostility to Incorporation not Hostility to the Law. Dangers of Incorporation. Needless Litigation. Home Rule for Unions. The New York Stock Exchange Unincorporated.

DURING recent years there has been a growing demand, urged persistently both by friends and enemies of organized labor, that trade unions should incorporate. It is argued that labor unions, at present for the most part unincorporated bodies not directly recognized by law, should become incorporated in somewhat the same manner as business enterprises. The law recognizes two classes of corporations, those "for profit" and those "not for profit," and it is held that unions should enroll themselves among the latter, and thus acquire ability to sue and liability to be sued. The result, we are told, would be to make labor unions more conservative and more responsible.

This solicitude on the part of many opponents of organized labor should, in a certain sense, be gratifying to unionists, since it is a flattering recognition of the power of organized labor. As long as the unions were small, feeble, and incompletely organized, no loud cry was raised for incorporation, since any employer could lock out his men or refuse to deal with the union. However, the extraordinary growth in the number and power of unions has evoked a strong sentiment for incorporation and for increased responsibility.

Viewed superficially, there appears at first glance some justice in the claim of employers that unions should incorporate. The employers assert that in making trade arrangements with labor unions they are risking vast sums of money invested in valuable properties. They aver that for any breach on their part of these contracts, they, the employers, are legally responsible, whereas for a similar breach on the part of the workmen, no one is answerable. Trade unions, it is maintained, should put themselves into a position where they may sue and be sued, and should accept all the benefits and all the responsibilities of a legal body incorporated under the laws of the state. If the union will not willingly incorporate, say some employers, then it should be forced to do so.

In all the vague talk upon the subject of incorporation one thing at least is clear, that incorporation must be either voluntary or not at all. The constitutions of the United States and of the several states protect the individual workman or group of workmen, as well as all other persons, from being forced against their will into an incorporated organization. No law compelling a labor union or any person or body of persons to incorporate would for a single moment be upheld by the courts. Incorporation is always a privilege, never an obligation, and a charter must be accepted before it becomes valid. The courts of the several states have repeatedly declared that "no man can be compelled by the legislature to become a member of a corporation without his consent." To refuse to allow a union to exist unless incorporated would be to deprive citizens of the right of lawful assembly as well as of the right to enter freely into contractual relations. Finally, apart from all other reasons, to legislate labor unions into the acceptance of charters would be unconstitutional, since it would be class legislation affecting only certain groups or associations, while leaving other classes unaffected. It is, of course, conceivable that stringent laws might be passed attacking labor unions with the purpose of compelling them to incorporate, rather than incur the animosity of the legislature. The general effect of such restrictive legislation, however, is simply heightened secrecy and increased irresponsibility, and not an approach to greater openness. It therefore seems clear that the question of incorporation or non-incorporation is one for the unions themselves to determine and is not a question to be decided for the unions by the legislatures of the states.

Even though the unions cannot be directly forced by the legislatures into incorporating, they should not, on this account, refuse to give due consideration to this or any other seemingly reasonable demand that may be made by the employing classes. The proposal to incorporate should receive a respectful hearing and should be considered upon its merits, the question of the advantages or disadvantages of incorporation being decided upon the probable effect which it will have upon the labor unions and upon the country at large.

If we look somewhat more closely into the arguments of those who favor incorporation of trade unions, we will find good ground for refusing to take a step in this direction without due consideration. The usual cry is that unions should become incorporated in order to become more responsible and, therefore, more conservative, but few people ask themselves what they mean by responsibility, or whether the unions are not already as responsible and scrupulous in keeping their engagements and agreements as they would be if incorporated. The chapter on trade agreements will show that arrangements made on a large scale between employers and employed have usually been conscientiously maintained and lived up to by both sides. There is such a thing as a moral as well as a legal responsibility, and in many cases the word of a man or an organization will bind him, when, if it were a legal agreement, he might hire a lawyer to drive a coach and four through it. As a rule the men keep their contracts with admirable fidelity. "I do not believe, under the present condition of things," says Marcus A. Hanna, United States Senator from the State of Ohio, "in incorporation of trade unions. . . . . . The test has come, for, when in their dire extremity, the anthracite miners of Pennsylvania appealed to their fellows in the bituminous fields in the West to come out and strike in sympathy, in order that conditions might be forced upon this country which would enforce a settlement of the trouble . . . . . the bituminous coal miners,

TIPPLE OF BITUMINOUS COAL MINE

In this mine coal is worked on the long wall system; all of the coal being taken out and no pillars left. Dirt dumps on the right

Tugboats Taking a Flotilla of Barges Filled with Soft Coal Down the Ohio River

with calm, cool judgment and loyalty to their agreement, voted unanimously against a sympathetic strike."

The way to make unions responsible is to give them something to be responsible for, in other words, to make a trade agreement with them. Such agreements for large industries should not be merely local, made upon the sole authority of a small body of men liable to be swept away by excitement, or of a single small employer, subject to the incalculable competition of the local market, but should be broad and general, involving, if possible, the whole industry and binding employers and men for a year or a period of years. The breach of an agreement of this sort involves consequences compared to which the damages that could be claimed by an employer or collected from even a wealthy union, whether incorporated or unincorporated, would be small indeed. Too much stress is laid upon the argument that the employer is responsible financially, whereas the employees are responsible merely morally. In the first place, it is not the fact. The great organizations of employers, the National Association of Manufacturers, the Typothetae, the associations of coal operators and of other employers are not incorporated. Apart from this fact, however, neither the workmen nor the union making a trade agreement for a particular city or for a whole region have, as a rule, a remedy at law for its violation. The union cannot recover damages, because its interest in the contract and the damage sustained by it are, from a legal point of view, merely hypothetical, while the individual workmen fail to secure damages owing to the fact that they are not parties to the contract and for various other reasons. Even where the damage can be proved, the amount is not easily ascertained. In the case of the Garment Workers, who had made contracts with the employers, it was recognized by the union that it was practically impossible to estimate losses or damage incurred, even if they were recoverable. In this particular instance bonds had been given by employers for the faithful performance of contract obligations, but even in this case, the union failed to recover by means of a forfeiture of the bond. The employers did not deny that violations had been made, but merely claimed—and their claim was sustained by the court—that their contract was not free, but obtained under duress, since, but for the contract with the union, they could not have remained in the business. There are many cases where a man's word is better than his bond or than a guarantee fund. The obligation resting upon the miners and operators to accept the award of the Anthracite Coal Strike Commission is purely moral, and in no sense legal, and yet both parties to the controversy have recognized and will continue to recognize that this obligation is stronger than any mere legal obligation, which might be avoided through technicalities of the law or the shrewdness of attorneys. Finally, it may be stated, as showing that both employers and workmen trust to the moral rather than the legal sanction of agreements, that where employers actually do break their contracts, the workmen strike and do not sue.

Even if the liability of the unions for the fulfillment of their contracts were not sufficient, and even if it were desirable and necessary to increase this responsibility, there is no good reason for believing that such a result would come from the mere incorporation of trade unions. Incorporation does not create funds, nor does it always make existing funds attachable. The object of incorporation in the capitalist world is not to create but to limit responsibility. Mere incorporation would not accomplish the purposes of those who advocate it and nothing short of a guarantee fund deposited by a union, whether incorporated or unincorporated, could have this effect, it being even doubtful whether this measure itself would be successful.

Perhaps one of the chief aims of some of the adherents of incorporation is to make the unions responsible for things for which the law does not at present hold them answerable. Some of the advocates of incorporation of trade unions seem to desire by this means to make the unions responsible in cases in which individual men strike or leave the employ of a company which has signed a contract with the union. Such a responsibility, however, is and should be beyond the legitimate province of the union. Except in such contracts as some made by the Longshoremen, the trade union is not a guarantor of a labor supply and does not agree to do a certain amount of work or to furnish a certain amount of labor. A contract entered into by a union merely determines the rate of pay and the conditions of employment for such members of the union as agree to work; and the union is no more compelled to furnish a sufficient and definite number of laborers than the employer to furnish a sufficient and definite amount of work. The union no more guarantees that any particular man will work than the employer guarantees that work will be provided for any particular man; and even if this guarantee did exist, the mere fact of incorporation would not render it more effective.

Some of the advocates of incorporation seem to desire to make the unions responsible not only for the authorized acts of their agents and officers, but for those of all members or of persons sympathizing with the unions but having no connection with them. The arguments of those who desire incorporation are curiously at variance in this matter. Some say that the unions should be forced to incorporate because they are not responsible for these actions; others claim that there is no reason why they should not incorporate, because they are even now liable for damages for such action, and that incorporation would really limit the responsibility of their members. They cite the recent Taff Vale decision in England, by which the court held that a trade union, though not incorporated, could be sued and mulcted in damages for unlawful acts of its agents in the course of a strike. At the same time, cases have recently been brought against individual members of trade unions, and these members have been held liable in damages for injury done or alleged to have been done by the trade union. A number of advocates of incorporation, therefore, believe that unions, even if unincorporated, are liable or at least that their individual members are liable.

It is probable, though not certain, that a union is already responsible for its own illegal acts and for those of its authorized officers and agents; and incorporation would neither increase nor decrease this responsibility. The individual unionist is equally responsible for his individual acts, and this responsibility likewise is not increased or diminished by incorporation. It would not be possible by incorporation to make the union responsible for the acts of unauthorized members or sympathizers, but if it *were* possible, this would constitute the strongest argument against incorporation.

One of the great drawbacks to incorporation is the vagueness of the law with regard to the rights of trade unions. There still remains in the minds of many of our judges a belief that trade unions have something in them inherently unlawful and of the nature of a conspiracy. There has been a tendency to consider trade unions in restraint of trade and labor and opposed to public policy. The judicial decisions upon the question of boycotting and striking have not been uniformly in harmony with modern ideas and ideals, and such things as peaceful picketing are not infrequently visited by the censure and punishment of the courts. It is questionable whether incorporation would really increase the responsibility and liability of trade unions, but as long as the law remains so vague and so capable of being used as a weapon against the unions, it is not to be wondered at that a proposal, such as that of incorporation, which is based exclusively on its supposed tendency to make the unions more liable to control by the law, should be inquired into with the utmost care.

Perhaps, to a certain extent, unionists have exaggerated the animosity of the judges of our superior tribunals. It is believed by many unionists that too many of our judges have secured and maintained their positions through services rendered or services to be rendered to large corporations. It has also been felt that many judges, while entirely honest and well-meaning, have been brought up to a manner of thought entirely at variance with the philosophy of trade unionism and without any appreciation of the dignity and rights of labor. The fundamental objection, however, is that the rigid application of a law, even if well conceived, might, through the fluctuating and ever-changing conditions of trade unionism, seriously affect the latter and prevent its growth along beneficent lines. There are some leaders of trade unions who believe that with the incorporation of the unions many of the present members would leave the organizations and many prospective members fail to join. This contingency is especially feared in the case of the non-English speaking elements in our laboring population, who might not understand the extent and limitations of incorporated unions and might harbor toward them an unfounded jealousy or fear. Moreover, it is recognized by both workingmen and employers that the laws of incorporation, as they now exist, are not adapted to the incorporation of trade unions. No law would encourage incorporation, unless it expressly provided for a form of association distinct from the ordinary business corporation, unless it protected collective bargaining and the ordinary legal rights of workingmen on strike, unless it made the union alone, and not its unauthorized members, responsible for a breach or violation of a contract, and, finally, unless it was so conceived that the unions could actually secure the same legal redress from employers that employers could secure from the unions. At all events, no law at present existing among either the federal or the state statutes would be sufficiently flexible and sufficiently in accord with modern ideas to permit of the incorporation of the unions on a large scale.

The intervention of the courts in the affairs of trade unionism is in actual practice not feared on account of any prohibition of, or punishment for, illegal acts. Even now the union and individual members and officers actually concerned are apparently responsible for illegal acts committed by them. What the unions dread, however, is the interference of the courts in matters which are not illegal, in other words, in the internal management and economy of the union. They also fear that the unions might become the victims of a definite policy of legal persecution. It would be possible for hostile employers to promote litigation between the union and individual members not in sympathy with the union upon questions of the internal policy of the organization; and the victory in such cases would rest with the longest purse. If an individual member were expelled from the union or suspended or even fined, it might be possible to carry his case by appeal to the supreme court of the state, if not to the supreme court of the United States. Litigation could be promoted upon the most trivial pretexts, and the funds of the organization could be spent in futile attempts to defend it. The union might be prevented from using the benefit funds for strike purposes, from exercising its judgment as to the proper and politic manner of treating an employer, or as to any one of the thousand and one questions of every-day policy.

The danger of submitting a union to the intervention of the courts in its every-day affairs is foreshadowed by J. W. Sullivan of the Typographical Union of New York: "A union has ways of its own in conducting the affairs that relate mainly to itself and its membership. It is a big self-governing family. In periods of strike the prescribed order of written constitution or by-law sometimes proves less desirable than the short cut obvious as a war measure. The members then become aware that in drawing up their laws they were unable to foresee the situation confronting them, and they may, for example, unconstitutionally confide absolute power temporarily in an officer or a committee. In times of peace a union often reaches conclusions and interpretations dictated by the common sense of a meeting rather than by the statutes as written, leaving the majority either satisfied or in a mood to accept the judgment for better or worse. Such proceedings may relate to trials of members, to executive session work, to appropriation of funds, to informalities or irregularities in elections or referendum votes, to the opening or closing of books for inspection, to the reading or the silencing of reports, to appointing or dismissing committees, to maintaining discipline, to accepting or rejecting candidates for membership, to suspending or expelling or reinstating members, to passing judgment on aggressions of employers tending to end in strike, to investigating the conduct of members prejudicial to the organization, and to settling questions in which rule or precedent or necessity of a local union conflicts with international union law. In all such proceedings two principles usually govern—self-preservation of the union and good fellowship. A popular employer, in general fair, who in a fit of temper has wilfully violated a clause in a contract or the union scale, will be adjudged innocent. A sound and active union man who has misappropriated a small sum will be found not guilty and given time to refund. In these matters an unincorporated union is in the main a law unto itself. It is free. It may make many changes in its internal methods and in administration without lessening its responsibility as a contracting party.

"But an incorporated union would in all these steps be subject to much revision and correction through the agencies of the law. Work, here, for judges, lawyers and enemies. The incorporated body, as a creature of the State, must be kept in health by the State. Disturbers, instigated by influences inimical to a union, might kindly aid the State. In incorporating, a union would have admitted non-kinsfolk as masters at the family table—the judge, of another blood, come to set things right; the sheriff, with keys to a jail and a money-sack for fines; the policeman, with a club and handcuffs.

"These officials occasionally regulate family affairs now in the unions, but the courts, only acting when called upon, refuse to interfere if the union's proceedings are in accordance with its own rules, which are subject to change at the will of the majority. But if these rules depended for regularity upon the terms of incorporation, and if informers were sent into the unions to report infractions, the sins of unions would be multiplied and the lawsuits ensuing would work pleasure to scabs. The knowing are fully conscious of what they are saying when they express a desire for an increase of the authority of the law over trade unions. They would wreck them from within."

It is a fact that while the unions are frequently berated by hostile critics because of their alleged unwillingness "manfully and courageously" to incorporate themselves, the typical capitalist organizations of this country have followed the same course. As has been before stated, the great associations of employers, the National Association of Manufacturers, the Illinois Coal Operators' Association, the National Typothetae, and so forth, are unincorporated. Even the New York Stock Exchange, an organization composed of the richest men in the world, and certainly not lacking the advantage of good legal advice, has always refused to incorporate. Other stock and produce exchanges have adopted the same course. In a certain sense, not entirely fanciful, the New York Stock Exchange is a labor union

—a union of men plying the trade of brokerage. It has at present an initiation fee of about $80,000; it restricts the number of its members, refuses to allow them to divide commissions with non-union brokers, and establishes a minimum piece price for work and a maximum working day of five hours. The reason given by the Stock Exchange for this refusal to incorporate is that it could not, if incorporated, maintain untrammeled powers of discipline and would be liable, in the case of any action which had that object, to interference by the courts and consequent delays. As a matter of fact, no injustice is worked through this refusal of the Stock Exchange to incorporate, and affairs are conducted as honestly and efficiently as though the Exchange were incorporated, and the same is true, upon the whole, of the manufacturers' associations and the labor unions of the country. What the unions desire is not immunity from legal penalties, not a special status under the law, but merely the opportunity to grow up unhampered by the constant oversight of judicial bodies, frequently antagonistic, and to shoulder in the form of trade agreements the responsibility which they believe they should actually assume.

Within a short time the demand for the incorporation of trade unions will probably grow less persistent and less insistent. Many friends of trade unionism now advocating incorporation are beginning to realize its limitations, and the foes of trade unionism are taking up other weapons closer at hand. It is coming to be realized that incorporation does not necessarily mean the ability to attach union funds, and the enemies of the unions now urge that an ounce of injunction is worth a pound of incorporation.

While, therefore, it is not possible to foresee exactly what will happen if the laws are so amended as to make incorporation a benefit, or what may ensue if hostile enactment or hostile interpretation of the law seeks to drive the unions into incorporation, it is probable that for the time being at least the great mass of workmen will resist a proposal the advantages of which are problematical and the dangers, real and imminent.

CHAPTER XXVII

THE CASE AGAINST THE TRADE UNION

Trade Unionism before the Bar of Public Opinion. Sentence First, Trial Afterwards. For Unions, but against Unionism. Grievances Old as Unionism. Does Trade Unionism "Destroy Individuality?" Does it "Tyrannize?" Does it "Dictate?" Does it "Lower Efficiency?" Does it "Foster Idleness?" Does it "Breed Discontent?" Does it "Monopolize Employment?" Does it "Reduce all Men to a Level?" Machinery and Equality. Minimum Wage and Maximum Wage. Do Trade Unions Run Counter to the Law of Supply and Demand? Recognition and Representation. Recognition a Means to an End Trade Unions Fallible.

IN the eyes of some critics the principal grievance against trade unions is the fact that they exist. From the beginning there have always been men so bigoted, so perverse, so blind to the progress and needs of their age that they can discover nothing but evil in popular movements. It has, it is true, become the fashion of late for men of this class to disguise in a measure their uncompromising hatred of trade unionism. They aver that they "have no objections to labor unions if properly conducted;" but this proviso, correctly analyzed, usually means that the unions must not do any of the things for which they are organized. The attitude of these men is as sensible as would be that of a keeper of a turnpike who, hating and fearing the progress of the age, should disclaim hostility to railroads, provided they did not run trains. These opponents of trade unionism are like the man who was "for the law, but against its enforcement."

There is nothing either good or bad which trade unions do or have done or can do that has not at some time been made the object of attack. They have been assailed because they have been local and because they have been national, because they have been mere fighting organizations without funds and because they have had benefit features and have subsidized their battles at the expense of innocent members desiring insurance, because they have raised wages and decreased hours and because they have not benefited the workman, because they have been marked by "bossism" and because they have been unable to control their members.

The case against trade unionism may be said to consist of charges against individual persons or organizations and of more sweeping charges against organizations in general. Everyone would resent the charge that the American is a drunken, lying, thieving, cheating, murderous criminal, although individual Americans have been convicted of these various offenses. It is not considered unfair, however, to bring a series of charges against trade unions or against "unionism as at present conducted," because individual unionists have shown that they share the failings and frailties of human kind.

Many of the charges against labor organizations, that they limit or restrict production, that they prevent the introduction of machinery, that they limit apprentices, that they resort to violence and intimidation, that they defraud and delude the workers, are considered in other sections of this book. The argument that trade unions do not keep their contracts is answered in the chapter on the trade agreement and elsewhere, the charge that they shirk responsibility is discussed under the subject of incorporation, and the allegation that they are law breakers is treated in connection with the subject of strikes and of the injunction. Sometimes these charges are made in good, sometimes in bad, faith, but in either case it is easy to show that, as a general rule, they are absolutely and entirely unfounded.

The complaints and grievances urged against trade unions in the present day are not new. Ever since workmen began to seek a higher standard of living through organization, they have been attacked by representatives of the employing classes. Thus, as early as 1741, when the English wool combers sought by organization to improve their condition, it was asserted that these wool combers had "for a number of years past erected themselves into a sort of corporation (though without a charter) their first pretence was to take care of their poor brethren that should fall sick, or be out of work; and this was done by meeting once or twice a week, and each of them contributing 2d. or 3d. towards the box to make a bank, and when they became a little formidable they gave laws to their masters, as also to themselves, viz., That no man should comb wool under 2s. per dozen: that no master should employ any comber that was not of their club: if he did, they agreed one and all not to work for him: and if he had employed twenty they all of them turned out, and oftentimes were not satisfied with that, but would abuse the honest man that would labour, and in a riotous manner beat him, break his comb pots, and destroy his working tools; they further support one another in so much that they are become one society throughout the kingdom. And that they may keep up their price to encourage idleness rather than labour, if any one of their club is out of work, they give him a ticket and money to seek for work at the next town where a box club is, where he is also subsisted, and suffered to live a certain time with them, and then used as before; by which means he can travel the kingdom round, be caressed at each club, and not spend a farthing of his own or strike one stroke of work. This hath been imitated by the weavers also, though not carried through the kingdom, but confined to the places where they work." (Webb, History of Trade Unionism, p. 31.) In 1815, we find the same sort of criticism directed against the journeymen calico cutters by the masters in their trade. "We have," says one of the masters, "by turns conceded what we ought all manfully to have resisted, and you, elated with success, have been led on from one extravagant demand to another, till the burden has become too intolerable to be borne. You fix the number of our apprentices, and oftentimes even the number of our journeymen. You dismiss certain proportion of our hands, and will not allow others to come in their stead, You stop all Surface Machines, and go to the length even to destroy the rollers before our face. You restrict the Cylinder Machine, and even dictate the kind of pattern it is to print. You refuse on urgent occasions, to work by candlelight, and even compel our apprentices to do the same. You dismiss our overlookers when they don't suit you; and force obnoxious servants into our employ. Lastly, you set all subordination and good order at defiance, and instead of showing deference and respect to your employers, treat them with personal insult and contempt." From that day to this, the assaults upon trade unionism have continued unabated.

The present chapter would easily be the longest in the book if an attempt were made even to enumerate the charges against trade unionism. Every possible accusation has at one time or another been brought against labor organizations, but many of these charges are so palpably absurd that their bare statement is a sufficient refutation. The unions have repeatedly been adjudged guilty by persons who have not taken the trouble to investigate the facts, the usual theory appearing to be "sentence first, trial afterwards."

If hypocrisy is a tribute which vice pays to virtue, then the smooth words which trade unionism, "if properly conducted," receives from its enemies should be a solace and a comfort. No one attacks the principles of trade unionism more fundamentally, no one inveighs against the actions of unionists more bitterly, than the man who claims to be a friend of labor organizations and to be writing in their interest. If ever a man was stabbed in the house of his friends, it is the trade unionist.

One of the most violent opponents of the trade union is the President of the National Association of Manufacturers. In discussing the opinions of this gentleman, I do not wish to appear to confound his criticisms of trade unionism with those of broader men opposed to us. As a physician studies a symptom in its most diseased and violent form in order better to make observations that will apply in cases of comparative health, so I prefer to discuss a few criticisms of trade unionism as they seem to appear to a one-sided, hostile, and evidently immature mind. The critic in question deplores trade unionism as "a system that coerces and impoverishes the worker, ruins the capitalist, terrorizes our politicians and destroys our trade —a system which seems to be hopelessly and irredeemably bad, a bar to all progress, a danger to the state and a menace to civilization."

Trade unionism does not coerce the worker, but is the expression of the united will of the members of the organization. It does not impoverish the worker, as is claimed by the very men who maintain that it forces employers to pay excessive wages; it does not ruin the capitalists, but rather tends to improve their condition and exalt their character. That it terrorizes our politicians is on a par with the other allegations.

Organized labor does not stand for physical force, "for the law of the Huns and Vandals, the law of the savage." Neither strikes nor boycotts are won by resort to violence, nor does either of these involve "a despotism springing into being in the midst of a liberty loving people."

Trade unionism does not demand "of the public and of Congress the privilege to violate the laws forbidding violence and property destruction;" it does not extend "its tactics of coercion and intimidation over all classes, dictating to the press and politicians, and strangling independence of thought and American manhood;" it does not deny "to those outside its ranks" any legal privileges whatsoever and does not interfere with any of the fundamental rights of American citizens.

Trade unionism does not seek "to place all men in each organized trade on the same dead level, as respects his daily output and his daily wage," and does not set "a premium . . . . on indolence and incompetence." It sets a minimum not a maximum wage, and is of more benefit to the efficient and industrious workingman than it is to the man of smaller ability and lower calibre. Its leaders are not "agitators and demagogues, men who appeal to prejudice and envy, who are constantly instilling a hatred of wealth and ability, and who in incendiary speeches, attempt to stir up men to seize by physical force that which their merit cannot obtain for them." Trade unionism is not opposed to wealth nor to the wealthy. It demands fair wages and fair conditions for all workers, but it will make as reasonable terms with a multi-millionaire as it will with the poorest or smallest employer in the industry. The enemies of trade unionism repeat and repeat again the economic fallacy that "organized labor stands for principles that are in direct conflict with the natural laws of economics," that they seek to impose a "man-made plan for the division of power," instead of "the natural law now enforced." If the law of supply and demand is unalterable—a law that cannot be changed—then the unions should not be convicted of changing it, and if the supply or demand can be altered, the critics should show good reason why trade unions should not influence them in the interest of the workingmen. It is also claimed that trade unionism is a trust and the "creator of other trusts," without mentioning, however, that it is a trust to which, as a rule, all may be admitted on the same terms as the original founders. The less irresponsible and unthinking of trade union critics vaguely mention that trade unionism is "foreign to our soil" and "destructive to the best interests of our country, industrially and socially;" although the only basis for this allegation appears to be the fact that trade unions are opposed to the merciless exploitation of children in Southern mills. Another charge against trade unionism by some of its critics is one which must be admitted, namely, that it tends to promote conciliation and arbitration. Conciliation, remarks the aforesaid critic, is "a myth;" and he continues, "an attitude of conciliation would mean an attitude of compromise with regard to fundamental convictions," while as to arbitration, that "is only putting off the day of reckoning." "The truth is," he continues, "that arbitration, to employers, means a surrender to the demands of labor, as surely as yielding to them direct."

According to a wiser and more temperate adviser of labor organizations, "trade unionism is an artificial institution built by man to counteract some natural law." This is an old and a false conception of trade unionism and an old and a false conception of natural law. If by natural law this critic means the state of society among savage tribes, then it is true that trade unionism is artificial, since it would have no place there. Trade unionism springs naturally from the needs of the workmen and is as natural as "the tendencies which it seeks to counteract." The same criticism might be levelled against all institutions, whether they be the school system, our system of law, or even the government of the United States. The law against highway robbery is as much an "artificial institution built by man to counteract some natural law" as is trade unionism.

The cry that trade unionism is un-American is raised by the very men who are opposed to the trade union demand for an American standard of living. Trade unionism represents a democracy of the poor—a government of workmen, by workmen, for workmen—and it stands for better conditions and more equal opportunities for the great masses. True, trade unionism arose in England earlier than in the United States, but it was not a direct importation to this country, like the English sparrow. It grew up spontaneously on American soil from the needs of American workingmen.

It is frequently urged against trade unionism that there have always been men who have risen from the ranks without the aid of any labor organization. The opponents of labor unions point out many self-made men who started as workmen and who rose to the highest positions in the industrial world. The workmen, therefore, they believe, should be encouraged not to join the union, but to attempt to do as these successful individuals have done—earn for themselves an exceptional position in society.

The error of this way of thinking is the ordinary mistake of believing that what anyone can do all can do. *Any* native American boy may become president of the United States, but it is not possible for *all* of them to do so. In the same way it is possible that one out of every hundred or every thousand workmen may rise from the ranks, and that one out of every million may become a Schwab or a Carnegie, but for the great majority this hope is as illusory as that of finding a fortune in the streets or of winning the first prize in a lottery.

It must be admitted that while the trade union can and does assist the exceptionally able workman it is not absolutely and entirely essential to him. The trade union appeals to the great mass of skillful, sober, industrious workmen, who are a credit to the trade, but the great majority of whom have no hopes of rising out of their present class. What the trade union seeks to do is not to enable carpenters, machinists, or track-layers to become railway presidents or bankers, but to render more favorable and more humane their conditions in the trades in which they already work.

The argument most consistently and repeatedly urged against trade unionism is that it tends to reduce all men to an equality. It is alleged by opponents of labor organizations that in the good old times before trade unionism, every man was enabled to earn as much as he wished and, therefore, the good men rose to the surface and the poor men sank to the bottom.

It must be admitted by unionists and anti-unionists alike that there is, in modern industrial life, a certain tendency toward equality of workmen in the same trade. In the days before industry upon a large scale existed and before division of labor was carried to its present extent, greater differences in the ability of individual workmen could be manifested than are possible to-day. All men are not equal before the machine, but they are more equal than without the machine, and in the unskilled trades the differences in skill and earning power are less than formerly. The substantial equality upon which many large classes of workers now rest, however, is determined by the employer, or, rather, by economic conditions themselves. In many large industries, the wages of employees of a certain group are fixed in a lump, irrespective of whether one workman is a little better or a little worse than another. There will be small difference in the pay of members of a gang of street laborers engaged in construction work on a railroad or in rough work around the docks, this being true whether these men are organized or unorganized. In many places a man who enters a large establishment leaves even his name at the door and becomes No. 647 or 123 as soon as he dons his working clothes. The growth of industry on a large scale necessarily wipes out many individual differences in skill and to a certain extent equalizes for large groups wages, hours of labor, and conditions of work to the point of merging the very identity of the workingman into that of the group to which he is assigned.

The trade union does not increase this levelling tendency and does not even perpetuate it. If there is a levelling at all in the trade union world, it is a levelling up and not a levelling down. The only levelling which the trade union does is the elimination of men who are below a certain fixed standard of efficiency. What the union asks for is not equal pay for all workers, but a minimum pay for all workers. The employer may not pay less wages than the minimum to any man whom he engages, but he may generally pay as much more to efficient workers as his sense of justice or of policy may dictate. On the mere matter of speed the union may indeed set limits, if the evident intent of the employer is to reduce wages by means of the employment of pace setters; but as a rule, higher wages may be paid for speed and may always be paid for more skilled, more efficient, more original, or better work, with the entire consent and approbation of the trade union. The trade union does not, except in exceedingly rare cases, set an upper limit to what men may earn, but this is frequently done by employers or their associations. Thus, the Illinois Coal Operators Association forbids its members paying premiums or supplemental wages to their employees, however great their merit. Notwithstanding the fact, however, that the union sets a minimum rate of pay and the operators, the same rate of pay as a maximum, there are great differences in the actual earnings of the men, corresponding to differences in their strength, industry, and general efficiency.

As a matter of actual practice, it must be conceded that in many cases the great majority of men at a given trade or operation receive the minimum wages demanded. The reason of this, however, is the unwillingness of the employer to pay, and not the unwillingness of the men to accept a higher wage. If a manufacturer is employing men with the right to engage and discharge them, he is probably not losing money on the laziest, least skillful, and least efficient man to whom he is paying the standard rate. If that is the case, it is probable that he is finding the labor of the most industrious and most skilled worker very profitable, and nothing in the rules of the union prevents him from giving a portion of this gain to the skilled workman in the form of an addition to his wages.

It is frequently urged against trade unionism that the increases in wages obtained are only temporary, since the higher wages attract more men from other industries or from other sections of the same industry. In a measure this is true. It is impossible to maintain wages in a given industry above wages in other sections of the same trade, but this merely emphasizes the necessity of more complete and general organization. If the pressmen of New York are fairly well organized, whereas no organization exists in any other American city, the result will probably be that any increase in wages in New York will cause the poorer paid workmen from other sections to flock there. To a certain extent, wages in a partially organized trade can even under such circumstances remain high, since the employer, obliged to pay high wages, will engage only the best and most efficient men, who thus become unionists. To be effective, however, a union should be national in its scope, and the organization of the few can be protected only by the organization of the many.

A similar argument against trade unionism is that it enables unionists to benefit at the expense of non-unionists. If, it is claimed, the Garment Workers, the Boot and Shoe Workers, the Cigar Makers, and the Building Trade operatives all receive increases in wages because they are organized, whereas the barbers and waiters receive no increase, then, it is claimed, the cost of clothes, shoes, cigars, and buildings (and their rent) will increase, and the barber, or waiter, with the same number of dollars per week as before, will be able to get less for his money. Even if this statement were true, it would constitute a strong argument not against, but in favor of, trade unionism. If by organization real wages rise and if by lack of organization real wages do not only fail to rise but actually fall, then the unorganized trades should take steps as soon as possible to establish trade unions. That the trade unionists do not themselves believe that they are taking their increased wages out of the pockets of other workmen is shown by the eagerness with which they themselves seek to organize these other trades. It has been shown, moreover, in another place that the increase in the wages of unionists do not come out of the pockets of non-unionists or of the general public, but chiefly out of increased production itself.

It is frequently made a reproof to trade unionists that they use their organization for the purpose of increasing their own wages or reducing their own hours, and this without thought of the wages of other men. The unionists are, therefore, accused of being materialistic and without ideals. In this claim, less than justice is accorded to the unionists, who, in many cases, work for the welfare of others. The sympathetic strike—whether justifiable or not—is, as its name implies, a sacrifice made by one body of men for the sake of the well-being of another, and the contributions from one union to another during periods of strike show the strength of the feeling of brotherliness and the willingness on the part of unionists in one trade to make sacrifices for unionists in another.

Where, however, the workingmen in a trade union are seeking their own benefit and are endeavoring to increase wages and better conditions in their own trade, it is not fair to make of this action a general reproof. The theory of trade unionism is that the whole army of workingmen can advance only by the progress of every part, and that each union should secure better terms for itself, so that better terms may be obtained for all. The carpenters, cannot, as a rule, strike for higher wages for brewery workers, nor the quarry men for higher wages for barbers, but if each of these organizations strikes for itself and each secures from the others such financial and moral aid as is possible, the result will be an improvement all along the line.

There can be no doubt that high wages and a fair working day are good things, and there seems to be at the present time no better way of securing them than by the tactics now pursued by trade unionists. It is impossible for the unionists of the country to get together and frame a wage scale for all employments. Unionists do not desire the same wage for all trades or employments, such as plumbers and tailors, railway engineers and stone cutters; and even hours of labor and conditions of work must be different in different industries. As a consequence, for at least an indefinite period, unionists will be obliged to secure their ends by each trade striving for itself, with such counsel and aid from other unions and from the general public as may be secured.

Many more charges are made against trade unionism with even less justice and foundation. Many of them are based on false information, or false interpretation of true information, or on broad generalizations from individual and exceptional instances. The argument that trade unionism destroys individuality is closely related to the charge that it reduces all men to a level, but is even less true. The union does not take away from the workman the opportunity of expressing his individuality in his work, while it gives him new opportunities of giving expression to himself, both in the administration of the union and in the extended leisure which it secures for him. When a man is permitted to work only eight hours a day and may devote three or four hours to self-improvement, his individuality will be brought out very much more than that of a man *permitted* by the union, but *compelled* by the employer, to devote twelve or fourteen hours a day to endless repetition of a single, monotonous, automatic movement. Trade unionism demands the freedom of collective bargaining between associated workmen and employers or associations of employers, and stands for an equality between the contracting parties. It therefore does not "tyrannize" or "dictate," but repels tyranny and dictation. It does not "foster idleness," but, by means of higher wages and shorter hours, compels greater steadiness and greater intensity of work. It may "breed discontent" or at least give expression to that already existing, but without hopeful discontent on the part of workman, as of employer, there can be no progress. It does not "monopolize employment," since the unions almost invariably admit to their ranks as many qualified workmen as apply. A monopoly which admits all applicants is no monopoly at all.

I do not wish to assert that trade unionism is perfect, or trade unions or unionists, infallible. Trade unionism is not a panacea for all the ills of life, and neither the unions nor the unionists constantly live up to the true principles of unionism. Labor conflicts evoke many unwise acts from both parties to the contest, and even in time of industrial peace, workmen err as do employers. I do not deny that trade unions and trade unionists have occasionally committed grave errors, serious indiscretions, and even actual crimes. But to build upon these failings a charge against the whole trade union world, or even against "trades unionism as at present conducted," is about as wise as uncompromisingly to denounce Christianity or the Christian churches, "as at present conducted," for the acts of individual men professing themselves Christians. The evil that trade unionism does lies upon the surface; the good is less apparent, buried deep in the grateful hearts of millions of men, who have been aroused by it to a new life and to higher and nobler aspirations.

Especially in a period like the present, when new recruits are flocking by the hundreds of thousands to the ranks of organized labor, it is wise and just to exercise a certain broad tolerance. The raw recruit, more zealous than understanding, commits errors and excesses impossible after a few years of membership in the trade union. There is a certain supercilious criticism and a certain intolerant haste of judgment toward the men who commit follies in the excess of their zeal for a noble cause. Far wiser in its judgment upon this matter was the United States Industrial Commission, which in its Report to the President, summarized the situation in the following weighty words: "Men," it said, "who have been accustomed to absolute submission in industry show the same faults when they first take up the burden of self-government as men who have been accustomed to absolute political submission. Only experience with democratic forms and methods can develop the good that is in democracy."

Trade unionism welcomes the criticism of sober-minded and well-intentioned persons of all classes. It will learn its lesson and will listen to the judgment of men who see its faults and point them out without malice and without exaggeration. It will not, however, be influenced by the swarm of hostile critics who openly or under the guise of a seeming friendship, assail its fundamental principles and impugn the motives of its most trusted leaders. The justification of trade unionism in the past has been its deeds in the past. Its future justification will be not any set form of promises or protestations, but the work which it will carry on through its millions of adherents.

CHAPTER XXVIII

THE RIGHT TO THE MACHINE

Have Machines "Lessened the Day's Toil of any Human Being?" Trade Unions Favor Machinery. Its Advantages. Union Attitude Misrepresented. Former Attitude of Workingmen. Machine Riots. The Old Evils of Machinery. The Machine-owning Class. Unemployment. Long Hours. The Loss of a Skilled Trade. Not Prohibition but Regulation. The Long Run and the Short Run. The Least Friction Possible. Differentials. The Right to the Machine. Time Work and Piece Work. How Trade Unions Introduce Machinery.

IN the year 1848 the famous political economist, John Stuart Mill, wrote as follows: "Hitherto it is questionable if all the mechanical inventions yet made have lessened the day's toil of any human being." These words, spoken not by a trade union leader, but by the most eminent economist of his day, may explain to some extent the instinctive hatred once felt by the workingmen for machinery. Since the days of Mill, however, there has taken place not only an improvement in the conditions under which machinery has been operated, not only an increase in the advantages and a decrease in the disadvantages arising from machinery, but also a gradual change in the whole attitude of the workman. Trade unions have been foremost in this change of opinion, and at the present time the great majority of labor organizations are desirous of promoting the introduction of machinery, although in such a way as to work the least possible injury to the wage earner and to confer upon him the greatest possible benefit.

Trade unionists recognize that machinery has enormously multiplied the productive power of the community. They realize that the work done at present in the United States could not, without the aid of machinery, be performed by three times the present population. They acknowledge that machinery has cheapened all manner of products and that the artisan can now purchase at a moderate price a variety of necessary, useful, and beautiful articles, wholly unattainable a century or even a generation ago. Finally, the trade unionists believe that machinery has not permanently deprived large masses of the population of the opportunity to work, and they recognize, amid the evils of machinery, great and enduring benefits.

Notwithstanding this attitude on the part of trade unions it has constantly been claimed by hostile critics that the unions are opposed to labor-saving machinery and endeavor, wherever possible, to prevent its introduction. This claim is false and erroneous, but it is none the less dangerous because with its falsity it contains a certain appearance of truth.

It is far easier to bear false witness and make reckless charges against trade unionism than to understand its real attitude. This attitude has been the result of an evolution taking place during a period of one hundred and fifty years. When machines were first introduced, men who were then not organized, not united into trade unions, struck blindly and instinctively at them, and there was violence, bloodshed, and arson. With the passing of each decade and with the steady growth of the power and intelligence of trade unionists, the former stupid opposition to machinery as such declined and diminished, until at the present time all but a small minority of workmen are converted to the view that machinery is a necessity, to which it is foolish and unwise, if not impossible, to offer permanent resistance.

It was about the year 1760 that the earlier machines were introduced with the result of herding former handworkers into the factories and large cities. The effect of these first inventions was intensified after 1785 by the application of steam power to the new machinery and the substitution of mechanical power for that of man. The invention of the locomotive and the steam railway and the newer applications of electricity, increased the field for machines. Eventually, not only were the products of industry made by machines, but these machines themselves were made by other machines.

Beneficent as machinery has upon the whole proved itself to be, there is no doubt that at first its effects were terrible. The despairing attempts of the old handworker to compete against the new machines, and the hunger, starvation, and degradation that resulted are among the most pathetic incidents in industrial history. The workingman felt that he was being deprived of his own in some curious way, which he did not understand, and the machine seemed to be his enemy. In hundreds of thousands of cases the machine drove the man from his work and in many instances substituted for patiently and painfully acquired skill the services of an untrained laborer, or a little boy or girl. The skilled men lost their positions and their only asset, their knowledge of a trade. Men advanced in years lost their employment and their hold upon life. Thousands of workmen were kept at home, while their wives and children worked inhumanly long hours in the dingy factories. The machine turned men into women and women into men. The old tool of the workers, like the sword of the soldier or the pen of the scholar, had been their friend, their assistant, their very own, but this new machine was a terrible, soulless monster, to which they were chained, to which they were subject, and over which they had no manner of control. The machines by displacing hundreds of thousands of workers, created intense hardship, even though the displaced workmen were eventually reëmployed in the same or other occupations. Even to-day the trade unionist sees the great loss entailed upon workmen, whose painfully acquired knowledge of a trade suddenly loses its value, and he also observes the manner in which machinery has encouraged the work of women and fostered the employment of children. Another drawback of machinery is found in the extent to which, in many occupations, the skilled mechanic is converted into a mere machine tender, occupied possibly for a whole life time in the manufacture of a hundredth part of a watch or a shoe.

While the trade unionist of to-day thus sees advantages and disadvantages in the use of machinery, he also sees the absolute necessity and inevitableness of its introduction and use. There is not even a respectable minority of trade unionists at the present day opposed to machinery as such. The accusation advanced by many writers, that machinery is dirty, ugly, disagreeable, monotonous, a blot upon the scenery, and an affront to the artistic sense, is not given much weight by unionists, even though a part

Coke Ovens

Far in the background men are seen with the apparatus which draws the coke out of the ovens. The product is then carried through the long trough by an endless belt, and thence by another belt, shown in the foreground, to the shipping sheds

THEODORE ROOSEVELT,
President of the United States.

of it is admitted to be true. Trade unionists know that they cannot do without further advances in machinery, just as they realize that they could not maintain their present status if all the machinery introduced in the past were to be suddenly withdrawn.

What the trade unionist desires is not the prohibition of machinery, but its regulation. The unionist demands first that machinery be introduced in such a way as to give the greatest possible benefit to all classes, with the least possible damage to the workman, and, second, that the introduction of machinery shall redound to the direct and immediate advantage of the workman, as well as to the direct and immediate advantage of the employer.

There have been many arguments advanced on both sides of the question as to whether, in the long run, machinery increases or decreases the amount of employment. It is claimed by some that the cheapening of production which comes with machinery, means an enormous increase in the number of positions to be filled. It is pointed out that there are now a million men employed on the railroads of the United States, whereas there were but a few thousand employed on the stage coaches which they displaced. It seems to be true that the total amount of employment has increased or, at least, has not decreased, with the introduction of machines; that while some industries have decreased, other industries have increased, the number of their employees, and that, on the whole, the labor force of the community is more advantageously employed at the present time than ever before.

Whatever may be the ultimate effect of the introduction of machinery, the immediate effect has been to work extreme hardship on the employee. The workmen who are obliged to work longer hours or more intensely for the same amount of pay, or who are thrown out of employment entirely, will not be consoled by the fact that in the long run prices will be reduced and the articles which they manufacture, cheapened to them. The unionists believe that machinery should be introduced with the least possible friction and the least possible hardship to individuals. When the employer is asked to increase wages or reduce hours, he frequently asks for an interval of a certain time in order to allow him to accommodate himself to the change, and the labor unions are now beginning to recognize the necessity of making great changes in industrial conditions by slow degrees. An equal duty should rest upon the employer to make alterations gradually, so as to extend the effect of the change over a series of years, and thus permit the workmen to accommodate themselves to the new conditions.

It is felt by the trade unionists, moreover, that the workman should receive some direct benefit from the introduction of new machines. Apart from the fact that machinery works damage indirectly by making work more irregular, apart, also, from the fact that the introduction of the machine often means increased intensity of work and increased wear and tear upon the nervous system, apart from all other considerations, the workman should receive a portion of the benefit which is derived by the employer from the introduction of machinery. Originally, the simple tool of the workman was his own property, and any improvement in this tool redounded to his own advantage. The machine was an extension and a combination of tools, and its introduction and improvement meant a gradual separation of the workman from the instruments of production. The vital fact of machinery was this—that it was too effective to permit the workman's tool to compete with it and too expensive for the individual workman to own it. As a result, there grew up, separate from the workman, a capitalist class, a class owning machines and hiring labor. The result of this separation was that every improvement in the machines was to the immediate, if not the ultimate, advantage of the employer and to the immediate, if not ultimate, detriment of the workman. The majority of trade unionists do not take the stand of the Socialists, that these machines should be taken away from the capitalist class and be owned by the whole body of workmen, but they do claim that whenever a machine is improved or a new machine introduced, a part of the advantage should go to them immediately in increased wages or decreased hours. It is felt by the unionists that this is only fair and just, and that such a distribution of benefits would compensate the workman for the increased intensity of his work, and would be to the ultimate advantage of the employer and of society. The claim sometimes made by employers that the whole benefit should go to them, since it will be eventually returned to the workmen in the form of cheaper products, is not reassuring to the workingman. He has so often found promises of this sort illusory that he is not unnaturally suspicious. If the force of competition can distribute the benefits of a new machine fairly when they are all in the hands of an employer, there is no reason why it cannot do so quite as effectively when part of them are in the possession of the workman.

Much of the supposed hostility of trade unions to machinery is due merely to the fact that the unions are not willing to allow the employer to secure the entire benefit from the new machine or the improved process. Even though the employer has bought the machine or the process, it does not entitle him to subject his workmen to it at a sacrifice to them and an advantage to him. The man who buys a machine does not and should not have the right to all the profit which the machine can exact and extort from the man who operates it; and the right to use a machine, or rather to be used by it, is one which should be paid for, just as the inventor is paid in the form of a royalty. A machine is in a certain sense the property not only of the man who buys it, but of the man who operates it, not only of the man who invents it, but of the society whose manifold work by men of research have made its discovery possible. The inventor receives his reward through royalties, or through a cash payment, society through the cheapening of the product; and the employer and employees should arrange among themselves for an equitable distribution among them, the employer to be paid for his increased expense, for the cost of equipment, maintenance, and risk, and for his enterprise while the workingman should be paid for his increased exertion and should be given a share of the bonus above that amount. The introduction of the machine should be done upon what may be likened to the coöperative system, and the machine should not be used to make the profits of the employer greater and the pittance of the employee less.

Where trade unions have in the past actually attempted to prevent or hinder the introduction of machines, they have signally failed. It is as impossible as it is undesirable for any body of men, however large or however well-organized, to prevent permanently the introduction of labor-saving devices. Where trade unions have in the past adopted this policy, the result has simply been to send the new machines into non-union establishments, and by means of the competition of the new with the old, of the better with the worse methods of production gradually to lower and reduce the union scale. While there can be no doubt that the sudden introduction of machines often works great hardship to workingmen, the method of securing redress is not by fighting the machine but by obtaining control of it. Both English and American unions have done this in a number of instances and have been accorded the right to man the new machines. The result has been an elevation of the standard of living of the men who worked upon the new machines as well as of men who worked by the old process. In this way the Typographical Union has entered into friendly relations with publishers, by which the linotype is kept in union hands, with the result that much better conditions have prevailed and larger wages and profits have been secured than would have been the case if there had been a struggle or contest between the new machine and the old union.

As a matter of history, trade unionism has not only not restricted the use of machinery, but has actually encouraged and stimulated its application. It was formerly cited as an instance of "trade union folly" that the insistence upon high wages and upon other expensive conditions led to the displacement of men by machines. During the last century there have been many instances where machines have been introduced because the men claimed high wages, and the employer was obliged to economize. The more costly labor becomes, the greater the advantage of economizing it, and in no country has the invention of machinery been so stimulated and gone on at so rapid a pace as in England and the United States, the countries in which trade unions are strongest. Even strikes themselves have had this result, and many of the most improved methods of production have originated from the necessity of doing with little labor. Trade unions, moreover, have consciously adopted the policy of encouraging inventions and the use of machinery. Unionists realize that, by insisting upon a standard rate of pay, a maximum working day, and a certain minimum of safety and comfort for the workman, factories which are not equipped with modern machinery must eventually be forced out of business. The theory of trade unions is that the manufacturer must either equip his factory with modern labor-saving devices or else suffer by competition, but that he may not pay lower wages because of his unwillingness to secure the best machinery. Where trade unions do not exist, employers with the worst and oldest machinery and the most antiquated methods manage to eke out a precarious existence by underpaying and starving their workmen, but where trade unionism is able to enforce a definite minimum wage, these less skilful and less adequately equipped manufacturers must either introduce the modern appliances or go to the wall. As a consequence, the countries, the industries, and even the individual establishments where trade unionism is strongest are those in which machinery is applied earliest and to the largest extent.

CHAPTER XXIX

THE RESTRICTION OF THE OUTPUT

The London "Times" on Restriction. Importance of the Question. Unions Opposed to Restriction. Efficiency *vs.* Restriction. The Attitude of Employers. The Amount of Restriction Exaggerated. Restriction by Unorganized Men. The Demand for Shorter Hours. Rushing and Rate Cutting. Speed and Health. Piece and Premium Systems. The Theory of a Work Fund. Attitude of Unionists on Restriction.

ABOUT two years ago there appeared in the London *Times* a series of articles attacking British trade unions for alleged restriction of the output of industry. The contributor to the *Times* asserted that many of the trade unions of Great Britain were consciously and deliberately conspiring to do as little work per man as possible, and that to this cause the comparative decline of British trade and commerce was to be attributed. It has since been shown that these claims were grossly exaggerated, and that there was but little fire in all this vast cloud of smoke; but the articles in question have evoked a timely discussion as to the manner and extent to which trade unions in the United States and Great Britain limit the output of labor.

No problem could be of greater importance to the workingman and to the country at large than this question of restriction. Upon this question there should be no room for difference of opinion or divergence in policy. The output of labor is the source of the reward of labor, the basis of national prosperity. While labor must defend itself against aggressive action upon the part of capital and while a seeming restriction of output may occasionally be necessary to avoid evils worse than actual restriction, the unions of this country should singly and unitedly take a firm stand against the policy of limiting the output except in so far as the output may be restricted by limiting the hours of labor. The slogan of trade unionists should be, and is, a fair day's work for a fair day's wage and sufficient pay for efficient work.

The whole question of restriction of output, however, throws a curious light upon some of the favorite contentions of anti-union employers. The employer has always taken a stand against what he terms the intermeddling of dreamers and sentimentalists. "Business," he has maintained, "is business. If the workman is not satisfied with the wages he receives and the hours of labor which I exact from him then he may go elsewhere at his own will and pleasure. I shall pay him as little as I must and get from him as much as I can; but if he can do better elsewhere, I have no objection to his trying." The moral aspect of the labor contract, however, suddenly emerges for the first time when the workingman has the advantage and seeks to profit by it. When the employers inveigh against the immorality of restriction of output, workmen might reply, with perfect logic, "We will give you as little work and extort as much wages as possible, and if you do not like it you may lock us out or close your factory." The workingmen would not be right in adopting such an attitude, but the indignation of the employers is a recognition of the fact that, after all, there *is* a moral aspect to the labor contract, and the workingmen in sweated trades have just as much right to appeal to the conscience of the nation as the employers would have if a deliberate policy of unjustifiable restriction of output were enforced against them.

The actual amount of such restriction of output has been magnified and exaggerated. It exists to a far less extent in England than has been claimed, and it is admitted by American employers that its extent in the United States is very much smaller than in England. In the vast majority of trades there is no restriction whatsoever, and the number and membership of trade unions which encourage restriction is small and unimportant. But such restriction as exists is not an invention of labor unions, since even unorganized workingmen do not desire, as a rule, to over-exert themselves unless they receive a compensating increase in wages. As a matter of fact, trade unions, by making wages higher and conditions of employment more favorable, tend to stimulate and increase the activity of the workmen rather than restrict it.

It frequently occurs, however, that when a union asks for a justifiable reduction in the length of the working day, the charge is erroneously made that the union is seeking to restrict the output. Again, it occasionally happens that a trade union is obliged to urge its men to go slow in order to prevent a definite, impending injury which may be threatened by the employer. In the machinery and many other trades it has been a common practice on the part of employers to resort to rushing and price cutting. This process is simple and, with unorganized men, effectual. Men engaged in a certain establishment who are earning three dollars a day and, we will assume, are finishing three pieces of work a day, are urged by the adoption of the piece system to greater activity, with the result that after a while they finish four pieces and secure four dollars a day. Immediately thereafter the piece price is cut to seventy-five cents, with the result that the men still earn three dollars a day. Again the workmen seek to increase their output, and by means of extra exertion a number of them manage to complete five pieces, whereupon, after a short time, the piece price is cut to sixty cents and the more efficient workers still earn only three dollars. By a final effort, and by the most intense exertion, by the partial sacrifice of the dinner hour, by over-rushing and the performance of poor work, the most able, skilled and indefatigable employees manage to complete six or seven pieces, with the result that after a short lapse of time the rate is cut again. The effect of all this is experienced in a constant tendency toward reductions in piece prices, which permit a few men to earn more than the standard rate while throwing the majority below it; and which results further in the breaking down of any stationary or reasonable rate of payment, in the deterioration of the quality of the work, in the ill health and often serious sickness of the workingman, and, finally, in the ceaseless, continual falling of piece price to a level where the work is inadequately paid. This example is not an isolated experience, but one which has repeatedly injured men in many trades. The alternate over-rush and under-cutting tend gradually or quickly to undermine the fair wage scale of the employee. Still another device of somewhat the same nature is the employment of men of exceptional skill and endurance as pace

Marcus A. Hanna,
Chairman National Civic Federation

Members of the Coal Strike Arbitration Commission

setters. There are always differences in the ability of men to perform work, and both employers and unions are willing to recognize these differences. Employers, however, where pace setters are employed, assume that the wages of the mass of the workers should be determined by the relation of their output to the output of the pace setter; whereas the unions insist that the remuneration of the great mass of workers shall be fixed at a fair minimum wage and that the man of exceptional ability or exceptional endurance may receive a bonus above the regular scale.

Where men are paid by the piece and are constantly urged by pace setters and employers to compete with one another for a job by working at a constantly increasing rate of speed, it is absolutely essential that the union should interfere to counteract this evil. If a man performs, through extra exertion, thirty per cent. more work for three dollars than his neighbor does, he will be preferred in the selection of employees, and the men will be constantly over stimulated to produce a given result. Where there is an undue and unusual exertion, the extreme tension of work injures a man physically and mentally, with the result that men break down and at an early age become totally incapacitated.

The pace setter has been frequently used as a club to depress the wages of men who are not thoroughly organized, and an attempt is constantly made to speed up the men beyond a point compatible with health and permanent good work. If a man is to be employed one day he may work at a tremendous rate of speed; if he is to be employed for a month without interruption and without illness, his rate of speed must be somewhat slackened, and if he is to be permanently employed and is not to be thrown upon the rubbish pile as soon as he attains the age of forty or forty-five, his speed and intensity of work must be regulated at a reasonable rate. As the president of a great railroad said to me, "We employers are responsible for the antagonism to piece work and are to blame for any restriction of output. We have made our employees do work running that it was difficult to do walking." In fact, many fair minded employers of the present day recognize that by ceaseless cutting of the price of work they have simply forced men to resort to some means of self defense, and the remedy applied by the workingman is apt to be harsher and cruder than that which the employers would have imposed upon themselves. The present agitation among some employers for a premium system, by which only a portion of the gain from increased exertion is to go to the employee, and by which the piece rates are to be considered as permanent, appears to be a wholesale admission on the part of the employers of their past folly in unfairly cutting prices and over-rushing workmen.

Where a temporary restriction of output has been invited and justified by over-rushing, pace setting, and price cutting by employers, it does not follow that such restriction would continue to be justified if the employer were willing to afford substantial guarantee that these evil practices would not be resorted to in the future. It is to the interest of workmen and of employers as well that all restrictions upon output, except in so far as they are clearly and obviously necessary to prevent loss of health or inferior workmanship, should be permanently and completely abolished. In the few trades in which restrictions exist, and in which they have been occasioned by the employers, the overtures for their removal should be made by the latter, and the workingmen should not put obstacles in the way of accomplishing this result, but should evince a willingness to meet the employer half way.

When the unions are simply attempting to mitigate the evils which result from pace setting or over-exertion it is not fair to accuse them of restricting the output. There still remains, however, a belief among certain workingmen that restrictions would be justified by the desire to make work. There seems to be prevalent among many persons, both employers and workmen, the idea that there exists only a certain fixed amount of work to go around and that the more work one man does the less work there will be left for others. This belief in a definite amount of work to be distributed occasionally tends to make a workman go slow with the job in order to make it last longer, or in order to make work for others who may be unemployed. To do too much work is supposed, sometimes, to be "hogging it," to be taking the bread out of another man's mouth. This may, occasionally, be more or less true, although even in such cases the employer has rights which should be respected and a man should do—as he ordinarily does do—a fair day's work for a fair day's wage. For the whole of society, however, the theory is not true. Within certain limits the more work done the more remains to be done. The man who earns large wages in a blacksmith's shop creates a demand for labor when he spends his wages in shoes, clothes, furniture, or in books, and a large production tends to make his product cheaper. To render work more expensive merely for the sake of restricting output, is to lessen the amount of work that will be done, and it is only by doing a fair day's work that a fair day's wages can be permanently maintained. The wages of workingmen, sooner or later, fall with any unreasonable restriction upon the output, and what is of still more importance, the habit of slowing up work permanently incapacitates the workman for continued and intense effort. It is, therefore, of supreme importance that the present policy of American trade unions, the policy of non-restriction, should be continued and enforced. The future of the trade unions of this country must rest upon an ever-growing emphasis upon efficiency of work and sufficiency of remuneration, and the theory of the restriction of output must never become a fixed program and must never be adopted as a policy.

CHAPTER XXX

THE PASSING OF THE APPRENTICE

Former System of Apprenticeship. System Older than Trade Unionism. Gradual Disappearance of the Apprentice. Wholesale Employment of Children. Apprenticeship in Certain Trades Increasingly Difficult. Lack of Training at Present Time. The Policy of Unions toward Apprenticeship. Do Trade Unions Unjustly Restrict the Number of Apprentices? The Exploitation of Child Labor. Industrial Schools.

ONE of the problems with which in the past the union has had to deal has been the question of apprenticeship, or the technical education of the workman. All work involves a certain preliminary training requiring years, months, weeks, or, it may be, only days, according to the skill and intelligence necessary. In the old days, this skill was acquired by the system of apprenticeship. At the age of fourteen or thereabouts a boy was indentured or apprenticed to the employer and remained with him for a period of seven years or more, obtaining in that time a thorough knowledge of the trade. The system was based upon the mutual advantage to both parties, the master instructing the youth, and the youth receiving small wages or none at all. The course of instruction was long and formal, as was the case with students of law, medicine, or divinity, and at its termination the youth was admitted to a trade, in which he was protected from the competition of interlopers, or men who had not served a like apprenticeship.

The system of apprenticeship was not invented by trade unions, but existed for many centuries before the modern labor organizations were formed. It was a definite formal relation between employer and youth, regulated by guild laws and later by the law of the land. There existed at the same time, however, an informal apprenticeship of the sons of journeymen to their fathers, the boys learning their trade directly from their parents and being paid or not as the latter determined.

As long as industries were of a simple nature and were conducted upon a small scale, the system of apprenticeship worked to the satisfaction of everyone. With the growth of modern industry, however, these conditions changed. The introduction of the machine destroyed the value of much of the knowledge formerly acquired by apprentices, and the division of labor frequently rendered it unnecessary. When an article was begun and completed by the same person, a knowledge of the trade was a thing difficult and tedious to acquire, but when this manufacture became divided into twenty, fifty, or a hundred different processes, each process a simple mechanical movement, the value of a complete knowledge of the trade became purely fictitious. The introduction of the machine and the division of labor meant specialization. It meant the performance by an unskilled man of a single, simple operation, not a whole series of operations by one skilled workman.

The apprentice system as it formerly existed began to crumble away about the middle of the eighteenth century. Children styled apprentices were worked at nominal wages, but were not taught any trade, being used merely as long as they were profitable and then turned adrift upon society. This unscrupulous exploitation of child labor under the guise of the apprentice system has been a standing grievance with many trade unions. Under the pretext of apprenticeship large numbers of boys, supported principally by their parents, are brought into the factory and kept there at low wages until they are old enough to demand more money, when they are discharged and a new relay of boys is taken on.

As a result of the breakdown of the apprenticeship system, the great mass of youths to-day receive little or no training in their particular trade. Even when there are no abuses on the part of employers, the unionists see their trade swarmed with crowds of boys who receive no regular instruction and who, as half-skilled workmen, are after a few years injected into the industry. Some of the unions, therefore, desire to secure the introduction of a system by which boys can obtain regular training and the number of apprentices to the trade be limited or adjusted to the real needs of the industry.

In consequence of their attempt to prevent the unregulated exploitation of children under the guise of apprenticeship, the unions have been charged with restricting their numbers and with attempting to establish a monopoly in the trade. This charge, however, cannot be maintained. A careful investigation, made by Mr. and Mrs. Webb, revealed that the British trade unions that actually and effectively restrict the admission of apprentices below the needs of the trade represented less than one per cent. of all unionists in the Kingdom. The percentage in the United States is probably smaller. Such a policy would necessarily be unsuccessful, since, as a result of unduly limiting the number of apprentices in union shops, the boys would learn their trade in non-union establishments, or the ranks of labor would be recruited from skilled immigrants. As a matter of fact, it is usually found that in the cases in which American trade unions actually determine the number of apprentices the employers in the trade are unwilling to take on as many apprentices as the union permits.

While in certain trades unmodified by the advent of machinery apprenticeship in its old-time form may still persist, in most cases the system of indenturing boys for a long period must be definitely surrendered. The boys themselves are no longer willing to serve this protracted apprenticeship, and, as a general rule, no opportunity is afforded in the great industrial establishments of to-day for a youth to acquire a thorough knowledge of the trade, even when such a knowledge would be necessary or advantageous to him.

The solution of the problem of training workmen is now being sought in industrial education. There is growing up in the United States an ever-increasing number of industrial schools, well managed and equipped, with all appliances and materials necessary for turning out efficient skilled workmen. It is probable that in the future many skilled mechanics will be graduated from schools of this nature. By means of special instruction in the manual arts, as well as in regular school studies, the boy receives a general education and is thus enabled to start life better equipped than the skilled workman of a generation ago.

However, there is one feature of the excellent industrial school system of this country which requires modification. It is a regrettable fact that a large number of the graduates from these schools are imbued with a hostile spirit toward trade unionism. In many cases the instruction is of such a nature as to fail to promote sympathy on the part of the boys for the doctrines and customs of labor organizations. This defect should be remedied. No line of cleavage should separate the shop-taught man and the school-taught man. The boys at an industrial school should learn not a trade alone, but methods for bettering their condition within the trade. I do not believe that graduates of industrial schools will permanently remain outside the trade union movement, but much needless friction and bitter feeling might be avoided if their instruction were of such a nature as to create in them a sympathetic feeling toward the great trade union movement.

CHAPTER XXXI

THE BOUNDARIES OF TRADES

The Definition of a Trade. Importance of Jurisdictional Disputes. The Old Trades and the Division of Labor. The "Trade" Union *vs.* the "Industrial" Union. Wastefulness of Jurisdictional Disputes. The Injustice to Employers. Federated Unions. The Representation of Unions. The Necessity of Peace between Unions.

IN the eyes of the ordinary man the most incomprehensible feature of trade unionism is the trade or jurisdictional dispute. It is difficult for anyone not versed in these matters to understand that there can be differences of opinion as to the trade to which a particular piece of work belongs. We speak of a trade as something clearly defined, as the trade of a carpenter, a blacksmith, a tailor, or a stone-mason. There are, however, hundreds of cases in which it is practically impossible to determine where one trade leaves off and another begins. A charge frequently brought against unions is that they themselves cannot agree upon questions of jurisdiction and cannot decide to which group of workmen a particular job should belong. The problem is extremely important, since it is injurious for union men earning three dollars a day to be displaced by men earning two, whether it be by workmen candidly non-union, or by members of a different trade union. If the employer is to decide which of two unions shall receive the work, he will invariably give preference to the one which does the cheaper work, and he may not hesitate to create organizations for the express purpose of underbidding the regular unions at the trade.

The conflicts over jurisdiction between various unions have been the result of the growth of industry itself. At one time the blacksmiths performed many functions now relegated to other workmen. The machinery trades have been divided and subdivided into hundreds of different processes. New materials have been introduced; iron has taken the place of wood, steel of iron, and copper and other materials of various metals since displaced. At one time a watchmaker made the entire watch, but now one set of men make the main-spring, another the hands, still another the case, and so on. The shoemaker, who makes a complete shoe, can no longer secure a position in the factories of Massachusetts, since the work has been subdivided into scores of simple operations.

This change in the character of industry has necessarily brought with it corresponding changes in the scope and organization of labor unions. According to the old theory, a trade union was an organization of men performing a certain given function. The union was based upon the fact that all its members performed essentially the same work and required essentially the same training. All the carpenters in the early trade unions performed practically the same work, and every shoemaker was likewise equal in all respects to his fellow-craftsmen. The trade union existed largely for the purpose of determining what period of apprenticeship should be served, for regulating the conditions of apprenticeship, and for keeping out of the trade men who had not had a particular training. This theory, however, while entirely suitable for the simple conditions of former times, is becoming less and less applicable. Division of labor has put an end to many old trades and has created hundreds of others; and with each new invention, with each change of tools or material wrought upon, the boundaries of trades become more dubious. With the change from wooden to iron ships, the boiler makers may come into conflict with the shipwrights, the carpenters, or any other of several trades. A given class of work may be contested for by a number of groups of workmen, one of which claims it because of the material worked upon, another, because of the operation performed, another, because of the tools used, another, because of the character of the establishment in which the work is done, another, for any one of a dozen apparently valid reasons.

The problem of the proper jurisdiction of trades is complicated by the fact that organization of men into unions is carried on upon distinct and conflicting bases. There are, roughly speaking, two classes of unions, the trade union in the narrow sense of the word[1] and the industrial union. The trade union endeavors to organize men according to the particular work which they do; the industrial union, according to the industry in which they are employed. An engineer engaged in a brewery might conceivably belong to a brewers' union or to an engineers' union, and there might therefore be a conflict of jurisdiction between these two unions. The problems thus created are extremely intricate, and I cannot in this book do more than merely state the questions at issue. The solution is difficult and depends in each case upon special and particular circumstances. However, a few observations may be made, which show at least the general direction in which a solution may be sought.

The importance of these jurisdictional disputes cannot be overestimated. Much of the opposition in this country to trade unions is due to the fact that they engage in strikes over jurisdiction, and it is claimed by Mr. and Mrs. Sidney Webb that in England "nine-tenths of the ineffectiveness of the trade union world" is due to the "competition between overlapping unions."

The necessity of a solution is more obvious than the solution itself. Competition between rival trade unions is prejudicial and injurious to both. In the matter of friendly benefits as well as in trade policy, the interests of two unions competing for the same jurisdiction will inevitably clash, with the result that competition for membership will ensue on terms harmful both to the members and to the unions. Such competition for membership on the part of unions is likely to lead to strikes without justification. It is also likely to lead, and in many cases has led, to reciprocal scabbing. When the members of one union claiming jurisdiction over a certain trade have struck, the members of another union have, at times, not hesitated to put in their own men at wages less than was demanded by the strikers, with

---

[1] In this chapter I use the word trade union in the narrow or strict sense, of a union organized according to the trade or operation, as distinct from an industrial union, like the United Mine Workers, organized on the basis of an industry or business. In other chapters I use the word trade union in its general sense of labor union.

the result of recrimination and subsequent retaliation on the part of the members of the injured organization.

There are difficulties in the way, both of trade and industrial unions. The trade union is frequently hampered by the fact of its comparative weakness, especially when its members constitute only a fraction of the men in the industry. It is further weakened by the fact that its policy may be out of harmony with that of other workmen in the same industry. In large industries a minority, however well organized, should not rule. Thus, in the anthracite mines it would be intolerable if the one hundred and fifty thousand men and boys were obliged to quit work owing to a disagreement between the employers and a few thousand engineers upon the question of wages, hours of labor, or recognition of the union, while the engineers themselves could not successfully cope with the operators without the assistance of the other men in the industry. The interests of all the men in a given industry are to a certain extent common. Their wages may differ but in a general way, they demand the same hours of labor, the same provision for safety and sanitation, the same methods and times of payment, the same holidays, and practically the same legal protection. It would, therefore, not be possible, and certainly not desirable, to have all these men organized in individual trades and to permit each separate organization to make whatever contract it desired with the employer, irrespective of the welfare of others.

An illustration of the manner in which industrial unions are organized may be found in the United Mine Workers of America. The anthracite workers include such diverse occupations as engineers, firemen, blacksmiths, pump men, machinists, carpenters, masons, laborers, teamsters, loaders, dump men, plate men, drivers, runners, door boys, fuel men, barnmen, ash men, oilers, culm drivers, slate pickers, and many other classes of workers, who could not be organized separately. The central fact of the organization, however, is that a large percentage of these men ultimately become miners, or other workers closely related to them, and in view of the similarity in interest of the overwhelming majority, an industrial union is formed. An industrial union, however, should embrace not only all the workers in an industrial establishment, but all the establishments in the industry.

The organization of mine workers must include not only all the anthracite mines of the country, but also the bituminous mines. The anthracite operators bitterly complained against the United Mine Workers of America because it was an organization which controlled the production of bituminous coal, which, they alleged as a grievance, was a competing product. A greater ignorance of the fundamental principles of trade unionism could not well be conceived. It is *because* anthracite coal competes with bituminous that the mining of both should be controlled by one organization. The Mine Workers have become strong both in the anthracite and bituminous fields, not *despite,* but *because* of the fact that these two products compete. There is a point, of course, where the competition of products may not be severe or direct enough to warrant the inclusion in the same union of the men engaged in the industry. Thus, for instance, it would be unwise to include in the Mine Workers' organization the men engaged in the production and refining of oil, but the position of the friends of industrial unionism will be made clear when it is stated that it would be better to include in the organization the producers of oil or of any and all sorts and kinds of fuel than it would be to include the miners of silver, gold, or copper. In other words, the industrial union follows the employer or the product on the market and does not concern itself chiefly with the particular and specific operation performed by its members.

There are drawbacks also to the system of organization on industrial lines. To a certain extent, such organization is more modern and more in accord with modern methods of business. Such organizations, moreover, overstep the bounds of the particular piece of work done by the members and are sufficiently elastic to include members engaged at varying kinds of work. On the other hand, they suffer the disadvantage of uniting men with more or less dissimilar interests, men able to pay high dues and men able to pay only small ones, and men whose wages and standards of living vary greatly. There is always danger in such a union that the interest of a minority will be sacrificed to that of a majority. The leaders of an industrial union should be careful to impress constantly upon its members the necessity of paying respectful attention to the demand of every constituent group, no matter how small, in order that the union may not suffer from secession. The danger of the trade union, in the narrow sense of the word, is constant conflict, owing to overlapping jurisdiction and inherent weakness resulting from small numbers and isolation. The peril of the industrial union is that of secession due to its frequent failure to represent the interests of all its parts.

The most satisfactory method of compromising the struggle between these two classes of unions is found in the formation of federated[2] unions. In the building trades the unions have become federated so that the individual unions may strive for certain of their demands, while the federation attempts to represent them in those cases in which their interests are general.

The only satisfactory or practicable method of reconciling the differences of conflicting unions is the formation of federated bodies and the delegation of authority to these federations to settle jurisdictional disputes, and to act as a body upon all questions affecting the common interests of the different unions exercising jurisdiction in any industry. Thus, the various unions in the wood-working industry should form themselves into a federation, and similar federations should be formed of all unions in the metal, the leather, the plumbing and steam-fitting, and other trades, working upon materials of the same class. Personally I believe that much good would result not only from the federation but from the actual amalgamation of many of the national unions now exercising jurisdiction over industries of the same character. There are, at the present time, five national organizations in the wood-working industry, each of these claiming juris-

---

[2] These unions, which are organizations consisting of separate, practically independent trade unions, should not be confounded with "federal" unions, which are single organizations of miscellaneous workers organized by the American Federation of Labor.

diction over certain kinds of work; in the metal trades an equal or a greater number of organizations exists. It seems to me that by amalgamating or consolidating these various organizations in the same trade, the interests of all the workers would be conserved. Of course, as a prerequisite, all unions should become affiliated with the American Federation of Labor. There are some obstacles in the way of the formation of these federations. The principal difficulty is that of the representation of the various unions within the federation. The larger unions desire to be represented according to membership, but this system may easily be used practically to deprive the smaller unions of all power. A single union in the federation, or a coalition of two or three, might outvote all the other members, so that the federated body would cease to be really representative. On the other hand, an equal representation of all unions might give a disproportionate power to a number of smaller and minutely specialized industries, which would give control to an insignificant minority. To reach a satisfactory compromise between equal representation of all unions and representation in proportion to membership is difficult though not impossible, and there will be, in the future, a movement toward the federation of unions in allied trades, especially where they are united in single industries or enterprises. Where, however, unions are strongly localized and where the vast majority of members are engaged at work which is approximately similar, or are apprenticed to such work, it is probable that the industrial union will persist.

While jurisdictional disputes are unavoidable from the very nature of industry, it is only fair that in so far as possible such disputes should be settled by the direct participants, the trade unions, without drawing into controversy the employer and the public. It is manifestly unfair that when an employer is willing to pay union wages and to observe union conditions generally, he should be prevented from so doing by two different unions, each of which claims the work and each of which will prevent the other from accepting it. The question of jurisdiction may be one of great, if not vital, importance, but such questions should, like family quarrels, be settled within the family itself.

To a large extent this is already done by the trade unions. The American Federation of Labor has accomplished a great deal toward preventing the outbreak of jurisdictional disputes and toward settling them where they have already occurred. In this matter the American Federation of Labor should be greatly strengthened. The various organizations claiming the same work should be compelled to submit the question in dispute to the arbitration of technically equipped special committees appointed by the American Federation of Labor. The respective claims of the parties to the dispute should then be passed upon and the award should be absolutely final. The national unions should support the Federation in its decisions, and all organizations which refuse to abide thereby should be punished according to the judgment of the Federation.

It is important that any decisions arrived at should be national and not merely local in their scope, and that they should be strictly enforced. Jurisdictional disputes must cease absolutely to be settled by strikes, and the employer must be relieved of the burden of inter-union struggles. Until some form of arbitration between unions is established upon a firm basis, there can be little hope of a permanent strengthening of labor organizations.

CHAPTER XXXII

THE UNIONIST AND THE NON-UNIONIST

Refusal to Work with Non-Unionists Entirely Legal. The Question of Policy. The Moral Question. The Rights of the Individual. The Right to Join the Union. Why is the Non-Unionist on the Outside? Initiation Fees and Limitation of Numbers. Monopoly, Open Unions, and the Exclusion of Non-Unionists. Kinds and Classes of Non-Unionists. Robinson Crusoes. The Men who do not Know. The Incapables. The Strike Breakers. Non-Unionists not Victims of Conscience. The Non-Unionist played off against the Unionist. Sentiment and Sentimentality. Even the Non-Unionist belongs to a Group. The Railroad and Section Hand No. 347. The Non-Unionist and the Fruits of the Strike. Loyalty and Gratitude. A Shop Divided against Itself.

BY a refusal to work with non-union men, labor organizations occasionally excite acute irritation among employers and criticism from press and public. The employer feels that in taking such action unions dictate how he shall run his business and encroach upon his rights and upon those of the non-unionist. A considerable section of the public seems to believe that by this course the unions monopolize employment and determine without the right of appeal who shall be permitted and who forbidden to work.

The question thus raised by the employer and by a section of the public is not legal, but ethical. From a strictly legal point of view, there can be no doubt that trade unionists or others have a perfect right to refuse to work with any person or persons for any reason good or bad. This was decided by the British House of Lords in the recent case of Allen *vs.* Flood, and American courts have closely followed this precedent.

Whether right or wrong in its preconceptions, the public is perfectly justified in insisting that a clear light be thrown upon the question of the treatment of the non-unionist. The welfare and moral health of the community depend upon the protection which it accords to the individual man.

It should not be permitted to any group of men, whether it be a thousand or five million, to deprive unjustly a single individual of his sacred and inalienable rights. The public, or at least a portion of it, feels that if a non-unionist may be deprived of the right to earn his living at the only trade which he knows, the same punishment may be meted out to others, and wage-earners may refuse to work with a man because he is Catholic or Protestant, Republican or Democrat, freckled or red-headed.

In discussing this question people are liable to form a false conception of what actually happens. The union workmen who refuse to work with non-unionists do not say in so many words that the employer shall not engage non-union workmen. The dictum of the trade union is not equivalent to an act of congress or of a state legislature prohibiting employers from engaging non-union men. What the unionists in such cases do is merely to stipulate as a condition that they shall not be obliged to work with men who, as non-unionists, are obnoxious, just as they shall not be obliged to work in a dangerous or unsanitary factory for unduly long hours or at insufficient wages. Of course, when unions are strong and include all the best men in the industry, this condition amounts to a very real compulsion. The compulsion, however, is merely the result of the undoubted legal right of workmen to decide upon what terms they are willing to give their labor, and the employer is always theoretically and often practically in a position where he may make his choice between union and non-union labor.

Another misconception arises from the frequent confusion in thought of refusing to work with non-union men and molesting, annoying, or injuring them. Much obscure and purposeless discussion might be avoided if these two essentially different policies were kept separate and distinct. The unionist has no right to molest, injure, or persecute the non-unionist, although he may very well have the right to refuse to work with him.

It is also frequently assumed in discussions of this subject, as of the strike and the boycott, that, because a certain compulsion is exerted by refusing to work with non-unionists, this compulsion is unjust and may be compared with the use of physical force. There could be no more flagrant error. There are many forms of compulsion which are not only legally but morally justifiable. If the workman refuses to work for less than three dollars a day, he compels the employer to pay him that sum or go without his services, and if the employer will only pay two dollars, he compels the workman to work for that sum or go without the job. Such compulsion may conceivably amount to extortion or to sweating, as the case may be, but it is absolutely necessary and is of the essence of every contract and every arrangement in life. To refuse to work with non-union men is to no greater and to no less extent compulsion than for a life or fire insurance company to refuse certain classes of risks, for a church to refuse membership to certain classes of people, or for any association whatsoever to set conditions under which it will have dealings with certain persons. The New York Stock Exchange does not compel men to join it (in fact, it costs about $80,000 for the privilege), but it refuses to allow non-members to deal on the floor and summarily dismisses members who split commissions with non-union brokers. The compulsion exerted by unions, whether towards non-unionists or employers, must be judged on its merits and must not be decried merely because it is compulsion.

The refusal of unionists to work with non-unionists is frequently made to look like a persecution of a religious sect. Employers are frequently heard to say, "I shall choose my own workmen, be they black or white, Protestants or Catholics, unionists or non-unionists." There is a wide distinction, however, in this matter. A man who is forced to join the church against his will is thereby obliged to surrender his liberty of conscience and to conform or pretend to conform to certain beliefs, which are possibly repugnant to him. The union, on the other hand, does not ask a man to believe in anything. A unionist may be a Catholic, Protestant, Jew, freethinker, protectionist, free trader, socialist, single taxer, prohibitionist, free mason, or anti-vivisectionist, and may have or profess any belief of any kind or nature whatsoever. In the matter of beliefs the trade union is as tolerant as the state when it grants citizenship, or the insurance company when it gives insurance. All that it requires is the performance of certain simple duties and the incurring of certain common obligations.

Much light could be thrown upon this subject of the relation between unionists and non-unionists by a knowledge of who exactly the non-unionist is and why he refuses to become a unionist. There are, of course, several types of non-unionists, just as there are several types of unionists. The character of the non-unionist will be different according to the character of the union to which he refuses or fails to belong. Naturally, all men are non-unionists in trades in which there are no unions, but in speaking of non-unionists we usually mean men who refuse or fail to belong to actually existing labor unions exercising jurisdiction over the trades in which they are employed. There are, therefore, as many kinds of non-unionists as there are reasons and causes for not joining a union.

To a slight extent and in a few and infrequent cases, men are non-unionists because of intolerable conditions existing in a union. It may and occasionally does happen that a local union is run for no good purpose, and matters may even come to a point where it is more of an honor to be outside than inside the organization. To right-minded men, however, the path of duty would even in such cases lie within the union, and an attempt would be made to prevent abuses by action within rather than by action without and against the organization. The moral right of leaving an organization is like the moral right of rebellion. It exists when conditions are intolerable, but it should not be exercised for light or trivial reasons.

Another class of non-union men, few in number and not unworthy in character, remain outside the unions because of strong but mistaken ideals. There are certain men who believe with fanatical zeal in individual action, in the right of every man to do as he will, no matter how it may affect or influence his neighbor. This is the philosophy of a Robinson Crusoe or of the backwoods, where each man may live by himself and be a law unto himself, but it is not possible in a civilized community. These men, therefore, however honest their beliefs, are in their apathy or active hostility toward labor organizations acting against the interest of their class and of society.

The great majority of non-unionists have remained so largely from a comfortable ignorance regarding labor organizations. Many men will welcome an idea if it comes to them, who will not leave the beaten track of thought to meet it half way. There are many workingmen who do not know the full possibilities of trade unionism, just as there are people who have never ridden in a steam car or used a telephone. These non-unionists represent the great mass of the unconverted, without active feeling for or against organized labor, and it is from this multitude that trade unionism is recruited. With each disturbance in the labor world, each growth of trusts and combinations of capital, larger and larger numbers of the unorganized non-union men see the advantage, the absolute necessity even, of joining the ranks of trade unionism, and, like all converts, they become the most ardent adherents. As a general rule, these men are below the level of intelligence found within the ranks of organized labor. Just as it is the more active and intelligent men who first migrate from one country to another, or from the country to the city, or who push forward as settlers into the wilderness, so it is the strong, intelligent workingmen who are the pioneer unionists. Men not wide-awake enough to be aware of the advantages of trade unions are not likely to be as intelligent as the average member of such organizations.

The majority of non-unionists are not malicious, only, at the worst, stupid and apathetic. However, there is one group of non-unionists, the professional strike breakers, but little removed from the criminal classes. Some of these professional strike breakers are former unionists, men who have been "dishononorably discharged" from the unions, cashiered for conduct unbecoming a unionist, if not actually indicted for defalcations or other offenses against the law. Others have never been in a union and have never been defiled or contaminated by work. There is growing up in our large cities a class of men employed like the mercenary soldiers of the middle ages, by anyone who will pay them for anything that may be asked of them. These men accept employment and "no questions" asked. They are men who loaf while honest men work and who work or pretend to work while honest men strike. Some of them, perhaps, are driven to this course by grinding poverty, or terrible distress, but this is true of the man who steals a purse or cuts a throat. There are regular organizations of strike breakers, men who do nothing else. Hostile employers have never been chary in their use of these reckless, desperate men, just as they have not refrained from engaging worthless hoodlums in the honorable capacity of private police. The instinctive "scabbing" of former days has been elevated into a fine art, and it is in the main in the interest of *these* men, frequently the lowest dregs of a corrupt city, that the employers invoke the sacred right of a man to work.

What is this right to work? It is commonly assumed in the argument for the non-unionist that every man has a right to work when and where he will, for what wages he will, and under whatsoever conditions he will. If this were true, it would follow that the unionist would have as much right to make the dismissal of all non-unionists a condition of his work as the non-unionist would have to work at less than union wages. As a matter of fact, no man and still less no woman or child, has even a *legal* right to work, except under certain prescribed conditions, and still less a *moral* right to do so. The laws of the various states and of all civilized nations prescribe the conditions and circumstances under which a man has "the right to work." Thus, a man may not work under certain unsanitary conditions, no matter what pay be offered to him or how anxious he is to secure the job. A man, no matter how skillful, may not work in any of the trades or professions in which a license is required without securing that license according to the law of the land. A Chinaman may not come over to this country to secure a position, and no immigrant is permitted to accept a job in the United States under a contract made previous to his immigration. A woman may not work over sixty hours in a Massachusetts textile factory, and a boy of ten may not be employed in or about the mines of Pennsylvania, however much he and his parents and his prospective employers may desire it. According to the decision of the Supreme Court of the United States, a Utah miner may not work over eight hours, no matter how ambitious he may be, and no man may work in factories or workshops that have not fulfilled the sanitary requirements of the law. A man has not the right to contract to work for another for the whole period of his life, however great the salary offered to him.

The legal right of a man to work is not absolute, but is based upon, and conditioned by, the welfare of society. A man has no more legal right to work when and where and how he will than he has to endanger his neighbor's property by burning his own, or to mingle with his fellow-men while suffering from some infectious disease. Such an absolute and unqualified right is conceivable in the backwoods or on a desert island, but inconceivable in a civilized community. Society endeavors to preserve to each man as great a measure of individual liberty as possible, but where the right of a man to work or to do anything else conflicts with the right of the state or the welfare of society, the individual is obliged to forego his right.

Subject to the limitations prescribed by the constitution and laws of the United States and of the several states, the non-unionist preserves and maintains a legal right to work and to take the place of the unionist. The unionist has no vested interest in his job, and the non-unionist may legally take it whenever an opportunity presents. The moral right of the non-unionist, however, is decidedly questionable. Just as the individual owes a duty to society, so also, though in a less degree, he owes a duty to his class. The non-unionist as well as the unionist is a member of a class in society, with class interests which, though not in necessary conflict with the interest of others, must be maintained by frequent and almost constant sacrifices. Nothing that the workman may do or refrain from doing will make him less a member of the class to which he belongs. As long as he works, he continues to belong to his class, with the interests and ambitions and aspirations of that class. The non-unionist has no moral right to seek his own temporary advantage at the expense of the permanent interests of all workingmen. It may pay an anti-unionist to defeat the hopes and aspirations of his fellow-men, just as it may pay a man to be a traitor to his country, but neither is morally justified. I hold it worse to be false to one's country than to be false to the great class of working men, which requires the support of every individual member, but it is a difference in degree and not in kind.

The argument for the non-unionist usually ignores completely the existence of a working class and assumes that in industry each man acts for himself and the devil take the hindmost. One would imagine from reading the tributes to non-unionists that each workingman acted as an individual, secured his position after an extended conference with the employer, after mature deliberation, and after having decided upon a mutually satisfactory rate of remuneration and mutually satisfactory conditions of work. Those who argue in this way cannot be aware of the conditions of industry as they exist to-day. The workingman of to-day, be he unionist, non-unionist, or anti-unionist, belongs to a group, and whether he will or not, acts with his group and is treated like others of his group. When a trackman or section hand asks for work on the Pennsylvania or Southern Railroad, he is not treated as an individual, and a special contract is not made with him. He is No. 347 or 651 and receives the pay given to other section hands. He works the time worked by other section hands, is given leave of absence, docked, taken on, and discharged, treated in every way, at every point, and under every circumstance, exactly as other section hands are treated. The Pennsylvania Railroad does not know that he exists, but simply knows that so many hundreds or so many thousands of men of his type are employed, at a given wage, for a given number of hours, and under certain given conditions. What affects one section hand affects all; a company's rule applying to one applies to all; an increase in wages given to one is given to all; the man is and remains, not an individual employee contracting with the railroad for the sale of his labor, but one of a homogeneous organized group, of which he is as much a part as he is of the city which shelters him or the state of which he is a citizen.

The fact that at bottom employers themselves so regard the workingmen is shown by innumerable circumstances. Thus, where a strike for higher wages has been successful, the companies invariably apply the increase not only to the men who have struck, but to the non-unionists, who ostensibly satisfied with conditions, may have worked throughout the strike. The employers say, "We must not let men who were loyal to us during the strike suffer through their loyalty." Therefore, these employees, although supposedly satisfied with past wages, are given an increase equal to that given to the dissatisfied strikers. The employers thus recognize that there must be one minimum rate prevailing within a shop and acknowledge at the same time that the non-unionist is to be considered in modern industry not as an individual workman, to be separately contracted with, but, like the unionist, as a member of a large industrial group.

It is generally felt by unionists that as the non-unionist obtains the advantage of all the sacrifices made by the union, he should also share in these sacrifices. The union feels and justly feels that he who reaps should sow. It is peculiarly galling to a trade unionist to find that the men who during a strike derided his ideals and combatted his efforts, the men who "scabbed" while he was striking and possibly starving, are the first to gain by sacrifices which he and not they have made. It is not in human nature to expect that a man who has borne the brunt of the conflict and the heat of the day should view with equanimity his enemies, or, at all events, his lukewarm allies, enjoying the fruits of his toil in the cool of the evening.

The non-unionist who refuses to assist his fellow-craftsmen, but draws benefits from their sacrifices, should not consider it a grievance if, at the conclusion of a successful strike, he should be invited to join the union or be obliged to work only with other non-unionists. To these men, who have not struck, who have not paid dues, who have not borne their share of the expense of organization and of struggle, the union opens wide its doors. Even at the eleventh hour these men are permitted to enter. The union is usually willing to let the dead past bury its dead, to clean the slate and allow the non-unionist, who has made no sacrifices, to join the union upon the same terms as others. All that is demanded is that the cost and burden of trade union management and action be fairly shared by these men in the future, and in the event of their refusal to join the union, the members simply refuse to work with them.

CONCILIATION BOARD

S. E. WARRINER, Lehigh Valley Coal Co.
ROLAND C. LUTHER, Sup't Phila. & Reading
WM. DETTRY, District President, No. 7
WM. CONNELL, Independent Operator
JOHN FAHY, District President, No. 9
T. D. NICHOLS, District President, No. 1

Presidents of Coal Roads during the Great Coal Strike of 1902

E. B. Thomas, Erie R. R.
Geo F. Baer, President Phila. & Reading
Wm. H. Truesdale, President D. L. & W. R. R.
Thos. P. Fowler, New York, Ontario & Western
R. M. Olyphant, President Del. & Hudson R. R.
Alfred Walter, Lehigh Valley R. R.

Apart from the justice of the non-unionist paying for what he gets, there is another question of equal importance. In many cases, it is almost impossible for non-unionists and unionists to dwell together in amity in the same shop. It is not a matter of personal animosity, because men who are on different sides of a question may oftentimes be friends, as the pickets of contending armies vie with each other in friendly services upon the eve of a great battle. A shop with union and non-union men is like a house divided against itself. There is a constant attempt to organize it entirely; an incessant struggle to disorganize it completely. If the non-union men in the shop are ready to work for less wages, or are pliant and more willing than the unionists to sacrifice their interests for the sake of retaining their employment, then these non-unionists receive all the benefits of the existence of a union, while, at the same time, rendering the assurance of their position doubly sure at the expense of the union which protects them. In such cases the employer discharges union men whenever there is necessity to reduce his force and takes on non-union men whenever there is need for more workmen, the only fact militating against this tendency being the general superiority and greater excellence of the union workmen.

Where non-unionists are permitted to work side by side with members of trade unions it is absolutely essential that their wages, hours of labor, and conditions of work be as good as those of the unionists. The great danger to the union lies in the fact that ordinarily a non-unionist who is not willing to pay dues is still less willing to abide by the union wages if it be to his advantage to undercut them. While accepting the union scale when work is plenty, he will immediately lower wages as soon as work becomes more difficult to obtain. The result of a number of non-unionists cutting wages or the price of work is like the existence in a community of healthy people of a man afflicted by a contagious disease. Many of the weaker-kneed unionists, seeing that they are losing their places or their work by the wage cutting of the tolerated non-unionist, will also either openly or secretly accept reductions in wages, so that eventually the whole wage scale is broken down and the shop or industry practically disorganized. In some trades it is possible to exercise a check upon such wage cutting, but in others this cannot be done, and in these latter the presence of non-union men practically means the loss of the shop to the union.

With the progress of trade unions and their growth in strength there will probably be a lessening in the intensity of feeling against the non-unionist, but no lessening in the policy of exclusion. The hatred of the non-unionist is not a new thing, and is probably less severe at the present time than it formerly was. In England much of the former animosity against the non-unionist, an animosity which took the form of physical violence and a refusal to have intercourse of any sort, has now abated, although the policy of exclusion has become more and more general. For instance, the British textile workers insist upon the employment of union men only, but in this and other trades the exclusion has become so complete that it has almost ceased to be felt. A union card is a matter of course and a matter of absolute necessity to a man desiring to engage in many British trades, and membership in a union is considered a privilege and not a burden.

In the United States the hatred harbored against the non-unionist is much more intense. The American unions are, upon the whole, younger and weaker than the British organizations, and the field is more favorable to the work of the non-unionists. This is especially true in the unskilled trades. While the number of non-unionists may be limited in the trades requiring skill and intelligence, the number of unorganized workmen flocking into unskilled trades is legion. In America workmen are extremely mobile and can be shipped from point to point by the train-load by any manufacturer who is willing to incur the expense. America is also the land of the professional strike breaker, and it is in this country more than elsewhere that racial differences and jealousies are played upon in order to crush the unions and defeat strikes. It frequently occurs that an Italian who would not take the job of another Italian may be persuaded to take the position of an Irishman or a Pole, or *vice versa*. The racial jealousies have been fanned by employers to the point of deadly outbreak, and the relations between negroes and whites have been intensified and aggravated by the deliberate policy of employers in using negroes as strike breakers. The United Mine Workers of America, however, have demonstrated that with proper organization and patient education, these racial animosities may be allayed and the problem of the non-unionist, at least to a certain extent, eliminated.

As before stated, the unionist has a perfect legal and moral right to refuse to work with the non-unionist, and as time goes on, the exclusion of the latter will become more and more complete. The employers, who are even now endeavoring to extend the responsibility of unions, will, to a greater extent, desire that these organizations be morally responsible for the conduct of all the employees. With the rapid extension of trade unions, the tendency is towards the growth of compulsory membership in them, and the time will doubtless come when this compulsion will be as general and will be considered as little of a grievance as the compulsory attendance of children at school. The inalienable right of a man to work will then be put upon a par with the inalienable right of a child to play truant, and the compulsion exercised by the trade union will be likened to that of a state, which in the interest of society forces an education upon the child, even though the child and its parents are utterly and irreconcilably opposed to it.

In stating that the unionists have a legal and a moral right to refuse to work with non-unionists, I desire to make two qualifications. If a union is working not for the interests of all the men at the trade, but of the members who at that time are actually in the union, if it is unduly restrictive, prohibiting apprentices, charging extortionate initiation fees, and excluding capable applicants for membership, then its refusal to work with non-union men is monopolistic, and such a union should not be put upon a par with unions that refuse to work with non-unionists in the general interests of the trade. I do not mean to say that a high initiation fee is always unfair. To a certain limited extent, it may be fair to capitalize the past sacrifices of members of the union and it may be necessary by reasonably high initiation fees to moderate a too rapid or too sudden rush into the trade. Especially where membership in a union means participation in a large accumulated surplus, it may be fair to charge an initiation fee somewhat higher than usual. One must look at the motive behind the regulation. But if the union is monopolistic, its refusal to work with non-union men is an aggravation of its offense, and an unduly high initiation fee may mean a tax levied upon capable men, willing to work according to union rules and regulations.

The second qualification is based upon policy rather than principle. While unionists have a perfect legal and moral right to refuse to work with non-unionists, it is not always politic to exercise this right, and the demand upon the employer for the complete unionizing of his plant is not always presented in a wise or politic manner. Many employers who are willing to have their shops unionized are not willing to appear to be forced into such a position, and many workmen can be persuaded who cannot be compelled to become unionists. No demand should be made for the unionization of a shop until all reasonable efforts have been made to secure the allegiance of every employee. It is unwise, moreover, to demand the unionizing of a shop or an industry where there is not sufficient strength to compel it. For every such demand and prior to every such demand there should be months of patient propaganda, *and in this, as in every other, line of trade policy, compulsion should not be used until persuasion has completely and signally failed.*

There is, it must be admitted, a certain danger apart from antagonism of employers in compulsory unionizing of shops. A man convinced against his will is of the same opinion still, and the union button does not make a unionist at heart. An enemy is sometimes more formidable within the lines than on the outside. Half a dozen obstructionists may defeat the purpose of an orderly meeting, while the presence of a few anti-unionists at trade union meetings may enable employers to inform themselves of the plans and projects of the organization, and may thus cripple the union more effectively than if the avowed friends were open enemies.

In conclusion, I believe that trade unions have a perfect legal and moral right to exclude non-unionists, but that this right should be exercised with the utmost care and only after persuasion has been tried and has failed. I also believe that with the growth of trade unionism in the United States the exclusion of non-unionists will become more complete, although animosity toward the non-unionists will diminish with the lessening of his power to do evil.

CHAPTER XXXIII

THE LABEL AND THE BOYCOTT

The Attack upon the Boycott. The Boycott and the Right of Free Speech. Boycott an Expression of Popular Feeling. Legality. Occasional Injustice. Difficulty of Drawing a Line. Secondary or Indirect Boycott. The Strike the Weapon of the Seller; the Boycott the Weapon of the Buyer. Boycotting, Advertising, and Modern Business. The Label the Reverse of the Boycott. The Union Label an American Invention. The White, Red, and Blue Labels. The Union Label and the Sweated Trades. Growth of the Label. Counterfeiting the Label. Legal Protection. The Label Organizes Workmen as Consumers. The Future Possibilities of the Label.

THE right to boycott, like the right to strike or lock-out, the right to vote, the right to bear arms, the liberty of speech, or the right to devise one's property as one will, is subject to misuse. There can be no personal liberty that does not, at some time or other, lead to abuse and cause individual hardship. There is no justification, however, for the widespread sweeping denunciation of the boycott, so lightly uttered.

The boycott presents one of the most difficult problems in labor disputes. It would be as foolish and wrong to defend all the various manifestations and instances of boycotts as it is for the critics of trade unions to attack them in a body. There are many instances of boycotts not only defensible but wholly praiseworthy, and there are other cases in which the boycott may be unjustifiable, mean, and cowardly.

It is not to be supposed that the boycott is a weapon merely of trade unionists, or even of working people. Every class in society and every society itself constantly makes use of this device. Speaking generally, the boycott is nothing more than an expression of moral disapproval, a method of social ostracism. A boycott, like a strike, is a means of compulsion, but it is not necessarily an unjustifiable means. Whenever a group in society, be it a church or a trade union, a temperance party, or a consumers' league, believes that it is necessary to discriminate against persons committing certain actions, a boycott exists. In political, industrial, and social life men are being constantly boycotted, because of their failure or refusal to attain to certain ideals.

Perhaps the most effective use of the boycott has been made by employers. Manufacturers have been boycotted by other manufacturers and by jobbers and by retailers, and these latter have been boycotted by manufacturers or associations of manufacturers. Individual firms have been boycotted by banks, and banks have been boycotted by the general business community. Railroads have been boycotted and, in turn, have boycotted, as they have specially favored, particular shippers in violation of the law. In the business world men of all classes and all occupations are boycotted for all reasons. A manufacturer may be boycotted by other manufacturers, simply because of his having made reasonable terms with labor. When in one of the early anthracite strikes a number of operators desired to submit to the demands of the striking miners, they were prevented from so doing by the railroads exorbitantly raising their freight rates, and thus shutting out of the market the coal mined under union conditions. As a matter of fact, during the last anthracite strike, one of the so-called "independent" operators personally told me that he would readily grant the demands of the union but for the fact that by doing so he would be discriminated against by the railroad companies, and consequently forced into bankruptcy.

The boycott of the union may be levied against a person or a thing. An anti-union employer or a non-union workman may be boycotted either in business or socially; a product may be boycotted either by a refusal to buy it or a refusal to work on it or with it.

The legal right of workingmen to boycott should not be called into question. Workingmen in boycotting one of their fellow-craftsmen are simply doing together what they have a perfect right to do separately. A man has a legal right to refuse to deal at a certain establishment, to give or withhold patronage, to buy where he sees fit; and what one may do a hundred or a thousand should have the right to do. No one can compel John Smith to buy goods from John Brown, and no one can compel him to enter the same car, to sit in the same church, or to eat at the same table.

The workingmen should not only have the right to boycott a person or a thing, but they should also have the right to present to the public in a fair and temperate manner a statement of their position, in order that the public may have the opportunity of judging and, in its discretion, of aiding or refusing to aid in the boycott. There are many cases of boycotts by organized workmen, in which other rights are involved than those of the laboring classes themselves. The occasional tyranny of unscrupulous employers over shop girls, amounting in many cases to a violation of the most fundamental laws of morals and decency, should be restrained by a boycott where legal redress is not possible. In many trades in which women, suffering under the double burden of their sex and their dependent position, or immigrants, pliant, ignorant, and unresisting, are exploited in the foulest dens of a foul tenement, the unions should have the right to appeal to the public by the boycott or the label to secure protection to these undefended creatures. The boycott should not be issued secretly, and the person or the owner of the thing boycotted should have the right to be heard before a boycott is imposed. The same rules that apply to a strike should apply to a boycott; it should be enforced only when a real necessity exists and under conditions which will promote the welfare of the working classes and of society in general. The morality as well as the efficiency of a boycott can be secured only by limiting its application to important cases and by preventing its abuse.

There is a great danger in the tendency of certain courts to adopt an attitude antagonistic to the boycott. If an attempt is made to render the boycott illegal, as has already been done, the result will merely be that the boycott or the concerted refusal to purchase goods at a certain place will become secret instead of open. The only safeguard against the occasional abuses of the boycott is openness and publicity; and if the law forces the boycott to become irregular and secret, it will undoubtedly be used to serve

"Captains of Industry"

EVICTION DURING THE COAL STRIKE OF 1902

These houses rent by the day, and tenants may be evicted at any moment.

the purposes of malice or spite, and unscrupulous employers or manufacturers will endeavor to use secretly this formidable weapon against their rivals and competitors. The endeavor should be to mitigate any possible evils without striking at the roots of a privilege of great importance and value to society.

It is to be deplored that the boycott occasionally is used tyrannously and unfairly and not infrequently is carried too far. It is very hard to draw the line as to just what length a people with a real grievance may go, but the rule should be adhered to always that the sins of the fathers should not be visited upon the children and that the innocent should not suffer for the sake of the guilty. Even this rule of simple justice is difficult to carry out, because in many cases the man who has struck at the welfare of his class or his town or society may attempt to recover his position under cloak of a relative, a friend, or an associate. Generally speaking, however, the same rule of justice which prevails in ordinary life should be applied to the boycott, and it is better here, as elsewhere, that ten guilty men escape than that one innocent man suffer. It is also true that trade unions, like other organizations, occasionally carry the boycott too far and much beyond the point where it is of value or of effect upon the original culprit. To boycott a street railway which overworks its employees and pays starvation wages is one thing; to boycott merchants who ride in the cars of the company is another thing, and to boycott people who patronize the stores of the merchants who ride in boycotted cars is still another and a very different thing. As a general rule, the further the boycott is removed from the original offender the less effective it becomes. It should be the aim of the union to seek, and not to force the alliance of the public, and to render the boycott as direct and personal as possible. There are many cases, however, where a secondary boycott is absolutely necessary. When a union is engaged in a contest with a newspaper, especially, as is usually the case, with a newspaper not largely read by the working classes, a secondary boycott is far more effective than a direct boycott. A newspaper can better do without a few hundred two-cent subscribers than without a few thousand-dollar advertisements, and a man who continues to pay large sums in advertising to a newspaper that is maltreating its employees may not unfairly be considered the ally of the journal, and as aiding and abetting it in its contest with labor. Especial care, however, should be used in the laying of a secondary boycott. A boycott of this sort, that is extended and extended from a central point like the waves made by a pebble thrown into a still pond, becomes of so little force and arouses so much just antagonism that discredit is thrown upon the original boycott, which in itself may have been perfectly just and reasonable.

There are other manifestations of the boycott, moreover, which are unduly intolerant. I do not believe that union men have a moral right to leave a church in a body when a non-unionist or a "scab" enters, since the struggles of the everyday world should not be carried into this place, and no one should leave a church because it is shared by a "scab," a thief, or even a murderer. I do not believe that it is right to secure or attempt to secure the dismissal of a school teacher because her father worked during a strike, or to urge or to allow children to boycott in school the children of a non-union or "scab" workingman. Last of all, I believe it would be utterly immoral and unjustifiable to refuse the last services to a dying man, whatever his past record may have been, or in any way to disturb or even hold aloof from the burial of such a man. A boycott itself, when used with temperance and justice, however severe its application, may be an admirable and entirely justifiable weapon against offenders; but the right to boycott can only be maintained by the community itself refusing to indulge in any merely savage or brutal manifestations of hostility.

While opposition to the boycott has always been strenuously urged by employers, the black list has at the same time been one of their common and successful expedients. As early as 1832 the merchants and ship owners of Boston held a meeting in order to discountenance and check the unlawful combinations of workmen, which were, it was claimed, driving trade from the city; and in this meeting, the merchants publicly resolved, "that we will neither employ any journeymen who at the time belong to such combinations, nor will we give work to any master mechanic who shall employ them while they continue thus pledged to each other and refuse to work the hours which it has been, and it is now customary, for mechanics to work." Since that time, the blacklist has been frequently used, either openly or secretly, both in England and in this country.

The cruelty of the boycott even in its worst phases is as nothing compared with the cruelty of the black list. Labor leaders and men interested in the labor movement have always been a shining mark for the blacklist, and many who have been willing to make sacrifices for the movement have been accorded that privilege by blacklist-using employers. Many a man has been hounded from position to position, driven as by the invisible wind from one part of the country to another, ceaselessly wandering, ceaselessly asking for positions, doomed inevitably after the shortest term of service to be dismissed upon some trumped up charge. There is nothing so terrible as this weapon of associated employers. According to the law a blacklist must be a conspiracy of a number of employers, but the injury is just as great in the case where a single company with its myriad plants monopolizes all opportunities of employment in the industry. Many a man has been driven to change his name and even to alter his appearance in the vain hope of escape from the omnipresent and omnipotent blacklist.

The boycott is, as a rule, a thing which is more or less open, because to secure action among a great body of employees a certain amount of publicity is necessary. The blacklist, however, is generally covert and secret. In former times and possibly still to-day, employers frequently wrote letters of recommendation to employees, discharged upon some trivial pretext or other, but by a secret sign, the employer who read the testimonial would know that the workman was blacklisted. In many cases, in fact, the blacklist has been negative and has been simply a secret arrangement by employers not to engage any workman without a specific recommendation from another employer.

In a certain sense the label and the boycott are different phases of the same thing, two sides of the same shield. The boycott points out those with whom one should not deal, the label, those with whom one should deal exclusively. When a man, whether he be a workman or any other consumer, insists upon a label, he is boycotting every article which does not bear that label.

All useful members of society are both producers and consumers of wealth. Whether a man is engaged at manual or mental work, whether he works with a pick or an axe, a plow or a pestle, a pen or a hoe, he is contributing either directly or indirectly to the wealth and prosperity of the country and may be considered as a producer. All this production, or, at least, the greater part of it, is intended for the purpose of consumption, since articles are made to be enjoyed, either by the man who makes them or by others.

In the early days, when the structure of society was simple, each family consumed the articles which it produced. The family raised its own food and made its own clothes from the fleece of its own sheep, and there was little assistance given by one to another and but little purchase or sale. To-day, however, society is organized on the basis of a minute and complicated division of labor and an extended change and interchange of commodities. A man no longer consumes more than the smallest fraction of the articles he produces, and perhaps he consumes none at all. The cigar maker may be a non-smoker, and the piano-mover certainly does not receive his wages in the form of grand pianos. Through the agency of money all producers are enabled to get the articles they wish to consume at the time and in the manner desired, and we thus have in modern society the example of all producing for all instead of each producing for himself.

The workingmen, as other members of society, are both producers and consumers. They are interested as producers in obtaining as high wages and as favorable conditions of life as possible; as consumers in being charged reasonable prices. When labor is organized, the workingman may be made to suffer as a consumer, through truck stores, forced credit, and other schemes, as well as through his being led without his knowledge to buy sweat-shop and other deleterious products. It is chiefly, however, as a producer that he suffers, and it is chiefly this phase of the workman's life in which trade unionism seeks to protect him.

Therefore, until recently, labor has been organized almost exclusively on the basis of the production of wealth. It was felt that the workingman as a consumer, if assisted by laws against truck stores, could amply protect himself. Where competition prevails, where monopoly has not yet obtained a foothold the consumer has a great advantage in modern society, and can, by granting or withholding credit, obtain such reasonable conditions as he desires.

It was due to the ingenuity of American trade unionists, however, and especially to that of the Cigar Makers that the power of the workingman as a consumer was enlisted in support of his demands as a producer. This was rendered possible in America, owing to the fact that largely through the agency of trade unionism wages had risen to a high point here, and a great part of the consumption of wealth in this country was on the part of the workingman. It was seen that workingmen purchased many articles and that their patronage was eagerly sought, and the expedient was therefore adopted and urged upon workingmen of not buying goods unless they were made under union conditions.

It is to this desire, to enlist the workingman as a consumer in support of his demands as a producer, that we owe the union label. Another fact, however, contributed to the same result. There is always a large section in the community more or less closely allied in thought, feelings, and habits of life with trade unionists, who are in sympathy with the general ideas of labor organizations, and many of the members of this class are willing to aid the unions as consumers, even if they cannot or will not do it as producers. The union label appeals to a still larger class and to an even more potent and more universal motive. When there is no check upon an unscrupulous employer or a hard-driven contractor, it is not impossible that work will be done under the filthiest and most unsanitary conditions and in circumstances which are a menace to the health and even the life of the consumer. The union label, by guaranteeing that the work was done under healthful conditions, relieves the consumer of the fear of disease or death from the purchased articles and is in a sense an insurance against noxious germs.

The union label originated in the United States among the Cigar Makers in the year 1874. It practically arose in the contest against the Chinese, who after the treaty with China in 1868 began to flood the country, especially the Western States. The workingmen of Australia had already been forced to exclude the Chinese on account of the imminent danger to the white population; but despite the agitation in California, no measure appeared to be immediately possible in the United States, and it was not until the year 1882 that the immigration of Chinese was prohibited in this country. In 1868 over 11,000 Chinese entered on the Pacific coast, and by 1872 a number of cigar manufacturers had already begun to employ Chinese workers. The number of Chinese so engaged was not large, but, owing to their willingness to work at starvation wages, the danger to the trade was felt to be very great. In 1874, therefore, the California Cigar Makers placed a white label upon the cigar box in order to indicate that the white workers were attempting to defend their standard of life against the lower standard of the Chinese coolies.

The use of the label was soon extended from a fight against Chinese labor to a fight against unorganized labor generally. In 1875 a red label was adopted by the St. Louis Cigar Makers in their conflict with non-union labor in that city, and the label received so much support that attempts were made to counterfeit it. The present blue label of the Cigar Makers was not adopted until 1880, when in the national convention at Chicago a dispute arose between the St. Louis and the California delegates as to whether the red or the white label should be adopted. The question was finally decided by an eastern delegate who said, "Let us take the other color of the flag," and from that time on the blue label has been the symbol of union cigars throughout the country.

The importance of the union label to the trade union movement can best be seen in the gradual extension of the use of the label by the Cigar Makers and other trades. The number of labels put upon cigar boxes increased from 1,590,000 in 1880, to 22,315,000 in 1900. Without this label it is doubtful whether the Cigar Makers could ever have attained the strength which they have secured. The trade has always been threatened by floods of unskilled immigrants working under the most unsanitary conditions in tenements and cellars, and women and children have been introduced by thousands to depress wages and to lower conditions of life.

The success of the label of the Cigar Makers soon led to the adoption of a similar label by other organizations. In 1885 the present label of the Hatters was introduced. This label, attached to the sweat band or linings of felt and stiff hats, soon became popular. By means of the label many formerly non-union establishments were brought under union control, and the number of labels rapidly increased. Up to November 30, 1897, over 115,000,000 labels had been issued, and as early as the beginning of 1901 the union was issuing a million new labels a month. The label was also adopted by the Garment Workers and has been of great service in the struggle of that organization against the domination of sweat-shop methods.

One of the most successful labels has been that of the Printers, which was adopted in 1891, and which is now general throughout the United States. Several cities have passed ordinances requiring the use of this label upon all public printing, thus endorsing the principle of trade union conditions for municipal work. Since 1891 the label has been adopted by a number of other trade unions, and the spread of this means of defense for unionism has been rapid and complete. At the present time a number of trade unions are expending large sums to advertise their labels, and several journals exist which are devoted to this purpose exclusively. In many states Label Leagues, composed of both men and women, have been formed, with the object of promoting the sale of goods made under favorable sanitary conditions and bearing the union label.

From the beginning employers have been found who were willing to counterfeit and imitate union labels. This was all the easier, since it was at first held by the courts that the label of a trade union could not be protected by an injunction or by a suit for damages. The courts took away from the union label the protection accorded under the patent and copyright laws of the United States, and ruled that the workmen who used the label were merely laborers who had no property rights in the results of their labor, suffered no financial injury from the counterfeiting, and should have, therefore, no redress. This adverse decision was rendered in the Minnesota case of the Cigar Makers *vs*. Conhaim, and was re-affirmed in several other cases. In order to overcome this difficulty the union secured in the principal states the passage of laws permitting labor organizations to adopt union labels, providing for the registration of the same, and imposing penalties for counterfeiting them. Laws of this sort were passed up to 1895 in twenty-four different states, in most of which the remedy by injunction or equity was expressly given to the workmen against any infringement or violation of their label. The constitutionality of these statutes has been sustained by the courts in several decisions, and the Illinois courts have even proclaimed that it was lawful for the label to contain a statement that it was used in the interests of an organization "opposed to inferior, rat-shop, coolie, prison, or filthy tenement-house workmanship."[1] It is said that imitation is the sincerest flattery, and the infringement of the label is a tribute to its success, and to the just and reasonable use to which it has generally been put.

All means are taken to prevent as far as possible the placing of the label on goods by anyone but a member of the union. Usually the label is a printed slip of paper, which is attached to the articles, or, as in the case of cigars, to the box or the package. The label of the Boot and Shoe Workers is printed on the sole or insole of the shoe with a steel stamp. The label of the Hatters is attached to the inside of the hat, and the labels of the Tailors and Garment Workers are sewed on the inside of each garment. The Horse Shoers print their label with a steel stamp upon the hot shoe, and the Brick Makers use a brass roller attached to the brick machine, which

---

[1] Many of the facts concerning the use of the label were obtained from an article by John Graham Brooks in the Bulletin of the Department of Labor.

stamps the label on the brick as the soft clay passes under it. The label of the Printers is too well-known to need description, but it, as well as all other labels, are put on in such a manner as to prevent fraud and unfairness. Loose labels are never sold; a manufacturer is not usually allowed to put on the labels himself; an accurate account is kept of all labels, and they are numbered consecutively in order that irregularities may be detected.

The label appeals both to the working classes and to general consumers, and it claims to stand, and usually does stand, for sanitary conditions, good workmanship and standard wages. When the label means sanitary conditions, it has been especially successful with the general consumer. No man desires to put upon his back a coat or shirt, or to put into his mouth a cigar, which he knows to have been made in the midst of filth and disease, and there is no guarantee against such conditions so effective as the union label. When the label stands for good workmanship, the general consumer is also interested. As a general rule, the unions endeavor to maintain a certain standard of excellence in goods bearing the label, and the cigar makers refuse to permit the label to be put on cigars which sell for less than twenty dollars a thousand.

The principal hold, however, which the union label has is the support of the working classes and their sympathizers. With each passing year the importance of the workingmen as consumers of the nation's products will increase, and with each year it will be more and more a matter of interest to the employer to appeal to this public. Through the label the workingmen of the country are organizing as consumers just as they have already organized as producers. The advertising of the label in the labor papers and other journals, in the street cars and elsewhere, the sending of lecturers to small towns, and the distribution of a vast amount of literature upon the subject, show that the workingmen are adopting business methods in increasing their strength. Like other features of the trade union movement, the label protects the scrupulous and just employer from the unfair competition of the man with less compunction. A union hat cannot be told from a non-union hat by its general appearance any more than a bushel of Iowa wheat can be distinguished from a bushel of Kansas wheat in a Chicago elevator, and the label serves the good purpose of separating the sweat-shop made goods from the goods made under fair and reasonable conditions.

If the label secures the support of the working classes and continues to be issued in a fair and honest manner, and if the boycott is judiciously and temperately used, the offensive and defensive power of the workingman will increase enormously. In a strike the workingmen are in general at a disadvantage as compared with the employer, because they are in the position of sellers whose commodity, labor, will spoil on their hands, unless disposed of immediately. The employer is at the same disadvantage in the case of a boycott, since he now becomes a seller of commodities to the working classes and finds through a boycott or through the absence of a label that he cannot make terms and has his products on his hands. Especially is this true at the present time when giant companies spending millions of dollars on advertising have become especially vulnerable to the boycott and especially desirous of securing the label. The label makes the consumer for the first time a responsible agent, capable of passing judgment and knowing good from evil. It coins the public disapproval of an act and becomes to the workman as a consumer what the union scale is to him as a producer—a standard and a rallying point. If the time should come when there are millions of workingmen acting together in common upon a boycott approved of by all, the power of the organized workmen of the country will be infinitely increased. The attainment of such a strategic position by the workmen is a matter, however, of slow growth and is the result of their education to the full comprehension of the ideals of trade organizations.

CHAPTER XXXIV

LABOR AND CAPITAL AT WAR

Normal Condition of Industry is Peace. Strikes Exceptional. Strikes a Method of Bargaining. Strikes Involve Freedom of Contract. Why Workmen Strike. Petty Grievances and the Last Straw. Strikes and Prosperity. Sympathetic Strikes and Sympathetic Lockouts. Does the Walking Delegate Cause Strikes? Labor Leaders and Labor Conflicts. The Responsibility of the Union Official.

THE normal condition of industry is peace. While we daily read of the outbreak of strikes or the declaration of lockouts, the average workingman, engaged in industries in which strikes occur, loses less than a day a year in this manner. A strike lasts upon the average about twenty-three days, but the average employer peacefully carries on his business for thirty years without the outbreak of a strike. The average lockout lasts ninety-seven days, but of a thousand establishments, less than two declare a lockout in the course of any given year.

The prevalence of strikes as of all dramatic occurrences is exaggerated. Every murder which occurs in the city of New York is reported in thousands of newspapers, and yet these crimes are so rare compared with the number of inhabitants that the average citizen has no fear or thought of such a calamity. Tragic, dramatic, or startling events are so impressed upon the mind that we fail to realize that they are highly exceptional.

A strike is simply a method of bargaining. If the grocers of a city would refuse to sell their sugar for less than seven cents a pound and the consumers would refuse to pay more than six, exactly the same thing would occur as happens in an ordinary strike. A strike does not necessarily involve animosity, hatred, dissension, recrimination, or any form of bitterness; it merely represents a difference between what the buyer of labor is willing to offer, and what the seller of labor is willing to accept. Until the buyer and seller of an ordinary commodity are agreed as to price and conditions, no sale can be effected. Until the wages and conditions of work are agreed upon and acceded to both by employer and workman, the industry must stop.

Strikes thus result from a failure to make a bargain or contract by men who are free to contract. Strikes in the true sense of the word, therefore, cannot exist before the freedom of contract is accorded. The concerted quitting of work by the Israelitish builders of the pyramids because of a refusal upon the part of their taskmasters to provide them with straw for the making of bricks was not a strike, because the workingmen were slaves and without the free power of contract. It was not for them to fix conditions of work, and their position was determined, not by contract, but by compulsion. The insurrection of the slaves at Rome and the peasant uprisings which occurred at the dawn of modern times in Germany, France, and England, were not in any true sense strikes, because the conditions of work against which these men rebelled were determined for them and not by them. Their various uprisings were met by the armed resistance of the State, since it was held that the men had no right to refuse to work in the positions assigned to them. The present conception of a strike or lockout is that of workmen or employers exercising their undoubted right to refuse to enter into contracts when the conditions are not satisfactory to them.

It is frequently stated that trade unions desire strikes because, it is alleged, they are organized for this purpose. This, however, is not true. The trade union is organized for the purpose of securing better conditions of life and labor for its members, and when necessary, a strike is resorted to as a means to that end. But it can no more be said that trade unions desire strikes because they are equipped for them, than that the United States desires war because it has an army and navy. It is true that, in a general way, strikes occur most frequently in those countries which are most progressive and in which trade unionism is strongest. In proportion to population, there are more strikes in the United States than in Great Britain, and more in Great Britain than in France, and more in France than in Italy or Austria, and this, in general, is the order of these nations in the prosperity of their working classes. The same conditions which cause the creation of trade unions are equally answerable for the constant demand for improved conditions on the part of the working class population, which demand frequently voices itself in strikes.

While strikes are occasionally called for senseless or trivial purposes, the great majority result from a justifiable desire on the part of workingmen to better their conditions. According to the Report of the United States Department of Labor, 41.4% of the strikes during the period from 1881 to 1900 were fought for higher wages; and 6.9% for the maintenance of present wages. In other words, practically one-half of all strikes in the United States during the last twenty years were declared either for the purpose of enforcing increases or preventing decreases in the rate of wages. Of the remainder of the strikes, one-half were attempts to enforce demands for a reduction of the working day. These demands looked to the regulation of the working time and of payment for overtime, as well as toward the granting of a Saturday half holiday. Only one strike out of sixteen was fought out upon the question of the recognition of the union, or the demand that the employer live up to union rules, and only one strike in nineteen was declared for the purpose of excluding non-union men, members of other labor organizations, unpopular foremen, or other persons objectionable to the union. Only 1% of the strikes were called for the purpose of enforcing the reinstatement or retention of particular union employees, while less than one in a hundred were fought out upon the question of apprenticeship. Despite the oft-repeated claim that trade unions obstruct the introduction of machinery, only one out of every seven hundred strikes in the United States during the last twenty years was called for the purpose of preventing or hindering the introduction or use of machinery, or other improved appliances.

It is admitted on all sides that strikes are to be avoided in all cases where the object desired can be obtained by peaceful negotiation. There is nothing immoral, however, in the workingman's striking, just as there is nothing immoral in his wanting higher wages. People with no interest in a labor conflict and inconvenienced by a strike, are liable to display an impatient irritation at workmen, who seem to be striking all the time and for no sufficient cause. It is true that strikes are occasionally called for light and trivial reasons, but the cause of a strike may be far deeper and far more important than the immediate incidents or occasions which precipitate the struggle. People frequently claim that workmen should never strike when the injury to be avoided or the gain to be secured is less than the cost of the strike, but if men were not willing, at least occasionally, to make great sacrifices to prevent even small losses, unscrupulous employers would take advantage of their unwillingness to strike. The principle of trade unions, as of all other organizations, should be "Millions for defense, but not one cent for tribute." Frequently workmen are subjected to a long series of petty aggressions by employers, who believe that no single one of these encroachments will be sufficient to provoke the men to strike. It is the last straw that breaks the camel's back, and a strike attributed to an apparently insignificant incident may be the outburst of pent-up feelings, resulting from months or years of repeated aggressions. The man who, in his haste, declares that a strike is ill-considered, because its immediate cause is slight, may be as wrong as the judge who, to discourage useless litigation, might decide against all plaintiffs in small cases, and would thus hold back the poor from the fountain of justice.

Trade unions are also frequently accused of lack of wisdom in calling strikes in prosperous times. The comic papers are filled with cartoons representing the foolish workman upsetting, by strikes, the precious jar of prosperity. But no matter when he strikes, the workman is called foolish. If times are bad and reduction of wages is threatened, the immutable law of supply and demand is quoted against him; if times are good, he is destroying prosperity; if times are normal, he is advised to leave well enough alone. As a matter of fact, if workingmen are to secure any advance or even to retain their present position, they are obliged to strike in good times. It is in good times that the prices of the necessaries of life rise; and it is at such times that employers are best able to grant fair conditions of work, for, if in good times the workingmen do not secure, either by strikes or negotiation, a share of the prosperity of the nation, the excessive profits of the employer will be capitalized, and the day for securing increased wages and better conditions of work will be indefinitely postponed.

While opposition to strikes as such is diminishing, there is still much disapproval of sympathetic conflicts, in which men strike, not to better their own conditions, but in order to express sympathy and grant aid to men unconnected with them, who are engaged in an industrial conflict. The public feels in a general way that sympathetic strikes are vicious and foolish and that they should be put down on all occasions.

To a certain extent and to a certain extent only, the public is justified in this attitude. Of course there are sympathetic lockouts as well as sympathetic strikes, though less is heard of the former. The opposition to sympathetic strikes arises from the fact that in actual practice they sometimes involve a breach of contract and from the further fact that the sympathetic strike is usually too remote and has too little bearing upon the main point at issue. Where a sympathetic strike involves a violation of a contract, it should under no circumstances take place, and this is true also of a strike which is not sympathetic. The right to strike, to strike sympathetically, or to boycott can never exist where such action involves a violation of an agreement with employers.

Another objection to the sympathetic strike is the fact of its remoteness. The public may sympathize with oppressed tailors who are struggling for better conditions, but it will not sympathize with waiters, teamsters, bricklayers, or railroad employees, if by any chance, they strike sympathetically with the Garment Workers. The public finds in the original quarrel no justification for the intervention of the new unions, and it fears that by means of sympathetic strikes a conflict originally limited in scope may become extended so as needlessly to involve the entire labor world.

Upon the whole, therefore, sympathetic strikes should not be encouraged. The caution which a wise labor leader exercises before involving his union in a strike should be multiplied manyfold in the case of an intended sympathetic strike. There are times, however, when sympathetic strikes are not only justifiable, but actually noble. A wise sympathetic strike which involves no violation of contract, and is of such a nature as directly and powerfully to influence the result of the original conflict, a strike carried out, not for the immediate good of the members of the union, but for that of other workmen, emphasizes, as no other event in industrial life, the universal brotherhood and solidarity of labor. There is nothing inherently and necessarily wrong in doing for others what we would that they should do for us, and a strike is not made immoral by the fact that the strikers permit others than themselves to be the gainers thereby. It sometimes happens that the weaker organizations, composed of oppressed workmen (and the more oppressed they are, the weaker their unions are apt to be), can only secure reasonable and humane conditions by and through the assistance of workingmen in other unions. In certain trades, moreover, where the unions whose members are engaged upon the same work are not affiliated, it may be necessary to involve all workers in a strike in which any one union is engaged, although, in such cases, it is better to secure uniformity by federation and by agreements binding all the unions equally. Some unions, in order to preserve their right to strike sympathetically—where such action is deemed essential to the welfare of the whole community—contract especially for this contingency and reserve this privilege in making their agreements. This is not unlike the strike clauses in contracts which one employer makes with another and which renders the contract or certain of its conditions void in case one of the parties thereto has a strike.

There can be no doubt, however, that upon the whole and in the long run, the policy of striking in sympathy should be frowned upon and discouraged. It should not be permitted at all where it involves a violation of a contract or where its influence will not be direct, powerful, immediate, and beneficent, not only to the men on strike, but to the community. Finally, in any and every instance, sympathetic strikes should be resorted to only in the most extreme cases and where the conditions fully and clearly indicate the necessity of making an exception to a settled policy. The number of sympathetic strikes appear to be small and diminishing, only 3% of the strikes occurring in the United States between the years 1880 and 1900 being sympathetic strikes.

It is frequently stated that the strikes in which unions engage are incited and brought on by the officials. There are many people who believe that labor leaders gain when strikes are declared, and that the men throw up their positions in order in some mysterious way to benefit "the labor agitators." As a matter of fact, the shoe is entirely upon the other foot. The work of the union official doubles and trebles as soon as a strike is declared, and, as likely as not, his salary is lessened. The remuneration of the union official is not unlike that of the Chinese physician, who, it is said, receives pay only while his patient is well. During the Coal Strike of 1902, the officials of the United Mine Workers contributed 25% of their monthly salaries to the strike fund, and officers of the union who had been slowly saving money on a salary of $70 or $75 a month, ran into debt while working for the union from twelve to fifteen and more hours per day. Unless, therefore, the union official stands for the principle of more work and less pay, he will not call strikes for his own selfish purposes, and what is more important, he cannot, if he will. The statement that strikes are caused by walking delegates is as naïve as the childish belief that it is the gong which makes the train move. Strikes, it is true, have sometimes been called for organization purposes, for propaganda, but no strike of this sort could be successful unless it were at the same time a protest against intolerable conditions, and unless it were generally desired and demanded by the men. In nearly all unions, the officials, from the local business agent or walking delegate to the international president, are elements for peace, not for war, and in actual practice the aggressive element is represented by the members of the union, and the steadying and conservative element, by the officers. The pecuniary loss which strikes may inflict upon a union official is the least of his difficulties.

I can conceive of few positions so unenviable, so filled with the peril of an evil choice as that of a labor leader on the eve of a great industrial conflict. Under the democratic constitutions of our unions, the decision to strike or not to strike rests in the final instance with the men themselves; but in the case of a particularly difficult problem, conditions may be such that the decision will depend upon votes cast under the influence of a single leader. The sobering sense of responsibility which under these circumstances comes to the union official, is radically different from the reckless spirit in which, it is claimed, the leaders of labor in this country evoke strikes. The potentialities of suffering, of want and destitution, the dread of a coming winter of idleness, bear with almost crushing force upon the man who is responsible. Either choice is fraught with the possibility, the absolute assurance even, of great evil. On the one hand, the leader feels the growing discontent, the increasing recklessness, the sullen irritation of idle men, the hatred between the men who strike and the men who work; he fears the clash between the more reckless on both sides; he fears blows and violence, perhaps even murder; he dreads the hardships, the suffering, the privation, the anguish of men whose wives and children are famished and freezing, the despair that comes at the end and destroys the slow patient work of long years. On the other hand, he sees unfolded before him, the whole history of labor; the upward striving through effort and courage and sacrifice; the temporary losses through cowardice or shrinking from the fear of evils, a movement ever upward and onward, but ever beset with difficulties, with danger, with suffering, and, it may be, with loss of life. A leader who in wanton recklessness and without thoughtful calculation of all the possible good and evil, a leader who makes his decision to strike, or not to strike, from any but the highest, the noblest, the most disinterested motives, is guilty of a crime against labor comparable to the treachery of a Benedict Arnold.

CHAPTER XXXV

STRIKES IN THEIR MORAL AND ECONOMIC ASPECTS

Strikes from an Ideal Standpoint. Strikes in Practice. Trade Unions Prevent Strikes. The Avoidance of Misunderstandings. The Initiative in Strikes and Lockouts. Do Strikes Pay? The Strike Bill of the Nation. The Loss in Time. The Shock from Strikes. Compensating Advantages of Strikes. A Strike Lost may be a Strike Won. Strikes have Benefited the Workman and the Employer. The Right "Not to Work." "Fools do not Strike." The Moral Gain from Strikes. Unrecorded Heroism.

STRIKES may be considered from the standpoint either of ideal or actual conditions. Viewed from ideal conditions, a strike is a barbarous method of settling industrial controversies. It is a struggle of endurance, a question of might, not right; it is war carried into the industrial field, and like all war, attended by cruelty and suffering; it is a feudal conflict, in which many besides the immediate contestants are grievously injured. Thus, from an ideal point of view, the necessity for even occasional strikes constitutes one of the strongest indictments against civilized society.

Doubtless, if in some way or other an all-wise, all-good, and all-powerful government could, without injury to the liberty and prosperity of individuals, determine the rate of remuneration and the labor conditions of all workers, either by some ideal form of Socialism or by so harmonizing the interests of all classes that no two men should covet the same thing—doubtless, in that event, strikes would come to be unnecessary. Even under present conditions, with humanity imperfect as it is, the frequency of strikes may be largely diminished by means of trade unions.

There can be little doubt that with the increasing strength and growing conservatism of labor organizations and with the growth of a fuller and better understanding between labor and capital, industrial conflicts will tend to become less frequent. There is an ebb and flow in the movement of labor conflicts, the number of strikes increasing rapidly in periods of great prosperity or sudden depression and decreasing in times of normal business activity. The trade unions, however, have largely stemmed the current of strikes. With each year the capitalists of the country, the men who are entrusted with the direction of great industries, learn to realize more fully the justification of labor organization, and, as a consequence, strikes for the existence of unions are becoming less necessary. Many strikes are due to misunderstanding and may be and *are* averted by friendly meetings of the parties in interest. When the employers and workingmen can get together about a table and discuss the various differences of opinion in a fair and open manner, many of the rash strikes and wanton lockouts of former times will disappear. More can be accomplished by education of both parties to their mutual interest than by strikes. It is only where either employers or employees absolutely refuse to do what is reasonable, whether in their interest or not, that a temporary cessation of work, in the form of a strike or a lockout, is better than a continuance of work.

Frequently strikes are inevitable, just as there are cases in which lockouts cannot be avoided. It is commonly believed by people unacquainted with the subject that workmen are responsible for strikes and employers, for lockouts. This is not true. When the decisive action is taken by the employees, a cessation of work is called a strike, and a lockout when the initiative is taken by the employers. The responsibility, however, for a strike or for a lockout does not necessarily rest with the person who takes the decisive step, but with the party at fault, either in making unreasonable demands, or in refusing to accede to reasonable demands. Employers are occasionally responsible for strikes, as workmen are occasionally responsible for lockouts. In fact, it is often extremely difficult to draw a line, or to make a distinction between the two, since in many cases it cannot be determined by which side hostilities were begun.

It is often said that strikes do not pay. The anti-union newspapers of the country are a unit upon this point, and even many friends of the workingman claim that it never pays to strike. We frequently hear it stated that by a strike workmen lose more in a month than they may hope to regain in years, and that consequently practically all strikes are useless and unremunerative. It seems to me that such a judgment, which is based on a calculation of mere dollars and cents, is inherently wrong, because incomplete. One might just as well impugn the common sense of the farmers of Lexington, since the cost of a war with Great Britain was a hundredfold greater than the whole amount of taxation without representation. There is more in a strike than wages or hours of labor, and a strike may be a loss from a money point of view and a great gain in a higher and nobler sense. The cost of strikes has been grossly exaggerated, and the benefits conferred by them unduly minimized. A careful compilation has been carried on during the last twenty years by the United States Department of Labor, and the cost to employers and employees of all strikes in all industries has been ascertained for the period from January 1, 1881, to December 31, 1900. As a result of this work, which was efficiently organized and well conducted, Commissioner Carroll D. Wright says: "The losses to employers and employees under all conflicts, both strikes and lockouts, occurring in this period, 1881-1900, amounted to the enormous sum of $468,968,681."

In other words, the direct losses resulting from strikes and lockouts during the last twenty years were about $469,000,000, of which about 5/6 were attributed to strikes and 1/6 to lockouts. This seems to be a large sum, but when spread over the whole period, it amounts to an actual loss of only 38¢ per year, or about 3¢ per month for each inhabitant. As a nation we spent during this period more than five times as much upon pensions as upon strikes, and the American people have expended more during the last four months for railroad transportation than they have lost in strikes and lockouts during twenty years. Roughly speaking, the average workingman has spent very much less than 1% of his income on strikes or lockouts.

The same is true of the time lost through strikes. If we multiply the number of days of unemployment by the number of men who are out of work, the total loss amounts to 194,000,000 days; but spread over the whole period, this loss amounts to very much less than one day per year for each adult worker. In other words, the workmen of the United States have lost less time from strikes and lockouts than from the celebration of the Fourth of July or any other legal holiday, and the leisure resulting from strikes has not been 1/50 of that caused by the general observance of the Sabbath. The total amount of time lost by strikes and lockouts during the last twenty years would be more than counterbalanced by the addition of four minutes to the average working day. Much of even this comparatively slight loss, moreover, is merely apparent. "The days so lost," says Commissioner Wright, "do not represent absolute loss, as cessation of work or production often does away with the necessity of stoppage at some other time for restricting the output to the demands of trade and making repairs." Thus, in the coal mining industry, which furnished almost one-third of all strikes during the last two decades, a large portion of the time lost through strikes would probably have been lost in any case, since the number of idle days in the anthracite regions, due to no fault of the miners, averaged 111 working days per year, while the days lost by strikes certainly did not exceed ten per year. The result of many of the coal strikes preceding that of 1902, had been to close the mines at one time, instead of closing them at another.

I do not wish to argue that strikes are not a great evil, nor that much hardship is not caused by them. The loss to the whole body of workmen may be very small, and still the hardship to individuals be acute and severe. In every strike individuals are bound to suffer, and the fasting of to-day is not compensated for by the feasting of to-morrow. There are many losses in a strike, moreover, which do not fall upon either of the two contestants. Thus, in many railroad and street railway strikes, the greatest sufferers are the public, who are deprived of comforts or even of necessaries. Another loss to the community results from a feeling of insecurity, which is shown in the strike clauses to contracts, as well as in the shock which the community experiences whenever a great strike is declared.

There are, however, great compensating advantages in strikes, especially when inaugurated for a good purpose and carried on in the proper spirit. The shock of which I have just spoken is in itself frequently of considerable advantage to the community. Workingmen, like employers, get into ruts, and the strike, or anything else which changes the ordinary constitution of industry, frequently leads to the adoption of better methods of production and to increased output. In many cases, strikes have resulted in the adoption of labor-saving devices or improved machinery, and the output of an industry after a strike has often been much greater than before its inception.

Apart from this fact, it can scarcely be doubted that the really justifiable strikes—and the majority of the strikes in the United States have been justifiable—have resulted in a great advantage to the workmen. Strikes have paid, and strikes, when for a good purpose and conducted in a proper manner, will continue to pay. While the workingman has lost during the last twenty years less than one per cent. of his wages in strikes and lockouts, and the loss in time from this enforced idleness has been less than one day per year, the gains derived from strikes, or what has been the same thing, the fear of strikes, have been very much in excess of one per cent. increase in wages. Not only have wages been largely increased, hours of labor reduced, and conditions generally improved, but the whole moral tone of the workingmen of the community has been appreciably elevated.

It is, of course, not true and it cannot be claimed, that all that has been gained by the workingmen has been obtained through strikes. Some of this advance has been due to, or, at least, has been rendered possible by, the increased intelligence and productivity of labor, by the adoption of new machines, and by the better organization of workmen in factories and mines; but a large percentage of gain, a percentage far in excess of the one per cent. cost, has resulted from the fact that through organization the men were able and willing, in case of necessity, to strike effectively. While any particular strike may not have been a paying investment, there can be little doubt that strikes in the aggregate have benefited the working classes much more than they have cost or injured them.

We have heard much of late of the right to work, and it cannot be doubted that under normal conditions, and without prejudice to the rights of others, all men should be permitted to earn their bread in the sweat of their brow. There is another right, however, as sacred and as inalienable, namely, the right not to work, the right to desist from work either singly or concertedly, when conditions are such as to render this action advisable and justifiable. There is no doubt that strikes are evil, but they are not so evil as industrial oppression, not so evil as the truck system, not so evil as the sweating in our great cities, not so evil as unregulated exploitation of woman and child labor. The great majority of strikes in the United States have had justifiable reasons. During the last twenty years, of all the strikes in the United States, 58%, as measured by the number of establishments affected, were fought out either for an increase of wages, a decrease in hours, or both, or against an attempted reduction in wages, while only $3\frac{1}{2}\%$ were sympathetic demonstrations with other workers, and less than $1\frac{1}{2}\%$ for the sole avowed purpose of obtaining recognition of the union. Moreover, of these strikes the majority were won, over one-half being wholly, and over one-eighth, partially, successful, while less than three-eighths failed completely. Moreover, it has been the intelligent and better class of workmen who have struck, and not the ragtag of the army. "Labor conflicts," says Commissioner Wright, "grow out of increased intelligence . . . . . fools do not strike. It is only men who have intelligence enough to recognize their condition that make use of this last resort." It is the states with the highest industrial development, such as New York, Pennsylvania, Illinois, Massachusetts, and Ohio, which have a disproportionately large number of labor conflicts; whereas in the more backward states, strikes are much fewer. It has often been observed that when a strike is justifiable demand for fair treatment, when it is only the possible expression of a "divine discontent," it is the heroes among the workmen who are in the van of the movement. What is true of states is equally true of nations. Strikes are most frequent in those countries in which civilization is most highly

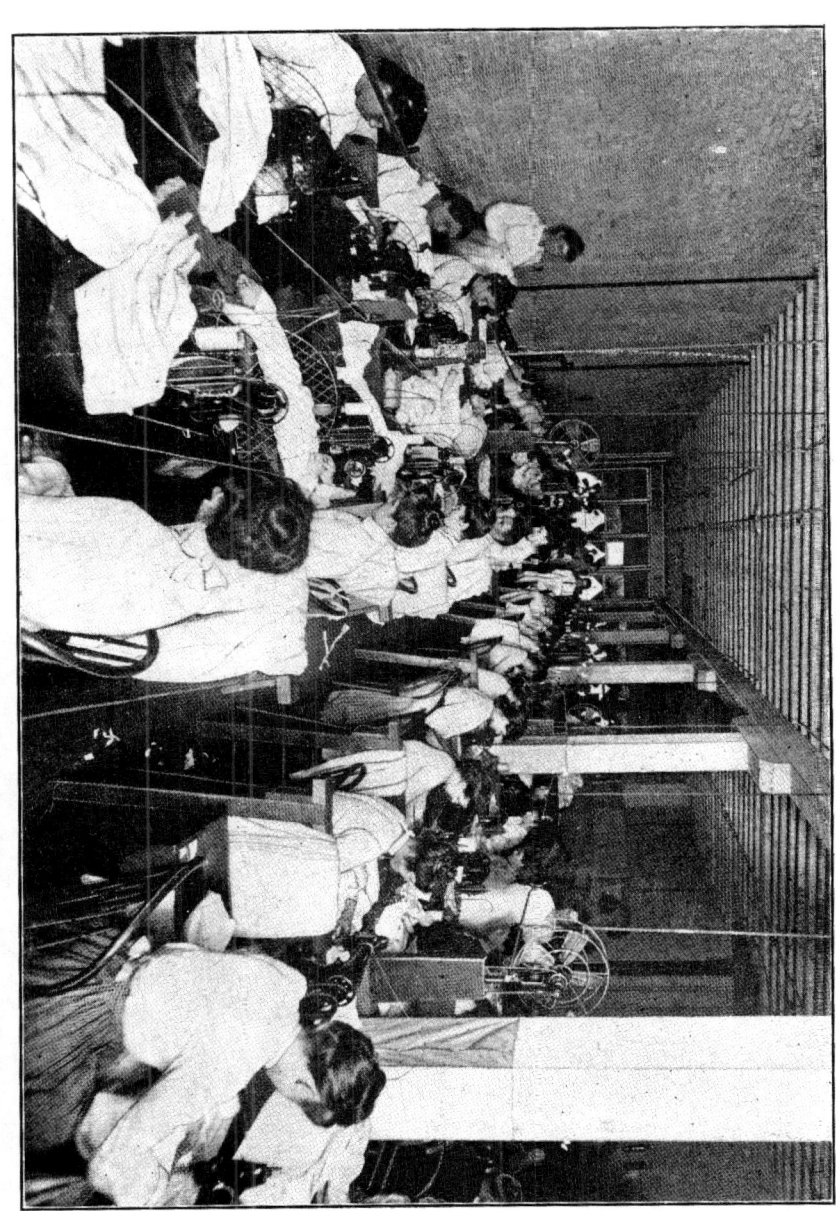

A MODEL GARMENT MAKING FACTORY

One of five floors, all heated with indirect steam, air exhausted by fan current, running ice water, windows on two sides and lunch rooms attached

A Non-Union Cigar Shop

developed. As a matter of fact, strikes are practically unknown in the less advanced nations.

In all conflicts of this sort, where men are fighting for a principle or for tolerable conditions of life, there is, apart from its material advantages, a great moral gain derived from the strike. It is difficult to overestimate the gain from a righteous labor uprising, and there are few moral forces more uplifting than the strike spirit that cements a vast army of crude men. It is to be accounted an evil in strikes that they cause bitter feelings between employers and employed, and between union and non-union men, although frequently a strike has the opposite tendency of clearing the atmosphere. Strikes have, however, at least this compensating advantage, that they unite with the bond of mutual self-sacrifice the men who are fighting together for the good of the whole. We conceive of strikes in a militant sense, but a strike is a siege rather than an assault. A strike cannot be won by a single action, but requires the greatest amount of endurance, patience, and self-control. The striker must husband his resources, must remain sober, must economize for the sake of his wife and children, must aid his neighbor who is needier than he, and must refrain from all manner of violence and all incentive to excitement. Day by day must he watch his supplies getting lower, must see perhaps his wife and children growing pallid under the stress of privation, must see other men work in his place, sometimes at wages higher than those for which he struck. The striker must refrain from manifesting any bitterness towards those who have taken his place, or towards the men who have been imported into his town for the sake of frightening him into submission. He must turn the other cheek to the swaggering bullies engaged as private police, and must in all cases refrain from entering into a contest with them. Temptation comes to such a man to sell out his fellows for the sake of great gain to himself. He is offered all manner of bribes, from a better position to a direct money gift, and he is told continually by agents of the employer that other men are deserting and that he is a fool to suffer that others may take advantage of his sacrifice. The courage, the steadfastness, the quiet endurance of workmen upon a strike verge upon the heroic. It is not good reading matter, not good "copy," and the papers make nothing of it. A hundred thousand men display exceptional self-denial and self-restraint, and the press of the country is dumb. A single man wields a club or heaves a brick, and the wires are hot with telegrams to all parts of the world. To the man who has lived through a strike, however, the great compensation for its evils is the quiet, modest, unrecorded heroism which it calls forth.

When a strike is thus fought out upon a moral basis, when men throw into the scale their bread and the bread of their wives and children, when men stand shoulder to shoulder and fight the dreary tragic battle of starvation and eviction, the contest cannot be lost. It is a commonplace among unionists that a strike lost is a strike won. The men may yield, they may be starved, shot, beaten, they may lose in wages and confidence, but others are encouraged by their struggle; and their fellow-workers and eventually they themselves gain by their sacrifice. The workingmen are saved from the aggression of unscrupulous members of the employing class, not only by their ability to win strikes, but by their willingness to fight even a losing battle.

While recognizing the advantages which may come from strikes, however, the approved policy of the best unions is to give their vote for peace wherever there is a reasonable measure of doubt. No more than employers do unions favor strikes and lockouts; like employers, they resort to them only in extreme cases. With the growth of unions in funds and membership the number of strikes tends to diminish. In its infancy an organization may be reckless and aggressive, but its approach to manhood almost invariably brings with it an increased sense of responsibility. It has been observed in England, as in the United States, that unions make for peace and not for war. The effect of the change from small, unorganized bodies of workmen to a single, homogeneous union has been similar to that of the change from little, reckless, fighting, cantankerous principalities to a single, strong, unified nation. Trade unions are the most effective, but not the most frequent strikers, and it is because they can strike so effectively that they are not obliged to do it frequently. The unions, moreover, approve the policy of conciliation, voluntary arbitration, and trade agreements, so that with stable conditions the number of strikes will diminish. There can be no doubt that the unions and those employers who favor trade agreements are doing their utmost to prevent the wastefulness of strikes. On the other hand, those employers who insist upon managing their own business and upon dealing only with their own employees are, because of their arbitrary and dictatorial methods, responsible for the majority of strikes. With the growth of a spirit of mutual concession and with a better understanding of the needs and aspirations of both classes, the necessity for, and justification of, the great majority of strikes will pass away.

CHAPTER XXXVI

THE PROPER CONDUCT OF A STRIKE

How a Strike Must be Conducted. Maintaining Enthusiasm. Informing the Public. Alertness and Vigilance. Errors Inevitable. The Moral Aspect of Strikes and of Lockouts. Violence Defeats its own Purpose. Better to Lose Strikes than Win by Violence. Violence and Peaceful Picketing. Individual Crimes and Union Responsibility. Exaggeration. The Sinews of War. The Financiering of a Strike.

THE responsibility of a labor leader does not cease with the calling of a strike. A strike may be perfectly justifiable both in morals and policy; it may be an inevitable revolt against intolerable oppression, and may be inaugurated with every likelihood of success. Unless properly conducted, however, a strike, be it ever so just, ever so noble in its purposes and aims, may very well be lost.

The problems involved in the conduct of a strike are many and pressing, and the whole strike may collapse through failure to meet any issue, however suddenly raised. It is necessary to keep up the spirit of the men struggling, it may be, against great odds, and to infuse the weaker members with the hope of the more confident. It is especially necessary to conserve the funds of the organization and to distribute relief in such a manner as to satisfy the needs and maintain the strength of the strikers. It is no less necessary to be aware at all times of the resources of the strikers as well as of the strength, tenacity and purposes of the opponent. The leader of the strikers must ever be open to any reasonable proposition made by the other side, and must give heed and respectful attention to any suggestion made by disinterested parties. The sympathy of the public must be secured by the fair presentation of the strikers side of the controversy, and this sympathy must be retained by reasonable conduct and moderate and temperate action throughout. The enthusiasm of the men for the strike must constantly be kept up, and those who have wavered or who have strayed from the fold must be approached and urged to return. Attempts must be made by peaceable methods to prevent the importation of new men, and where this has already occurred, efforts must be made to induce them or aid them to seek employment elsewhere. Above all and beyond all, the leader entrusted with the conduct of a strike must be alert and vigilant in the prevention of violence. The strikers must be made constantly aware of the imperative necessity of remaining peaceable. They must be urged to remain in their homes except when picketing, and attempts must be made to prevent them from drinking, or from engaging in brawls with men upon the other side. The strike leader must secure the sympathy of other unions and of all reasonable men in the community, and must endeavor to prevent the abuse of power or opportunity by his opponents. However careful he may be and however great his foresight, there will arise daily scores of situations claiming his immediate attention and requiring for their solution a clear judgment, great tact and patience, and the ability and willingness to make an immediate decision.

No man can conduct a strike without making at least some errors. No labor leader pretends to be infallible, and no one who has gone through a strike and has been entrusted with its leadership, can believe that it is possible to carry such a conflict to a successful conclusion without being involved in errors of commission and omission. At such times every letter may be a trick, every message from supposedly disinterested parties a snare intended to defeat the aims of the strike. But the leader in such emergencies must endeavor to render his mistakes as few as possible and to approach each problem with the single view of taking the action best calculated to advance the interests of the men and the welfare of the public.

There is very much more written about the proper conduct of a strike from the moral point of view than about the proper handling of a lockout, or the proper conduct of employers during strikes. The responsibilities of labor leaders are treated as fully and exhaustively as are the rights of employers and of non-union men, but one looks in vain for any adequate consideration of the rights of labor unions in a strike, or of the responsibilities of employers and the duties of non-union men. The discussions all turn upon what unionists must do and refrain from doing, what rules they must obey, just what points of etiquette and procedure they must observe. We hear many statements as to how the men must or must not strike and how, what, and when they should boycott, but nothing is said of the duties or responsibilities of employers to men locked out, the use of the blacklist and the injunction, the arming of private police, the orders "to shoot to kill" on the wholesale, the eviction of helpless tenants, etc. I do not desire to thrust advice or criticism upon employers, however, and I shall therefore limit my remarks to a statement of how the men and officers of a union should conduct themselves during an industrial conflict.

Under no circumstances should a strike be allowed to degenerate into violence. There are times, when a great issue is at stake and the struggle seems about to be lost, when the use of brute force appears for a moment to be desirable. This, however, is a shortsighted policy and brings with it its own punishment. A single act of violence, while it may deter a strike breaker or a score of them, inflicts much greater and more irreparable damage upon the party giving than upon the party receiving the blow. Violence invariably alienates the sympathy of the public. No matter how just the demands of the men, no matter how unreasonable and uncompromising the attitude of the employer, the commission of acts of violence invariably puts the strikers in the wrong. The public absolutely closes its eyes to the merits of a controversy when one party or the other has actively stimulated or has condoned acts of violence. The use of force is properly considered a sign of weakness. The leader who desires to carry a strike to a successful conclusion must, therefore, even as a matter of policy, endeavor to prevent the commission of such acts.

It should not be permitted to plead in defense of lawbreakers that a strike is war. Just as in actual war the contestants, under penalty of forfeiting the sympathy of all other nations, are compelled to govern themselves by the principles of international law prescribing the rights of combatants and of non-combatants, so the two parties engaged in a strike must abide scrupulously by the provisions of the law. A strike or a lockout is coercion, but it is lawful, whereas a resort to physical force is both immoral and unlawful.

It is sometimes claimed that no strike can be won without the use of physical force. I do not believe that this is true, but if it is, it is better that the strike be lost than that it succeed through violence and the commission of outrages. The cause of unionism is not lost through any strike or through any number of strikes, and if it were true that all strikes would fail if physical force could not be resorted to, it would be better to demonstrate that fact and to seek remedy in other directions than to permit strikes to degenerate into conflicts between armed men. If it be shown that strikes cannot be won without violence, then it will be necessary to secure reforms for workingmen exclusively through political action.

As a matter of fact, the conduct of strikes without violence is as advantageous and successful as the use of violence is futile and immoral. In the long run, violence acts as a boomerang and defeats its own purposes. No group of workmen can resist the force of the state militia, or of the regular army of the United States, and if it should come to an armed conflict, the Federal government would, with the approval of the community, raise, if necessary, as many hundreds of thousands of troops to maintain peace as were used against the seceding states in the War of the Rebellion. The whole force of public opinion and the undivided sentiment of the wage earners of the country would be united upon the suppression of acts of violence and of insurrection against the constituted authorities.

Workingmen gain by their abstention from violence as they gain by every acknowledgment of the rights of employers and of the public. It is essential to workingmen on strike that the right to picket be maintained, but picketing itself depends upon abstaining from violence. The best picket is the man who is not violent and who does not threaten, but relies entirely upon the power of persuasion and appeals to the manhood of the strike breaker. A man with a club in his hand or a pistol in his pocket has not the time or the patience to waste on argument, and by refraining from violence or threats of violence the unions secure the services of a much more efficient class of pickets. There are men, it is true, who can be intimidated, but not persuaded; it is better, however, to suffer the injury that these men can inflict than to inflict violence upon them. The struggle of labor is not for a day or a month or a year. The employer cannot permanently keep the strike breakers. Even when successful, the employer who has had a strike fears its recurrence as a burnt child fears the fire. The strike will more likely be won if violence is not resorted to, but even should a case arise where violence is necessary to the victory of the men, it is better to trust to the hope of snatching victory from defeat itself than to put the union and the strikers irretrievably in the wrong by resorting to force.

The employers are perfectly justified in condemning as harshly as they desire the acts of any striker or strikers, who are guilty of violence. I welcome the most sweeping denunciation of such acts and the widest publicity that may be given to them by the press. In this the employers and the newspapers are simply supplementing the work of trade unionists themselves who are endeavoring to stamp out all incentive to acts of violence. What the trade unionist, however, does object to, is the use which is made of the occurrence of acts of violence to discredit persons and parties who are in no wise responsible. The union should not be held responsible for the acts of individual members done without its consent, sanction, or approbation, and even in direct contravention of distinct and specific orders to maintain peace. The United Mine Workers of America is no more legally or morally responsible for the three or four murders or for the other acts of violence committed by individual mineworkers or by sympathizers during the coal strike of 1902, than would the Philadelphia & Reading Railroad be for the unwarranted actions of a coal and iron policeman in the course of a drunken brawl. In fact, the railroad corporations should have been held more responsible for lawbreakers directly employed by them, than the Union for men who were not its agents. A union is no more responsible

A Model Union Cigar Factory

Manchester, N. H., Cotton Mills—The Largest Cotton Mills in the World

for the violence of individuals than is a corporation for the unwarranted actions of its several stockholders.

The unlawful conduct of individual men is also used by employers to exaggerate the amount of violence and to make it appear as though a state of lawlessness and anarchy prevailed. There is also a constant temptation on the part of some newspapers to exaggerate, to make as dramatic as possible any act of disorder that may occur. Peaceful conventions of trade unions are made to appear like wild gatherings of excited and irrational men. Accounts of meetings conducted with decorum and due regard to parliamentary procedure read, oftentimes, in some of the newspapers, like reports of incipient riots. A group of two or three pickets peacefully stationed outside a factory grows, in some newspaper stories, into a surging and intractable mob, and a drunken brawl between men in no wise connected with the union becomes a deliberate attempt on the part of unionists to molest, cripple, and injure non-unionists. The amount of violence actually committed is grossly exaggerated and that which is fairly traceable to the officials of trade unions is almost infinitesimal. What little there is should be visited with the strong disapproval of public opinion and swift and condign punishment by the courts; but the amount should not be exaggerated, and the responsibility should be fixed upon the perpetrators. Above all, the theory and justifiable practices of trade unionism should not be assailed on account of violence or other illegal acts committed in its name.

There are more men killed on the Fourth of July from explosions or from resulting lockjaw, than are killed in all the strikes in all the cities of the country on all days of the year. More men are killed in election brawls and more violence is committed on election day, than can be charged to the account of all strikes in the United States during the whole year. There are more arrests made in the city of Chicago or in the city of New York in one month, than have probably been occasioned by all the strikes in these United States for one hundred years. No one would argue from this, however, that the Declaration of Independence is at fault, or that elections should be abolished, or that the mayor of New York or Chicago is responsible. Critics of trade unionism do not make a distinction between the making of law and its enforcement. The state of Illinois or of New York, specifically condemns murder, arson, burglary, and theft, but the governments of these states are not necessarily responsible when these crimes are occasionally committed. A trade union, moreover, is not even in the position of a sovereign state, it has not the right to punish the offender. The United Mine Workers of America was accused of aiding and abetting violence because, in advance of the trials of a few perpetrators of such violence, it refrained from expelling them from the union. It would be as fair to condemn the Christian Churches for failing to exclude from membership men who were accused, but not convicted, of crime. These churches are sincerely opposed to the perpetration of crime, but do not conceive it to be within their province to inflict a punishment of this nature, especially in advance of action by the courts. The attitude of the trade union is identical.

During the five months of the anthracite strike eight men were killed, three or four of these deaths being caused by men on strike or claiming to be in sympathy with the union, while if the mines had been operated during this period and had maintained the average number of accidents, two hundred men would have been killed and six hundred seriously maimed or injured. Of course I do not put the murder of men in brawls upon a par with the killing of men as a result of dangerous occupations, or through the negligence of operators or their foremen. It is well, however, that acts of violence not only diminish, but absolutely disappear. Life is sacred, though it be in the body of an incurable, a lunatic, an epileptic, a criminal, or a professional strike breaker willing to assume the risk of his profession; and the union should assist the state in the maintenance of order and the preservation of the life of even the men opposed to it. With the advance in strength and the growth in age of the unions, the amount of violence accompanying strikes, small as it now is, will be even lessened, and strikes will be in practice what they are in theory, simply and solely a peaceful abstention of men from work.

A most important feature in the conduct of a strike is the collection and distribution of funds. No protracted strike can be carried on without money, and since the burden of the strike, no matter when it comes, must fall largely upon the strikers, all unions, however peaceable, should provide themselves with a defense fund, to be used only if absolutely necessary. Strikes called by or with the approval of a national organization should receive the entire financial support of the union. The maxim should be, "Beware of entrance to a quarrel, but being in, bear't that the opposed may beware of thee." The union should be chary of engaging in strikes, should not call them as "bluffs" or threats, but when once launched upon a justifiable conflict, in which there is the slightest hope of success, it should be determined to sacrifice the last penny of its funds.

There needs more than good intention in this matter; more is necessary than money. Some system must be arranged, efficacious, reliable, and not open to abuse either in the collection or the distribution of the funds. During the anthracite strike of 1902 a well-thought-out system was perfected. The money contributed to the support of the strike was sent by the national union to the district organizations, by the districts it was forwarded to the locals, and by the locals in turn, was given to the strikers, in the form of store orders, and according to the needs of each. A system of checks and balances was devised, so as to prevent the slightest misappropriation of the money. Thus, as contributors to the fund were assured of the proper use of their money, outside support was willingly given, so that the men were stronger and more able to resist at the close of the contest than at the beginning.

CHAPTER XXXVII

THE INJUNCTION IN LABOR DISPUTES.

Injunctions against Strikers. History of the Injunction. Temporary Injunctions. Contempt of Court. No "Trial by Jury." Nullifying Fundamental Constitutional Rights. Injunctions in Criminal Cases. Injunctions, the Anti-Trust and Interstate Commerce Laws. Blanket Injunctions. Government by Injunction. The Bias of the Appointed Judges. Judge Jackson and the "Vampires." Injunctions against "Feeding the Hungry." Attempts to Abolish the Use of Injunctions in Labor Disputes. The Liberties of the Whole Nation Assailed. The Virginia Law Unconstitutional. Deep Iniquity of the Injunction. Ceaseless Agitation. An Amendment to the Constitution.

NO weapon has been used with such disastrous effect against trade unions as the injunction in labor disputes. By means of it trade unionists have been prohibited under severe penalties from doing what they had a legal right to do, and have been specifically directed to do what they had a legal right not to do. It is difficult to speak in measured tones or moderate language of the savagery and venom with which unions have been assailed by the injunction, and to the working classes, as to all fair-minded men, it seems little less than a crime to condone or tolerate it.

Trade unionists do not object to the injunction in itself. If properly used in its own sphere, as determined by English and American judicial decisions prior to 1890, the injunction may be useful and necessary. An injunction was merely an order by a court in equity, commanding a certain person or persons to desist from some action proposed or actually begun, and it had been effectively used for the protection of property where the injury contemplated would have been irreparable, or of such a nature that adequate damages could not be calculated. The injunction was in the nature of an ounce of prevention, and was intended to obviate certain civil injuries by applying to them what was practically, though not technically, a criminal punishment.

It was not until the opponents of trade unionism and the enemies of the working classes decided upon concerted movement against labor organizations, that the full possibilities of the injunction, as distorted and perverted by the courts, became apparent. The method of procedure in injunctions is inimical to the perpetuity of free government, since it sweeps aside all constitutional safeguards. The judge, upon application and under certain prescribed conditions, issues a preliminary injunction against a person or persons, known or unknown, or against all those engaged in a given industry, without service upon any of these parties and without an opportunity to them to appear and be heard before the preliminary injunction is granted. This restraining order may be and often is issued upon false information and perjured statement, by illegal and improper method, and upon a matter entirely beyond the legitimate province and jurisdiction of the court. The preliminary injunction is usually prepared by the plaintiff's attorney, who states therein whatever he wishes; and no opportunity is offered to the defendant before the granting of the order, to make counter-affidavit or to show cause why the preliminary injunction should not be issued. During the often unreasonably long time which elapses between the grant of the preliminary injunction and the time set for the hearing to determine whether that injunction shall be continued, a strike may be lost and thousands or tens of thousands of men defrauded of their rights and disappointed of their justifiable expectations. The preliminary injunction thus produces exactly the evil which it was intended to obviate or prevent, but for the workingman there is no remedy against the incalculable and irreparable damage inflicted upon him by a temporary injunction illegally and wrongfully granted. If, during the time before the hearing, anyone in the whole wide world is known or is supposed to be guilty of a violation of any part of any clause of any section of an injunction, he may be summarily arrested, either then or later, and put upon trial. Upon such trial he may insist upon none of the rights guaranteed to him as a citizen of the United States. A trial by jury is denied to him, and the judge passes sentence upon the sole ground of whether or not the preliminary injunction, issued without a hearing, has been disobeyed. The constitutional guarantees of liberty and property are denied and nullified by this judicial process. The court, after hearing the case in its own way, decides in its own way. The man is condemned to pay such fine or to suffer and undergo such punishment as the court in its supposed wisdom may determine. In a civil action the amount recovered should not be greater than the proved damages, but by injunction a man who commits precisely the same offense for which civil action is brought, is punishable by fine or imprisonment according to the discretion of the court. In a criminal action the law specifies a maximum punishment that may be inflicted, but if the same offense is committed in violation of a temporary injunction, issued without a hearing, or without personal service, the punishment may be whatever the judge decrees, however much in excess of the maximum punishment fixed by the law of the state or the nation. From this decision of the judge there is no appeal, and even if an appeal is taken upon the question of the jurisdiction of the court issuing the injunction, it is possible that the active men of the union may lie in jail during the appeal. In many cases, however, the striking workingmen are not in possession of sufficient funds to take an appeal, and generally the injury inflicted upon the defendants and those they represent is irreparable, even if the temporary injunction is eventually set aside.

It would naturally be supposed that the courts would exercise this extraordinary power of injunction in a conservative manner and with the most scrupulous care, but this has not been the case. Injunctions in labor disputes have been granted by judges in chambers, without notice and without a hearing of the parties against whom they are issued; or they have simply been written out by some clerk of the court in the absence of the judge. Such an injunction thrown out upon the spur of the moment may restrain the union or its members from giving food or money to strikers, forbid peaceful picketing, or prohibit other actions equally lawful. Under this injunction persons or parties who might be punished civilly are made criminally liable for offenses or for actions which are not offenses at all.

One of the worst features of the injunction in labor disputes is that the court enjoins not only civil but criminal acts, and thus deprives the workingman of his constitutional guarantee of trial by jury for such offenses. For centuries Anglo-Saxons have struggled incessantly for the right of trial by jury in criminal cases, and this right has been specifically guaranteed by the English Bill of Rights, by the charters of the various colonies and by the constitutions of the United States and of the several states. "In all criminal prosecutions," says the Constitution of the United States, "the accused shall enjoy the right to a speedy and public trial, by an impartial jury of the State and district wherein the crime shall have been committed; which district shall have been previously ascertained by law—and to be informed of the nature and cause of the accusation; to be confronted with the witnesses against him; to have compulsory process for obtaining witnesses in his favor, and to have the Assistance of Counsel for his defense." This constitutional guarantee has been swept aside by the courts. The apologists for judicial aggression and for government by injunction maintain that an act may be an attempt to effect irreparable injury and at the same time a criminal offense, and that in case of doubt an injunction may always issue. This, however, offers no solace to the man who is hauled up before an omnipotent federal judge, upon an alleged criminal offense, and is severely punished without being allowed to defend himself by ordinary constitutional methods. The action of the courts in issuing injunctions in criminal cases in contravention of what had always been supposed to be the plain and evident intention of the Bill of Rights of the Constitution of the United States, has been sustained by the United States Supreme Court in the Debs case, even though the overwhelming opinion of lawyers and laymen, until within the last ten years, had been that in such cases injunctions could not apply.

In every way and in every direction possible, the use of the injunction has been extended and enlarged. It was formerly held that an injunction could only be used to protect a particular property right of a particular person, and then only in cases in which that right was clearly and obviously threatened. The courts have now held that the government may itself enjoin persons in order to protect the laws, to prevent combinations in restraint of trade or interstate commerce, or to protect the mails, in which the government is said to have a property right. This process has also been extended by the "blanket" injunction. In this case, besides certain specified persons, the injunction is addressed to "all other persons whatsoever, who are not named herein, from and after the time when they shall severally have knowledge of such order." It was not, of course, possible to serve a notice of this injunction upon all against whom it was directed, since it apparently included the inhabitants of Senegambia, Cochin-China, and, possibly, the inhabitants of the moon. The picturesque term "government by injunction," became almost literally true. The order of the court in the Debs case supplanted all laws and all constitutional rights and immunities of all the parties affected, and thus each and every inhabitant of the United States was placed in jeopardy of his liberty and property, despite anything which the constitution of the United States or of his own state might determine. The process of injunction has gone even further, and, in order to prevent strikes it has been used to pervert the evident intent and purposes of laws not directed against labor organizations. By the Anti-trust Law of 1890, "any contract, combination in the form of trust or otherwise, or conspiracy in restraint of trade or commerce among the several states," is declared to be illegal; and by the Inter-state Commerce Act of 1887 railroads as well as their officers and employees are prohibited from refusing to perform their services as common carriers or from refusing the cars and passengers of other railroads and of other companies. By this combination of laws, with a judicious admixture of judicial interpretation, a strike of employees becomes a conspiracy against inter-state commerce, and therefore in violation of the law, and the injunction is specifically recommended in the Anti-trust Law as a means of securing the enforcement of the law. In the case of the Southern California Railroad *vs*. Rutherford, thousands of men were specifically required by injunction " to perform all of their regular and accustomed duties" while they remained in the employment of the company, and when strikes have been contemplated, injunctions have been granted to prevent the leaders from issuing the strike order or doing anything else which might be necessary to inaugurate the strike or to carry it to a successful conclusion.

In speaking of the application of the injunction to labor disputes, Mr. F. J. Stimson states that "the objections are three:

"1. This course of things does away with the criminal law and its safeguards of indictment, proof by witnesses, jury trial, and a fixed and uniform punishment. Most of these offenses might well have been the subject of criminal prosecution; and the bill of rights of our constitution says that in all criminal prosecutions the accused shall enjoy the right to a speedy and public trial by an impartial jury of the State, and district wherein the crime shall have been committed; to be informed of the nature and cause of the accusation; to be confronted with the witnesses against him; to have compulsory process of obtaining witnesses in his favor, and to have the assistance of counsel for his defense.

"2. It makes the courts no longer a judicial, but a part (and it bids fair to be a most important part) of the executive branch of Government. More briefly and picturesquely: the Federal courts may thus grow into mere Star-chambers and run the country.

"3. It tends to make our judiciary either tyrannical or contemptible. If we do not fall under a tyranny such as might have existed in the England of Charles the First or such as does exist in the South America of to-day, we shall fall into the almost worse plight of finding an injunction of our highest courts a mere *brutem fulmen*—an empty threat, a jest and a byword; so that through their own contempt process the courts themselves will be brought into contempt." . . . . .

The rights, privileges, and immunities of the citizens of the United States depend upon the permanent separation of the powers of the executive, legislative, and judicial branches of the government. If the executive is to grow at the expense of the legislative or the latter at the expense of the judiciary, or if the judiciary is to encroach upon the rights of both executive and legislative branches of the government, as well as upon those of the people, the liberties of the citizens will be vitally and seriously endangered. There have been times of great stress and peril when the courts have been obliged to take, or have been granted, extraordinary powers. During the fourteenth century in the reign of Richard the Second of England, the turmoil of civil wars and the aggressions of the great barons made the decision of common law judges nugatory and unenforceable, and the king was therefore obliged to grant extraordinary judicial powers to the chancellor. The court of Star Chamber itself was originally intended to correct abuses and violations of the law, but when this tribunal unduly extended its powers to the detriment of the people, it evoked a revolt and contributed finally to the rebellion against King Charles the First and to his execution. The extension of the injunction in recent years, with its abrogation of the fundamental rights of the citizen, is a similar instance of encroachment on the part of the judiciary, an encroachment, moreover, during times when there is no civil war and no internal disturbance.

In my judgment this extension of the use of the injunction is the most disturbing factor in our national life, the darkest cloud upon our horizon. The elements who favor the injunction as it is now used are, either consciously or unconsciously, inimical to true democracy and are apparently like the adherents of Hamilton in the early days of the Republic, in favor of what is practically a monarchical, even a despotic government, and in favor of the limitation and restriction of the rights of the people. Those who, like Justice Brewer, advocate the still further use of this formidable weapon, are undermining the faith of the people in the Constitution and the laws of the land and are destroying the confidence of the working classes in the impartiality of the courts.

The final argument of apologists for judicial aggression and the unlimited extension of the injunction is their faith in the wisdom and honor of judges. "In the last resort," they say, "our rights, liberties, and immunities are safe in the hands of judges selected for their probity and integrity as well as for their profound knowledge of men and things." This argument, however, is not conclusive even if true. The tyranny of the best of men is bad, and the liberties of the American people should ever be in their own keeping and never entrusted to the wisdom and moderation of even the most upright judge. Personally, I believe, with most trade unionists, that the judges of the Federal and State courts are men of honor, in this respect equal or superior to the average of men. There is, however, a bias in every one, especially in close corporations of individuals selected from a particular group in society and usually for a long or for a life tenure of office. As we proceed from the lower to the higher courts, from short tenure judges to long tenure judges, from judges by election to judges by appointment, we find a constantly increasing prejudice against workingmen and a constantly lessening ability to understand the fundamental principles of trade unionism. The fact, also, that many judges of superior courts have in the past been servants of the great corporations and intend in the future to return to that service, while not necessarily affecting their honor, undoubtedly tends to create an unconscious bias.

While I have no desire to impugn the honor of the judges or their profound knowledge of the law, the practical wisdom of the judiciary, as manifested by many recent decisions, seems to me to be at least open to question. The judicial attitude of some of the eminent judges of our federal courts may be indicated by their demeanor towards workingmen brought before them in alleged contempt of court. Thus, the eminent District Judge, John J. Jackson, of the Southern District of West Virginia, stated to the defendant miners that they and other officers of trade unions were "a professional set of agitators" and "vampires that fattened on the honest labor of the coal miners." It is not so much what the judges say as what they do that arouses the antagonism of workingmen, but the manner in which Judge Jackson spoke is at least an index of the attitude of mind in which many injunctions have been issued.

There is no labor leader who has not had a bitter experience with these injunctions. In what was probably the first injunction ever issued in a labor dispute, the injunction against the Cigar Makers during their strike at Binghamton, N. Y., the strikers and all others acting for them or in their behalf were enjoined by the court not only from being in the vicinity of the factory, but also from being upon the street in which the factory stood, while the court further enjoined the union from paying money or giving support to non-union workmen. Even though this injunction was appealed and subsequently set aside, the damage done to the union through the unwisdom of the judges was irreparable, and no advantage was gained by the appeal. In many cases unions have been enjoined from picketing, from giving money or support to strikers, and from doing any one of the many legal acts which are absolutely essential to the gaining of a strike or to resistance to a lockout. In the case of the injunction against the Amalgamated Association of Iron and Steel Workers, the strikers were enjoined even from peaceable talk with workers, while in the case of an injunction against the International Typographical Union, which was at that time in conflict with the *Buffalo Express,* the members of the union were enjoined from boycotting and were even refused the right to discuss or talk about the paper in any way that might affect it or its business. The Industrial Commission received a large amount of testimony showing clearly the folly of many injunctions, some of which were set aside and some upheld, although all of them worked irreparable injury to the workingmen and brought the judiciary into disrespect and contempt.

In order to avoid even the semblance of misrepresenting the position of the judges or misstating the terms of injunctions, I prefer, rather than give my own account of the injunction issued against strikers, to quote from a pamphlet carefully prepared by five members of the New York Bar and issued during the year 1900 by the Social Reform Club of that city. "In the case of the Sun Printing and Publishing Company *versus* Delaney and others, in December, 1899," says the pamphlet, "the Supreme Court of New

York, among other things, enjoined the defendants from the exercise of their right to give the public their side of the controversy with the Sun, as an argument against advertising in a paper which they claimed had treated them unjustly. It also forbade them from attempting to persuade news dealers from selling the paper, and finally wound up with a sweeping restraint 'from in any other manner or by any other means interfering with the property, property rights or business of the plaintiff.' It should be added that on appeal the Appellate Division struck out these commands, but they were so plainly subversive of fundamental rights that it is difficult to see how they could have been granted in the first instance.

"In still another case last year the 'Wheeling Railway Company *versus* John Smith and others' (so runs the title of the action, without naming the others) in the United States Circuit Court, West Virginia, two men not parties to the action nor found to be agents of 'John Smith and others' whoever they may have been, were punished for contempt of court for, among other things, 'reviling' and 'cursing' the Court?—not at all, but for 'reviling' and 'cursing' employees of the railroad company. If these men had not actually served out an imprisonment in jail for thirty days as a punishment for contempt of corporation, it might be thought your committee had taken this example from opera bouffe. The legality of this punishment was never passed on by the Supreme Court, for the reason, as your committee understand, that the parties were unable to bear the expense of taking it there, and so served their term in jail.

"During the final drafting of our report a temporary injunction has been granted by a justice of the Supreme Court in New York City. . . . . This injunction forbids the defendants (certain members of the Cigar Makers' Union) even from approaching their former employers for the laudable purpose of reaching an amicable result. It forbids them from making their case known to the public, if the tendency of that is to vex the plaintiffs or make them uneasy. It forbids them from trying, in a perfectly peaceful way, in any place in the city, even in the privacy of a man's own home, to persuade a new employee that justice is on their side and that he ought to sympathize with them sufficiently not to work for unjust employers; and finally it forbids the union from paying money to the strikers to support their families during the strike."

During the last decade attempts have been made by organized labor to secure by legislative action or otherwise the limitation of the use of injunctions to their proper sphere. In other words, the trade unions of the country are endeavoring to protect the right of jury trials in labor disputes, which right is hazarded by the aggressions of the judiciary. The American Federation of Labor has petitioned Congress and the legislatures of the various states for laws restraining the power of the courts in the issue of injunctions, and the railway brotherhoods have also been active in this direction. The Hoar-Grosvenor Bill introduced into the House of Representatives and reported from the Judiciary Committee attempts to define conspiracy and to take away the power of the courts to issue injunctions in the case of a combination or agreement of persons to do anything in furtherance of a labor dispute. The bill provides: "That no agreement, combination or contract by or between two or more persons to do or procure to be done, or not to do or procure not to be done, any act in contemplation or furtherance of any trade dispute between employers and employees in the District of Columbia or in any Territory of the United States, or between employers and employees who may be engaged in trade or commerce between the several States, or between any Territory and another, or between any Territory or Territories and any State or States or the District of Columbia, or with foreign nations, or between the District of Columbia and any State or States or foreign nations shall be deemed criminal, nor shall those engaged therein be indictable or otherwise punishable for the crime of conspiracy, if such act committed by one person would not be punishable as a crime, nor shall such agreement, combination, or contract be considered as in restraint of trade or commerce, nor shall any restraining order or injunction be issued with relation thereto. Nothing in this act shall exempt from punishment, otherwise than as herein excepted any persons guilty of conspiracy, for which punishment is now provided by any Act of Congress, but such Act of Congress shall, as to the agreements, combinations and contracts hereinbefore referred to, be construed as if this act were therein contained."

Members of trade unions and all other citizens should agitate ceaselessly against the abomination of the injunction. Legislators and judges must be constantly and always brought to a realizing sense of the deep iniquity of the denial of the right of trial by jury. It is possible that laws passed by the state or national governments to repel judicial aggression will be set aside by the courts as an infringement or impairment of their supposed rights. The Supreme Court of the state of West Virginia declared unconstitutional the law of that state, passed in 1898, limiting the exercise of the injunction, with the statement that the courts were coördinate with the legislature itself, and that therefore the legislature had no right to restrain the powers of the judiciary, or to prevent the courts from protecting themselves by proceedings in contempt.

It seems to me that the question of the legality of a law restricting the indiscriminate use of injunctions should be inquired into, and if it is seen or contemplated that such a law will not be upheld by the courts, then other methods should be used. The courts themselves should be constantly appealed to for relief from their own oppression. As a matter of history the injunction, which is a procedure in equity, was originally intended to protect citizens from the very sort of wrongs which the injunction as used in labor disputes actually causes. The complexion and convictions of courts change, and perhaps equity will give to the workingman what equity has taken away. Perhaps, through the agitation of the wage earners and through the willingness of men to go to jail in this good cause, the courts themselves will come to an understanding of the manner in which they have departed from their own precedents and invaded the liberties of the people. Personally, I share with the vast majority of trade unionists a respect for the judiciary, which even a decade of wrong-minded, tortuous, and illogical decisions cannot entirely destroy. If, however, there is no remedy from present judges, then we must look to reform from an amendment to the constitution of the United States relegating the judiciary to its proper place, as a law-interpreting and not as a law-making body, or else, by the appointment of judges of character and knowledge, we must gradually change the trend of decisions by altering the calibre of the men appointed. I do not approve of stocking the Supreme Court or of doing anything to impair the independence or lessen the legitimate control of that body, but it does seem to me that the Executive, in appointing judges, should bear in mind that the legislature needs as much protection from the judiciary as the judiciary from the legislature.

As to the attitude of trade unionists, I believe, in the first place, in ceaseless agitation for a redress of this intolerable grievance. Moreover, when an injunction whether temporary or permanent, forbids the doing of a thing which is lawful, I believe that it is the duty of all patriotic and law-abiding citizens to resist, or at least to disregard, the injunction. It is better that half the workingmen of the country remain constantly in jail than that trial by jury and other inalienable and constitutional rights of the citizens of the United States be abridged, impaired, or nullified by injunctions of the courts.

CHAPTER XXXVIII

THE STRIKE VERSUS COMPULSORY ARBITRATION

Recent Strikes of Greater Magnitude. The Interests of the Public. Compulsory Arbitration Proposed as a Remedy. Compulsory *vs.* Voluntary Arbitration. Compulsory Arbitration Means State Control. Corrupt *vs.* Honest Government. Contrast between New Zealand and the United States of America. Compulsory Arbitration in New Zealand. Conciliation Board and Arbitration Court. Methods of Procedure. The Recognition of the Unions. Preferential Treatment of Unionists. Compulsory Arbitration and Rising Wages. Why Compulsory Arbitration can not be Generally Adopted in the United States. Possible Exceptions.

AS long as employers were many and unions of employees few, as long as strikes were carried on in a small way and with purely local effect, the theory prevailed that a strike was a matter of importance to the contestants only. It was believed that employers were right to buy labor as cheaply as possible and employees were right to sell their labor as dearly as possible. The haggling over the price of labor might cause a temporary cessation of work, just as a merchant and his customer might spend time in haggling over the price of a coat or a spade. The best interests of the community, it was assumed, would be subserved by permitting employer and employee to fight the matter out to their own satisfaction.

With the growth of large labor unions, however, and with the increase in the resources of individual employers and groups of employers, the interest of the public in these industrial conflicts became more vital. It was soon felt that in many strikes the public suffered more acutely than either contestant. For instance, during the recent coal strike both operators and miners commanded sufficient resources to enable them to hold out almost indefinitely, while the public would have suffered irreparable injury and untold hardship, had the strike lasted but two or three months longer. A strike of a month's duration upon all the railroads centering in Chicago would not, perhaps, affect the bonds and stocks of the corporations more seriously than a complete failure of the crops, and the workmen themselves could bear the strain quite easily. Long before the month had elapsed, however, the country would be in the throes of a frightful crisis, and steps would probably be taken by the state or national government to put an end to a contest in which the interest of the public was not only as great as, but infinitely greater than, that of either combatant.

The only infallible remedy against strikes and lockouts is sometimes held to be the adoption of compulsory arbitration. By this is meant an obligation imposed upon employers and employees to submit their differences to an official tribunal and abide by its decision. There are, of course, other ways of avoiding strikes, but no other method, it is held, can be considered a specific. Conciliation or an attempt to avoid strikes by conferences between the two parties, with or without the intervention of a third, is frequently successful in obviating misunderstandings and preventing strikes. The same is true of voluntary arbitration, or the submission of the matter in dispute to an impartial tribunal by both parties to the controversy.

Voluntary arbitration is entirely different in its effects from compulsory arbitration. In many cases of actual industrial conflict the weaker party to a controversy is inclined to submit the matter to arbitration, while the stronger party will have nothing to do with it and says "there is nothing to arbitrate." Consequently, voluntary arbitration, while in many cases a vast improvement over striking, and preferable to it, is often neither more nor less than the victory of the stronger over the weaker party to the contest; that is to say, the decision is frequently given to the side that would have won, and in proportion to what it would have won, had the issue not been submitted to arbitration, but been fought to the end through a strike or a lockout. Of course, there are many instances of voluntary arbitration in which a decision has been reached without reference to, and uninfluenced by, either the numerical or the financial strength of the contestants; although, generally speaking, what is called voluntary arbitration is resorted to only when one side is strong enough to compel the other to submit to it, or when public sentiment becomes so thoroughly aroused that arbitration is practically forced upon the belligerents. Compulsory arbitration, on the other hand, introduces a new element—the power of the State. It is binding upon both parties irrespective of their comparative strength, and the decision or award is not in accordance with the strength or weakness of the employees, but with the wishes and purposes of the State, which compels the arbitration. Compulsory arbitration is, therefore, apart from all other questions, largely a matter of the strength, stability, wisdom, impartiality, and honesty of the government; and the experience of honest governments with compulsory arbitration cannot be conclusively cited for countries with corrupt governments or *vice versa*.

In the present chapter it is proposed to describe the workings of the compulsory arbitration laws passed in 1894 in the Australasian Colony of New Zealand and subsequently adopted by New South Wales and Western Australia. The author of the New Zealand law was the Honorable William Pember Reeves, Minister of Labor, and the law has been one of the most widely discussed measures ever passed by any legislature or Parliament.

The agitation in New Zealand for some form of arbitration law dates from 1890. In that year there occurred the Maritime Strike, a labor conflict which spread sympathetically from the shipping world to all forms of industry in Australasia and practically divided the society of the continent into two hostile camps. In order to obviate experiences of this sort in the future, the New Zealand Minister of Labor made a special study of efforts to avoid strikes in England, France, Germany, and the United States, and finally came to the conclusion that neither conciliation nor voluntary arbitration would suffice, but that the only practicable remedy for his country was compulsory arbitration. Attempts to secure the passage of a compulsory arbitration law failed in 1892 and 1893, but were successful in 1894, when a bill providing for compulsory arbitration passed the colonial Parliament.

The law as passed in 1894, and as subsequently amended, applies only to those industries wherein trade unions are established, but permits a trade union to be formed in any industry by the action of any seven workmen. The law does not in any way hinder conciliation or prevent voluntary arbitration, and only after conciliation has been exhausted is resort had to compulsory arbitration. The obligation to arbitrate, however, is final and conclusive whenever the two parties do not come to an agreement voluntarily, and a breach of the award may, in the discretion of the Arbitration Court, be visited by fine or imprisonment.

The method of procedure in New Zealand is as follows: there is in each of the seven districts into which the colony is divided a Board of Conciliation composed of from four to six men chosen by the unions and by the associations of employers, together with a chairman elected by all, who is usually an outsider and casts the deciding vote. There is only one Court of Arbitration for the country, this court consisting of three persons appointed by the governor for three years. Of these three members one is a judge of the Supreme Court, and the others, nominees of the unions and of the employers respectively. In cases of unusual difficulty, or requiring exact and technical knowledge, two experts may be chosen, one from each side. From the Board of Conciliation an appeal always lies to the Court of Arbitration, but the action taken by the Court of Arbitration is final and without appeal. "No award or proceeeding of the court," says the act, "shall be liable to be challenged, appealed against, reviewed, quashed, or called in question by any Court of Judicature on any account whatsoever."

Neither the Board of Conciliation nor the Court of Arbitration may take the initiative in any dispute between employers and employees, but each acts only when called upon by one or the other of the parties. This, however, does not detract from its powers, since any single aggrieved employee may bring the matter in controversy before the Board and ultimately before the Court and secure an award. These awards, moreover, are made binding not only upon the particular employer or association of employers involved, but also upon all employers in the same district or even in the entire colony. The court thus establishes uniform rules for the whole industry for the period of one, two, or three years

The scope of the Court of Arbitration in making such general or common rules is not limited. Since 1894 the act, which was originally intended chiefly to prevent strikes, has been extended continually in its scope and jurisdiction, until it is now used as a means of establishing minimum rates of wages, maximum number of hours, and such general conditions of labor as the relations of union to non-union men, the use of safety appliances, the prohibition or permission of Sunday work, and regulations for the health of workers. The court, according to the act as amended, is allowed to settle all disputes about industrial matters, by which are meant "all matters affecting or relating to work done or to be done by workers, or the privileges, rights and duties of employers or workers in any industry, not involving questions which are or may be the subject of proceedings for an indictable offense." Besides other matters, the court has jurisdiction over wages, allowances or remuneration of workers; piece prices; hours of employment; sex, age, and qualifications of workers; modes, terms and conditions of employment; employment of children or young persons or of any other class of persons; dismissal or refusal to employ particular persons or classes of persons; preference of union over non-union men, together with all established customs or usages in an industry, whether in the whole colony or in a particular district. The commission thus practically has power to decide all questions relating to the wage contract and practically to legislate for existing factories as well as for those to be established during the life of an award.

The law not only prevents strikes or lockouts during the time of the award, but prevents recourse to such measures when made for the purpose of escaping the jurisdiction of the court. No man may discharge his employees on the eve of their appeal to the Board of Conciliation, and a strike may not be called for a similar purpose. There is no compulsion upon any workingman to join a union, but if he does join he may leave it only upon three months' notice. One of the most interesting phases of the awards of the Court is that where the ordinary custom of the trade is not to the contrary, the employer is obliged to grant to the member of a union preference over the non-unionist in the matter of employment, provided he be equally capable.

The effect of the act upon workingmen has been to change their status and practically to compel the incorporation of trade unions. The unions are given corporate rights and responsibilities, including the right to sue and the liability to be sued, the power to buy or lease land and authority to punish defaulting officers or members. A violation may result in the visitation of a fine, which may be collected against the union or against its members individually in the same manner as against associations of employers, or individual members of such associations.

When the system was first introduced in New Zealand it was anticipated that not one case in ten would be taken from the Board of Conciliation to the Court of Arbitration, but this prediction has not been verified. On the contrary, in two-thirds of the cases an appeal has been taken from the Board to the Court. The proceedings of the Court have been conducted, as a rule, in a sensible, rapid and untechnical manner. According to the law, professional attorneys may be excluded at the wish of either party, and useless or frivolous litigation is discouraged and may be summarily dismissed and visited with costs. Most of the costs of the Court are defrayed by the State, the theory being that it is better to encourage useless litigation than to prevent the poorer members of society from securing justice.

While the cases arising under this law were at first few, they have rapidly increased within the last four or five years. There have been, on the whole, some few hundred cases before the Court, most of which have been decided in favor of the workingmen. It must, of course, be remembered that during practically the whole of this period New Zealand has been progressing industrially and has been enjoying good times, and the success of the workingmen before the Court is to be largely attributed to this fact. A severer test of the act will be made during periods of depression, when a larger percentage of the awards of the Court may be adverse to the unions.

The Compulsory Arbitration Law of New Zealand has become increasingly popular with workingmen. At first wage earners were somewhat lukewarm in their attitude toward it, but with each year it has gained ever greater favor with them. The employing class seems to be somewhat divided. A number of them take a stand similar to that taken by employers in this country toward the trade agreement. There are many New Zealand employers who resent any retrenchment or limitation of their right to manage their own business as they see fit or to deal with their own employees as they desire. As, however, the award in any particular case is made binding upon the whole district and in some cases even upon the whole colony, the employer enjoys the same benefit as under the trade agreement, namely, that of a certainty that no other employer will undercut him or secure an advantage over him in the matter of wages. He has still another advantage similar to that given by the trade agreement, namely the certainty of no strike during the period of the award. The result has been that employers have become more and more friendly to the act, and at the present time, there appears to be no considerable class or section of the New Zealand population which is adverse or hostile. In fact, the adoption of similar acts by the Parliaments of New South Wales and Western Australia have strengthened the hold of compulsory arbitration upon the New Zealanders. In New Zealand and during the period of prosperity in which it has been in operation, the Compulsory Arbitration Law seems to have been successful. Enemies of the bill predicted the direst evil as a result of its enactment. Capital, they said, would leave the country, employment become scarce, and wages fall as soon as the law became operative, but its effect has been the direct contrary. The number of men employed in New Zealand industries has increased, wages have risen, business has progressed and become more prosperous than ever, and employers have been reassured by the stability of wages and the practically total absence of strikes and lockouts. The act has had a steadying effect upon associations both of employers and employees and has promoted a peaceable solution of many difficulties outside the court room. The classes beyond the jurisdiction of the act have clamored for the intervention of the court, and both sides appear to have been, on the whole, well pleased with the honesty and efficiency of the judges and the expeditious and untechnical methods of procedure adopted. The objection usually urged that you cannot by force of law make a man pay more wages than he is willing to pay is not valid, since the Compulsory Arbitration Law of New Zealand does not compel a man to continue in business, but merely prohibits his paying anything less than a stipulated wage if he does so continue. Equally inapplicable is the argument that you cannot by law compel a man to work against his will. The New Zealand law does not compel a man to work any more than it does an employer to continue in business, but merely states that if the man does work, or if the employer does contract for work, it shall be at certain rates and under certain conditions.

It cannot, however, be predicted that what has apparently succeeded so well in New Zealand would, if adopted, be equally successful in the United States. It must be remembered that New Zealand is a new country with a small and practically homogeneous population and without the sharp contrasts between wealth and poverty which exist in the United States. The entire population of the colony is below 800,000, less than one-fourth of the population of the city of New York, and most of its inhabitants are engaged in agricultural and pastoral pursuits. Thus, in 1896, there were only 27,389 persons in New Zealand employed in factories, workshops, meat-preserving, and other similar establishments, whereas in the United States, there are over seven millions of persons engaged in manufacturing and mechanical pursuits.

There are still other reasons which render the example of compulsory arbitration in New Zealand, inapplicable to American institutions. In the first place, there is the separate, independent, partially sovereign government of each of our forty-five states, with inter-state competition in all forms of industry. A decision favorable to labor and to the conscientious manufacturers in one state could be immediately nullified by adverse action or simply lack of any action whatsoever in another state.

An Interior View of a Manchester Cotton Mill.

Blast Furnaces of a Great Steel Mill

The tendency of backward states is to oppose remedial industrial legislation, while in the more progressive states such legislation does not meet with the same opposition, and the present lack of uniformity in the factory and mining laws of the various states would be felt a thousandfold more acutely in the event of the adoption of compulsory arbitration. Again, the intricate and complex character of American industry, the necessity of recognizing and maintaining differentials because of the location of the various industries, and above all the diverse and heterogeneous nature of the people composing the American republic would render compulsory arbitration, if adopted by the various states, inadvisable if not absolutely repugnant to the great mass of both the employing and working classes.

There is, moreover, a deep-seated distrust among workingmen as to the fairness and impartiality of the judiciary, and even apart from this difficulty, it would be impossible in our American states to create a court of arbitration the findings of which would not be subject to review by the superior courts. Any other proceeding would probably come under the head of acts depriving citizens of property without due process of law, and would therefore be in conflict with the state and federal constitutions.

While for the states of the American republic a general compulsory arbitration law is not practicable, there are particular instances in which compulsion might possibly prove beneficial. It would be perfectly feasible, as is done in some European cities, to compel street railway companies or other companies obtaining valuable state or municipal franchises to submit all differences with their employees to arbitration, and the failure or refusal so to arbitrate could be considered, like the failure to keep the property in running order, as a violation of the franchise and a waiver of all rights. There are certain industries, such as railroad and street railway transportation, where the power of the state might occasionally be exercised in order to secure the country from incalculable damage. In the case of railroads engaged in inter-state traffic, possibly in certain circumstances, it might become necessary for the federal government, under its right to regulate commerce between states, to compel such railroads to arbitrate differences with their workmen. Many of the arguments against compulsory arbitration laws enacted by the states would not apply to a specific law of this sort with a limited scope, if passed by the federal government for certain definite, prescribed cases, but even such arbitration should be resorted to only as an extreme measure. It is probable that no action of this or a similar sort will be taken unless a crisis should arise, such as that which occurred in the coal strike in the fall of 1902. Until such a crisis comes, however, it will be better and more in accord with the spirit of American institutions to seek industrial peace wherever possible in trade agreements and not in compulsory arbitration.

CHAPTER XXXIX

THE STRIKE VERSUS THE TRADE AGREEMENT.

The Trade Agreement and Industrial Peace. The Agreement and Union Recognition. Difficulty of Reaching Agreements. The True Coöperation between Labor and Capital. The Essence of Trade Unionism. The Agreement in its Simplest Form. Local and National Agreements. How Agreements are Reached. The Treaty-Making Power of the Union. Sentiment and Business. The Agreement and the Future Relations of Labor and Capital.

THE hope of future peace in the industrial world lies in the trade agreement. There is nothing so promising to the establishment of friendly relations between labor and capital as the growing tendency of representatives of both sides to meet in friendly conference in order to settle conditions of employment. These conferences are as impressive as important. The men assembled in national joint convention represent two great estates, the employers and the workmen of a vast industry. It is like a congress legislating for a nation, or, rather, like a coming together of the representatives of two great nations, upon the basis of mutual respect and mutual toleration, for the formulation of a treaty of peace for the government of industry and the prosperity and welfare of the contracting parties.

The trade agreement is the clearest and most unmistakable recognition of the importance of labor to capital and of capital to labor. The coöperation between these two factors of production, a coöperation more spoken of than believed in, receives in these formal treaties of peace and amity definite expression and complete confirmation. The bituminous coal operators, representing an approximate yearly output of 200,000,000 tons, and the bituminous mineworkers, numbering about 250,000, recognize in their annual conferences their dependence upon each other for the furtherance of their respective needs and for the promotion of their joint interests. The trade agreement represents the highest form of coöperation in modern industry.

The formulation of a trade agreement which will be satisfactory to both sides and will meet with the approval of all parties, is by no means easy. Those who deny to workingmen capacity for self-government should study the making of agreements as worked out in Great Britain and the United States. These agreements and the conferences which precede them require a high degree of intelligence and wise moderation upon the part of the workmen and diplomacy and skill on the part of the leaders. Before such an agreement is possible, a basis of reasonable demands must be evolved. One section of workmen may have to make concessions in favor of another, and frequently the whole body must postpone the presentation of justifiable demands until a more opportune moment. It is necessary, moreover, for both the leaders and the rank and file to appreciate the attitude and position of the employers. An agreement, to be made and lived up to, must be reasonable and fair to both sides; and it is unwise, even if it were possible, to insist upon terms that are ruinous or seriously detrimental to employers. The formulation of such an agreement, moreover, requires great patience and forbearance and necessitates an unusual degree of technical knowledge. The problems taken up and discussed are complex and difficult. The workmen or their representatives must be informed concerning wages in their own as well as in other industries; the cost of living; the cost of production to the employers; the charges for transportation; the state of the market; the price, cost, and quality of competing products; the character of machinery and processes used, as well as many other factors entering into the question of the ability of employers to pay higher wages. The workingmen must recognize the difference between what is desirable and what is attainable, and must exercise an unusual degree of self-restraint.

The trade agreement secures to the workingman what various beneficent and coöperative schemes in the past have failed to secure—a real coöperation between employer and employee and a measure of control by workingmen over the conditions of industry. Coöperative schemes, suggested by the philanthropy or justice of employers, are, in a sense, an acknowledgment of the claim that workingmen should have a say in the conduct of business. These schemes, however, are not as a rule successful, and where the employer has, as he should have, the complete control of buying, selling, advertising, accepting credits, making contracts, etc., the effect of extra exertion by the workingman often has but an inappreciable influence upon his share of the profits of the enterprise. The sliding scale is a more important form of coöperation and is of advantage where a high, definite, minimum wage is made the basis. These coöperative plans, however, prove as a rule but a slight stimulus to the workman and rarely give him any real interest in, or any real control over, the business. The employees of the United States Steel Corporation could not, at the present rate of subscription, secure control of the stock within a century, even if the stock were not increased during that time. The plan of securing even a partial control of industry by workingmen through the purchase or allotment of stock is as chimerical as a scheme suggested to me by a friendly correspondent, during the recent strike, viz., that I use the strike fund to purchase the various railroad and mining properties under the control of the antagonistic corporations, and thus bring the strike to a close.

The gift of money, the payment of premiums, and the grant of small favors and privileges do not constitute in any true sense a coöperation between employer and employee. While individual employers have made splendid benefactions, the influence of these gifts is small, except in a few instances. The creation of model towns, the establishment of libraries, gymnasiums, natatoriums, and assembly rooms for workmen are entirely commendable and highly praiseworthy, if they do not involve such a dependence of the workingman upon his employers as will render it impossible for him to voice his grievances or present reasonable demands. It is well that the workman be provided with free napkins, towels, ice water, and other conveniences and comforts; but the maintenance of factories as clean and as pleasant as possible should not be a matter of the individual bounty of employers. After all, the American workingman does not want to be favored or coddled. The total amount of benefactions of this sort is probably much less than one-tenth or one-twentieth part of one per cent. of the annual wages of the American workingmen. Whatever their amount, however, these benefactions, whether they be good or evil in their purpose and in their result, do not create or constitute that real coöperation which can be obtained only through the trade agreement.

The trade agreement represents the very essence of trade unionism. In its simplest form the agreement is nothing but a determination of wages, hours of labor, and conditions of work by men in a single establishment or a single local community. From the very beginning of labor organization, agreements of this nature have been made by men working in the same establishment or the same town, and these agreements, whether verbal or written, have been binding upon all the men so engaged. These agreements have sometimes been nothing more than the simple formulation of shop rules, the determination of the length of the working-day, and similar matters, which have thus been taken out of the realm of individual bargaining between the employer and each separate employee, and have been incorporated into a contract binding upon all.

Trade agreements, therefore, even in their simplest form, represent the central idea for which trade unionism stands, viz., the collective or joint bargain, and they presuppose the existence of a union and, in the case of agreements upon a large scale, associations of employers as well as of workmen. The difficulty in the way of forming trade agreements in the past has been this lack of organization upon the part of employers, and it has been largely due to the stimulus of trade unionism that employers have organized upon a national basis and have entered into yearly contracts with their workmen. These agreements were made in England at an earlier date than in the United States, because of the earlier development of national organizations in that country. They have, however, become increasingly popular in the United States, and in about a dozen important trades they now regulate the conditions of industry.

The machinery of the trade agreement has been evolved in each trade in answer to the necessities of that trade, and the systems in vogue differ, therefore, in various particulars. In the main, however, the same principles are observed. As far as possible, the machinery has been simplified and has been rendered effective and easy to control. There is, as a rule, a joint convention consisting of employers on the one side and representatives of the union upon the other, and no provision is made for the presence of paid attorneys or of experts. The number of representatives differs in the various conventions. It is usually provided that the vote must be unanimous, and there is, therefore, no possibility of the formation of a contract without its being clearly satisfactory to all interests represented.

Joint agreements are, in fact, treaties of peace determining the conditions under which the industry will be carried on for a year, although longer agreements have been made and maintained. The agreement usually provides for the settlement or arbitration of all controversies which may arise under it. It is provided, however, that the arbitration shall be in the nature, not of negotiation, not of a change in the conditions fixed by the agreement, but shall be limited entirely to the interpretation of the agreement. In the contracts existing in the bituminous coal mining industry, it is provided that in the case of a dispute arising between any operator and miner over a point covered by the inter-state agreement that cannot be settled between the parties directly at interest, appeals may be taken from one tribunal to another until the court of last resort is reached. During the course of the dispute, however, the men remain at work, and as a result of the trade agreement and of the provisions therein contained for the adjustment of all questions in controversy, the number of petty local strikes has been minimized and conflicts of this nature have almost entirely disappeared.[1]

---

[1] The following is quoted from the agreement between the coal miners and operators of Illinois:

"(13 b) In case of any local trouble arising at any shaft through such failure to agree between the pit-boss and any miner or mine laborer, the pit committee and the miners' local president and the pit boss are empowered to adjust it; and, in the case of

Trade agreements almost identical in character and formulated in practically the same manner, exist in numerous other industries. Such agreements made by labor organizations have been rigidly and strictly maintained, even at the sacrifice of temporary advantages. Employers as well as workmen have shown a well-defined tendency to live up to the spirit of the agreement and not to bind themselves solely by its letter.

The advantage of the trade agreement, apart from its democratic character and its recognition of the rights and obligations of both sides, is the knowledge which it gives to employer and workman of the conditions under which labor is performed and the manner in which the industry is conducted. Before the era of trade agreements, the workmen were wont to exaggerate the profits of the employers and to believe, frequently without cause, that they were being exploited. The employers, on the other hand, often failed to realize the effect upon the wages of the workmen of rising prices and increased cost of living and were liable to obtain from their foremen or others a false idea of the conditions under which their employees lived. There was often a feeling of superiority over the workmen and their representatives, which, as a result of the trade agreements, is now being obliterated. Both sides enter the convention with the hope of securing a rea-

---

their disagreement it shall be referred to the Superintendent of the Company and the President of the miners' local executive board, where such exists, and shall they fail to adjust it—and in all other cases—it shall be referred to the Superintendent of the Company and the miners' president of the sub-district; and, should they fail to adjust it, it shall be referred in writing to the officials of the company concerned and the State officials of the U. M. W. of A., for adjustment; and, in all such cases, the miners and mine laborers and parties involved must continue at work pending an investigation and adjustment, until a final decision is reached in the manner above set forth.

"(13 c) If any day men refuse to continue at work because of a grievance which has, or has not been taken up for adjustment in the manner provided herein, and such action shall seem likely to impede the operation of the mine, the pit committee shall immediately furnish a man or men to take such vacant place or places, at the scale rate, in order that the mine may continue at work; and it shall be the duty of any member, or members, of the United Mine Workers, who may be called upon by the pit boss, or pit committee, to immediately take the place or places assigned to him or them in pursuance hereof.

MAKING TIN CANS BY MACHINERY
Where thousands of tin cans are turned out daily for salmon canneries, etc.

INTERIOR VIEW OF A LARGE WIRE MILL

sonable settlement, and any proposition made by either side is given a respectful hearing.

Trade agreements are a matter of business. The representatives of the employers do not desire to pay higher wages than are necessary, and the workmen do not wish to take smaller wages than they must. To this very fact, that the two parties meet upon the plane of business, it is due that the best results are obtained. The attitude of mind which dictates the making of the ordinary business contracts prevails in the formulation of trade agreements. Instead of a loose, verbal arrangement, the trade agreement is usually a written document, stating in precise terms its various provisions, so that there is little possibility of error Moreover, for such difficulties as arise in interpretation, a system of arbitration is usually provided. Trade agreements thus obviate hundreds of little misunderstandings which might otherwise lead to recrimination and to strikes and lockouts. In the course of a few years of experience, therefore, the trade agreements become fixed upon a settled basis, and their general provisions become universally known.

The difficulties, dangers, and misunderstandings which trade agreements obviate may be seen from a study of the joint conventions in which these agreements are formulated. It usually happens that during the first few days, the radical speakers on both sides make extravagant claims or give utterance to more or less violent speeches, so that the two interests appear absolutely irreconcilable. As the convention progresses, however, the conservative men on both sides gradually approach a common understanding, and by the time the matter is referred to the scale committee, the differences of opinion have been minimized, and a general agreement is almost invariably reached. In the United Mine Workers' conventions, the agreement recommended by the scale committee, which is a small committee representing the miners and operators of the various states and appointed by the two sides, is referred to the general convention, the miners and operators voting by states. In the past the reports of the scale committee have been unanimously adopted in every instance. It does not, of course, follow, nor is it true, that every man or even the men of every district believe that the provisions are what they should be; but in view of all the circumstances, each man and each district is willing to make certain concessions, and a satisfactory arrangement based upon mutual compromises is made and adhered to.

It must not be supposed that the trade agreement will prevent all strikes. It will undoubtedly minimize these industrial conflicts, by obviating misunderstandings, by showing each side the position of the other, by creating a more friendly feeling between employers and employees, and finally by making strikes and lockouts, when they do occur, so wide-spread, general, and expensive, that their recurrence will be avoided. The fact that failure to reach an agreement would result either in a great strike or a general lockout, impels each side to respect the reasonable demands of the other. If it were not for that possibility, the more radical and uncompromising elements could not be induced to forego their claims. With each new agreement, however, both sides become more conservative and more willing to sacrifice a part of their demands, and with each passing year, the industries in which trade agreements prevail become established on a firmer and more permanent foundation of peace.

CHAPTER XL

THE COAL STRIKE OF 1902.—THE ADVENT OF THE GREAT RAILROAD CORPORATIONS.

The Strike of 1902 a Landmark in the History of Labor. Importance of Conflict—Enormous Interests Involved. The Strike an Incident in a Struggle of Two Generations. History of Labor in the Anthracite Regions. Early Equality. Deep Mining and Monopoly. Coal and the Civil War. "The Good Old Times" of Oppression. The Extinction of the Old Union. The Advent of the Great Railroad Corporations. The Influx of New Races. A Surplus of Labor. Work and Pay Insecure. The Elastic Ton The Car of Live Oak. Exactions and Deductions. The Docking Grievance. One Dollar Powder at $2.75. Company Stores. Exorbitant Prices. Company Houses. The Markle Evictions. Competition at the Expense of the Miner.

THE struggle of labor to secure control of itself and to better its conditions is a slow, incessant, upward movement. The contest is fought out, not by a few brilliant strikes or by the sudden emergence of a few great leaders, but by slow upbuilding forces acting upon vast bodies of men and giving to them increased confidence and an increased sense of solidarity and brotherliness. However, at infrequent intervals events occur of startling or dramatic nature, which, fastening upon the working classes the attention of the whole community, aid and contribute to the furtherance of the labor movement.

An event of this nature was the Anthracite Coal Strike of 1902. This strike in point of the number of men engaged, the length of the contest, the determination with which it was fought out, and the losses which it entailed upon both parties, and, unfortunately, upon the general public, stands out prominently in the history of labor conflicts. At a signal almost one hundred and fifty thousand men and boys dropped their tools, and during a period of over five months, despite the pangs of hunger, despite temptations to desert the cause, none but an inconsiderable minority returned to work.

The contest was memorable also for the enormous strength of the associated corporations opposing the mineworkers. The railroad and mining companies and their financial backers represented a capital of hundreds of millions, if not of billions of dollars. The financial losses resulting from this strike were such as to make it an object lesson in the costliness of labor conflicts. It was estimated by the Anthracite Coal Strike Commission that the loss to railroads and coal companies in reduced freight and coal receipts was not less than $74,000,000, and the loss in wages to the mine workers not less than $25,000,000, the total loss being placed by the Commission at the enormous sum of $99,000,000. The coal strike of 1902 was finally memorable for the great hardships which it entailed upon the public and for the resolute intervention of the President of the United States, with the settlement of the strike as a direct consequence.

The strike was, however, rightly considered, not an event in itself, but merely an incident in a great drama which has been going on for over fifty years. During the last two generations a slow, stubborn contest has been waged by labor in the anthracite coal fields against the ever-growing power of monopoly and the strike of 1902 was but the culmination of a development lasting through three-fourths of a century.

Although anthracite coal began to be shipped to the seaboard during the War of 1812, its production was, until 1850, extremely slight. At that time the business of mining hard coal was unimportant, and the number of miners, only about six or eight thousand. The veins were largely outcropping or were easy to reach, the amount of necessary capital was small, and wages were low and employment irregular. There was no monopoly of the mines, no connection between transportation and mining companies, and no labor problem in the modern sense of the word.

During the period from 1850 to 1860, however, despite setbacks and hard times, the coal mining industry grew rapidly, and after the breaking out of the Civil War, the industry became extremely profitable. During the years from 1861 to 1865 the coal miners for the first and only time in their history received large earnings, and although prices had risen at the same time, they were still able to secure more for their wages than they have subsequently been able to obtain. After the war, however, although the operators themselves had made large profits, an attempt was made to depress wages and to break up the miners' union. For eight years, from 1867 to 1875, an active and aggressive war was carried on by the operators against the union, the Workingmen's Benevolent Association, and by the close of the latter year, the organization had ceased to exist.

It was especially during the quarter of a century that elapsed between 1875 and 1900 that the abuses leading to the strikes of 1900 and 1902 were inaugurated or intensified. During this period of practically unorganized labor, the conditions of the miners grew worse and worse. The object of the operators seems to have been to keep the miners in subjection by defeating all efforts to form trade unions, and in this endeavor they practically succeeded. The miners became organized from time to time in various parts of the field, but the old expedient was resorted to of playing off one section against another, so that divided, all of the sections fell. During this period the operators also introduced large numbers of laborers from Austria, Hungary, Poland, Russia, and Italy with the idea of lowering wages through competition and of defeating attempts at organization by keeping on hand an oversupply of unorganized men. It is interesting to note in this connection that poetic justice has been meted out to those who initiated this plan. The surplus of labor has been a curse not only to the men themselves, but to the operators, and the non-English speaking men introduced to break the unions have in the course of time become the staunchest and most loyal adherents of labor organization.

In their unorganized, or only partially organized state, the miners suffered in many ways. The constant accession of new bodies of men willing to work hard and long for small pay depressed wages to a minimum. The old English, Scotch, Irish, German, and Welsh miners were obliged to accept the wages for which newly arrived Poles, Hungarians, and Italians, under the stress of a merciless competition, were compelled to work. Much of even these low wages, moreover, was never paid in cash to the mine-workers. There were in vogue many systems for cheating the men. While some companies were reasonably and some scrupulously conscientious about such matters, others incessantly abused the ignorance and impotence of their employees. The early union, the Workingmen's Benevolent Association, had secured a law compelling the weighing of coal and the adoption of a standard ton, that every man might know what he mined and be paid accordingly. Upon the dissolution of the union, however, the operators compelled the disorganized miners to surrender their rights under this law. The size of the ton increased, so that 2,800 and even 3,190 pounds came to be considered a ton, while the price remained at the same level. The operators who paid their royalties by the ton of 2,240 pounds and who sold their coal to the railroads or to the consumers by the ton of 2,240 or less, exacted from the miner as high as 3,190 pounds to the ton. Where the coal was paid by the car, the same system was adopted, and the car grew, as the men said, as though it were made of live oak. Thus, the encroachments upon the wages of the miners were insidious. If a man were being paid a dollar for filling a certain car with coal, he was paid no more when three or four inches were added to the size of the car, nor was he paid more when he was obliged to add nine or ten inches of "topping" above the railing of the car. In fact he was more likely to be paid less. The companies adopted a system of docking, which in many cases was arbitrary, unjust, and tyrannous. The miner had no opportunity to test whether or not he had been docked fairly for impurities or underweight, but a round sum was taken from him at the sole discretion of the docking boss. This device led on the part of some companies to a system of unblushing theft and reacted by making many of the miners careless. According to the testimony adduced by the operators themselves before the Anthracite Coal Strike Commission, the amount docked even by fair companies diminished 50% as soon as the miners were allowed to employ check docking bosses.

In still other ways were the miners subject to deductions and exactions. As the result of an antiquated agreement, the miners were obliged to buy their powder from the companies and to pay $2.75 for a keg which was not worth over $1.10. Since it is impossible to blast coal without powder, the powder grievance became an increasingly serious one as the veins of coal grew thinner and harder to mine.

Not only was the miner mulcted as a producer, but he was controlled and in many cases directly, clearly, and unscrupulously cheated and defrauded as a consumer. The legislature of the state of Pennsylvania had passed anti-truck store laws, but the operators, who have always cried loudest against illegal action by miners, openly and unhesitatingly violated the act and subsequently evaded it by various devices. In many collieries the mine worker was not paid in the legal coin of the realm, in good, hard, money, but was given an order on the store, where he was obliged to buy inferior goods at exorbitant prices. At first, no doubt, the company stores were instituted for the real advantage of the workingmen, since in those days there were practically no stores in the mining towns, and during the earlier period it seems that many of the company stores, as well as many of the company houses, were run with reasonable regard to the interests of the employees. The stores, however, as well as the other institutions, were at best harmful in their tendency, since they were calculated to increase the dependence of the workingman upon his employer; and in many cases they had, intentionally or unintentionally, the effect of defrauding the mine workers. Often a man together with his children would work for months without receiving a dollar of money, and not infrequently he would find at the end of the month nothing in his envelope but a statement that his indebtedness to the company had increased by so many dollars. Many companies earned as much through their company stores as through mining coal, or, as the mineworkers themselves expressed it, many of the companies earned the money not only by mining coal but by mining miners. The company houses also served in some cases as a means of extortion, in other instances, as a weapon to be used against the miners, the cruel and merciless eviction of the Markle tenants showing what could be done in this way against unorganized workingmen.

During this whole period of unorganized labor, during these halcyon days, upon which the operators have never ceased to look back with regret, the conditions of the workingmen were extremely bad and wages were low and fluctuated violently. The miners averaged only one hundred and ninety ten-hour days per year, and the mine workers were, of course, paid only for the time which they were allowed or permitted to work. In very good times the men were able to work a fairly large number of days, but in times of depression conditions grew rapidly worse. Whatever advantages resulted from the reckless and unrestricted competition of the time accrued to the coal companies or the railroads, and whatever disadvantages or hardships ensued fell to the lot of the workmen. The coal operator played with the mine worker a game of chance, in which it was "Heads, I win; tails, you lose."

Even when the mines changed from ownership by the coal companies to ownership by the railroads, the condition of the miners did not appreciably improve. In the early 70's the anthracite railroads, with the Reading at their head, began to invade the field and to buy up coal properties on all sides, and this process has been continued for thirty years. The mine workers, however, disorganized as they were, did not secure any advantage from the economies which it was claimed were effected by the railroad companies' owning the mines. No increase in wages could be paid as long as the railroads felt themselves obliged to pay dividends on an enormous and excessive capitalization. The former owners had not only extorted money from the mine workers, but had capitalized their future chances of extortion in the price which they asked for their property. In the purchase of these lands, the railroads, in an era of unbounded optimism, launched into the wildest extravagances, and some of these companies have since been chronically in the hands of receivers in an attempt to sweat out of their system the excess water. The cry for dividends raised by stockholders, loaded down with securities bought at a ruinous price, had the effect of further stimulating the directors to look for more earnings out of the wages of the workingmen. Some of these coal companies, moreover were and still are "mine poor," possessing properties which will be of enormous value in the future, but which are necessarily idle now, and the burden which should be borne by future generations was shifted to the shoulders of the mine workers.

In one respect the advent of the great railroad corporations has been of advantage to the mine workers. By means of these large organizations, controlling vast sums of money, the industry of mining coal has been systematized and some check placed upon the indiscriminate and cut-throat competition prevailing in former times. The railroad companies have, perhaps, been foremost in introducing reforms on the technical side of mining, in improving ventilation and the general conditions of work. It is only fair to state that the worst abuses of company stores, company houses, company doctors and various other means and forms of extortion, were practiced to a less extent by the railroads than by some of the independent operators, although it is claimed by these latter that they were forced to such courses by the extortionate freight rates on coal to the seaboard. Upon the whole, however, the railroads failed to improve or ameliorate the conditions of the men under their control. Wages were not increased, hours not reduced, grievances not removed, and the unions of the workmen not recognized by or through any voluntary action of the railroad corporations. Whatever small advantage the mine workers secured from the advent of the railroad companies was purely incidental to the improved methods of mining which had come into vogue. In their hostility to trade unions, moreover, and in their refusal to grant any reform or redress until extorted from them, the railroad corporations failed signally in their obligations toward the great body of workingmen, upon whose labor their profits and their general welfare ultimately depends.

CHAPTER XLI

THE COAL STRIKE OF 1902.—THE ADVENT OF THE UNITED MINEWORKERS OF AMERICA

Organization Necessary in the Anthracite Region. Difficulty of the Problem. The United Mine Workers of America. Its Predecessors, 1861-1890. Its History, 1890 1900. The Strike of 1897. Rapid Growth. The Mineworkers not exclusively a Bituminous Organization. Necessity of a National Organization. Successful Strikes. Inter-State Agreements in the West. Confidence in the Organization. The Work of the Organizers. Appeals from the Anthracite Region. Demands of the Men. The Strike of 1900. The Surrender of the Operators. After the Strike.

AS late as 1899 the idea of organizing the anthracite miners of Pennsylvania was scouted by all but a few of the leaders of the United Mine Workers. The difficulties in the way of such organization appeared insurmountable. The differences in race, religion, and ideals of the twenty nationalities in the region, the variations in the standard of living, the mutual distrust among the races, and the former failures of attempts to form permanent unions, all conspired to make the men distrustful of the new movement. Among the three districts of the anthracite region, the Lackawanna, Lehigh, and Schuylkill, keen jealousy existed, and conditions varied to such an extent as to render it difficult to formulate the grievances in a series of general demands. The market was glutted with coal, and the region was glutted with men. The operators were united in a bitter and uncompromising hostility towards any form of organization among the miners, and the pioneers in the movement were threatened with the possibility of a blacklist. Many miners grown old in the anthracite fields shook their heads and gloomily predicted that organization would never secure a foothold in the anthracite region. Within a year all this had changed, and the anthracite miners had won the greatest victory ever secured in the seventy-five years of mining in that region.

The experience of the fifty preceding years seemed to justify the pessimism of the workers who had spent their entire lives and whose fathers before them had toiled from boyhood in the anthracite mines. To form unions of mine workers in the past, many efforts had been made; but either through internal jealousies or by the hostility of the operators, each attempt was doomed to failure. As early as 1849 a union of mine workers was organized in the anthracite region by an Englishman named John Bates, but this as well as several other organizations of a local character speedily collapsed. In 1861 an organization called the American Miners' Association was established in Illinois and gradually extended to the eastern states, but following the unsuccessful strikes of 1867 or 1868, the association collapsed. In 1869 a union, known as the Miners' and Laborers' Benevolent Association, was formed in the anthracite region under the leadership of John Siney. This organization grew rapidly, and notwithstanding the intense antagonism of the operators, maintained its existence until the year 1875, when a general strike was inaugurated, which practically closed every mine in the region; but, owing to the opposition of the mine owners and to internal dissensions and racial and religious prejudices, the strike failed, and the organization was destroyed.

During the period in which the Miners' and Laborers' Benevolent Association was attempting to ameliorate conditions in the anthracite region, the Miners' National Association flourished in the bituminous fields. In the year 1874 its membership exceeded 20,000, but this union, like the others which had preceded it, disintegrated and shortly disappeared. Following the dissolution of these organizations, came the Knights of Labor, which spread rapidly through both the bituminous and anthracite regions, and for a time exerted considerable influence in improving the conditions of life and labor of the workmen employed in the coal industry. The same forces, however, which had destroyed other organizations were put into operation against the Knights of Labor, and its membership declined as quickly as it had grown. By 1885 its power for good in the mining fields had passed, and in that year the Miners' National Progressive Union was formed. This organization was more successful in the bituminous fields than any of its predecessors. Through it, joint conferences and trade agreements with the operators were established in West Virginia, western Pennsylvania, Ohio, Indiana, and Illinois; but owing to constant friction with what remained of the Knights of Labor, its efforts were hampered and its influence neutralized. By 1890 its membership had dwindled away, and it became patent that the thorough and successful organization of the mineworkers depended upon the consolidation of the Progressive Union and Assembly No. 135 of the Knights of Labor, which claimed jurisdiction over the men employed in the coal mines. Accordingly, in 1890, the Miners' National Progressive Union and District Assembly No. 135, Knights of Labor, amalgamated, forming the United Mine Workers of America.

For several years thereafter this union gradually extended its influence and organized a considerable number of both anthracite and bituminous men. In 1894 a general strike was inaugurated in the bituminous fields, which resulted in only partial success, and at its close membership rapidly declined in both the anthracite and bituminous regions. The spring of 1897 found the total number of members of the United Mine Workers of America reduced to less than 9,000, there being practically nothing left of the organization in the anthracite field, and the bituminous men again sought relief from their hard and grinding conditions in a general strike. After a stubbornly fought contest a compromise settlement was made which, while giving the miners only a slight advance, lent an impetus to the organization, and from that time on membership speedily increased in all the bituminous coal-producing states. In the following year joint conferences and trade agreements between operators and miners were reëstablished and comparative peace and prosperity assured.

But during all this time the conditions of the anthracite men were growing steadily worse. Every effort to organize them or to ameliorate their condition having met with failure, it seemed that the anthracite workers had abandoned hope. Organizers were assigned to that district, but wherever they went they were told that there was no use wasting either time or money, as membership in the union would be followed by dismissal and the blacklist and that, therefore, the anthracite men could not be organized. Thousands of them declared that while they would not join the union and jeopardize their chances of retaining their work, they would participate in a strike if they were given assurance that such a movement could be made general.

Early in 1900 an increased force of organizers was stationed in that region, and while they were unable to form any considerable number of local unions, they were successful in reviving hope, allaying fear, and preparing the mineworkers for the struggle that seemed inevitable. In the month of July the time seemed propitious for a decisive movement. Mutterings of discontent were heard on every hand, especially among the mineworkers of the Lackawanna and Lehigh districts, and the sentiment in favor of a strike became quite general. In view of these circumstances a convention was called to meet about the middle of July in the city of Hazleton, for the purpose of deciding upon a definite policy for the future guidance of the anthracite mineworkers. Many delegates in this convention favored an immediate strike, but better counsel prevailed, and drastic measures were not then resorted to. On the contrary, the officers of the union were directed to invite the operators to meet representatives of the mineworkers in joint conference in the month of August, in order that a scale of wages might be formulated which would be satisfactory to all parties in interest. The operators, ignoring this invitation, failed to attend the August convention; whereupon the representatives of the mineworkers drafted a series of demands covering wages and conditions of employment, and decided to strike for their enforcement unless they were acceded to within ten days. The mine owners still continued to ignore the representatives of their employees and refused to make any concessions. Consequently, a strike was declared, to take place on September 17th.

Although the membership of the union at this time was less than 8,000, the organization represented so clearly and so unmistakably the attitude of the overwhelming majority of the mineworkers that from 80,000 to 100,000 men and boys quit work on the first day of the strike, and with each succeeding day the number increased until, at the close of two weeks, fully 90% of the 144,000 employees were idle. The strike, which lasted through the month of September and the greater part of October, aroused intense public interest. The sympathy of the press and the people became enlisted on the side of the mineworkers as soon as it was realized under what terrible conditions they were compelled to toil.

The operators, as in 1902, repelled all overtures for a settlement of the strike and protested that the vast majority of the strikers were prevented from remaining at, or returning to, work by the turbulence and violence of a small minority. They tried in vain to explain why they should charge miners $2.75 for a keg of powder which they (the companies) purchased for 90 cents. They endeavored to convince the public that "pluck-me" stores, company doctors, and exorbitant house rents were necessary adjuncts to the successful operation of coal mines; that they were really a benefit to the mineworkers and were conducted in their interest. But the public was not deceived, and sympathy for the strikers and indignation against the companies were expressed on every hand. As the strike progressed, as the supply of coal diminished, as winter approached and the demand for fuel increased, press and public became provoked at the unreasonable and unyielding attitude of the operators. A circumstance which proved of incalculable assistance to the mineworkers was the fact that a Presidential election was to take place on November 5th. Senator Hanna, Chairman of the National Republican Committee, had endeavored to avert the strike; during its progress he had made repeated efforts to bring about an amicable settlement, and on the 3rd of October the operators offered an increase of 10% in the wages paid prior to the strike. The operators did not make this proposition directly to the mineworkers, but notice of it was posted in conspicuous places about the mines. The proposal of the operators was unacceptable for the reason that no promise or guarantee was given that the increased wages would be paid for any definite period, and no provision was made for a reduction in the price of powder, the abolition of the company stores, the discontinuance of company doctors, or the semi-monthly payment of wages, all of which had been demanded as conditions of settlement. As a consequence, the offer was rejected and the strike continued. About the 20th of October the operators withdrew the notices embodying their first proposition, and substituted for them notices in which it was proposed to grant a 10% increase in wages, to reduce the price of powder,[1] to pay wages semi-monthly in cash, and to adjust some of the other grievances against which the men so bitterly complained. This latter proposition, while not all to which the mineworkers believed themselves entitled, nevertheless afforded some relief from the intolerable conditions which had formerly prevailed, and when submitted to the executive committees of the miners' organization, it was accepted. Work was resumed on October 29th.

In deciding to instruct the miners to resume work the officers of the union were confident that the victory achieved would result in building up among the anthracite men a strong, compact organization, and they were imbued with the hope that a year later the operators would enter into contractual relations with the union. In this hope of recognition they were disappointed, but the organization grew in numerical strength, and within a short time after the strike practically every man and boy in the anthracite fields was enrolled as a member of the United Mine Workers of America.

---

[1] The reduction in the price of powder, it was understood, was to be taken out of the advance in wages.

CHAPTER XLII

THE STRIKE DECLARED

Labor Problem in Anthracite Region not Settled in 1900. Attempt to Disrupt the Union. Stockades, Coal Depôts, and Washeries. The Local Bosses, the Railroad Presidents, and the Financiers. Organized Labor's Struggle for Existence. The Invitation to a Joint Conference. The Refusal of the Railroad Presidents. The Shamokin Convention. Intermediation of the National Civic Federation. The Scranton Meeting. The Offer of Arbitration. The Railroad President and the "Eminent Prelates." The Hazleton Convention. The Strike Declared.

THE coal strike of 1900, while resulting in a victory for the men, did not solve the problem of the proper relation between labor and capital in the anthracite field. Instead of fairly meeting the men face to face and arranging by joint agreement the wages, hours of labor, and conditions of work to prevail in the region, the operators simply posted notices upon their breakers and towers, and the men accepted the concessions thus announced. There was no meeting between representatives of the two sides and no formal treaty was made. The concessions were wrung from the operators under the stress of a political campaign and were silently accepted by the mineworkers under advice of their union.

It was felt by both sides that the struggle was not conclusive. Just as the American colonies secured their independence in the Revolutionary War, but did not secure its confirmation until the War of 1812, so the anthracite mineworkers of Pennsylvania gained their liberty in 1900, but did not firmly establish it until 1902.

The great railroad corporations owning and operating mines in the anthracite region were in 1900 officered by men who had no sympathy with the principles and purposes of trade unionism. They had no eyes to see, nor sense to appreciate, the achievements of the union in raising the standard and improving the calibre of the men employed in and about the mines, and they could not realize or discern the new spirit of independence and hopefulness infused into the mineworkers by their organization. To them the union was nothing but a fighting machine to be fought, and the demands of the union, nothing but an increase in wages and a reduction in dividends. The union seemed to prevent them from running their business as they saw fit, from exercising despotic sway over the lives of their tens of thousands of workers. The men in charge of these vast industries were trained in the school of unorganized labor. They understood the art of obtaining work for low wages, but they utterly failed to comprehend the new spirit which would resist oppression at no matter what cost in suffering and privation. The ideal of these men to whom the anthracite coal industry of the country was entrusted was the annihilation of the union, its destruction root and branch. In the past the operators had destroyed the miners' unions, and what had been done once could surely be done again.

The aggressive policy of the operators was evident from the first. Immediately after the strike of 1900, stockades were built about many of the mines, depôts were established for the storage of coal, washeries were opened in many places, and preparations were made for the battle which was bound to come. The efforts of the union to better the conditions of the workmen were resisted at every point, and the bosses discouraged the mineworkers from joining the organization or remaining members of it. Agents of the companies circulated freely among the unionists, and records of the proceedings of the organization were immediately available to the presidents of the roads. The minor officials and petty bosses, men skilled in the exploitation of labor, constantly sent reports to their superiors of the alleged misdeeds of the unionists; and the antagonistic spirit of the men in control of this great industry was whetted by misleading accounts of the supposed doings of the United Mine Workers.

The desire on the part of the great railway presidents to involve the United Mine Workers of America in a contest which would mean its defeat and dissolution, was apparently shared by men of even greater dominance and power. There is growing up in these United States a small body of multi-millionaires, men exorbitantly rich and tremendously powerful, but apparently without those ideals of free and democratic government which should be the distinguishing characteristic of every American citizen. The coal strike of 1902 seems to have been merely the first battle in a destructive war to be waged by the greatest monopolists of the country against the democratic organization of trade unionism. The battle was more than a struggle between operators and miners. It was rather a gigantic contest between organized and concentrated wealth upon the one side, and organized labor, extending to every section and every industry in the country upon the other. The attempt to defeat and disrupt the United Mine Workers of America was apparently only a part of a much larger program —the defeat and destruction of all the trade unions in the country.

In contrast to this the attitude of the United Mine Workers was one of conciliation and peace. In 1900 the men accepted the concession, which was flung at them rather than granted to them. In 1901 the union again maintained peace by a continuance of the agreement of 1900. In an interview held in 1901, in which President Thomas of the Erie Railroad, Senator Hanna, the Presidents of the Anthracite Districts of the United Mine Workers, and I, took part, it was agreed that the conditions of 1900 should be maintained, and the representatives of the Mine Workers left the conference with the hope, if not the anticipation, that the union would be ultimately recognized. These hopes, however, were doomed to be unfulfilled.

In the following year, 1902, every attempt consistent with the preservation of dignity was made by the representatives of the union to secure a joint conference with the operators in order that a strike might be avoided. On February 14th, 1902, the officials of the Mine Workers' Union addressed a letter to the various railroad presidents asking for a joint conference between operators and miners to be held in Scranton on the 12th day of March. This request was unanimously refused by the operators, who claimed that "there cannot be two masters in the management of business" and stated their opposition to any agreement or arrangement with the union. The replies of the operators further attacked the union and held it responsible for the local strikes which had occurred during the last two years and which had really been traceable to the failure of the operators to meet the representatives of the union and settle grievances amicably.

Upon the refusal of the operators to meet them in joint conference, the mineworkers, in convention at Shamokin, formulated a series of demands to be presented to the operators. The increase in the cost of living had rendered of no effect the advances conceded in 1900, and the Mine Workers demanded a twenty per cent. increase in pay for men paid by the piece, a corresponding increase in the shape of a reduction in hours for men working by the day, the weighing of the coal, and the incorporation of these reforms in an agreement with the union. On March 22, by direction of the Mine Workers' convention, a telegram was sent to the railroad presidents, asking them to meet the representatives of the mineworkers for the purpose of discussing grievances. An immediate strike seemed unavoidable, but as a result of the intermediation of the National Civic Federation, a conference was arranged between the representatives of the miners and of the operators. An interview was accordingly held on the 26th of March, and action was delayed by the miners for a month in the hope of reaching an agreement. During this month, the National Civic Federation made every possible effort to bring about a satisfactory adjustment and urged upon the operators the necessity of making some concessions. Public opinion, as reflected in the various newspapers of the country, also advised this course. The operators, however, remained obstinate, and at the second meeting with the representatives of the mine workers again refused to make any concessions whatsoever or to grant the slightest part of the demands made upon them. The officials of the Union, while realizing the justice of their position, offered to compromise their original demands by accepting a 10% instead of a 20% increase, and a nine-hour instead of an eight-hour day. This policy was dictated not by fear of losing the strike, but in order to avert the terrible suffering which, it was clearly foreseen would inevitably result from the desperate conflict. The peaceful attitude of the union, however, was mistaken for weakness and cowardice, and each attempt at conciliation increased the obduracy of the railway presidents.

Up to the final moment, the mineworkers made every reasonable effort to avert hostilities. The justice of the men's demands was subsequently conceded, at least in part, by the United States Commissioner of Labor, by the Award of the Anthracite Coal Strike Commission, and even by the President of the Reading Coal and Iron Company, by Mr. Baer himself. During the negotiations, however, the operators refused to concede a single point and insisted upon the men surrendering their whole position. The president of the miners' union in conjunction with the district presidents had been empowered to call a strike, but it was felt that no step should be taken without the consent of the men, expressly given in convention, and without the fullest opportunity being afforded to the operators to arrange matters upon a satisfactory basis. On the 8th of May the representatives of the Mine Workers, with a lingering hope of averting the impending strike, sent a telegram to the railroad presidents, offering to submit their demands to the arbitration of a committee of five persons selected by the Industrial Branch of the National Civic Federation, or, if that proposition were unacceptable, to a committee composed of Archbishop Ireland, Bishop Potter, and one other person whom these two might select. This offer of arbitration was also unanimously refused, President Baer of the Reading Coal and Iron Company declaring that "anthracite mining is a business, and not a religious, sentimental, or academic proposition," adding, "I could not, if I would, delegate this business management to even so highly a respectable body as the Civic Federation, nor can I call to my aid as experts in the mixed problem of business and philanthropy the eminent prelates you have named." But neither Mr. Baer nor any of the other railway presidents suggested arbitrators more acceptable to them.

On the 9th day of May, the District Executive Committee of the United Mine Workers, assembled at Scranton, after having exhausted all efforts to bring about an amicable settlement with the operators, ordered a temporary suspension of mining to take place on May 12th, and called a convention of delegates to meet in Hazleton on the 14th of May to determine whether the suspension should be made permanent. In the call for the convention it was specifically requested that the delegates, when elected by the various locals be instructed to vote either for or against a strike. It was important, as it always should be, that the strike if declared, should represent the true and actual attitude of the men who were to bear the brunt and burden of the conflict. Even after the convention met on May 14th, hope was not entirely abandoned that a strike could be averted. The National Civic Federation, as well as a number of men acting in the public interest, made noble efforts to avert the threatened calamity, but no word came from the operators and no concessions were made by them. On the eve of the conflict, one of the railway presidents predicted that, come what might, the men would not strike, but would submit to any rebuff. For my part, I was still opposed to the declaration of a strike at this time if it could possibly be avoided, despite the provocation which the miners had received from the operators. I foresaw that the conflict would be long and severe, and I hoped that it might be averted until the late fall, when the men could have struck more effectively. I was even in hopes that by that time the operators would see the folly of their course and make concessions, which would have preserved the mineworkers and their families, as well as the general public, from the hardships and horrors of a protracted conflict. More important, however, than the question of strike or no strike was that of the control of the union by its own members. I made as strong a plea as possible for the maintenance of peace at least until the fall, but I insisted even more strenuously that the men remain bound by their instructions and vote against me, if they had been instructed by the vote of their local body to favor an immediate strike. A large number of delegates adopted my view of the advisability of postponing the conflict, but the majority were bound by instructions from their locals and remained true to the promises which had been made to their constituents. By a vote of $461\frac{1}{4}$ to $349\frac{3}{4}$, it was decided, on May 15th, to continue the suspension, and the greatest strike in American history was declared.

CHAPTER XLIII

THE INDIANAPOLIS CONVENTION.

The Early Days of the Strike. Peaceable Conduct. The Strike of the Steam Men. Attempts at Conciliation. The Investigation of the Commissioner of Labor. Distress in the Anthracite Region. The Indianapolis Convention. The Preservation of the Union and The Sanctity of Contracts. The Miners Maintain Faith.

THE news of the declaration of the strike came as a shock to the country, although a labor conflict had seemed inevitable in view of the unyielding and uncompromising attitude assumed by the operators. The public had hoped against hope that some general arrangement could be reached by which the strike might be averted.

At the time of the calling of the strike, it was confidently predicted on many sides that the contest would be of short duration. The union was known to be without large funds, and the ability of the miners to hold out was greatly underestimated. Many of the papers opposed to the organization stated that the strike would not last for more than five or six weeks and that by the first of July, at the latest, it would begin to disintegrate.

These hopes were doomed to be shattered. The strike, like all great movements, began in a quiet, noiseless manner and continued for many weeks without incidents of note. The anticipations of violence were not realized, and the men showed great wisdom in maintaining unbroken peace. The officials of the union urged the members to exercise absolute caution, to abstain from contests or contact of any sort with the coal and iron police, and to refrain entirely from drunkenness or street brawls. Thousands of members took the pledge of total abstinence during the strike, and peace reigned throughout the region. There was nothing to indicate that a great struggle was going on. The men remained quietly at their homes, cultivating sometimes a little garden patch, making necessary repairs about the houses, or engaging in baseball games and other sports. The breaker boys, many of them for the first time in their lives, enjoyed an uninterrupted holiday, and play took the place of work. From the very start, a number of miners felt the pinch of want, but their needs were relieved by the generosity of their neighbors, and the spirit of brotherliness and reciprocal help for a long time prevented any suffering.

In 1901 the engineers, firemen, and pumpmen had desired to strike owing to the excessive hours which they were obliged to work. These men were employed for twelve hours a day, and on alternate Sundays, when the shift changed, they were compelled to work uninterruptedly for twenty-four hours. The United Mine Workers of America had promised that if they postponed their strike, the organization would assist them, and accordingly, in the early part of June, the engineers, firemen, and pumpmen were called out upon strike.

Much unjust criticism has been directed against the officials of the Mine Workers, and especially against myself, for calling out the steam men. We were accused of attempting to "hold up" the operators, and it was claimed that the steam men, in striking, deserted their posts of duty and engaged in a sympathetic strike with the miners. The truth, however, is that the pumpmen, engineers, and firemen were called out in their own interests absolutely, by their own request, and for the sole purpose of removing grievances against which they alone complained and against which some of them had inaugurated an independent but unsuccessful strike the year before. The position which they held was not a post of duty, but a post of contract. The obligation of the steam men to the companies was not like the relation of soldiers to the army in which they enlist or sailors to the navy of which they form a part, but was merely a contractual relation which might be terminated at the will of either party, there being no agreement between the steam men and the operators, obligating them to work for any given period. Had the operators desired to reduce wages, they would have locked out the steam men without compunction, and the right to strike should have been frankly conceded to the steam men when they desired to better their conditions. It was realized that to call out these men suddenly and without sufficient notice to the companies, would mean the destruction of many valuable properties by the flooding of the mines. Consequently, the steam men were not called out for some time, ten days warning being given to the operators in order that no calamity might ensue. The steam men were ordered to strike only in case their own demands were not granted, and no provision was made that the demands of the miners themselves should be conceded before the steam men returned to work.

As the strike progressed, the public evinced a keen interest in its outcome, and attempts were made at intermediation by various public-spirited citizens. Marcus A. Hanna, United States Senator from Ohio, was especially active in this direction. In the course of several months no stone was left unturned to bring the operators to a fitting sense of their responsibilities to the public, but in these endeavors, Senator Hanna, as well as the National Civic Federation, which was also active, failed completely. By the early part of June the price of coal began to rise and consumers began to complain. Under the direction of President Roosevelt, Carroll D. Wright, United States Commissioner of Labor, went to New York where statements as to the causes and the status of the strike were made to him by the railway presidents and myself. The report of Commissioner Wright justified in part the demands of the men, but was not made public until much later, and no action was ever taken upon it.

When the strike was declared, on the 15th of May, many of the anthracite mineworkers believed that help would be forthcoming from their brothers in the bituminous fields. About 150,000 men and boys in the anthracite regions had been thrown idle by the strike, and these, together with the miners of West Virginia, who were also on strike, constituted one-half of the membership of the national union. It was therefore hoped by many of the anthracite workers that the bituminous men might be called out in order, by means of a general suspension of mining throughout the country, to force the hand of the operators. The President of the United Mine Workers of America is compelled, according to the constitution, to call a special convention upon the demand of any five district organizations. When, therefore, I received requests from five districts, I issued a call for a national convention of all mineworkers to meet in Indianapolis upon the 17th of July.

By the time of the convocation of the Indianapolis convention, distress had already begun to show itself in the anthracite region. Many of the men, who, two months before, had entered the strike in high hopes, had long since been reduced to their last penny and had pawned or sold all their small valuables. Many of the strikers, especially among the foreign element, had gone to other parts of the country, or to Europe, but large numbers still remained, and these now began to feel the pangs of hunger. But the question uppermost in the minds of the men was the winning of the strike and the manner of assistance they should receive from the soft coal men. The bituminous miners were in full sympathy with the sufferings of their brothers in Pennsylvania and were willing to make any sacrifices in order to aid them. Some of the delegates argued that a complete suspension of all miners throughout the country would mean speedy victory for the anthracite men, since the railroads would be obliged to surrender as a result of the lack of fuel. The men in the soft coal fields would undoubtedly have struck in sympathy but for one deterring fact.

This fact was the existence of a contract between them and the bituminous operators. For several years the miners and operators had met in joint convention, agreed upon a scale of wages, and fixed conditions of employment, the contracts so made being binding for the period of one year. To strike in July, 1902, the soft coal miners would have been obliged to break contracts which did not terminate before April, 1903. It was argued, as in the steel strike of 1901, that where the life of the union was at stake, no agreement should be regarded, since the duty of self-preservation takes precedence over the sanctity of any contract. It was further held that a mere suspension of work without a demand for a change in wages or conditions would not be a strike in the technical sense of the word, since by the contract the men were obliged to work only at a certain rate of pay, but not for any particular number of days. It was also represented that the attack of the operators upon the anthracite miners was but the beginning of a concerted effort to disrupt the entire organization of mineworkers and that, if the anthracite men lost their strike, it would be but a short time before the bituminous miners would also be crushed. The miners, however, did not pay the slightest attention to what they regarded as quibbles, but insisted absolutely upon the maintenance of their agreements. Even the anthracite delegates adopted this view, believing that it was the part of honor for the soft coal men to stand by their contracts, though as a result the union might be shattered and destroyed. In my speech before the convention I took the same stand and urged the men not to break their agreements. The honor of trade unionism, based on the willingness of organized workingmen to make sacrifices in order to maintain the absolute integrity of their contracts, was at stake, and the friends of organized labor looked anxiously to Indianapolis for signal proof that workingmen consider their contracts sacred. By a unanimous vote the convention, consisting both of anthracite and bituminous delegates, decided that the existing agreements should be kept inviolate and that no strike should be declared in violation of the annual contracts, no matter how strong the temptation or how pressing the need.

CHAPTER XLIV

THE INTERVENTION OF THE PRESIDENT

The Bituminous Miners Provide the Sinews of War. Over Two and One-half Million Dollars Contributed. Delay and Discontent. The Critical Period. The Shenandoah Riot. The Campaign of Vilification. Exaggerated Accounts of Violence. The Coal and Iron Police. Sympathy of the Public. Contributions to the Strike Fund. The Price of Coal Rises. Suffering of the Poor. The Operators Still have "Nothing to Arbitrate." The Lengthening of the Contest. The Irresistible Force and the Immovable Body. The Intervention of the President. The Third of October. The Operators still Unyielding. The Calling out of the Pennsylvania National Guard. The Surrender of the Operators. The End of the Strike.

THE Indianapolis convention did not result in a suspension of work by the soft coal miners, but action was taken that proved of greater benefit. The delegates voted unanimously against a sympathetic strike, but voted with equal unanimity to extend moral and financial support to the anthracite mineworkers until such time as victory should be achieved, or the mine owners should agree to submit the matters in dispute to the arbitrament of an impartial tribunal.

By this action the various members of the United Mine Workers of America in the bituminous coal fields pledged themselves to subscribe weekly either one dollar or ten per cent. of their weekly earnings to a fund to be used for the assistance of the anthracite strikers; and the officers of the organization agreed to pay thirty-five per cent. of their salaries for the same purpose. In this manner, during a period of sixteen weeks the enormous sum of $2,645,324.42 was collected, and there can be no doubt that the contributions would have continued at an increasing rate, had the termination of hostilities been delayed. The bituminous miners alone paid into the relief fund an average of from $7.00 to $16.00 per man, and at no time was there any disposition to withhold from the anthracite mineworkers the assistance so generously and spontaneously given; as a matter of fact, toward the close of the strike many local unions voluntarily increased their donations, and in some instances members offered to contribute twenty-five per cent. of their gross earnings.

The action of the Indianapolis convention in refusing to vote in favor of a sympathetic strike and in providing, instead, for financial support, appeared to meet with the strongest possible commendation from the press and the public. The press, however, in its endorsement of our proceedings, unintentionally over-estimated the amount of money which would be contributed to the anthracite men, and it under-estimated the time that would elapse before collections and arrangements for distribution could be made. The money voted by the bituminous miners was not paid into the treasury until a full month after the adjournment of the convention. This delay was due to the fact that the men in the bituminous regions receive their wages semi-monthly, and the money earned in the last half of July was not paid to them until the 15th day of August.

In calculating the amount of money that would be available for distribution, the newspapers estimated that each person on strike would receive not less than $5.00 per week during the continuance of the struggle. Such claims, of course, were utterly ridiculous, involving, as they would, an expenditure of about $3,500,000 per month. As a consequence of these extravagant statements the striking mine workers became imbued with the hope, if not the absolute belief, that they were actually to receive this amount; and when these payments failed to materialize, many of the strikers were seized with a feeling of despondency, and mutterings of discontent were heard on every hand.

During the first week of August a crisis was reached. The agents of the companies, taking advantage of the opportunity temporarily afforded them by this loss of confidence, circulated rumors among the strikers to the effect that the money contributed by the bituminous miners was being withheld, if not actually misappropriated. I am fully convinced that the strike would have collapsed, had the operators at this time opened their mines and invited the strikers to return to work. It was the crucial moment, the only time during the long, stubbornly fought contest in which there was any sign of wavering. The operators, evidently, did not realize the extent of the disaffection in the ranks of the strikers and failed to take advantage of the opportunity open to them.

Following this period a riot occurred at Shenandoah, precipitated by the hasty and unnecessary action of a deputy sheriff in firing upon a crowd of striking mine workers, who, incensed by this action, assaulted him. Several mineworkers or their sympathizers, who came to the sheriff's rescue, and a merchant were seriously injured, the merchant subsequently dying from the effects of his wounds. This violence, following upon a period of tranquillity, was taken up by the hostile press and grossly and maliciously exaggerated. From this time on there appeared daily, in many newspapers, reports of assaults and riots, many of which never occurred. Street brawls, entirely unconnected with the strike, were magnified and distorted, the officials of the union were charged with instigating violence, and the statement was repeatedly made that a reign of terror prevailed throughout the region. The efforts of the union officials to maintain discipline, to inspire confidence, to prevent illegal acts among the 150,000 striking men and boys in the region were greatly hampered by a torrent of abuse and by the misrepresentation of those opposed to them.

The leaders of the strike, however, patiently maintained their position, plainly and honestly stating to the mineworkers the condition of the treasury and the possibilities of relief; they refrained from making extravagant promises and continued to encourage the men to maintain a silent, passive struggle until the very end. Official and public proclamations were issued, directing the strikers to refrain from deeds of violence, to be ever on their guard against being provoked into the commission of any act that would bring discredit upon them or would alienate the sympathy and support so generously given to them by the public and by the vast majority of the newspapers.

One week later contributions began to come in, and, as fast as funds were received, they were hurried to the weaker points and distributed among those most in need or most likely to surrender. Circular letters were also addressed to each of the local unions, explaining the delay in the distribution of funds and instructing relief committees as to the manner in which money should be expended. At no time during the strike were there sufficient funds to provide for all who were idle. Men who had bank accounts, those who owned property, or those who could, in any way, shift for themselves, were required to subordinate their claims to the more pressing wants of the needier and less provident. There is, of course, a certain injustice in thus discriminating against men who have been saving and economical, but in a strike of vast magnitude, involving over half a million men, women, and children, a union is oftentimes compelled to husband its resources and to provide only for those who cannot provide for themselves and who, if not relieved, will be forced to accept the alternative of returning to work on the employer's terms or starving to death.

Meanwhile, public-spirited men in every walk of life renewed their efforts to settle the strike. The hardships suffered by the mineworkers also found answer in the sympathy of the public, and large sums of money flowed into the union treasury. These contributions came from all classes and from all ranks of society. Occasionally a broker in a New York office would send a check, with a request that his name be not made public; in like manner, checks for various amounts came from manufacturers, merchants, lawyers, doctors, ministers, workingmen, and farmers. Even little children sent the nickels from their money boxes, and the widow's mite was added to swell the fund. Of course, the great bulk of the money from other sources than the union funds came from the organized workers in other trades, who contributed several hundred thousand dollars. Even the toilers of foreign lands were moved by the tale of the heroic struggle of the anthracite mineworkers, and money was received from England, Wales, and other countries where men had similarly struggled in their efforts to improve conditions.

As the summer advanced the hardships and privations of the great body of American people, especially those in the eastern and seaboard states, sensibly increased. The operators had stored considerable coal during the thirty days' truce which had been arranged prior to the inauguration of the strike, but with each week the visible supply diminished, and prices mounted higher and higher. Coal that could formerly be purchased for six dollars per ton was now selling for eight, ten, twelve, and eventually rose to above twenty dollars. The effect of these high prices was felt by every member of society; the burden falling most heavily upon the very poor in the great cities, who were compelled to purchase their fuel by the bushel or by the pail, in many instances paying at the rate of $30.00 per ton. Railroads were obliged to discontinue running many trains, factories closed down, and men were thrown out of employment in various industries; the cost of living appreciably increased, and the work of many people became unremunerative. The scarcity of anthracite coal and the extortionate prices being charged for it created an abnormal demand for the product of the bituminous mines, and as a consequence the price of soft coal rapidly increased.

As a result there was a fear of coal riots in the city of New York and elsewhere—riots in comparison with which the bread riots of London and the meat riots of New York's East Side would have faded into insignificance. Even the more responsible members of society occasionally took coal by force, following, in this instance, the example of the railroads, which in many cases confiscated coal entrusted to them by shippers. The smoke ordinances of New York and other large cities were openly violated, and the cities were covered with a pall of black smoke. In view of the ever-diminishing supply of anthracite coal, the health authorities found themselves powerless, and the law was openly disregarded.

The discomforts and inconveniences endured by the people of the Eastern states during the months of August and September were many. To any but the near-sighted, however, it was evident that the perils which were coming were infinitely worse. Had no coal been mined in October or November, had the strike lasted until December or January, the hardships would have been beyond endurance. Despite the fact that winter was approaching, the coal operators remained singularly stubborn and obdurate; they showed no sign of yielding. They had been misled, and they themselves had misled the public repeatedly throughout the conflict. They had, at first, declared that the strike would not take place; when it did come, they maintained that it would not last more than a few weeks, but that it would collapse and coal would be mined by the first of August. When, however, each prediction failed of fulfillment, renewed prophecies were made with increased confidence. From week to week the opening of the mines was postponed, and the inevitable dissolution of the union, so often and so confidently predicted, was prophesied again and again. Despite the suffering of the public, the presidents of the great railroads in control of the coal industry refused to budge an inch. Just as they were willing to have the mines flooded and destroyed rather than grant to the steam men a reasonable reduction in hours, so they were willing to plunge the whole country into irremediable distress rather than acknowledge for a moment the existence of the United Mine Workers of America. On the other hand, the union, from the very beginning, offered arbitration and never ceased in its efforts to arrange for an amicable adjustment. These efforts were seconded by many leading men, including Senators Hanna, Quay, Penrose, Platt, Governor Odell, and others. Again and again, the miners were buoyed up by the hope of an early and satisfactory settlement of the difficulty, but in every case their hopes were doomed to disappointment. The letter of President Baer, in which he said that the welfare of the workingmen would be cared for, not by the agitators but by the Christian men to whom God, in His infinite wisdom, had entrusted the property interests of the country, was indicative of the uncompromising attitude of the managers of the coal properties. These men, although undoubtedly conscientious and sincere, seemed utterly unable to comprehend the progress that had been made in the requirements, thoughts, and aspirations of workingmen during the last five centuries. The cry was still "We have nothing to arbitrate," and the claim was made and reiterated that only the violence of the mine workers prevented the reëstablishment of industry in the coal regions.

Nothing could be more significant than the manner in which the operators emphasized every disturbance occurring in the anthracite field. It cannot be denied that there was a number of clashes between the more reckless or impetuous strikers and the more irresponsible of the coal and iron police, hired by the operators for the purpose of protecting their mines. Testimony before the Anthracite Coal Strike Commission revealed the calibre of many of these defenders of the sacred right of property. Some of them were men of good character, but many of them were thugs, recruited from the lowest slums of the great cities, uniformed, armed, and invested with police authority. Some were, indeed, the most desperate characters, and in the case of one man the Commission absolutely refused to allow him to be cross-examined, because of his own shameless acknowledgment that he was a crook, a thief, and a confirmed criminal. There were several cases of wanton assault and unprovoked murder by these coal and iron police; and, on the other hand, there were instances in which violence was done and murder committed by strikers, or by men who claimed to be in sympathy with them. It is utterly impossible to control every act and deed of every single individual in a population of 150,000 men and boys, who have been idle for months and many of whom are on the verge of despair, if not of actual starvation. But the claim that the majority of the men were prevented from working in the mines by the force and intimidation of a minority was utterly misleading, utterly false, and, as was subsequently shown, easily and completely disproved.

During the months of August and September the operators opened up a few mines and washeries in various parts of the region. In the official statements given out by the companies, the output of these mines was exaggerated, or else the coal produced by them must, for the most part, have been unaccountably lost before reaching market. What became of it has remained one of the unsolved mysteries of the coal strike. The output, as reported, increased steadily with each succeeding day, but importunate demands of would-be consumers were met with the stereotyped statement that no coal was being received. There can be no doubt that, whatever the production of coal by washeries and by mines, the output was much below the needs of the community, and the demand for fuel became daily more pressing.

Meanwhile, the coal operators remained firm. They attributed the inauguration of the strike to the uncontrolled ambitions of the short-sighted, self-seeking agitators; its continuance they attributed to the violence of a small minority of the men, who, they claimed, terrorized a vast majority; and they felt, or seemed to feel, that, if the public suffered for lack of fuel, it was because that public, in its generous but stupid sympathy, had encouraged the striking mineworkers. The serene indifference of these men to the demands of their employees and to the pressing needs of the public, is one of the most curious anomalies of this most remarkable of contests. All efforts at intermediation were met by a determined rebuff. Week after week the railway presidents met, as directors of the Temple Coal and Iron Company, but they did nothing to bring the strike to a close. Even the prosecutions brought against them as the creators of a trust were met by the same stolid indifference, and their policy of masterly inactivity was not shaken even by the concentrated indignation of the whole people or by the threats, made in various states, of legislation seeking to control the industry. The remarkable power of the union to continue the strike, although it desired peace, was perfectly evident. The ability and willingness on the part of the operators to prolong the struggle were equally clear. The strike had resolved itself into a contest in which, figuratively speaking, an irresistible force struck an immovable body. But the horror of the situation lay in the fact that between the two great powers, one struggling for the right to live, the other animated by the determination to be alone dominant —to be sole master—there stood the public, suffering, sensitive, and panic-stricken at the approach of winter.

At this critical moment the President of the United States intervened. There seemed no possibility of reaching the operators by other means; they refused to yield to advice of friend or threat of foe; they appeared utterly oblivious of the demands of a suffering public. President Roosevelt, however, conscious of the hardship that would follow in the wake of a coal famine, sent invitations to the various railroad presidents, to the presidents of the anthracite district unions, and to myself, to meet him in the temporary White House on the 3rd day of October. This meeting has become historic. The President, in stating the purpose of the conference, disclaimed any right or duty to intervene upon legal grounds or by reason of any official relation to the situation; he also advised against a discussion of the merits of the case, but requested both parties to "meet upon the common plane of the necessities of the public." "I appeal to your patriotism," he concluded, "to the spirit that sinks personal considerations and makes individual sacrifices for the common good."

The address of the President, short as it was, could not but arouse his auditors to a sense of the grave responsibility resting upon them. At its conclusion, I stated that I was impressed with the gravity of the situation, and I proposed on behalf of the anthracite mine workers that all matters in dispute be submitted to the arbitration of a tribunal selected by the President. At this juncture the President suggested that further discussion of the matter be deferred until three o'clock in the afternoon, in order that the operators and miners might think the situation over and come to an understanding.

The afternoon meeting was one of the most astounding events of the strike. The railway officials, disregarding the request of the President that the merits of the controversy be not discussed, launched forth upon a series of tirades and invectives against the union and its officers, which left no ground for discussion or conciliation. This abuse, so openly showered upon the organization, was not spontaneous or instinctive, not made upon the spur of the moment, but was read from carefully prepared statements, which, no doubt, had been written and re-written and should therefore have represented the cool judgment of the operators. The presence of the Chief Magistrate of the nation did not in the least restrain some of the operators from giving way to unseemly outbursts of feeling. It was intimated that the President had failed in his duty toward the public and the operators, and one of the speakers ended an impassioned, but utterly baseless invective, by a demand upon the President that he do his duty. The union was denounced as illegal, and a large number of cases were quoted in an effort to demonstrate that the union had no legal status and should be prosecuted. Some of the gentlemen representing the anthracite industry did not limit themselves to their carefully prepared statements, but injected into their reading a number of extemporaneous remarks bitterly assailing the organization of the United Mine Workers; and, instead of accepting our proposal of peace and arbitration, the railway officials concluded by urging that the President station United States troops in the anthracite coal fields.

The character of these attacks was such as to provoke indignation, but we preferred to disregard them, and I limited my reply to an acknowledgment that there had been some violence, which I regretted, and to the further statement that this violence had been exaggerated. I did not; however, desire to put anything in the way of a reconciliation with the operators and therefore refrained from replying to the attacks in the spirit which they naturally aroused. Instead, I submitted, in writing, a formal proposition for arbitration and pledged its acceptance by the mine workers.

While the effort of the President to bring about a settlement of the strike had apparently failed, it nevertheless opened the way for an ultimate adjustment. The attitude of the operators in refusing to accept the mediation or the arbitration of the President of the United States, caused a wave of indignation to sweep over the country, and the general judgment was that the wishes of the Chief Executive should be regarded and peace established. President Roosevelt continued his efforts to bring the strike to an end and on the 6th day of October requested me, through the Hon. Carroll D. Wright, Commissioner of Labor, to secure the return of the men to work. The assurance was given that after mining was resumed a commission would be appointed to investigate the conditions of life and labor in the anthracite field, and that when the report and recommendations of this commission were received, the President would do all in his power to induce the operators to accept its findings. This request was taken under advisement, but after most careful thought I concluded that, inasmuch as the operators had not agreed to accept the decision of a commission appointed in this manner and as the President had no power legally to enforce the award of a commission appointed by him, compliance with his request would mean surrender of the cause for which the miners had so heroically fought. I was therefore reluctantly compelled to decline to advise the men to return to work, much as I sympathized with the efforts of the President in behalf of the people of the United States.

A few days after the conference with the President, the Governor of Pennsylvania ordered out the entire National Guard, which was directed to proceed to the coal fields. I was fully aware that the calling out of the troops would not have the effect desired by the operators. I knew that the presence of ten thousand or one hundred thousand soldiers would not result in the strikers returning to work, and the order, therefore, for the mustering of the entire National Guard did not shake my confidence in the ultimate victory of the men. In order to demonstrate the falsity of the claims made by the operators, that the strikers were deterred from resuming work through fear of violence, I directed that all men on strike—union and non-union—should assemble in mass meetings and by vote determine whether or not they, or any of them, desired to return to work. On the very day on which 10,000 members of the Pennsylvania National Guard were being stationed in various parts of the coal fields, and when every man who desired to work was guaranteed military protection, 150,000 mine workers, without one dissenting voice, voted to continue the strike until victory was achieved or until they were ordered by the union to reënter the mines.

The operators had repeatedly promised that, if given military protection, they would be able to mine sufficient coal to meet the necessities of the public; but the arrival of the troops had no appreciable effect upon the output of the mines. As a matter of fact, some who had previously deserted from the ranks of the strikers or had been imported to take their places, now refused to work. The failure of the operators thus became evident through the very measure which they had urged to insure success.

With coal at famine prices, with the press and the country clamoring for the resumption of mining, the operators finally realized the absolute necessity of surrender, and on the 13th of October, Mr. J. Pierpont Morgan called upon President Roosevelt and, in the name of the operators, offered to submit the matters in dispute to a commission consisting of five men to be appointed by the President and selected in the manner prescribed in the letter of submission.

At the time the offer of arbitration was made the mine workers had practically won the strike. The funds of the union were increasing at a rapid rate, and the amount of money on hand was greater than at any time in the previous history of the organization. The men had demonstrated conclusively that the presence of the troops had no effect and that they were in a position to continue the contest indefinitely. At the same time I felt that, as we had struggled for the principle of arbitration, we would not be justified in refusing to accept it because victory was within our hands.

The only objection that I had to the proposition submitted by Mr. Morgan was that it stipulated that the arbitrators be selected from certain avocations and certain classes of society. I therefore insisted that the President be free to exercise his own judgment in the selection of the commission and that, if the operators have a distinctive representative on the commission, a representative trade unionist be also appointed. The justice of this position was acknowledged, and a modification of the original proposition submitted by Mr. Morgan was accordingly secured. As soon as it was learned that the President would have full latitude, a delegate convention of the striking mine workers was called to meet in Wilkesbarre on October the 20th. After a full day's deliberation, it was unanimously decided that work should be resumed October the 23rd, and all questions in dispute were submitted to the arbitration of the commission appointed by the President of the United States.

CHAPTER XLV

THE AWARD OF THE ANTHRACITE COAL STRIKE COMMISSION

The Miners Gain Arbitration. Organized Labor Represented on the Commission The Work of the Commission. Testimony and Argument. Nature of the Investigation. Its Cost. Bulk of Testimony. Elaborate Report. Award, Recommendations and Discussions. Temporary and Permanent Awards. Wages. Hours of Labor. Weighing of Coal. Check Weighmen and Docking Bosses. The Union Recognized. The Board of Conciliation. Its Recognition by the Operators. The Convention of June, 1903. The Redress of Grievances.

THE coal strike, which had endured for five months as a result of the operators' refusal to arbitrate, was brought to a close about the middle of October by the submission of the questions at issue to arbitration. During the whole course of the strike, the miners had vainly struggled for the recognition of this principle, and the retreat of the operators from their untenable position, constituted a clear victory for the men and justified the declaration of the strike. As originally presented in the letter of the operators dated October 13, the offer of arbitration was entirely unacceptable. This defect, however, being remedied upon the demand of the miners, a return to work was immediately recommended by the District Executive Boards and unanimously approved in general convention on the 21st day of October. The suspension of mining, which for one hundred and sixty-three days had been general throughout the region, thus came to a close.

The appointment of the Anthracite Coal Strike Commission will remain a landmark in the history of labor. By this act, the President of the United States asserted and upheld the paramount interest of the public in conflicts affecting injuriously the welfare of the community. In a certain sense, the appointment of the Anthracite Coal Strike Commission was a signal proof of the power of public opinion, and a clear demonstration of the wise manner in which this power can be exercised at critical periods.

The sessions of the Commission were destined to become historical. Preliminary meetings were held on October 24th and 27th, 1902, and with few intermissions, the Commission sat in Scranton and Philadelphia from the 14th of November, 1902, until the 5th of February, 1903. This period was devoted to the taking of testimony and was succeeded by five days of argument from February 9th to February 13th inclusive. The sessions aroused the liveliest public interest, and thousands of people attended, while hundreds of others were unable to obtain entrance to these meetings.

The attorneys presented the cases of both operators and mine workers with great skill and knowledge, and the legal contest between the representatives of the two sides evoked intense interest and general enthusiasm. The sessions were marked by a series of dramatic incidents, chief among which was the testimony of the little children, who worked in the silk mills and the coal breakers. In all, 558 witnesses were examined, of whom 240 were called by the Union, 153 by the attorneys for the non-union men, who were specially represented, 154 by the operators, and 11 by the Commission. The testimony was extremely bulky, amounting to over 10,000 legal cap pages, besides a vast number of statistical and other exhibits. The award, which was given on March 18th, 1903, was also lengthy, and, with the exhibits appended to it, made a document of some 120,000 words.

The findings of the Anthracite Coal Strike Commission consist of a report and an award. The report is a more or less theoretical discussion of general principles, while the award consists of specific injunctions and specific recommendations bearing upon the anthracite struggle. I shall not discuss the report, which is, in my opinion and in that of the great body of unionists, a document prepared by fair-minded and intelligent men, but showing, upon the whole, a lack of appreciation of some of the fundamental principles of unionism and based upon premises which cannot be maintained.

The award, however, displays great practical wisdom and illustrates the tendency of wise men to surrender theoretical prejudices when they come into contact with a real and pressing problem. While it did not give the men all that they had demanded or were entitled to, still the award of the Commission secured to them substantial advances in wages and material improvement in conditions. What was perhaps even more important, it recognized the United Mine Workers of America as one of the contracting parties, thus fixing the status of that organization. According to the award of the Commission, which is to remain in effect from April 1, 1903, to April 1, 1906, all contract miners were to receive an advance of 10% in their rates of pay for cutting coal, for yardage, and for other work, for which standard rates or allowances previously existed. The engineers engaged in hoisting water were to have a reduction of hours from 12 to 8, with no reduction in pay, or, in other words, an increase of 50% per hour, while the engineers who were already working eight-hour shifts were to have no further reduction in hours, but a 10% increase in wages. Hoisting engineers and other engineers and pumpmen, except those before mentioned, were awarded an increase of 5% in their wages and relieved from duty on Sunday, with full pay, or, in other words, an hourly increase of 22%. The firemen were also awarded an eight-hour day instead of a twelve-hour day, this being an increase of 50% in the hourly rate of remuneration. The company men or men who were paid by the day—representing about one-half the employees in and about the mines—were awarded a nine-hour instead of a ten-hour day, and as these men are practically paid by the hour, this award amounted to an increase of 11 1/9% in their wage rate. These awards bearing upon wages were to be further advanced with every increase in the price of coal. When White Ash coal of sizes above pea coal sold at or near New York harbor at a price above $4.50 f. o. b., the employees were to have for every 5¢ in excess of this price, an increase of 1% in their wages. This will probably amount to an average increase of 5% during the entire year, this being in addition to the increases before mentioned. The total addition to the wages of the anthracite mineworkers secured through the strike of 1902 will probably average between seven and eight millions of dollars annually.

The Commission awarded the payment of the miners' laborers directly by the Company instead of by the miner; provided that the mine cars should be equitably distributed, that the men should be granted the right to have check weighmen and check docking bosses, whenever a majority at a colliery demanded it, and decreed that no person should be refused employment because he belonged or failed to belong to a labor organization.

The recommendations of the Commission, were, upon the whole, such as would commend themselves to well-intentioned and well-informed men. "The Commission thinks that the practice of employing deputies . . . . . is one of doubtful wisdom, and perhaps tends to invite conflicts between such officers and idle men rather than to avert them." The Commission further stated that the employment of coal and iron policemen "militates against the very purpose for which they are employed." It recommended laws against the employment of young children and the compulsory investigation by the Federal Government of controversies of the nature of the Anthracite Coal Strike.

The most important feature of the award was the provision for a board of conciliation. While disclaiming the wish to compel the recognition of the United Mine Workers of America, the Commission in actual practice made that recognition inevitable and immediate. The Commission recognized the fact that it could not itself settle future disputes as they arose; it realized that it was not a perpetual body, and it feared, with good reason, that if no machinery were provided for the interpretation and enforcement of the award, such award would soon be nullified, and conditions would lapse into their former evil state. The Commission seemed to realize, moreover, that there existed no machinery except the organization of the United Mine Workers of America capable of guaranteeing the integrity of the award, and in forming a board of conciliation, therefore, it saw itself compelled to rely upon the machinery provided by the Union.

The Commission adjudged and awarded: "That any difficulty or disagreement arising under this award, either as to its interpretation or application, or in any way growing out of the relations of the employers and employed, which can not be settled or adjusted by consultation between the superintendent or manager of the mine or mines, and the miner or miners directly interested, or is of a scope too large to be so settled or adjusted, shall be referred to a permanent joint committee, to be called a board of conciliation, to consist of six persons, appointed as hereinafter provided. That is to say, if there shall be a division of the whole region into three districts, in each of which there shall exist an organization representing a majority of the mine workers of such district, one of said board of conciliation shall be appointed by each of said organizations, and three other persons shall be appointed by the operators, the operators in each of said districts appointing one person.

"The board of conciliation thus constituted, shall take up and consider any question referred to it as aforesaid, hearing both parties to the controversy, and such evidence as may be laid before it by either party; and any award made by a majority of such board of conciliation shall be final and binding on all parties. If, however, the said board is unable to decide any question submitted, or point related thereto, that question or point shall be referred to an umpire, to be appointed, at the request of said board, by one of the circuit judges of the third judicial circuit of the United States, whose decision shall be final and binding in the premises.

"The membership of said board shall at all times be kept complete, either the operators' or miners' organizations having the right, at any time when a controversy is not pending, to change their representation thereon.

"At all hearings before said board the parties may be represented by such person or persons as they may respectively select.

"No suspension of work shall take place, by lockout or strike, pending the adjudication of any matter so taken up for adjustment."

The significance of this award is evident and those who run may read. The organizations of the three districts meant, of course, the District Organizations, 1, 7 and 9, of the United Mine Workers of America. The presidents of these districts, Messrs. T. D. Nicholls, Wm. H. Dettrey, and John Fahy, were appointed as representatives of the Union upon the board of conciliation, and the operators appointed Wm. Connell, independent operator, Roland C. Luther, General Manager of the Philadelphia & Reading

Coal and Iron Co., and S. F. Warriner, General Superintendent of the Lehigh Valley Coal Co. These appointments were made in June, 1903, but the operators at first refused to recognize the three district presidents, and for a time feeling ran high in the anthracite region. The men were determined upon striking, unless they were assured that their duly accredited representatives would be accepted by the board. A convention of all anthracite mineworkers was held and the appointment of the mineworkers' representatives confirmed. The railway presidents, recognizing the unwisdom of their policy, agreed to be bound by the action of the convention, and at the present time the board of conciliation, is succeeding in satisfactorily solving all questions of interpretation as they arise. The institution of a board of conciliation augurs well for the continued peace and prosperity of the anthracite region. The present award remains in force until the first day of April, 1906, and will, no doubt, be scrupulously adhered to, both by operators and miners. At that time, there is every reason to believe that the operators will appreciate the wisdom of remaining upon good terms with their employees, and will enter into yearly agreements with the United Mine Workers of America. If the men and the operators can work together for three years under the award, if they can learn to understand each other's motives and to realize that they have large interests in common, the future of a clear and definite recognition by means of trade agreements need not be despaired of, and wage disputes in the anthracite industry will then be adjusted as they are in the bituminous fields to-day—by joint conventions representing the capitalists and the laborers. The award, however, must be lived up to according not only to its letter, but to its spirit. If either the men or the operators try to see how far they can diverge from the intention of the award without actually breaking it, instead of trying to see how clearly and consistently they can live up to it, no award and no agreement will ever endure. I have no doubt, however, that with each month relations will continue to improve, and that from 1906 on, labor conditions will be fixed annually by joint convention, and peace and contentment reign in the region so lately distracted and ravaged by a great industrial conflict.

CHAPTER XLVI

LABOR FEDERATION IN THE UNITED STATES

Federation an American Idea. The Principle of Federation carried further in the United States than in England. Local Unions the Base of the Pyramid; the Federation the Apex. Federation Begins after the Civil War. The National Labor Union. Platform and Principles. Politics and Dissolution. Knights of Labor. "The Five Stars." Secrecy and Publicity. Methods of Organization. Rapid Growth. Principles. The Rise of the American Federation of Labor. Its Constitution and Government. National Organizers. Federal Unions. Contrast between the Knights and the Federation. Program of the Federation. National Conferences. Scope and Nature of Work. The Future of Labor Federations in the United States.

THE history of trade unionism in the United States has shown the development of national or international unions from local unions and the evolution of a trade union federation out of the various national organizations. The base of this huge pyramid is formed by tens of thousands of local unions, representing various trades and scattered throughout the cities, towns, and villages of the country. Exclusive of state branches, there are one hundred and twelve national and international unions, exercising jurisdiction over their locals, and, finally, there is a single federated body, to which the national, international, and other unions send delegates.

The federation of trade unions, as we understand and practice it, may be said to be an American idea, as the principle of associated effort among trade unions has been carried further in this country than in Great Britain or elsewhere. There is nothing in British trade unionism that may fairly be compared with the American Federation of Labor, although loose attempts at federation were made earlier in England than in the United States. As has been said, both local and national unions developed later in this country than in Great Britain. Attempts at federation were not made until even a more recent date. Until the year 1850 there was nothing in the United States corresponding to a national trade union, and until the close of the Civil War there existed no federation of national unions.

The first organization in the nature of a national federation was formed in the city of Baltimore on August 20, 1866. This organization, the National Labor Union, which was political in its purposes, left but small impress during its short life upon the labor movement. The organization held conventions every year from 1866 to 1870 inclusive, and in the year 1868 adopted a formal platform which was devoted chiefly to the money question. The organization claimed credit for the eight-hour law passed by Congress in 1868, but except this victory, which may or may not have been due to the National Labor Union, the organization effected but little good apart from the agitation which it carried on. The union suffered the fate of organizations which are solely political in their aims, and have no central idea or program and no definite industrial policy.

A federation of much greater scope and power, and of much more lasting influence was the Knights of Labor. This organization, which, in 1869, resulted from a series of conferences in Fairmount Park, Philadelphia, was formed through the efforts of Uriah S. Stephens and six other garment cutters. At first the organization was secret, and a ritual was enforced which resembled that of the Masonic Orders, Mr. Stephens himself being a Free Mason. A new member was initiated with the greatest possible solemnity, oaths were administered, and under no circumstances was the name of the organization, "The Noble Order of Knights of Labor," to be mentioned in writing or in speech.

The result of this secrecy was the creation of a considerable amount of unnecessary antagonism on the part of the community, especially of the clergy. When it was found that the five stars chalked in front of Independence Hall in Philadelphia could bring together several thousands of men from all parts of the city, the community became alarmed, and all manner of incredible stories regarding the doings of the order were circulated and gained currency and credence. The opposition of Protestant and Catholic clergy was so great that it was decided, in 1878, to make known the name of the order, and the oath of secrecy was made not binding with reference to the confessional. With the throwing aside of the veil of secrecy, the Noble Order rapidly increased in membership. In 1883 there were 52,000 members, in 1885, 110,000, and in 1886 the membership was reported to be 703,000, although the estimate by Mr. Powderley, the General Master Workman, was less than 600,000.

From 1886 on, the power and prestige of the Knights of Labor began to decline. The American Federation of Labor had already been formed, and the trade unionists were turning from the old to the new federation. In 1888, the convention of the Knights of Labor reported an apparent loss of 300,000 members, and in the following years membership continued to diminish. The order became involved in a number of unsuccessful strikes, as well as in other troubles, and by the beginning of the nineties was in debt and was obliged to remove from the headquarters in Philadelphia to a less pretentious building in Washington. Since that period, the Knights of Labor have steadily declined in membership and have also declined in influence, representing at the present time an entirely insignificant proportion of the organized workers of the country.

The passing of the Knights of Labor was due to the fact that the organization disregarded trade lines and sought to merge all unions into one. During the period of its ascendency, however, the order did much to infuse the workers with high ideals, and its efforts in behalf of unskilled workmen and of women workers are deserving of great praise. The order, however, was inevitably destined to failure, and it will probably not be many years before the principle upon which the Knights of Labor was founded will be given up, and its few remaining members will join national unions affiliated with the American Federation of Labor.

The American Federation of Labor was formed upon a basis entirely different from that of the Knights of Labor. Although the Knights of Labor was originally constituted as an organization of separate trades, being composed primarily of garment workers, the policy changed as a result of the accession of members from other trades, until the union came to be an organization of all workers in all trades. The central thought of the Knights of Labor was the identity of interest of all productive workers, and the organization was conceived in the sense of a union of all members of the working classes, irrespective of trades. The Knights practically set no standard of admission, and included not only the professional classes but many employers. Farmers were freely admitted as well as manufacturers, doctors, and men engaged in mercantile pursuits, the rules providing that any person over sixteen years of age might be admitted, if he was not engaged as an employer in the handling of intoxicating drinks, and if he was not a banker, a lawyer or a professional gambler. Representation was based not upon trades or industries but upon location, the organization being divided geographically or territorially. The fundamental theory of the union was that an injury to one was the concern of all, and it was argued therefore that all men engaged in productive labor, irrespective of the nature of their work, should be admitted into a single, unified organization.

The failure and subsequent decline of the Knights of Labor resulted from the fact that it thus disregarded trade lines and was too inclusive in its membership. No trade union federation can be permanently successful unless it respects the autonomy and self-government of the various unions of which it is composed. The miners of Illinois, Ohio, Arkansas, and West Virginia have practically identical interests, but in any given state or territory there is a wide divergence and dissimilarity in interest between its miners and its locomotive engineers, its carpenters and its garment workers, its glass blowers and its waiters, its doctors and its farmers, its manufacturers and its newspaper writers, even though these various people live and work in the same city or on the same street. It is almost impossible to organize all these various occupations into a single compact body, and it is utterly self-destructive to allow representatives of all these classes to decide upon the merits of a controversy between, let us say, the garment workers and their employers. The American Federation of Labor, therefore, was organized upon the basis of trade autonomy. While at first there appeared to be some disposition to organize territorially, the Federation disclaimed the intention of merging its several unions into a single, compact body, and restricted its efforts to affiliating or federating them. The American Federation of Labor is based upon the idea of the independence of the various unions composing it, and it permits each union to regulate its internal policy as it will. The government of the Knights of Labor was centralized and unified, the organization exercising the same sort of control over its constituent parts that the Republic of France exercises over its various departments, or the State of New York over its various counties. The American Federation of Labor, on the other hand, is based upon the idea of a loose federal government such as that of the United States, or, better still, such as existed in this country under the Articles of Confederation. The American Federation of Labor is really less a federation than a confederation, and it is owing to the looseness of its organization and the power which the confederated unions reserve that the organization has attained so preeminent and secure a position in the labor world.

The preliminary meeting to form the Federation of Labor was held on August 2, 1881. It was the result of a combination of the Knights of Industry and the Amalgamated Labor Union, which latter organization was composed of members who had seceded from the Knights of Labor. The organization, which was formed at Pittsburg, Pa., November 15, 1881, was originally styled The Federation of Organized Trades and Labor Unions of the United States of America and Canada, and claimed at the start the adherence of labor organizations with an estimated membership in excess of a quarter of a million. This membership, however, as well as the number of unions affiliated with the Federation, rapidly declined during the succeeding years, and in 1886 it was agreed to merge the weakened Federation with a number of independent trade unions which were then about to form a new federal organization. The result of this combination, which took place in the year 1886, was the present American Federation of Labor; but the organization dates its existence from the formation of the original Federation of Organized Trades and Labor Unions in 1881.

From the date of this amalgamation the American Federation of Labor grew once more in strength and power. By 1890 it again claimed a membership of 250,000, and since that time its members have gradually increased. During the last years in particular its growth has been exceedingly rapid. Exclusive of the membership of local central and state branches, the organization had, in 1898, 264,400 members, in 1899, 334,100, 1900, 515,400, in 1901, 742,600, and in 1902, 957,500. These figures, however, are very much below the actual membership of the organization, since they exclude all the members of 678 federal and local unions, and all the members of 425 central labor bodies, as well as those of 27 state branches. The method of calculation adopted, moreover, is based upon the receipts of the per capita tax, which invariably show a number much smaller than the actual membership. No member of a local union is counted as such unless he has paid up to the last month, and members temporarily in arrears, of which there are always many, are not counted. The locals in paying dues to the national union oftentimes fail to report upon their full membership, and the national organizations in turn, in paying their tax to the Federation, are also inclined to pay less rather than more than their just amount. Moreover, the estimate of members is based, not on the number at the close of the year, but on the average paid-up membership reported each month. It is probable that at the present time the actual number of *bona fide* members, ordinarily paying their dues, connected with national and local unions affiliated with the American Federation of Labor, and omitting all or any repetitions, is in excess of two millions.

The funds of the organization have also increased at a rapid rate. From 1881 to 1886 inclusive, the total annual receipts ranged between $125 and $690. From that time on the receipts quickly increased, reaching a total of almost $24,000 in 1890. No increase, however, took place after this point was reached until the year 1899, when the receipts amounted to $37,000. In 1900 the receipts increased to $71,000, in 1901, to $115,000, and in 1902 to $144,000. The income during the present year will be very much in excess of that of the preceding year.

It may be said that the American Federation is the sovereign organization in the trade union world and represents the apex of a pyramid, the foundation of which consists of one hundred and twelve national unions and many thousands of local organizations. The steady and, at times, rapid growth of the Federation has resulted from its adoption of a wise, conservative policy and from its adherence to the interests and purposes for which it was instituted. The object of the Federation has been, and still is, to foster and encourage the formation of local and national organizations, to secure the institution of local and state central bodies, to establish friendly feelings between the various national and international organizations, though without destroying their autonomy and self-government, and to encourage and promote the labor press of the country, as well as the use of union label goods.

The administrative government is carried on by the president and an executive council, consisting of the president, six vice-presidents, a secretary, and a treasurer, all of whom must be members of some local union. The legislative power is vested in a convention, in which the national organizations are represented in proportion to their membership, a national union having one vote for each one hundred members. The Federation also includes in its membership separate local unions not affiliated with national organizations, but wherever possible it encourages the merging of these locals into national unions. Such locals are under the direct control and supervision of the Federation, which stands to them in the same relation as a national union to its constituent locals, directly aids and advises them in the matter of strikes or lockouts, and provides for their support and maintenance.

The revenue of the Federation is derived from a per capita tax of $\frac{1}{2}$¢ per month, or 6¢ per year, for each member of the affiliated national organizations. The tax for local unions not affiliated with national unions is 10¢ per month, which is twenty times as great per member as is that of the national unions. It should be remembered, however, that these local unions are simply paying to the Federation dues which they would otherwise pay to the national organizations of which they formed a part. Consequently there is no injustice in these locals, which are directly chartered by the Federation, paying this amount to their parent body. A considerable portion of the money obtained from local unions is devoted to the support of their strikes and to other purposes connected with their welfare. The Federation further applies a large part of its income to the formation of new locals, which is, perhaps, one of its greatest and best works. At the present time it has upon its rolls twenty-five salaried organizers, who devote their entire time to forming new unions and to settling the strikes or controversies of such unions as are formed. It is also assisted by one thousand one hundred and seventy-eight volunteer organizers, who receive a small commission for each local union established by them.

The political activities of the Federation have been discussed in another place; but it may be proper in this connection to discuss the problem in its more general aspects. The Federation has done yeoman service in proposing legislation and in attempting to secure its enactment and enforcement. Up to the present time it has not as yet had sufficient power or control over its various constituent local, central, and state bodies to become as effective as it will doubtless be in the future; but, despite defect in its power, much progress has been made. The Federation is debarred by its constitution from directly affiliating itself with political parties. According to Article III, Section 8, "Party politics, whether they be Democratic, Republican, Socialistic, Populistic, Prohibition or any other, shall have no place in the conventions of the American Federation of Labor." Numerous attempts have been made by Socialist members of the Federation to secure control of the body and to commit it to the Socialist platform; but these efforts have been unsuccessful. The trade unions and the Federation of Labor itself stand for a number of reforms contained in the platform of the Socialist party, but the great majority of the members, whatever their political sympathies, refuse to permit the Federation to be committed to any definite political party, existing or to be formed.

While the American Federation of Labor has performed good and effective work in the past, it has not as yet been able to accomplish all that is possible, owing to the fact that it has not received the entire, enthusiastic, and ungrudging support of its affiliated unions. Its policy of respecting the autonomy and right of self-government of its constituent or affiliated bodies, should win for it the loyalty and staunch support of the unions composing it. The Federation cannot grow strong by itself, but can prosper only through the fidelity and cheerful adherence of the unions. Many phases of activity commending themselves to the trade union world can be carried out only through the American Federation of Labor; and if necessary the unions should even subordinate their own immediate interests to those of the great mass of the workmen of this country and should under all circumstances endeavor to unite for political and industrial purposes by strengthening the hands of the Federation. The political program of the American Federation of Labor should be carefully considered by the officers as well as the members of the various unions composing it, and the action of the majority of unionists, as determined by a vote in the Federation, should be binding upon all members of all affiliated trade unions. The state federations and the local central bodies should be more directly under the control, guidance, and supervision of the Federation, and the national organizations should enforce this control by refusing to permit their locals under penalty of fine, suspension, or expulsion, from belonging to any local, central, or state body which has been suspended by the Federation. The political program of the American Federation of Labor should be worked out in detail and should be sent to the various national, state, and local central bodies, in order that the proper influence may be brought to bear upon members of Congress or other legislators residing in the particular district. State and municipal legislation should remain in the hands of the state and local bodies, but no action should be taken that will conflict with the national aims and aspirations of American trade unions, as formulated by the American Federation of Labor.

The American Federation of Labor should also receive the hearty support of all national and local organizations in the matter of jurisdictional disputes. When a dispute cannot be settled by the parties to the controversy, arbitration by the American Federation of Labor should be compulsory, and punishment should be meted out to any organization which refuses to live up to the award. At the present time, the American Federation of Labor can not always enforce its decisions upon strong unions, owing to the fear that a number of large national organizations may possibly take sides with the union which has lost in the arbitration. If, however, the national unions would all remain loyal to the organization and would insist upon both parties to the controversy living up to the award, a vast amount of injury might be avoided, and both the Federation and the several trade unions themselves would be infinitely strengthened in public estimation. The prestige and power of labor unions of the United States will be enhanced by any increase in the prestige and power of the American Federation of Labor, and will be lessened by any diminution of the estimation in which the Federation is held by the American people.

One of the most deplorable facts in the present status of labor organization in the United States is the refusal of the railroad brotherhoods to throw in their lot with the other workingmen connected with the trade union movement. There was ample and sufficient reason for refusing to join the Knights of Labor, which claimed jurisdiction over the individual members and endeavored to fuse the laboring people of the country into one single, unified body. There is, however, no such objection to joining the American Federation of Labor. By doing so the railroad brotherhoods would not surrender any part of their autonomy or power of self-direction. They could not be drawn against their will into sympathetic strikes or boycotts, and they could not be prevented or hindered from engaging in any strikes or other movements in which they desired to engage. Their adherence to the Federation would mean increased strength to that body and increased power to themselves, and it would bring to an end the policy of aloofness and separatism which has not yet completely died out in the labor movement.

CHAPTER XLVII

THE WORK BEFORE THE UNIONS

What Trade Unionism has Done and What Remains to be Done. Further Organization. Improving the Quality of Unionists. Labor Lyceums and Labor Journals. Raising the Efficiency of Workers. Maintaining Agreements. Raising Wages, Lowering Hours, Improving Conditions, Preventing Accidents. Compensating for Accidents. Progress and Social Reform.

TRADE unionism has accomplished much in the past and has behind it an honorable record of good work well done, but the time is not yet, nor will it ever come, when the unions may cease their activity, as a warrior takes off his armor and say that the task is done. With new conditions new problems arise, and with each advance in trade unionism, the amount of work to be done increases and the duty resting upon trade unions becomes more imperative.

The first work which lies before American trade unions is further organization. The strength of trade unions increases much more rapidly than does membership. Six million trade unionists in the United States would not be twice, but four or five times as powerful as three millions. Each new adherent to the unions makes firmer and stronger the position of every other unionist in the country. Especially should the unions endeavor to organize the men and women in the unskilled trades, and by making sacrifices for the less fortunate members of the working class, intensify the feeling of solidarity and brotherhood among all wage earners.

There are many ways in which trade unions might extend the beneficent influence which they now exert upon workmen. To a larger extent than at present, they should become social and intellectual centres. The locals or aggregations of locals should have permanent club rooms, where men might go to spend an evening, and they should possess a few books, so that the leaders as well as the rank and file might be kept informed upon the subjects connected with their work or their position as workingmen. In every town one or more union assembly rooms should be found, where workingmen might secure the various trade union journals, and other labor papers, as well as books and magazines. In order that unionists might be enabled to obtain information upon many points and be afforded opportunity for mutual improvement, speakers from other trades or from other branches of the same union, as well as men entirely outside the movement should be invited to address local meetings.

One of the most effective methods of solidifying trade union sentiment is by the combination of various unions in the same locality for the maintenance of a common labor lyceum. Frequently, the local unions meet in the dingiest and worst kept of places, or often in bare rooms, back of saloons. These surroundings can not but have their effect upon the whole tone of the meeting, and the proximity of the place of meeting to a saloon renders intemperance easy and tends in many cases to drive away from the meetings the better class of unionists. Where unionists combine and share jointly in the expense of a common lyceum, with a sufficiently large assembly room and with suitable committee rooms, there is a greater chance that the meeting will be conducted in a sensible, orderly, and business-like manner and a better opportunity is afforded for men of various trades to meet and obtain from such intercourse a wider outlook, than is possible within a single local union.

The intellectual improvement of the trade unionist can also be furthered by means of the official journals of the unions and by other labor newspapers. The increase in the number and circulation, and the improvement in the quality, of trade union papers have been one of the most promising signs of progress in the past, and this improvement must continue in the future. The labor journals, besides giving the news and the gossip of the trade, already discuss matters of interest to labor and in the case of a number of journals afford the reader an opportunity to acquire a vast amount of technical information and thus promote his knowledge of his trade. These journals should never be run for profit or in the interest of advertisers, and the price should be kept so low and the quality so high that the circulation will be extended as far as possible.

Trade unionism should also aim constantly to elevate the moral standard of workingmen. The members of trade unions must respect themselves, if they desire their unions to be respected. A strong union is not in itself sufficient to gain the regard, esteem, and good wishes of the community, and a union cannot be strong unless it is founded on the unselfish adherence of self-respecting men. Trade unionism, moreover, must do all in its power to make the workmen efficient and valuable employees. The trade unionist should in the future, even more than to-day, be distinguishable from the non-unionist by the cheerfulness and efficiency of his work. A union card should be the badge of honest effort and good workmanship. The unions cannot hope permanently to advance the wages and welfare of their members, unless they continue increasingly to enhance the ability and industry of the individual workman.

Trade unions must further extend the sphere of the trade agreement and must do everything in their power to improve the relations between employers and employed. The unions can even afford occasionally to forego slight and immediate advantages, if by so doing they can secure the permanent esteem and confidence of the employers of the nation. Above all, trade agreements, whether national or local, general or particular, formal or informal, written or oral, should be adhered to religiously and scrupulously. The word of the union must be better than its bond, and the action of the individual unionist must, under penalty of expulsion, be in accordance with the spirit as well as the letter of agreements.

Trade unionists have still much to do towards securing proper wages, reduced hours of work, and reasonable conditions of labor. The wages of workmen should be considerably higher than they are at the present time, and for the ordinary unskilled workingman, residing in towns of usual size, and working eight hours a day, an irreducible minimum of six hundred dollars should be secured. The hours of labor should, in practically all industries, be reduced to eight, and the Saturday half-holiday should be everywhere secured. The unions should obtain the prevention of Sunday work except where it is a matter of absolute necessity or charity, and overtime should in all trades be so regulated that it will not become systematic. By means of trade union effort the conditions of the factories should be rendered far more sanitary than they are at present. Stringent laws should be enacted in securing the minute regulation of dangerous trades, and it should be taken out of the power of the individual workman to ruin his health, undermine his constitution, and poison and destroy his whole system by working under conditions annihilating to human kind. The factories themselves should be places where the workingmen of this country can find their work a source of pleasure instead of a wearisome round of tasks under degrading and disgusting conditions.

The trade unions should take the child off the street, out of the breaker, the mill, and the factory and put him to school; they should foresee and guard against every evasion of the laws regulating the employment of children. The abomination of the Southern cotton and tobacco factories should be wiped out entirely. The woman who toils should be protected in her capacity as bread winner; she should toil only under proper conditions, and the trade unions should persist in their efforts to improve conditions of women workers, upon whom so much of the burden of our factory life falls. Trade unions should protect the health and save the life and limb of the workers. They should enforce conditions which will guarantee the security of the men, women, and children at work and diminish the number of preventable accidents. Moreover, the unions should endeavor to obtain laws which will compensate workmen for accidents which cannot be prevented, so that men killed in the performance of their duties shall not leave widows and orphans dependent upon the charity of the community.

The protection of the widows and orphans of workingmen killed in the performance of their duties, is of grave importance to the community, but the right to such protection has not been fully recognized or adequately conceded. This is especially true in the United States. In this country, the economic development has been without a parallel in the history of all times and all peoples. The wheels of progress have revolved at an ever accelerating speed, and things have been accomplished with an instantaneous suddenness, which reminds one of the miraculous events of the "Arabian Nights." The country has grown from a few millions of farmers and fishermen living near the margin of existence to a great, wealthy nation of eighty millions. Machine has supplanted tool, improvement followed improvement, new methods displaced old, until the country has become almost choked with its prosperity and embarrassed with its riches.

In the meanwhile, however, we have been so dazzled by our own achievements that we have failed to perceive the other side of the shield. For this vast prosperity we have paid a large price. We have been carried along upon a wave of materialism and have too largely made the dollar the unit of success, both personal and national. We would judge everything upon the basis of cheapness, upon our ability, in other words, to compete for foreign markets. In no other country has life been so lightly regarded, has the workingman been so mercilessly exposed to violent death or to grievous injury. In no other country is there less organized compensation for those who are killed or maimed, for those who are sacrificed and slaughtered that others may grow rich. The country which spent billions of dollars for the pensioning of its soldiers, which at another time wiped out at once other billions of dollars of human property, has disregarded almost utterly the claims of the men, women, and children who have died that our industrial supremacy might be maintained. In no other country are the laws against the exploitation of women and children so lax, so absurdly inadequate, so cruelly ineffective as in the United States. In no country does the workingman age so rapidly, nowhere is he cast aside with so light a heart and with so little compassion. Trade unionism should not put a brake upon the progress of the community, but should endeavor to render it more rapid. At the same time its mission should be to mitigate the evils which have flown from the unregulated condition of industry and the indiscriminate and heedless pursuit of purely materialistic aims.

CHAPTER XLVIII

THE IDEALS OF ORGANIZED LABOR

The Ideals of Trade Unionism. The Ideals of Anti-Unionists. Feudal Lords and "Loyalty." The Father of his Workmen. Paternalism *versus* Fraternalism. The Ideal of Free Collective Contract. The Ideal of Better Conditions and Better Men. Trade Unionism and "Wage Slavery." Trade Unionism and the Wage Contract. Contentment *versus* Progress. What Unionism Stands for.

THE average man, whether or not he belong to a labor organization, has at the bottom of his nature a certain more or less distinct aspiration for a more or less exalted thing. There can be no combination, association, or union of men without common ideals; for without ideals there is lacking the internal bond that carries men along despite the temptation to pursue selfish aims. No one can understand trade unionism unless he has some conception of its fundamental ideals.

It will be easier to comprehend these ideals of trade unionism if we consider for a moment the ideals of men opposed to it. The conception of many people, although they are fewer now than a generation or two ago, is that the employer is a man of a different class, a different race, one may almost say, a different species from his workmen. In the eyes of these people the ideal state of affairs is one in which the beneficent employer is surrounded and served by throngs of faithful servants called wage earners, loyal to his interests, protected by him, and grateful for the bounties which he in his goodness and at his sole discretion bestows upon them. Employers frequently speak as though two or three dollars a day were enough for a workingman, although they themselves may be spending twenty or fifty or a hundred dollars a day. These employers talk of the "loyalty" of some of their men and of the "disloyalty" of others, thus assuming that the wage earner is bound to his employer by ties of personal allegiance, instead of by a contractual relation, supposedly based upon the interest of both parties. There is something feudal in the manner in which the great lords of industry occasionally speak of disloyal employees on strike. They seem to believe that they possess what is almost a property right in the services of the men engaged by them. They are more incensed at a competitor who takes away from them the services of a valued employee by offering him a higher wage, than is the striker at the competition of a non-union man. They speak as though they were conferring a benefit upon a man by letting him work for them, but they would consider the world topsy-turvy if the workman should for a moment assert that, in accepting work, he was conferring an even greater advantage upon them.

This feudal theory of a high-born or high-placed employer "giving work" to his loyal employees finds its best expression in the attitude of the employers who seek to be fathers to their workmen. Many well-meaning and philanthropic employers have done admirable service in providing their employees with reasonable or sometimes excellent accommodations, with comforts, with small privileges, with opportunities to improve their minds, and with many other advantages. Trade unionists, whatever their attitude toward employers in general, must hail with pleasure any manifestation of this spirit or any act of generosity or justice upon the part of well-meaning employers. The ideal of trade unionism, however, is not a state of affairs in which the employer is a father to his workmen. The time has gone by for any wholesale reversion to this plan. Every day the employer is being separated further and further from his workmen, and personal supervision and personal interest in the welfare of employees are becoming less possible. As soon as the generous employer capitalizes his establishment or sells out to the trust, the day of favors and benefits is practically over. While trade unionists do not oppose, but actually favor, such welfare work, if not intended to undermine the union and destroy the independence of the workers, they fail to find in it even a temporary solution of the labor problem. It would not be possible to re-introduce the paternalism of the past, and, even if possible, it would not be desirable, since the ability to confer favors brings with it also the opportunity to vent spite or to discriminate.

Trade unionism does not stand for paternalism of the employer, but for a broad, all-inclusive, self-forgetting fraternalism of all workers. It does not stand for the "loyalty" of the worker to his employer, but for a fair reciprocal contract between these two parties. It does not stand for the recognition of a difference in species between employer and workman, or for a spirit of blind, silent content on the part of the employee, but it insists upon the substantial equality of all men and upon the right of the workers to secure all that they can by fair and reasonable methods. Finally, it does not accept the doctrine of the employer who in giving work to a man assumes that he is conferring a benefit upon him, any more than it stands for the opposite doctrine, that the acceptance of work confers a favor upon the employer. The ideal of trade unionism is not that of a superior class conferring favors upon an inferior, not one of "loyalty" on the one side and generosity upon the other, but the ideal of two separate, strong, self-respecting and mutually respecting parties, freely contracting with each other, and with no limitation upon this right of perfect and absolute freedom of contract, save that which a community in its wisdom may determine to be necessary for its own protection.

In the ideals of trade unionism, the freedom of contract between associated workmen and associated employers, equal in position and in opportunity and power to make agreements, is but a means or a step to a higher and better ideal. The true and final ideal of trade unionism is the elevation and the material and moral improvement of the workingman. Trade unionism is essentially optimistic. It realizes the progress which has been made and bases its hope of future advance upon past improvement. Trade unionists do not adopt the logic of their opponents, that, because conditions are better than formerly, the workingmen should be satisfied, but consider the progress already made as the best and fullest justification for continued efforts to improve conditions. Neither does trade unionism accept the theory of a certain section of socialists, who believe that conditions must grow worse before they can grow better. If conditions were first to grow worse, the power of the workingmen to better themselves would ultimately decrease, and they would be so depressed and degraded that they could not utilize or improve any concessions made to them. The theory of the trade unionist is that things must improve a little in order to improve a great deal, and that every advance in the condition of the workingmen is an earnest of still further advance in the future.

Trade unionism is not based upon a necessary opposition to the so-called "wage slavery" of the present time. By the phrase "wage slavery" is usually meant a condition of practical enslavement, brought about, not by legal, but by economic subjection, a slavery enforced, not by the lash, but by pangs of hunger. The trade unionist recognizes that in certain sections of the country and in certain industries, the wage earners, especially women and children, are in a condition so debased and degraded, and are so subject to oppression and exploitation, that it practically amounts to slavery. Where such wage slavery exists, however, trade unionism is opposed to the slavery as such, and not to the wages as such. Trade unionism is not irrevocably committed to the maintenance of the wage system, nor is it irrevocably committed to its abolition. It demands the constant improvement of the condition of the workingmen, if possible, by the maintenance of the present wage system, if not possible, by its ultimate abolition.

The history of trade unionism in the past seems to indicate that by the aid of the State and by the concerted efforts of workingmen, a vast and wide-spread amelioration of their condition can take place under the present system of wages. No limit, however, should be set to the aspirations of the workingmen, nor to the demands for higher wages and better conditions of work which they may ultimately make. At any given moment in the history of society, there is a limit set to the remuneration of labor by the amount of its production and by other causes. But with the gradual growth in the productivity of society, there should be a gradual, even a rapid, increase in the rate of wages. The skilled workingmen of to-day earn wages undreamed of fifty years ago, and, doubtless, fifty years hence they will earn wages in comparison with which the present rate of remuneration is a beggarly pittance. The existence of the wage system does not at the present time appear to preclude the possibility of a very high rate of remuneration to the workingman. Therefore, trade unionists should endeavor to insure a more equitable distribution of the products of industry, so that wages may still continue to rise. The fact that the remuneration of the most highly trained and successful leaders of industry is frequently paid in the form of salary or wages, would indicate that there is no necessary connection between the payment of the workingmen in the form of a weekly or monthly stipend and a low rate of remuneration or a low standard of life. Trade unionism, however, is not absolutely bound up with the existence or maintenance of the wage system, and if it were ultimately to be shown that the system is incompatible with a high standard of living and a full development of the capabilities of the American workingman, the hosts of organized labor would unite in an effort to secure its abolition.

The advance in the material condition of the American workingman, important as it is, is still not so essential as the absolutely vital ideal of trade unionism—the moral and intellectual improvement of the worker. The result of the development of modern industry has been to throw ever larger and larger classes of the community upon the necessity of earning wages, and a greater percentage of the men and women of this country now depend upon wages than at any previous time. The migration from country to city, from farm to factory, increases with each year the proportion of wage earners, and it is not improbable that at some future date a large proportion of the men engaged in tilling the soil will be actually, if not legally, in a position resembling that of the wage earners of the cities. It thus becomes imperative, if the American democracy is to endure, that the moral and intellectual improvement of these masses of wage earners should be raised to the highest possible level. Much work has been done in this direction by means of the school system of the country, by means of our cheap and popular newspapers, by means of the admirable postal system of the United States, and by means, lastly, of the trade union movement. The ideal of trade unionism is to become an ever more important element in the life of the wage earner, and by means of its activity continually to raise the standard of its members. This has already been done to a considerable extent, but in the future, progress will be more rapid. To secure this advance, there must be an increase in the material prosperity of the workingmen. High thinking is not incompatible with plain living; but it is impossible, when men work for excessively long hours, for a pittance scarcely sufficient to maintain their families, and with the constant fear of dismissal and penury staring them in the face, that they develop mentally or morally. When every workingman is assured of his ability to earn fair wages under fair living conditions and is guaranteed against the possibility of undeserved indigence, he will be able vastly to improve his intellectual and moral being.

To realize these ideals, trade unionism builds upon the foundation of a hopeful discontent. A considerable advance in wages or a considerable reduction in the hours of labor may be no boon if the extra wages and the extra leisure can not be employed to the profit and sane pleasure of the workingman, and the wage earner cannot and should not secure these extra wages or this extra leisure until he *wants them,* and, therefore, until he *demands them.* Our public schools and our newspapers endeavor constantly to stimulate the wants of the people, and, as a consequence, they require more wages and more leisure in which to spend them. I do not mean that this progress in the wants and needs of the people should keep too far in advance of the possibility of satisfying them, or that the workingmen should demand grand pianos, Turkish rugs, or extra dry champagne. Wage earners, however, should constantly seek to widen and broaden their desires for material, intellectual, and artistic satisfactions, and thus make life worth living in the highest sense of the phrase.

Trade unionism stands for liberty, equality, and fraternity; it stands for the liberty of workingmen to arrange their own lives and to contract jointly for the manner in which they shall be spent in mine or factory; it stands for equality, not of wealth, but of opportunity, and it stands for fraternity, complete and absolute.

CHAPTER XLIX

ORGANIZED LABOR AND PUBLIC OPINION

Necessity for Securing Public Favor. Self-help and the Help of the Public. Justice and Public Opinion. The American People in Sympathy. Power of Public Opinion. Necessity of Educating the Public. Education and Agitation. How Public Opinion has veered towards Trade Unionism. The Popular Conception of Trade Unionism in the Past and in the Present.

THE growth of trade unionism in popular favor is one of the most promising indications of the present time. It is of vital importance to unionism that it secure the approbation of the public, and its actions should be guided by the desire to retain and augment this favor through a just and reasonable attitude toward all classes.

No one can help the workingman unless he helps himself. If the wage earners of this country did not associate themselves into trade unions, did not defend their own rights, and did not take a stand against aggression and oppression, it is improbable that other classes in society would offer to assist them. Indeed, if American workingmen were so supine, so nerveless, so lacking in courage and initiative as not to unite for purposes of defense and justifiable offense, they would not *deserve* intercession or assistance. The success of the workmen, therefore, and the maintenance of their standards of living and liberty must depend primarily upon their own efforts and upon their faithful allegiance to their labor organizations.

In the conduct of trade unions, however, it is essential that they do what is right in the eyes of the community. There are times when the American workingman can exploit the employer, just as there are times and occasions when the employer can exploit the workingman. In the long run, however, such exploitation of employers or such unfairness on the part of workingmen is bound to alienate public sympathy and to injure the cause. A union may secure a temporary advantage by a breach of contract, but if, as is inevitable, it thereby destroys public sympathy, the temporary gain is offset by a permanent loss. Breaches of contract, unjustifiable restrictions upon output, or needless and wanton jurisdictional contests will affect the public unfavorably and will completely alienate its sympathies.

Trade unions are strong, but they are neither invincible nor omnipotent; and it is well that they are not so, for the wisdom they have shown has been largely due to the ever-present necessity of appealing to the public for sympathy and support. Far-sighted leaders, as well as the great mass of intelligent unionists, have constantly borne in mind the vital importance of squaring trade union action with the policy and purposes of the public; and this view of the obligations and responsibilities of trade unions to the public should ever be firmly impressed upon any members who might tend to forget their duty to the community. In the long run, the success or failure of trade unions will depend upon the intelligent judgment of the American people. That judgment now points to an unqualified success for the trade union movement. The public is in sympathy with the chief demands of the organizations, and it desires for the workingmen of this country increased wages, shortened hours, protection of women and children, proper sanitary conditions, education, technical and general, and everything which makes for the welfare of workingmen, organized and unorganized. But upon each problem as it arises, upon each controversy or strike, the public reserves its opinion and passes judgment upon the particular point at issue.

The force of public opinion may be exerted in different directions. If adverse to the unions, as it formerly was and as, in many countries, it still is, it may cause the passage of laws restricting their activity and hampering them in many ways. The law is an instrument which may be used with great effect, either to the advantage or the disadvantage of trade unions, either for the protection or the destruction of the workingmen. In the course of strikes, moreover, the public may throw the weight of its active sympathy upon one side or the other, and by contributing to, or withholding from, the strike fund, may seriously affect the result. In many instances, also, the force of public opinion, acting directly through the newspapers and other channels of publicity, has forced one or the other side to submit, or has compelled both to reconcile their differences.

One of the chief purposes of trade unionism is to appeal constantly, directly, and openly to the general public. The mission of the union, frankly stated, is to agitate. The labor leader is and should be an "agitator" and an educator. The unions of this country must educate their members, as well as unorganized workingmen, to a proper realization of their ideals and a proper method of securing them; and they must always make to the American people temperate statements of those demands, and must educate the people to a point where they will endorse them. Through peaceable and progressive agitation and education, trade unions have already accomplished wonders. Workingmen have learned to go into a strike and come out of it without violence; they have learned to hold together through thick and thin, to make sacrifices, to obey orders, to vote on their own affairs, to stand shoulder to shoulder and to abide the issue of an industrial conflict in peace and patience. Workingmen have also learned to pay their contributions regularly, to make contracts and stand by them, to be fair and reasonable in their attitude toward employers and toward non-union men, to be temperate in their statements and equally temperate in their demands. They have learned, as well, through the contact afforded by organization, the lesson of respect for the wishes of other members and have acquired a willingness to subordinate themselves for the good of the whole. In the same way the public has been educated to a knowledge of the purposes of organized labor and to an appreciation of the value of organization. There was a time in the history of this country when labor organizations were proscribed and punished by law, when the right to strike was not fully conceded. There was a time, not very remote, when trade unionists were regarded as dangerous revolutionaries, when the peaceable efforts of unions were looked upon as desperate attempts of fanatics violently to overthrow all government. Only two generations ago the unions were denounced as enemies to religion and morals, and during even the last fifty years the stigma of belonging to a labor union has only slowly been changed into an honor. The public, however, has now been educated by the unions to a recognition of the essential merits of organization and to an appreciation of the wisdom and temperance of many leaders, as well as of the rank and file, although much still remains to be done to bring to the public a realizing sense of its full duty toward labor organizations.

The change in the attitude of public opinion toward trade unionism is traceable in large measure to a fundamental revolution in the thoughts of the people with regard to the rights and privileges of workingmen, and to a change in the current theories concerning the distribution of wealth. In the eighteenth and in preceding centuries it was commonly held that low wages were good, and high wages bad, for society. When wages were high, the workingman, it was believed, would become lazy and would not work; when wages were low, he would be obliged to work continuously in order to sustain life. Society would thus progress better when wages were low and the price of food, high. As long as society fixed its eyes upon profits and not upon wages, as long as it considered wages as a cost which it had to pay, like the cost of an army or a navy, low wages continued to be held good and any organization or union tending to improve wages, bad.

In the half century from 1817 to about 1867, the theoretical opposition to trade unionism took a different form. During this period it was generally assumed that wages could not rise, since there was only a certain fund or amount of wages to be given out at any particular time, and if some workman received more, other workmen would have to content themselves with less. It was believed that if a union temporarily raised wages, other workmen would seek employment in the trade, and wages would again fall to the former level, while, if by any means, all workmen secured a temporary advance in wages, the birth rate would rise and the increase in population would again reduce wages. According to this theory, trade unionism was foolish, if not harmful, and was, therefore, undeserving of the support of wise and intelligent people.

It happened in this instance, however, as it has happened many times before and since, that the wise men were wrong and the "foolish" men right. The healthy common sense of the unionist, who saw the advances of wages and the improved conditions and did not fear the ghosts in the economist's closet, has been completely vindicated by subsequent events. The men who, instead of taking the lead in the movement for reform, remained in their studies and proved by all the laws of logic that reform was impossible, have at last recognized that the trade unionists were right. The theory of limiting wages to a certain pre-determined part of a preëxisting fund, has been overthrown and has finally been relegated to the lumber room of false theories, while the trade unionists, who builded even better than they knew, are now acknowledged to have been in advance of the wise men of their time. During the last forty years, therefore, organizations of labor have constanty grown in popular esteem. The unionists have worked patiently, while others predicted their failure. They have paid dues, which, it was asserted, was an unprofitable expenditure of wealth; they have declared strikes, a thing denounced by employers, economists, and ecclesiastics, as both useless and immoral; they have slowly worked out their salvation and have justified their existence by what they have accomplished.

Even at the present time, though to a less extent, trade unionism meets with the same sort of objections as it encountered fifty or seventy-five years ago. Just as it has been compelled to fight for each petty increase in wages and each slight reduction in hours, recording a small gain here and a small gain there, advancing gradually like the waters of a slowly rising flood; so it has been compelled to contest each inch of ground and to struggle continually, patiently, and painfully toward the distant goal of public favor. Moreover, just as the material advance of trade unionism is marked by occasional setbacks, so the gradual clarifying of public opinion is retarded by occasional recessions. Even now organized labor must meet with opposing ideals held by society, ideals born of past conditions and destined to disappear, abstract ideals, like those of the wage-fund and the immutable law of supply and demand, independent of human action. Some of these ideals, such as the uncontrolled right of a man to work, the right of a man to run his own business, the right of a man to do what he will with his own, while still held firmly and absolutely by good and sincere men, who therefore oppose trade unionism, are slowly dissolving and disintegrating, and before long will cease to exist, except in the minds of men who are *in* their generation, but not *of* it.

Just as trade unionism is not one and indivisible, so public opinion is not one and indivisible. There are many separate and distinct eddies in the great stream of public opinion, and there are many who fail to realize the direction in which the main current is flowing. Moreover, public opinion is not infallible, just as trade unionism is not infallible. There are times and occasions, especially in periods of great stress and excitement, when the voice of the people ceases to be the voice of God. Generally, the opinion of the public, though broad and sweeping, is in the main just and fair and reasonable. Trade unionism should adopt the policy, and subscribe to the principle, of attempting to follow the best and most enlightened public opinion of the day. I do not mean that trade unionists should surrender any of the fundamental doctrines or ideals of organized labor to what may be but a passing whim of the public, but broadly speaking, the organized workingmen of the country cannot and should not hope for any permanent success unless their actions are in accord with the ideals of the American people. There is more than mere policy in this obedience to the popular will. The wage earners of the country, like the manufacturers, the farmers, the professional classes, the small tradesmen, are all a part of society, and in the long run, no one of these classes can succeed unless it has the support, approval, and sanction of the whole community. The welfare of society is even more important than the welfare of organized workmen, and the welfare of each is bound up in the welfare of the other. Trade unionism will prosper as it respects the will of the people, and with its prosperity will come a clearer recognition on the part of the great, humane public of the justice of its ideals and the wisdom of its policy.

CHAPTER L

TRADE UNIONISM AND THE AMERICAN DEMOCRACY

King Log and King Stork. The Democracy of the Unions. The Local President. Walking Delegates and Business Agents. Democracy of National Unions. Democracy and Efficiency. The Danger of Bossism. The Duty to Vote.

DURING the anthracite coal strike of 1902, a number of newspapers upbraided me for headlong, reckless conduct, and spoke as though I personally had called out one hundred and fifty thousand men. From a perusal of these journals, one would imagine that I, unaided, or, at best, assisted by a few officials, had compelled this army against its will to desist from work.

The same charge is made in a scarcely less ridiculous form against all trade unions and their officials. The critics of labor organizations pose as kind friends seeking to place their protecting cloak about the poor union workman, oppressed by a cruel and merciless organization. It is asserted that the employees are compelled to strike against their will, and to give up their work and the bread of their wives and children at the whim of an irresponsible walking delegate. The tyranny of the employer, it is claimed, is as nothing to the tyranny of the union official over the defenseless worker enmeshed in the trade organization. It is the story of King Log and King Stork, a transition from the frying pan into the fire.

One must have lived and worked in a trade union atmosphere fully to realize how baseless are these statements, which imply a careless or a wilful ignorance of the fundamental principles of trade union life. The labor union in the United States, as elsewhere, rests upon the firm basis of democracy. It secures its power from the ungrudging consent of the governed, and its spirit is that of our political constitutions—the spirit of a broad democracy. The American ideal of a government of the people, by the people, and for the people, is assured and secured in the trade union world. In fact the trade union government is even more democratic than the political organization of our cities and towns, of the states, or of the nation. There is probably no organization within the boundaries of the United States which is more essentially and entirely democratic than the American trade union.

The foundation stone of the trade union structure is the local union. The government of these local bodies is extremely democratic. The essence of democratic government is equality; and socially, industrially, and politically, the members of local unions are approximately equal. As a general rule, all who attend the weekly, fortnightly, or monthly meetings of the unions are men working at their trade, men who have enjoyed about equal educational opportunities and are obtaining approximately equal wages. The president of such a local union is a man who also works at his trade and who devotes his time gratuitously to the welfare of the organization; and the democratic temper of the union is manifested in the manner in which it restricts the power of even this trusted official. Notwithstanding the fact that the members of the union are usually able to know all the principal facts in connection with the work of each of their local officers, every precaution is taken to prevent any abuse or excess of power. Thus, most of the committees, even those of the slightest importance, are selected by members of the union, rather than by the local president, and the principle of rotation in office is commonly in force, the term of office being often not greater than six months or one year.

The same is true, as a general rule, of the walking delegate, or, as he is more properly called, the business agent. The walking delegate has been more maligned than any other official in industrial life. He was called the walking delegate, not because he preferred walking to working, but because in the olden days he had not enough money to pay cab or 'bus fare and was obliged to walk instead of ride. The business agent is usually a man whose duties are so manifold that he cannot work at his trade. He it is who meets with the employer and attempts to secure redress of grievances or maintenance of rules; who collects dues from members of the union; secures new adherents, and obtains work for the unemployed. The great majority of men of this sort are hard-working and perfectly honest and disinterested, although there are exceptions, as there are among bankers or lawyers. Where a business agent has the right to order a strike and where his decision is practically ultimate and final, the door is opened to bribery and corruption; but even here the essentially democratic nature of the union is shown by the fact that the business agent with unusual powers is ordinarily chosen for a short term, and the inefficient or dishonest are gradually weeded out.

The local unions are thus as democratic as it is possible to make any body of men. There is no restriction put upon the voting power of any union man or woman, and in some unions the principle goes so far as to permit boys to have a vote or, at least, half a vote. Even in these local meetings the man of ability naturally rises to the top and exerts a dominating influence, and no one is hindered from making his mark. The American principle of majority rule is applied rigorously, and upon the whole the action of the local is usually a clear and obvious expression of the will of the majority. The national unions are almost equally democratic, although the arrangements are not so simple. It is not possible for all of the members of an organization like the Railway Conductors or the United Mine Workers to get together and to vote *viva voce* for any measure; but the attempt is made to attain the nearest possible approach to this. The unions have adopted the principle of representation which has been worked out by the political parties. The national conventions of the unions, consisting of delegates from the locals, correspond to the legislatures of New York, Massachusetts, or any other American state, or to the House of Representatives of the United States. The various local bodies send their delegates or representatives to the conventions, either with or without instructions, and the vote of the conventions is thus the vote of the various locals. The representation of the locals is sometimes in direct proportion to the membership, the smaller locals have a larger representation than their members would secure to them. In the conventions, the majority rules, and the vote of the convention represents more nearly the opinion of all the members of the union than does the vote of a primary, or a ballot for the election of governor or president. The union, moreover, has gone even further in an approach to pure democracy than have the states of the American nation. The conventions, which are held in most unions annually, and in others every second, third, fourth, or fifth year, are relatively losing importance, and much of the work there is now done by direct vote of all the members of the union, or, in other words, by the referendum. In many unions, no constitutional amendment can be adopted without a referendum vote, and many of the organizations elect their officers by referendum. This election or legislation by popular vote does away with much of the danger of machine control and insures a clear expression of the popular will. Legislation may be proposed and nominations made by a local or a number of locals without the intermediation of representatives in convention. In some unions much of the discussion and voting is done by postal card or letter, and numerous devices have been hit upon to combine the greatest amount of freedom of action on the part of officers with the highest development of the democratic principle.

No one who has not been an officer of a union can appreciate the extent to which the vast body of men, nominally under his control and direction, makes its wants felt. In every crisis men forge to the front and interpret the wishes and feelings of their fellow-men, but in the trade union, as in few organizations in society, the real movement is that of the great mass, and the decision upon important subjects is that of the members themselves. It is well that this is so. In this rude democracy, in this deep and abiding jealousy of officials and of insignia of rank or of office, is found the most hopeful sign for the future of trade unions.

It is quite probable that at the time of the miners' convention preceding the anthracite strike of 1902 a considerable majority of the delegates elected to declare in favor of or against a strike, were of the opinion—which I myself held—that in view of the hardships which the strike would inflict upon the miners and upon the country at large, it would be better for us to endure our evils for a time, and, if they still remained unredressed, to strike at a later period. It is a sign, however, of the democracy of trade unionism that the president of the organization, the national and district officials, and even the representatives in the convention, were powerless to refuse to obey the clear mandate of the majority of workmen as expressed by a series of votes in the various locals. The mineworkers of the whole region, English, Irish, German, Welsh, Scotch, Poles, Russians, Hungarians, Lithuanians, and members of a dozen nationalities. had voted upon this question, each man registering his will, each man having a vote irrespective of race or language; and when this vote was finally counted and crystallized into instructions to the delegates, there was no power within the union to prevent its taking effect.

In some cases the effect of these extremely democratic principles is to detract from the strength of the action of the union and to bestow power upon weak and irresponsible men; but on the whole the power of the union over its officials is exerted for good, and acts as a check against the grosser forms of dishonesty and incapacity. A trade union leader notoriously corrupt cannot maintain his position as easily as in the political world. Even the majority of the inhabitants of a city may be held in subjection by a well-organized but corrupt minority; but in a union the disaffection of even a minority will cause a split which will immeasurably weaken the organization and loosen the hold of the officers. The democratic spirit of the organization is strengthened by the substantial equality of all its members and by the ability of a minority to secede from the union if conditions become unbearable. The controlling powers in a state can generally exercise through taxation and the law compulsion over all persons in the state, but even a majority in a union would find it difficult to exert compulsion upon a strong, determined, and disaffected minority. The government of a trade union, therefore, must constantly receive the sanction of practically all of its members. The resulting democracy is occasionally a hindrance to rapid and effective action on the part of the officers, but it precludes likewise the possibility of a minority of men or of a small group of officials holding and keeping out of work or at work a majority of the members of an organization.

The democratic spirit of the trade union, while showing itself most clearly in the local unions, is found in every part of the organization up to the office of president. The majority of officials of trade unions receive salaries which are much smaller than those paid for like abilities in the business world, and the method of life of many trade union leaders is not fundamentally different from that of their constituents in the mine and at the forge and bench. No union official can prevent or seek to prevent free access to his person by any member of the union, and an official of a union, even if he had the means, would not maintain a standard of living which would tend to separate him in thought and feeling from the men over whom he is placed. In the political world the old-time democratic simplicity has largely worn away, and the President of the United States or the Governor of a state can no longer maintain the simple manners of the days of Jefferson. The president of a labor organization, however, even though the members of his union—with their families—number a million, must combine with an executive ability, which will enable him to perform the thousand and one duties of his office, the willingness to give a respectful hearing at all times to any individual unionist.

There exists in the trade union world, as in the political world, though by no means to the same extent, a certain danger of the building up of inside rings and the creation of a boss system. This danger is not immediate or imminent, but even as a remote possibility, it merits the thoughtful consideration of unionists. At the present time our political system is threatened by the existence of rings securing their power by means of preying upon, or being bribed by, large corporations, and receiving contracts, favors, or direct gifts from the money of the city or state. It is essential to the democratic spirit and continued prosperity of labor organizations that no such state of affairs be permitted in the trade union world. There are many reasons why the danger is much smaller than in the political field. In the first place, there is as a rule no means of coercing or taxing an unwilling majority of unionists. Even a respectable minority of workingmen could, by secession from a boss-ridden union, utterly destroy it, and thus end the power of an unscrupulous dictator. A trade union "boss," moreover, would not have the power which a political boss has, of using the entire machinery of a state for enforcing his demands. The essential equality of the members of a trade union, and, further, the comparative absence of conflicting desires and ideals, would not be favorable to the tyranny of a boss, which usually represents the subjection of certain classes in society to the rule and dictation of others.

Notwithstanding the remote possibility of bossism in the trade union movement, however, no effort should be neglected to make the assurance of perfect freedom, democracy, and autonomy within the union doubly sure. By this I do not mean that power should not be vested in the hands of a few men, since this is necessary to energetic and successful action, especially in times of crises or emergencies; but the machinery of the union should be of such a nature that the fullest publicity may be given to the acts of its officers, or at all events such acts should be subject to review by officials independently elected. Wherever possible, matters of great moment and importance—unless they involve special and technical knowledge—should be referred to the vote of the members. The referendum should be extended as far as practicable, in order to allow a constant expression of the will of each individual member. Finally and above all, every individual member of every trade union should on every possible occasion register his vote. The prosperity and good government of all institutions depend upon the intelligent interest of all members. The non-attendance of union members at trade union elections is as dangerous as the non-attendance of qualified voters at the polls, or at the primaries of the political parties.

CHAPTER LI

"THE UNIVERSAL VITAL PROBLEM OF THE WORLD"

An Army of Unionists. What Unionism has Done. The Future of Trade Unionism. Labor Expensive and Effective. The Wage Earner of Tomorrow. Pleasure in Work. The Treatment of the Incapables. Trade Unionism a Phase of the Organization of Labor. The Universal Vital Problem of the World.

THERE are at present from two and a half to three million trade unionists in the United States. These men, though divided according to trades or industries, are united by more or less common ideals and aspirations and are struggling towards a common goal. Back of these unionists are millions of other workingmen more or less in sympathy with the unionists, and back of these is the vast working population of the United States.

The great new fact of American labor is its organization. The workingman has risen from his knees and now stands upon his feet; he has joined with his fellow-workmen, and has obtained, as a right and not as a privilege, higher wages, shorter hours, and better conditions of life and labor. Finally, through the trade agreement, he has secured the right to be consulted as to the conditions under which his work shall be carried on. The union has meant an improvement in the manner of life of the workman and a revolution in industry from autocratic to democratic government.

In the future, the union movement will mean even more than at present. Trade unionism in the United States is still in its infancy; American labor is still far from being organized. In the future, as in the past, labor organized will exert itself in making labor expensive and efficient. The progress of society depends upon this development. It is only where labor is dear and the product of labor cheap that a high state of civilization is possible. If the trade union movement is permanently successful, it will be so only by compelling the constant invention of improved means and methods of production and the continual saving of labor. Labor must become a thing too valuable to be wasted, and as society advances wages will increase, hours of work still further decrease, and the most elaborate machinery will be introduced to save labor. Trade unionism by making labor valuable and expensive will compel employers to save it wherever possible and will make the competition among workmen one of efficiency and not of cheapness.

There is no limit to the possibility of advance in this direction. With every year, the productive power of society will advance, and the remuneration of the workman will increase. Wages will rise not through the expropriation of the capitalist but through the increase in production. By political action, the trade unions will be able to equalize the burdens and benefits of government and will be able to lessen the power of monopoly to extort an unfair share of the products of labor. The remuneration of labor will increase relatively to the reward of capital, and, absolutely, it will increase enormously. Just how the workingman will eventually come into his own is a question which trade unionists do not feel called upon to answer. The first steps in this progress are clear, but the latter part of the journey is veiled in the obscurity of the distant future. Whether or not this ideal will be attained by socialism or by an improvement of the present state of society, whether it will be secured by the abrogation or by the elevation of the wage contract, is a problem which is not yet ready to present itself. The unionist does not cross bridges until he reaches them. It is conceivable that the highest attainable form of society may be reached without any fundamental change in its political and economic structure. The wage earner of tomorrow may possess a comfortable house, ample leisure, an excellent education, a high social position; he may be a man of culture and refinement, and still a wage earner. The productive capacity of modern society, as improved by machinery and by the application of science, is almost boundless, and the problem of providing an ample revenue for all members of society may very well be solved in the future. A few generations ago it would have seemed ridiculous for bricklayers to secure through organization a remuneration of sixty-five cents an hour; and it is not impossible that within a few generations the skilled workmen will through their unions secure a minimum wage equivalent in purchasing power to several dollars per hour in the currency of to-day. Commodities will continue to become cheaper and labor or personal service dearer. The cheapness of things and the dearness of men are the goal toward which trade unionism and society itself should steer.

With a reduction in hours and an increase in remuneration of labor the workingman should find an increased pleasure in his work. The distinguishing characteristic of modern life is the joy of service. The skilled workers to a certain extent, and in much greater measure the professional classes, even now derive more pleasure from their work than from their recreation. The employer who works more hours per day than any man in his employ obtains a zest and a pleasure from his work greater almost than any other satisfaction in life. It may easily come to pass that with the progress of the age a man will secure through trade unionism absolute pleasure from five or six hours of work. The result of this will be to render the recreation of such a man saner, better, and nobler than heretofore. A workman jaded by excessive toil will seek pleasure in the most banal or degrading amusements. The man, whose work is his pleasure, will make his pleasure his work, and the men will have a life outside the factory. Time was when the pursuit of arms was the chief concern of a nation. The time will also pass when the desire or necessity for earning enough to subsist upon will be the chief concern of the people of a country. There was a time when education was a thing to be feared, when children crept unwillingly to school and came from it gladly, but it is now becoming a pleasure even to the smallest of little children. Through a reduction in the hours of labor, an improvement in factory conditions, an increased right to share in the control of his labor, a diminution in the fear of discharge or dismissal, and a lessening of the compulsion under which men labor, work may become less onerous and be converted into a pleasure.

I do not believe, as many seem to do, that the work of the majority of men will with increasing civilization become more artistic and more individual. The prosperity of society and of the wage-earning class is dependent on, and conditioned by, not an increase in manual skill, but by an ever-growing perfection of automatic machinery. If men are to be released from the tyranny of poverty, if they are to be relieved from excessive toil in the factory, it will be only through an ever-increasing perfection of production upon a large scale. Only through the machine can man hope to escape from the machine, only through the perfection of the iron man can the man of flesh and blood gain his full freedom. What is probable is that a large amount of the leisure of society will be devoted to the production by hand of things of beauty; but this will be art, not industry. The patrons of industry in the future will not be the wealthy few, but the comfortable many.

The ideal of American trade unionism must be to uplift even the unskilled workingmen, to raise the standard and remuneration of woman's work, and to make underpaid toil as obsolete, as non-existent as slavery or serfage. The ideal of the American working class must be an organization so effective that even the poorest and weakest of men and women may receive a reasonably large amount of the pleasures and satisfactions of life. Those who cannot attain this standard, the incapables, the men and women smitten with physical disease, with mental weakness, with moral laxity, or with any of those vices which sap the strength and weaken the fibre, should be supported by the state and allowed to live out their lives. There should be for the incapables a charity which will relieve, but not dishonor, a charity that shall be what its name implies, goodness unmixed with moral reprobation. The conditions will not then be as they are to-day, when an army of blind, halt, and lame, of imbeciles, idiots, and drunkards, of diseased, beggars, and criminals are saddled, unfed, unclad, unhoused, upon the unskilled workingmen, almost equally unfed, unclad, and unhoused. At the present time the labor of men and women unfit to engage in the industrial combat is used to lower the wages of men who are capable. It would be cheaper for the workingmen of this country themselves to assume the whole burden of supporting the incapables of society by direct contribution from their wages, than continue the present method of forcing these persons to compete with unskilled workmen, just as on a much smaller and less important scale the prisoner in his cell, subsidized by his crime, is allowed to compete with free labor.

Trade unionism will not cease when conditions are improved. On the contrary, the higher wages become and the more humane and reasonable the conditions of work, the greater will become the need of trade unions and the clearer their justification. Trade unionism is not only negative, but positive. It is a weapon for defense, and also an instrument for further progress; it is both the sword and the plowshare. Even if oppression by capitalists were to vanish from the earth, the need for continued organization of workingmen would not disappear.

The great and noble aspirations of trade unionism should not blind its adherents to the problems of the immediate present or to the difficulties in the way. One must keep his feet upon the ground, though his eyes are upon the stars. It is necessary to pursue the path slowly and painfully, at the same time keeping in mind the ideals which will be ultimately realizable. It has been said that society progresses only by crawling upon its belly. Progress is always slow and accompanied with great cost in tears and blood. Evolution is long and life, both of man and man's institutions, short.

There will be recessions and progressions of the trade union movement, like the ebb and flow of the tide. The movement will be helped on in days of prosperity and retarded, or apparently retarded, in the rays of adversity, although the moral chastening and the hard lessons learned in the period of adversity constitute, perhaps, the greater and truer and surer progress of the two. There can be no doubt, however, that the movement is onward and upward. The workingman who once crawled upon his knees is now upon his feet, and though he may suffer buffets in the future or may be temporarily cast down, he has at least learned to walk and will no longer crawl. It takes generations to implant dignity in the human breast, but once implanted, it is ineradicable.

The movement called the trade union movement is not a thing by itself with its own beginning and its own end, but a step in a long development, which began many thousands of years ago and which will not have ended many thousands of years hence. It is a single act in a drama as long as the history of humanity itself, a single act in the uplifting of the human race. We are told that man rose from a lower scale of existence, that at a certain time he was tapped upon the forehead, and it was said, "Let there be light." There was a gradual rise of man from the savage to the barbarian, from the barbarian to the semi-civilized, from the semi-civilized to the civilized man. Even this civilized man is himself merely a link in a gradual evolution. The evolutionary and educational forces which have been at work for thousands of years have not spent themselves, but will continue, so that the least civilized man of a future age may be higher in the scale than the noblest, purest, and best man that lives to-day. There may come a time when the generations for whom we are struggling will look upon us as barbarians, but little removed from the cave dwellers or the prehistoric savages who ranged the dense forests. There may come a time when labor will no longer be degrading, when the last vestige of slavery of any sort will have disappeared, when work will be a pleasure and an honor and an ambition. When that time comes, when men will have advanced from, and evolved out of, the present degrading conditions, the generations to come will look back with gratitude and approval upon the institution of trade unionism, which has contributed and will have contributed so much to the ultimate goal of society, the ascent of man.

"This," said the great humane philosopher, Thomas Carlyle, "This that they call the Organization of Labour is the Universal Vital Problem of the World."